Dennis O. Rinehart

Park United Methodist Church
122 Park Avenue
Coshocton, Ohio 43812

APR. 5 1984

The Biology
of Anxiety

The Biology of Anxiety

Edited by
ROY J. MATHEW, M.D., D.P.M., M.R.C. Psych.
Chief, Psychosomatic Research Unit, Texas
Research Institute of Mental Sciences

Technical Editors
LORE FELDMAN and KAREN HANSON STUYCK

PROCEEDINGS OF THE FOURTEENTH ANNUAL SYMPOSIUM,
NOVEMBER 5-7, 1980
TEXAS RESEARCH INSTITUTE OF MENTAL SCIENCES, HOUSTON

BRUNNER/MAZEL, Publishers • New York

Library of Congress Cataloging in Publication Data
Main entry under title:

The Biology of anxiety.

  "Proceedings of the fourteenth annual symposium,
November 5-7, 1980, Texas Research Institute
of Mental Sciences, Houston."
  Bibliography: p.
  Includes index.
  1. Anxiety—Congresses. 2. Anxiety—
Research—Congresses. I. Mathew, Roy J.
II. Texas Research Institute of Mental Sciences.
RC531.B47   616.85′22307   81-21560
ISBN 0-87630-295-9   AACR2

CONTENTS

IV. PSYCHOSOMATIC MANIFESTATIONS OF ANXIETY

V. SLEEP

CONTRIBUTORS

ROBERT E. ALLEN, M.D.
Associate Professor of Clinical Psychiatry and the Behavioral Sciences, University of Southern California School of Medicine, Los Angeles

EDWARD B. BLANCHARD, Ph.D.
Professor and Director of Clinical Training, Department of Psychology, State University of New York at Albany

JAMES L. CLAGHORN, M.D.
Assistant Director and Head of the Training Division, Texas Research Institute of Mental Sciences, Houston

GREGORY CAREY, Ph.D.
Assistant Professor of Psychology in Psychiatry, Department of Psychiatry, Washington University School of Medicine, St. Louis, Missouri

VICTOR H. DENENBERG, Ph.D.
Professor of Biobehavioral Sciences and Psychology, University of Connecticut, Storrs

S. J. ENNA, Ph.D.
Professor of Pharmacology and Neurobiology, Departments of Pharmacology and Neurobiology and Anatomy, University of Texas Medical School at Houston

MAX HAMILTON, M.D., F.R.C.P., F.R.C. Psych., F.B.P.S.
Emeritus Professor of Psychiatry, University of Leeds, England

LORRAINE ROTH HERRENKOHL, Ph.D.
Professor of Psychology, Temple University, Philadelphia, Pennsylvania

DIANTHA HOWARD, M.Sc.
Biometrics Facility, University of Vermont, Burlington

ISMET KARACAN, M.D., D.Sc. (Med.)
Professor of Psychiatry and Director, Sleep Disorders and Research Center, Baylor College of Medicine; Associate Chief of Staff for Research, Veterans Administration Medical Center, Houston

CHASE PATTERSON KIMBALL, M.D.
Professor of Psychiatry and Medicine, Division of Biological Sciences, and Professor in the College, University of Chicago, Illinois

MALCOLM LADER, D.Sc., Ph.D., M.D., F.R.C. Psych.
Professor of Clinical Psychopharmacology, University of London, England

ROY J. MATHEW, M.D., D.P.M., M.R.C. Psych.
Chief, Psychosomatic Research Unit, Texas Research Institute of Mental Sciences, Houston

HARVEY MOLDOFSKY, M.D.
Professor of Psychiatry, University of Toronto; Psychiatrist-in-Chief, Toronto Western Hospital, Ontario, Canada

CONSTANCE A. MOORE, M.D.
Resident in Psychiatry, Baylor College of Medicine, Houston

ALEXANDER NIES, M.D.
Professor of Psychiatry, University of Connecticut, Storrs; Chief, Psychiatry Service, Veterans Administration Medical Center, Newington, Connecticut

FERRIS N. PITTS, Jr., M.D.
Professor of Psychiatry and the Behavioral Sciences, University of Southern California School of Medicine, Los Angeles

KATHLEEN M. RICE
Doctoral Candidate in Psychology, State University of New York at Albany

DONALD S. ROBINSON, M.D.
Chairman and Professor of Pharmacology, Marshall University, Huntington, West Virginia

HERBERT WEINER, M.D.
Professor of Psychiatry and Neuroscience, Albert Einstein College of Medicine; Chairman, Department of Psychiatry, Montefiore Hospital and Medical Center, New York

MAXINE L. WEINMAN, Dr.P.H.
Research Specialist, Psychosomatic Research Unit, Texas Research Institute of Mental Sciences, Houston

ROBERT L. WILLIAMS, M.D.
D.C. and Irene Ellwood Professor and Chairman of Psychiatry; Co-Director, Sleep Disorders and Research Center, Baylor College of Medicine, Houston

INTRODUCTION

Recent years have seen an upsurge of interest in the biology of psychiatric illnesses. While extensive research has been conducted on illnesses like schizophrenia and affective disorders, anxiety has received only minimal research interest. This is ironic in view of the ubiquitous nature of anxiety. There is general consensus that anxiety is present in varying degrees in all psychiatric and physical illnesses. A clearer understanding of the biology of anxiety will facilitate the development of effective preventive and therapeutic techniques. Furthermore, separation of anxiety-mediated biological changes is imperative to the understanding of the pathology of other psychiatric illnesses.

This book represents an attempt to bring together recent studies of the biology of anxiety. Most of the authors address issues to which the average psychiatrist has had only minimal exposure. Such topics as physiology of anxiety, stress and catecholamines, and clinical pharmacology of benzodiazepines have been omitted as an extensive literature is already available on these topics. This book, which emphasizes the biological aspects of clinically relevant phenomena related to anxiety, is meant for the biologically oriented clinician who is interested in current research trends.

ROY J. MATHEW

The Biology
of Anxiety

I.
STRESS AND ANXIETY

1

DIAGNOSIS OF ANXIETY STATES

MAX HAMILTON, M.D.

The anxiety states or neuroses have long been regarded as essentially psychogenic disorders or personality disturbances for which the fundamental treatment was psychotherapy. The usual statement in the textbooks concluded that "simple" psychotherapy was sufficient for most patients but that severe or long-standing cases required deep analysis. Unfortunately, the continual multiplication of psychotherapeutic procedures indicates that such treatments are by no means as satisfactory as their proponents suggest. Probably for this reason and partly also because of the success of biological treatments in psychiatry, psychiatrists have begun to take another look at the anxiety states.

The word "anxiety" is used with different meanings and it would be well to make clear what is being considered here. Anxiety is a particular mood, a modified and more or less continuous state of fear. It is a normal reaction to a threat or danger of some kind and as such can be recognized easily. We also talk of a pathologically anxious mood in which the anxiety either bears no relation to an external threat or is grossly exaggerated in relation to the precipitating stress. Thus, it is normal to be afraid of falling over a cliff but pathological to be afraid of a mouse. Pathological anxiety can occur as a symptom in almost all psychiatric disorders. The term is also used in the form "anxiety state" or "anxiety neurosis," by which is meant a pattern of symptoms which are more or less dominated by a pathologically anxious mood and which is diagnosed rather than recognized. For the purpose of classification, the anxiety state can be regarded as a member of the group of affective disorders. This implies that it is related to the manias and depressions.

There are good reasons for this classification: Genetic studies have shown a high concordance in twins for the diagnosis of anxiety states with or without anxious personality. This concordance is higher in monozygotic than in di-

zygotic twins. Thus, there is good evidence for the significance of constitutional factors in this disorder. The anxiety states have a remittent course,
though this is not as clear as in the depressions and manias. Anxiety states
can occur sometimes as a prodromal phase occurring prior to an acute depressive illness (Hays, 1964). Some patients respond remarkably well to
treatment with monoamine oxidase inhibitors. Although this proves nothing
by itself, such a response to a drug which is not essentially an anxiolytic or
sedative indicates the need to take into account some underlying biological
process. The popular belief that a clear recognition of constitutional factors
in illness leads to therapeutic nihilism is worth mentioning here. This is, of
course, quite untrue, as can be seen from the examples of Addison's anemia
and Parkinson's disease.

All these features indicate the close relationship between the anxiety states
and the other affective disorders. In particular, there is a considerable overlap in the symptoms of anxiety states and the depressions. Anxiety, for
example, is present in over 80 percent of patients suffering from a depressive
illness.

It is customary at present to make a distinction between anxiety states
and depressive illness even though the symptoms are similar. The evidence
for this is based on research using psychometric, physiological and biochemical techniques. The distinction is important not only from the point of view
of classification but also clinically because current treatments are quite different. For depressive illnesses we prescribe antidepressive drugs or elec-
troconvulsive therapy; for anxiety states we recommend some form of
psychotherapy, supplemented by anxiolytic drugs for acute episodes. Some
patients with phobic and depressive symptoms may respond to monoamine
oxidase inhibitors.

SYMPTOMS

There is no need here to give a list of the symptoms, which are very well
known, but a few special points are worth considering. The symptoms can
be classified as psychological and as somatic. In the first group anxious mood
is a central feature. Even during remissions it may not be wholly absent.
During a phase of illness, anxiety is fluctuating and reactive. The fluctuations
are irregular, and any sudden increase makes the patient search for a precipitating cause in the same way that a patient with indigestion always blames
his or her last meal. One should therefore beware of false precipitating
stresses. The anxiety also responds quickly to situational changes and is
easily exacerbated by minor stresses which would not affect a normal individual. In other words, the patients have a low threshold for the development

of anxiety. The anxious person responds well to comfort and reassurance. In a drug test I conducted, control subjects were given placebos for as long as five weeks and their symptoms diminished steadily during this time (Roberts and Hamilton, 1958). Mere attendance at a clinic will relieve the symptoms (Kellner and Sheffield, 1971). It is this which makes the evaluation of therapies so difficult.

In addition to the more or less continual anxiety, patients also experience attacks of panic, associated with sweating, dizziness, chest pains and, above all, palpitations. These attacks often constitute the basis for agoraphobia. Much work has been done recently which indicates that many of these attacks are associated with mitral valve prolapse (e.g., Kantor et al., 1980). Undoubtedly, this work is of great importance, but its full significance for our understanding of anxiety states and their management is not yet clear. Agoraphobia, despite its name, appears to be distinct from those phobias which occur in the "phobic anxiety" states. Evidence is accumulating that these constitute a special subgroup (Marks, 1969).

Most of the somatic symptoms can be regarded as arising from overactivity of the autonomic nervous system. Excessive sweating is a common complaint and occurs in the muzzle area of the face, hands and feet, axillae and perineal regions. A minor sign not often mentioned is that these patients may show greatly dilated pupils. Muscular symptoms are extremely varied. The most obvious is a coarse tremor in the hands, but the patient may complain of "trembling" in the trunk and abdomen. Increased muscular tension may be the basis for complaints of aching in the jaws and neck and even in the tongue. It may also explain the difficulties some of these patients experience in the wearing of dentures. Some patients grind their teeth during sleep.

DIAGNOSIS

The diagnosis of anxiety states can be considered from two aspects: the differentiation from organic conditions and from other mental disorders. The first is very much the problem of the general practitioner and the internist, the second is the problem of the psychiatrist.

In regard to the first, it must be made clear that it is not merely for convenience that we distinguish between psychological symptoms and somatic ones. In fact, the symptoms of anxiety states tend to fall into two groups which have low intercorrelations. Patients usually complain of either one group or the other—so much so, that in Europe the somatic symptoms have received the distinct label of "autonomic dystonia." The symptoms which patients complained of are also influenced by their attitudes; sophisticated patients will emphasize their psychological symptoms, and less sophisticated patients will place greater emphasis on the somatic symptoms. For this reason, the first step in the diagnosis of patients who come complaining of cardiac, digestive or respiratory symptoms is taking a full history. Of course, background information which points to a psychological disorder does not exclude the presence of organic disease, but it does add to the probabilities which underlie all diagnosis. Whatever the presenting symptoms, a careful search for the other symptoms of anxiety states will often reveal the full clinical picture and make the diagnosis easy. It is usually considered advisable to carry out some investigations to rule out the possibility of organic disease. This is part of the medical tradition which regards not recognizing an organic disease as a serious error, but the misdiagnosis of a psychological disorder as of little consequence. This tradition is unfortunate. For example, a patient with gastric carcinoma may be misdiagnosed as having functional dyspepsia, but the outcome of treatment of this condition is so lamentable that it could be argued that a delay of six months in making the diagnosis does not affect the outcome and does give the patient an extra half-year of peace of mind. Similarly, early coronary disease is probably better left well-enough alone, rather than subjecting the patient to vigorous treatment which is likely to produce side effects worse than the primary condition.

It is therefore sufficient to carry out a few simple tests and examinations and, if these are negative, to make a final decision. The physician should not engage in innumerable investigations in the hope of detecting some obscure disease. This procedure merely convinces the patient that he or she is indeed suffering from something serious and obscure, and when finally informed, "There is nothing organically wrong," or worse, "There is nothing wrong," will believe rather that something has been found and is being concealed. It is in this situation that one sees clearly the difference between treating a patient and treating a disease, or, from another point of view, the difference between the true physician and the mere mechanic. In view of the rapid amelioration of symptoms produced by proper reassurance and explanation, the importance of sound clinical judgement cannot be over-emphasized.

Paroxysmal tachycardia can be differentiated from anxiety states by the history of repeated attacks of palpitations which come on very suddenly and without reason. The patient's pulse rate is usually well over 140 per minute, whereas in anxiety states the rate is usually lower. Sweating, pallor and faintness during attacks occur in both conditions. During an attack, the electrocardiogram will make the diagnosis immediately. Thyrotoxicosis is always mentioned as a diagnosis to be excluded, even though it is much less common than anxiety states. When this is mild, patients complain of palpitations, tiredness, tremor and anxiety, but they look much more anxious than they are or admit to being. The tremor of the fingers is fine, not coarse, and the hands are warm and pink, not cold and clammy. The increased pulse rate does not slow during sleep. The diagnosis can be confirmed in the usual way by looking for a raised protein-bound iodine or serum triiodothyronine. "Spontaneous hypoglycemia" may need to be considered for acute attacks, but the history will generally reveal that the attacks are relieved by eating. During an attack the blood sugar is obviously low, and a glucose tolerance test shows a flattened curve.

The problems of diagnosis are much more difficult for the psychiatrist. In the first place he or she should not place too great faith on the reports of others that organic conditions have been excluded. The diagnosis of peptic ulcer or urinary infection is not infallible. The difficulty is that anxiety can occur as a symptom in most psychiatric disorders, and a proper history is not always easy to obtain. In the early stages of schizophrenia, the patient may be very alarmed by the symptoms when they first appear but be reluctant to talk about thought-blocking or hallucinatory voices. Much the same applies to the obsessional neurotic who will talk about anxiety but not of lurid obsessions concerning aggression, sex or blasphemy. The fact that the symptoms are atypical should be a hint that further questioning is desirable.

The most important distinction to be made is between a depressive illness and anxiety. The overlap of symptoms often makes this difficult. The history and family background are of the utmost importance here. Depressive patients are likely to have a family history of depressions with or without suicides. Previous attacks may have been obviously depressive in nature. Depressions can occur in patients with well-adjusted personalities, sometimes even euthymic, sociable and extraverted, whereas patients suffering from anxiety states tend to have anxious dispositions. If there is a psychological precipitant to the attack, its nature can be helpful. This is often epitomized with the aphorism that depression is precipitated by a loss while anxiety is brought on by a threat. Of course, the psychological stress has to be assessed in relation to the personality of the patient.

The patient's pattern of symptoms needs to be evaluated carefully. Those indicative of depressions are predominantly of a biological nature. The patient suffers from a loss of appetite and even a loss of weight. There is a loss of energy and rapid fatigability. The patient loses interest in work, activities and hobbies. Loss of libido can be an early symptom, though patients often will not mention this unless they are asked. The same applies to suicidal thoughts, which may be no more than a feeling that life is not worth living. Guilt and self-accusation may be no more than a preoccupation that the illness is the patient's fault or that he has let himself or his family down. Depression may be denied, minimized or even explained away as a reaction to the other symptoms. One should always ask the patients about their attitude to their previous life and to the future. They tend to view the past in the worst light: It has not been worthwhile; it has been pointless or a failure. The future is regarded pessimistically.

It is easy to explain how the anxieties can be distinguished from the depressions; yet, even with the best efforts, there will always be a residuum of patients on whom it is impossible to make a decision. What is to be done in such cases? The one thing which should *not* be done is to prescribe blunderbuss treatments, a bit of this, that and the other. In all branches of medicine, illnesses are more easily distinguishable in their severe form than in the mild. There is no difficulty in differentiating a severe anxiety state from an agitated depression. The patients who present the greatest diagnostic difficulties are those who are only mildly ill. When the patient is not obviously ill and the diagnosis is in doubt, the best course is to wait until time makes the diagnosis clear. The old joke about "masterly inactivity" is sound advice. Reassurance about the nature of the illness and its prognosis is surprisingly helpful and it has no adverse side effects. Sound judgement is always better than enthusiasm in the treatment of patients.

REFERENCES

HAYS, P. 1964. Modes of onset of psychotic depression. *Br. Med. J.*, 2:779-784.
KANTOR, J. S., ZITRIN, C. M., and ZELDIS, S. M. 1980. Mitral valve prolapse syndrome in agoraphobic patients. *Am. J. Psychiatry*, 137:467-469.
KELLNER, R. and SHEFFIELD, B. F. 1971. The relief of distress following attendance at a clinic. *Br. J. Psychiatry*, 118:195-198.
MARKS, I. M. 1969. *Fears and Phobias.* New York: Academic Press.
ROBERTS, J. M., and HAMILTON, M. 1958. Treatment of anxiety states. I. The effects of suggestion on the symptoms of anxiety states. *J. Mental Sciences*, 104:1052-1055.

2

BIOLOGICAL DIFFERENTIATION OF ANXIETY, AROUSAL, AND STRESS

MALCOLM LADER, M.D.

My task is to discuss the biological differences between anxiety, arousal, and stress. These terms are concepts rather than biological phenomena. Therefore, the conceptual and semantic ground must be carefully prepared lest one seek biological relationships among fictitious or philosophical factors, among noumena rather than phenomena.

Mindful that I am writing for a predominantly medical audience, I will emphasize pragmatism rather than dogmatism, clinical relevance rather than theoretical symmetries. I shall avoid an esoteric exposé of the intricacies of psychophysiology but I shall concentrate on a few key studies and crucial concepts which illumine our clinical problems. But first I shall outline my schema for considering anxiety.

ANXIETY

Definition of Anxiety

Anxiety has two main meanings. To be anxious can mean "full of desire and endeavor to effect some act." For example: I am *anxious* to keep your interest and attention. The low-key emotional tone attached to this urge is directed toward the act to be effected. The second meaning is "being troubled in mind about some uncertain event, being in disturbing suspense, being fraught with worry." The first type of anxiety is goal-directed and controllable; the second type is diffuse, causing the person to feel passive and helpless.

The latter meaning is relevant to the clinical situation as the ineffable feeling of foreboding is the core of anxiety. It is irreducible scientifically,

11

which means that ultimately one must rely on subjective reports of this state. However, observations and inferences from those observations come close to allowing objective detection of anxiety. It is interesting that hand movements give the best clues to anxiety (Waxer, 1977).

Anxiety as part of everyday experience is a *normal* emotion. Fear is also a common normal emotion; the distinction between anxiety and fear is quantitative not qualitative. If the cause is clear, the emotion induced is labeled "fear"; if the cause is clouded, or, although readily identifiable, its potential impact is unpredictable, the more diffuse emotion experienced is termed "anxiety." But anxiety may also be an *abnormal* emotion, and distinctions between normality/abnormality and normal/clinical can be difficult. It is best to regard clinical (morbid, pathological) anxiety operationally as a need of the sufferer to seek relief from his or her anxiety. Such anxiety may be too severe, too persistent or too pervasive for the person to tolerate. He or she seeks medical advice, thereby becoming a "patient" and the condition an "anxiety state." Normal anxiety may thus refer to an emotional state for which the subject does not seek help, although the anxiety levels might actually be greater than those of the patient who welcomes help.

Another distinction of normal anxiety involves the nexus between the intensity of the emotion and the magnitude of the apparent cause. If the anxiety reported by the person and conjectured from the person's behavior is commensurate with the apparent precipitating cause, it may be deemed "normal." If, by contrast, the anxiety seems disproportionate to the cause, or, as often transpires, no cause is detectable, the anxiety is abnormal. This type of anxiety may also be termed "neurotic," as the emotion reflects symbolic, nonconscious interactions and processes. That, of course, is a separate, vast topic.

Yet another distinction is between *state* and *trait* anxiety. State anxiety refers to anxiety felt at one particular time, the moment of study. Trait anxiety is the habitual tendency to feel anxious. Some individuals have such high levels of trait anxiety that they are chronically in a condition of state anxiety.

Psychophysiology of Anxiety

I have described several ways of considering anxiety and tried to pick my way through the semantic minefield. The distinctions are of obvious clinical relevance, for the biological differentiation of these various types has not so far proved rewarding. Put simply, the biological changes that accompany states of anxiety reflect the severity of the condition rather than its operationally defined type. The correlation between physiological changes and anxiety tends to be higher when the anxiety is assessed objectively than by a subjective report, but there are no qualitative differences among the various facets of anxiety.

Feelings of anxiety are accompanied by physical signs and symptoms: palpitations, a sense of constriction in the chest, tightness in the throat, difficulty in breathing, epigastric discomfort or pain, dizziness and weakness in the legs, dryness of the mouth, sweating, vomiting, tremor, screaming, running in panic, and sudden micturition or defecation. The detailed evaluation and precise measurement of the concomitant physiological changes are the particular interest of the psychophysiologist (Lader, 1975). However, other emotions such as rage and ecstasy also produce physiological changes, and patterns of changes pertaining to each emotion are not easily differentiated (Ax, 1953; Schachter, 1957). Thus, these indicators of anxiety demand continuous concurrent validation by reference to other indicators of anxiety, such as subjective reports and observation of facial expression.

Normal Subjects

Anticipation of a painful stimulus such as an electric shock has been used as a "model" of anxiety. Katkin (1966) told half his subjects to expect a shock and the others merely to rest quietly. Neither group was given shocks, but the expectation group showed greater sweat-gland activity. The subjects were considered high or low in affect according to their scores on the Affect Adjective Check List. The high-affect subjects in the expectation group were slower to return to resting levels of sweating after the stress period than were the low-affect individuals.

The intravenous infusion of adrenaline induces a variety of emotions including anxiety. In medical students such an infusion produced tachycardia, a rise in systolic and a drop in diastolic blood pressure. The relationship between the intensities of the physiological and the subjective reactions was unclear. Subjective estimates of effects declined steadily during each infusion (Frankenhaeuser and Järpe, 1963).

The estimation of plasma catecholamines is becoming technically easier with the development of radio-enzymatic assays and high-pressure liquid chromatography. In the past, however, the urinary excretion, a semiquantitative index, was often used for want of something better. Levi's (1963) stressful task, for example, involved the sorting of steel ballbearings of four very similar sizes in the presence of a loud noise and variations in the intensity of a bright light. Soldiers comprised the experimental subjects; 20 were rated as able to cope with stress, 20 as having low tolerance to stress. Adrenaline and noradrenaline excretion both increased during the task period, the rise in adrenaline being especially pronounced, but catecholamine excretion was unrelated to the ratings of stress tolerance.

Physiological concomitants of anxiety in sport parachutists were evaluated in detail by Fenz and Epstein (1967). Skin-conductance levels (sweating) and heart rate were recorded for 10 experienced and 10 novice parachutists throughout the day before the jump, in the aircraft before the jump, and on landing. The physiological measures were similar in novices and veterans when arriving at the airport and during take-off. Then the curves diverged. The novices' heart rates rose rapidly to an average of 145 beats per minute just before the jump, while those of the experienced parachutists diminished at this point to increase again immediately before landing. The experienced jumpers' pattern coincides with the realistic time of physical danger.

Several studies have examined the relationship between anxiety-proneness (trait anxiety) and psychophysiological measures. Habituation of the finger blood volume response measured photoplethysmographically (pulse beat) was slower in high scorers on the IPAT (Institute for Personality and Ability Testing) anxiety scale than in low scorers (McGuinness, 1973). Similarly, high scorers on the Test Anxiety Questionnaire had higher skin conductance levels than low scorers, and subjects with high neuroticism scores on the Eysenck Personality Inventory were more reactive with respect to sweat-gland activity than were low-neuroticism subjects.

Anxious Patients

An early finding, replicated several times, is that anxious patients have much higher plasma cortisol concentrations than normal subjects. Also, the cortisol levels seem related to the intensity of anxiety, with panicky patients having the highest concentrations. In 13 patients hospitalized with anxiety and depression, plasma catecholamine concentrations correlated with anxiety ratings but not with ratings of depressive affect.

Goldstein (1964) measured electromyographic (EMG) activity in anxious women by recording potentials from seven bodily sites. While resting, the patients had significantly higher levels than normal subjects with respect to masseter and forearm extensor EMG. An auditory stimulus induced greater responses in the patients at the sternomastoid, frontalis, forearm extensor, and gastrocnemius muscle sites. Thus, anxious subjects are more easily differentiated electromyographically from calm subjects during stimulation procedures than at rest.

Not only do anxious patients have high levels of activity but they adapt slowly to the changing exigencies of an experimental situation and habituate only gradually to a series of repeated, identical, discrete stimuli. Impaired habituation of the skin conductance response in anxious individuals was described many years ago (Lader and Wing, 1966), and this observation has been replicated several times, for example, in patients (Raskin, 1975) and in anxious normals (Goldwater and Lewis, 1978). However, the mechanisms of abnormal physiology underlying the lack of response habituation are unclear.

Chronically anxious patients have high "resting" levels of forearm blood flow, react *less* than normals to a difficult performance task and adapt more slowly. Other findings in this area include impairment of adaptation of pupillary responses in anxious patients and inefficient respiratory functions.

The electroencephalograms (EEG) of anxious patients show more beta and theta activity than do those of normal subjects. Alpha activity, however, is about the same (Bond et al., 1974; Hoffmann, 1980). Any alpha activity that is present in anxious patients tends to be at a higher than normal dominant frequency.

The CNV (contingent negative variation, expectancy wave) is a negative-going potential which develops in the interval between a warning and an action signal. The CNV is smaller than normal in anxious patients, suggesting that a state of expectancy to an external stimulus is not readily maintained. Also, patients are much more distractible so that the CNV can be easily attenuated. It also habituates more slowly than normal in the anxious patient. As with the EEG itself, the physiological basis for the CNV is not firmly established so interpretation of the data must be cautious.

Symptom Mechanisms

Physiological research has a direct clinical application in evaluating the symptoms of anxious patients. Sainsbury and Gibson (1954) administered an inventory to 30 anxious and tense patients, recording their symptoms, feelings, and any bodily complaints attributable to muscular overactivity (head sensations, backache, etc.). Then, electromyographs were recorded from the frontalis and forearm extensor muscles. The patients were divided into two groups according to whether their symptom scores were above or below the median on the inventory. The high symptom scorers had higher EMGs at both sites than the less anxious and tense patients. Seven patients complained of headache or head sensations at the time of recording: They displayed higher frontalis EMG levels than the remainder of the patients but their forearm levels were not different. Conversely, 14 patients complaining of stiffness, "rheumatics" (without joint pains), and aching in the arms had higher forearm muscle potentials than the others.

AROUSAL

Concepts of Arousal

The salient feature of the psychophysiology of both anxious patients and normal subjects made anxious by some stratagem is general physiological overactivity. Attempts have been made to relate the special case of over-activity in anxiety to a more general concept of arousal.

The concept of arousal has occupied an important but controversial role in psychophysiology. Briefly, it combines several strands of developing theory (Malmo, 1959). The earliest derives from the work of Cannon on the general and specific responses of the sympathetic and parasympathetic nervous systems to threatening stimuli. These physiological changes prepare the organism for fight or flight; thus arousal was regarded as a physiological activation. This arousal model was developed in terms of behavior energetics by Duffy (1951, 1957, 1962, 1972) and by Freeman (1948). It incorporates the motions of stimuli threatening the integrity of the organism, activation of the autonomic nervous system, and the activation of vigorous adaptive behavior.

The second tradition derives from Hullian learning theory and postulates a nonspecific component of drive that energizes the behavior of the organism. The drive may be aversive or appetitive. Again, the concept of physiological energy-mobilization is present.

Thirdly, physiological studies revealed the importance of the reticular activating system as a possible anatomical substrate for nonspecific arousal mechanisms. The EEG was used as a marker in human beings of the state of arousal—fast-wave, low-voltage activity denoting high arousal, slow waves of high power denoting low arousal (Hebb, 1955; Lindsley, 1951). The reticular activating system was found to be a multisynaptic sensory channel which could modulate the cortical appreciation of stimuli arriving there via the paucisynaptic classical sensory pathways.

Problems arose in attempting to assimilate all these concepts into a single theory of arousal. The simplest model was to refer to a continuum of arousal in a psychological behavioral sense, ranging from drowsiness and an inalert state at one extreme, to an alert state, and then on to high arousal states with emotional behavior increasing to the extreme states which accompany rage, panic, and ecstasy. It has generally been assumed that behavioral efficiency is an inverted U-shaped function of arousal, both high and low levels of arousal being associated with behavioral inefficiency or even disintegration.

Lacey (1967), however, reviewed the evidence for a unitary concept of arousal and found it wanting. At least two arousal systems seemed necessary, a reticular activating system and a limbic system. The limbic arousal system was regarded as more closely related to behavioral activation. Recently, a third arousal system (Fowles, 1980) has been postulated, based on Gray's (1975) two-process theory of learning. The third component is a behavioral inhibitory system which mediates the effects of threatening stimuli on anxiety and produces an increase in anxiety. Aversive stimuli and their arousal-increasing effects are explained by this approach.

Such theorizing may be useful in animal studies where physiological studies can be used to identify anatomical substrates and linkages. In humans, a simpler, more empirical approach must suffice, and the concept of a dimension of general *behavioral* arousal is still useful. The intensity of behavior and its integration and purposefulness can be related to the level of general arousal. Superimposed on the general arousal is a more specific dimension of arousal. For example, an organism indulging in sexual behavior will be at a particular general level of arousal. Superimposed on this will be specific arousal pertinent to the sexual aspect of the behavior. Another organism avoiding a predator will also have a particular, but different, level of general arousal, on which is added specific arousal related to the flight reaction which may eventuate. The concept of general arousal thus allows comparisons between different behavioral states in terms of a common behavioral continuum.

Relationship of Anxiety to Arousal

Can anxiety be viewed simply as a state of high arousal? Behaviorally, the actions of an anxious individual intuitively resemble those expected of an aroused individual. The psychophysiological findings outlined earlier, which are essentially refinements of clinical observations, are also consistent with this view. But this simplistic statement leaves many questions unanswered. For instance, is anxiety the only high-arousal state? Can anxiety be present without a high-arousal state? Why feel anxiety and not some other emotion?

The most convincing attempt to relate emotions to a general arousal level was by Schachter (1966), who presented a new theory of emotions. According to this theory, emotions arise from an interaction between a state of physiological arousal and cognitive information derived from the situation. Three assumptions underlie the theory:

1. An individual labels a state of physiological arousal for which he/she has no immediate explanation according to the cognitive clues derived from the situation.
2. If an immediate and totally congruent explanation is forthcoming, the person will not generate an emotional feeling.
3. Even if cognitive clues are forthcoming, an emotion will be engendered only to the extent that the underlying physiological arousal is raised.

In an ingeniously conceived experiment, Schachter and Singer (1962) injected students with either saline or epinephrine (adrenaline). In the case of the epinephrine injections, half the students were given incorrect information about what effects to expect, the rest were correctly informed. The students were then placed with a stooge who behaved in either a "euphoric" or an "angry" way. The significant results, though limited, were taken as evidence for the theory. However, several methodological problems included:

1. The placebo and epinephrine groups did not differ in the degree of emotional reaction whether euphoria or anger was induced. Thus, clear evidence was not obtained that the degree of emotional reaction depends on the degree of arousal evoked. Against this must be set the limitation that epinephrine does not induce a true arousal state; as many studies have shown, subjects injected with catecholamine report feeling as if they were anxious: the physiological state induced lacks full credibility.
2. The emotional situations were poorly standardized in that the behavior of the experimental confederate was not strictly controlled and varied with the subject's behavior. Thus, some confounding of effects could have occurred.
3. The emotional situations were also poorly comparable. The euphoria-inducing situation and the anger-inducing situation differed with respect to duration, the type of subject's activity and the type of behavior ratings as well as the intended affective differences.
4. False information about the injection may not have prevented the "misinformed" subjects from inferring correctly that their bodily symptoms were caused by the injection.

I have labored these problems because they illustrate the difficulties in designing and executing informative experiments in this area. Surprisingly, in view of the pivotal importance of the theory in the area of emotions, few experimental replications have been attempted. Erdmann and Janke (1978) tried to obviate as many as possible of the above objections. Drug administration (ephedrine) was disguised so the subjects did not realize they had been administered anything. Four situational conditions were used—a neutral condition and "anger," "happiness," and "anxiety." The subject read a report on his or her performance on a previously completed intelligence test and answered supplementary questions designed to elicit angry or happy responses or was threatened with electric shocks. Even there, the four conditions differed in respects other than the emotion to be induced. Mood was assessed using an adjective checklist which yielded a scale of general well-being, an anxiety scale, and an excitement scale.

The results were only partly in accordance with Schachter's theory. The effects of the "happiness" and "anger" situations were consistent with the theory and the ephedrine increased the emotional ratings. With the "anxiety" situation, which is our present concern, the results were unexpected. Differences between anxiety scale ratings with the anxiety and the neutral situation were found with placebo administration but not following ephedrine, when the two states were indistinguishable. This result is contrary to Schachter's theory. The authors were at a loss to explain their results. Speculations about the paradoxical effects of ephedrine could be made invoking the Law of Initial Values so that anxiety was already maximal under the placebo condition, but why did this not occur under the other conditions?

Another explanation concerns the limited effectiveness of ephedrine in raising the level of arousal. Ephedrine is a sympathomimetic that produces standard effects such as tachycardia and pupillary dilatation. But, as with epinephrine, it does not induce a true state of anxiety, rather a state of sympathetic overactivity which partly mimics anxiety. Patients with anxiety states may have learned to associate such sympathetic hyperactivity states with their anxiety states, but normal subjects have not done so and are not deceived by the physiological effects alone (Tyrer, 1976). In Erdmann and Janke's experiment, under placebo conditions the anxiety-provoking situation seemed effective in actually inducing anxiety. The ephedrine increased physiological activity under neutral situational conditions which raised the ratings of anxiety. Under the anxiety-provoking situation, the ephedrine may have resulted in physiological changes which were inconsistent with the changes being induced by the situation, an "occluding effect" resulting.

In a further experiment, Erdmann and van Lindern (1980) administered the beta-adrenergic antagonist, oxprenolol, or placebo, or the beta-adrenergic agonist, orciprenaline, to students in one or two situations, one designed to induce anger, the other neutral. The expected physiological changes were induced by the drugs, and the "anger" situation led to a significant rise in blood pressure, especially diastolic. The "anger" situation led to an increase in self-reports of anger only in the placebo subjects but to increases in anxiety ratings both in the placebo and the orciprenaline subjects.

The circulatory effects of the beta-stimulant, orciprenaline, more closely resembled those accompanying anxiety than those associated with anger (Ax, 1953; Schachter, 1957). But this implies that the self-perception of the physiological pattern outweighed the cognitive promptings provided by the anger-inducing situation, as anxiety, not anger, ratings were increased.

These studies should not be overinterpreted. The pharmacological agents used are quite limited in their ability to induce high arousal states centrally in contrast to sympathetic overactivity peripherally. A more pertinent pharmacological observation is that chronic overindulgence in caffeine-containing beverages or in amphetamines may result in a state of anxiety indistinguishable from the naturally occurring syndrome. Why is anxiety the emotion reported rather than anger or ecstasy? Caffeine is a phosphodiesterase inhibitor and 3'5' cyclic adenosine monophosphate (cAMP) has been claimed to be raised in states of anxiety (Moyes and Moyes, 1977). Maybe this is relevant.

To summarize, the literature is both scanty and confusing. Both high arousal and cognitive clues seem important in the genesis of an emotion. Anxiety may be more pivotal an emotion than others as attempts to induce another emotion may increase anxiety instead. Perhaps one may speculate that anxiety is somehow the most primitive emotion, that which is experienced when the emotional parts of the brain are active but disorganized.

STRESS

The concepts of anxiety and arousal and the relationship between them are difficult enough to clarify. The task of defining stress is beyond mortal endeavor. So many conflicting ideas concern this concept that it is useless scientifically as a general term. Any use of stress can only take place after a careful definition by the user of what is meant. Such *de novo* definitions carry the danger of further confusing the chaos.

The term "stress" in lay usage means "hardship, affliction, an adverse force or influence." In physics it is defined as "the physical force exerted upon a material object." The term "strain" implies any definite change in a material object produced by an external force. Thus, although the distinctions are not total, stress is generally taken to mean the external agencies, strain the internal changes. This is still the general usage: Stress is an external adverse circumstance, people are under stress.

Selye, nearly 50 years ago, described a syndrome in animals with the gross changes induced by pituitary-adrenal dysfunction. Selye defines stress as "the nonspecific response of the body to any demand made upon it." It is immaterial whether the demand is pleasant or unpleasant. This definition is too wide-ranging to be useful, too inexact to be heuristic. Both "nonspecific" and "demand" are awkward terms, the latter especially containing the germs of a tautology. Stress is the body's response to demands, but demands can only be defined in terms of producing stress. Also, stress is the wrong term—Selye studied changes in the animal which he misadvisedly labeled "stress" instead of "strain." Attempts to rectify the mistake and to clarify the issue by introducing the term "stressor" have made things worse.

Luckily we can obviate these definitional problems by avoiding the term altogether. The adverse influences causing the responses are stimuli, admittedly severe or of special type. But being stimuli they can be defined in physical or psychological terms without any assumptions concerning special properties. The changes in the organism, strictly "strain," can be described and defined operationally, again without the confusing assumption that "stress" has been induced. In this way, powerful stimuli produce changes in people including an increase in arousal. If the cognitive clues are appropriate, or perhaps if they are absent, anxiety is experienced. I prefer not to regard this as an aspect of stress but as a stimulus-response paradigm.

A useful psychophysiological distinction may be between self-imposed and externally imposed stimuli, the latter producing more changes in arousal (Beaumaster et al., 1978). This, again, throws into prominence the role of cognitive factors. We need stimulation in our lives in order not to become bored: If so, it should be self-imposed! Threat may also be important and produce cardiovascular changes (Bloom and Trautt, 1977). But this process of subdividing stimuli into elements of greater and lesser relevance to psychophysiology again leads us to specifying stimuli without the need to invoke the global concept of "stressfulness."

REFERENCES

Ax, A. F. 1953. The physiological differentiation between fear and anger. *Psychosom. Med.*, 15:433-442.

Beaumaster, E. J., Knowles, J. B., and MacLean, A. W. 1978. The sleep of skydivers: A study of stress. *Psychophysiology*, 15:209-213.

Bloom, L. J., and Trautt, G. M. 1977. Finger pulse volume as a measure of anxiety: Further evaluation. *Psychophysiology*, 14:541-544.

Bond, A. J., James, D. C., and Lader, M. H. 1974. Physiological and psychological measures in anxious patients. *Psychol. Med.*, 4:364-373.

Duffy, E. 1951. The concept of energy mobilization. *Psychol. Rev.*, 58:30-40.

Duffy, E. 1957. The psychological significance of the concept of "arousal" or "activation." *Psychol. Rev.*, 64:265-275.

Duffy, E. 1962. *Activation and Behavior*. New York: Wiley.

Duffy, E. 1972. Activation. In N. S. Greenfield and R. A. Sternbach (eds.), *Handbook of Psychophysiology*, pp. 557-662. New York: Holt, Rinehart and Winston.

ERDMANN, G., and JANKE, W. 1978. Interaction between physiological and cognitive determinants of emotion: Experimental studies of Schachter's theory of emotions. *Biol. Psychol.*, 6:61-74.

ERDMANN, G., and VAN LINDERN, B. 1980. The effects of beta-adrenergic stimulation and beta-adrenergic blockade on emotional reactions. *Psychophysiology*, 17:332-338.

FENZ, W. D., and EPSTEIN, S. 1967. Gradients of physiological arousal of experienced and novice parachutists as a function of an approaching jump. *Psychosom. Med.*, 29:33-51.

FOWLES, D. C. 1980. The three-arousal model: Implications of Gray's two-factor learning theory for heart rate, electrodermal activity and psychopathy. *Psychophysiology*, 17:87-104.

FRANKENHAEUSER, M., and JÄRPE, G. 1963. Psychophysiological changes during infusions of adrenaline in various doses. *Psychopharmacologia*, 4:424-432.

FREEMAN, G. L. 1948. *The Energetics of Human Behavior*. Ithaca, N.Y.: Cornell University Press.

GOLDSTEIN, I. B. 1964. Physiological responses in anxious women patients. A study of autonomic activity and muscle tension. *Arch. Gen. Psychiatry*, 10:382-388.

GOLDWATER, B. C., and LEWIS, J. 1978. Effects of arousal on habituation of the electrodermal orienting reflex. *Psychophysiology*, 15:221-225.

GRAY, J. A. 1975. *Elements of a Two-Process Theory of Learning*. New York: Academic Press.

HEBB, D. O. 1955. Drives and the C.N.S. (conceptual nervous system). *Psychol. Rev.*, 62:243-254.

HOFFMANN, E. 1980. EEG frequency analysis of anxious patients and of normals during resting and during deep muscle relaxation. *Advances in Biological Psychiatry*, 4:119-130.

KATKIN, E. S. 1966. The relationship between a measure of transitory anxiety and spontaneous autonomic activity. *J. Abnorm. Psychol.*, 71:142-146.

LACEY, J. I. 1967. Somatic response patterning and stress: Some revisions of activation theory. In M. H. Appley and R. Trumbull (eds.), *Psychological Stress: Issues in Research*, pp. 14-44. New York: Appleton-Century-Crofts.

LADER, M. 1975. *The Psychophysiology of Mental Illness*. London: Routledge and Kegan Paul.

LADER, M. H., and WING, L. 1966. *Physiological Measures, Sedative Drugs and Morbid Anxiety*. London: Oxford University Press.

LEVI, L. 1963. The urinary output of adrenalin and noradrenalin during experimentally induced emotional stress in clinically different groups. *Acta Psychotherapeutica* (Basel), 11:218-227.

LINDSLEY, D. B. 1951. Emotion. In S. S. Stevens (ed.), *Handbook of Experimental Psychology*, pp. 473-512. New York: Wiley.

MCGUINNESS, D. 1973. Cardiovascular responses during habituation and mental activity in anxious men and women. *Biol. Psychol.*, 1:115-124.

MALMO, R. B. 1959. Activation: A neuropsychological dimension. *Psychol. Rev.*, 66:367-386.

MOYES, I. C. A., and MOYES, R. B. 1977. Urinary 3'5' cyclic adenosine monophosphate (cAMP) as a measure of anxiety. *Postgrad. Med. J.*, 53:(suppl. 4)41-46.

RASKIN, M. 1975. Decreased skin conductance response habituation in chronically anxious patients. *Biol. Psychol.*, 2:309-319.

SAINSBURY, P., and GIBSON, J. G. 1954. Symptoms of anxiety and tension and the accompanying physiological changes in the muscular system. *J. Neurol. Neurosurg. Psychiatry*, 17:216-224.

SCHACHTER, J. 1957. Pain, fear and anger in hypertensives and normotensives: A psychophysiological study. *Psychosom. Med.* 19:17-29.

SCHACHTER, S. 1966. The interaction of cognitive and physiological determinants of emotional state. In C. D. Spielberger (ed.), *Anxiety and Behavior*. New York: Academic Press.

SCHACHTER, S., and SINGER, J. E. 1962. Cognitive, social and physiological determinants of emotional state. *Psychol. Rev.*, 69:379-399.

TYRER, P. 1976. *The Role of Bodily Feelings in Anxiety*. London: Oxford University Press.

WAXER, P. H. 1977. Nonverbal cues for anxiety: An examination of emotional leakage. *J. Abnorm. Psychol.*, 86:306-314.

3

ANXIETY AND CEREBRAL BLOOD FLOW

ROY J. MATHEW, M.D., MAXINE L. WEINMAN, Dr.P.H.,
and JAMES L. CLAGHORN, M.D.

The study of cerebral blood flow has been made easier by the recent advent of noninvasive and accurate assessment techniques (Meyer et al., 1978; Obrist et al., 1975). Regional cerebral blood flow (rCBF) measurement is especially relevant to psychiatric research because of the close correlations that have been demonstrated between rCBF and brain function (Risberg, 1980). Such indices of neuronal metabolism as oxygen and glucose utilization have been shown to be tightly correlated with rCBF (Raichle et al., 1976). The map of the cerebral cortex, depicting levels of regional activity, which rCBF measurement provides may assist in evaluating regional brain function in functional illnesses.

ANATOMIC AND PHYSIOLOGIC CONSIDERATIONS

Blood supply to the human brain is normally provided by the two internal carotid arterial systems and a single basilar arterial system; the two vertebrals join together to form the basilar artery. These three major arteries are joined by the anterior and posterior communicating arteries to form the circulus arteriosus. The anterior, middle, and posterior cerebral arteries originate from the circulus arteriosus and supply each hemisphere. The circulus arteriosus also extends central branches to the interior of the brain. The arterial systems of the brain communicate with one another and with the extracranial arterial systems through anastomotic channels. Anterior, middle, and posterior cerebral arteries reach the cortex via the pia mater and form branches that penetrate the brain perpendicularly to form short cortical branches, which supply the middle zone of cortical gray matter, and long transcerebral branches (medullary arteries) which pass through the gray matter to supply underlying white matter. The angio-architecture of the brain is believed to be characteristically different in different parts of the brain. Capillary density in any given brain region seems to be related to regional blood flow, density of synapses, and the local metabolic rate for oxygen.

The brain is drained by three venous systems: the superficial external group, the deep internal group, and the dural sinuses. These three systems are connected by anastomotic channels and join to form the internal jugular veins (Baptista, 1976; Deshmukh and Meyer, 1978).

An adequate supply of oxygen and glucose is vital to brain function as the brain has only limited ability to store either one. Anoxia or hypoglycemia may lead to neuronal death in a short time. Several physiological auto-regulatory mechanisms are designed, therefore, to insulate the brain blood flow from the vicissitudes of peripheral circulatory and metabolic influences and intracranial pressure. Brain blood flow is normally regulated by such factors as neuronal metabolism, oxygen and carbon dioxide levels, and auto-nomic nervous system activity. Products of neuronal activity such as lactic acid, carbon dioxide, potassium, and adenosine diphosphate produce vaso-dilation while oxygen is a vasoconstrictor (Deshmukh and Meyer, 1978; Ingvar and Lassen, 1976; Olesen, 1972).

All major arteries supplying the brain have a rich adrenergic supply. Pial and superficial cortical arteries and arterioles are innervated by adrenergic fibers while most of the intraparenchymal vessels have little or no inner-vation. Most of the postganglionic adrenergic fibers that supply the intra-cranial blood vessels originate in the superior cervical ganglion. There is also some evidence of cholinergic innervation of cerebral vasculature (Chan-Pa-lay, 1977; Chorobski and Penfield, 1932; Owman et al., 1974; Rennels and Nelson, 1975; Rosenblum, 1971).

The influence of the autonomic nervous system on CBF is somewhat unclear. Electrical stimulation of the superior cervical ganglion has been demonstrated to cause reduction in cerebral blood flow which can be re-versed by alpha-adrenergic blockage. Norepinephrine (NE) and its agonists have been found to cause cerebral vasoconstriction; however, the cerebral arterioles are less sensitive to NE than the peripheral vessels (Hardebo et al., 1979; Lavyne et al., 1975; Raichle et al., 1975). Since ablation or phar-macological blockage of the superior cervical ganglia does not produce any significant change in brain blood flow, it seems that the sympathetic system does not influence resting CBF (Skinhøj, 1972). Cholinergic fibers which reach the brain capillaries through the facial nerve and the superficial petrosal nerves have been reported to bring about vasodilation (Chorobski and Pen-field, 1932). Studies with cholinergic agonists and antagonists, in general, support the concept of cholinergic vasodilation of cerebral blood vessels.

The cholinergic mechanisms have not, however, been researched as extensively as the adrenergic ones (Kawamura et al., 1975; Sokoloff, 1959).

AROUSAL AND CEREBRAL BLOOD FLOW

Nonspecific arousal, mediated by the reticular activating system (RAS) is believed to be the physiological basis for anxiety (see Lader, this volume). The concept of nonspecificity of arousal has been questioned because of the absence of anatomic homogeneity and regional differences in neuronal activation within the RAS, and because different physiological indices of arousal have not been shown to correlate (Siegel, 1979; Taylor and Epstein, 1967). The limbic system also has been implicated in arousal (Kelly, 1976; Routtenberg, 1968). Stimulation and lesion studies involving the limbic system, compared to the brain stem reticular activating system, indicate clearer functional localization in the former. Such functions as sexual stimulation, aggression, autonomic arousal, thirst, hunger and satiety have been ascribed to different parts within the limbic system by these studies (MacLean, 1973; Olds, 1976). The hypothalamus plays an important role in the arousal mechanism. Arousal is associated with such symptoms of hypothalamic origin as changes in sleep, libido, appetite, and neuroendocrine mechanisms (Antelman and Caggiula, 1980). The hypothalamus is connected to limbic structures such as the septum, amygdala, and hippocampus as well as to brain stem structures and thalamus through the hypothalamic-mesencephalic continuum (Kelly, 1976). More precise functional localization is possible in the hypothalamus than in the lower brain stem (Olds, 1976).

The cortex forms the end organ of the arousal chain. Neuronal activity in the cortex, midbrain, and reticular formation measured through multiunit recording techniques have been shown to be highly correlated with one another and with the observed arousal level (Bambridge and Gijsbers, 1977). The arousal system is responsible for the maintenance of optimal tone for the execution of the higher mental, motor, and sensory functions by the cortex (Luria, 1973). The frontal lobe has been described as the neocortical representative of the arousal system. Of the whole cerebral cortex, only the frontal lobe is known to project directly to the septal-hypothalamic-mesencephalic continuum (Nauta, 1964, 1971; Luria, 1973). Functional differentiation of the cortex is clearer and more complete (Luria, 1973; Nauta, 1964, 1971).

MacLean (1976) described three basic stages in the brain's evolution: the primitive reptilian (brain stem structures), the intermediate paleomammalian (limbic system), and the most highly developed neomammalian (cortex).

Progressive functional differentiation from brain stem to limbic system to cerebral cortex is in keeping with the axiom of evolution, that phylogenically older systems show less functional differentiation.

The connections between the components of the arousal mechanism are bidirectional, that is, higher centers can stimulate or inhibit the lower ones and vice versa (Nauta, 1964, 1971). Sensory stimulation is well known to increase reticular activation. As they ascend to the cortex, sensory signals stimulate the brain stem reticular activating system through collateral fibers (Siegel, 1979). Motor activity has also been demonstrated to be preceded by firing of reticular neurons as decending corticospinal tracts make collateral connections with the reticular activating system before they reach the spinal motor neurons. Behavioral studies show an increase in reticular formation unit firing in association with anticipated pain, pleasure, and aggression, which are believed to be frontal-lobe functions (Philips and Olds, 1969; Pond et al., 1977; Vertes and Miller, 1976). The foregoing information makes clear that sensory, motor, and mental activities can activate the RAS. This leaves intriguing questions about spontaneous activity of the system.

Studies of cerebral blood flow and metabolism may provide new insights into the physiology of arousal as close correlations have been demonstrated between blood flow and brain activity levels. Conditions characterized by increase in arousal, such as REM sleep, mental activation, and epileptic seizures, are known to be associated with increased blood flow to the brain (Knoblich et al., 1979; Meyer, 1978; Sakai et al., 1979a and b), whereas hypo-arousal marked by drowsiness, slow-wave sleep, semicoma, and stupor are associated with reduced cerebral blood flow (Ingvar and Lassen, 1976; Sakai et al., 1979a and b; Sokoloff, 1959). Changes in EEG and cerebral blood flow have been shown to run in parallel in conditions characterized by altered levels of awareness (Ingvar and Soderberg, 1956; Ingvar et al., 1976). Amphetamine sulfate, which is known to increase arousal, had also been reported to increase CBF (Berntman et al., 1975).

That the brain stem reticular activating system plays an important role in arousal mechanisms is further supported by findings that stimulation of the brain stem increases brain blood flow (Ingvar and Soderberg, 1958). Ingvar et al. (1964) reported reduction in cerebral blood flow in a comatose patient with an upper brain stem lesion, and brain stem cerebellar blood flow changes have been reported to be correlated to levels of arousal in conditions characterized by altered levels of awareness (Juge et al., 1979).

Under conditions of resting wakefulness, normal human brain shows increased blood flow to the frontal areas. This is in keeping with the hypothesis that the frontal lobe which is connected to the limbic system and RAS is responsible for maintaining the cortical tone. In states of reduced or absent consciousness, the hyperfrontal rCBF pattern disappears and the flow becomes almost uniform (Ingvar, 1979). Activation has been found to be associated with two types of rCBF increases: a diffuse, global increase with more marked changes in the frontal areas and a focal increase in the anatomically appropriate brain region depending upon the sensory modality through which activation was induced. The former is believed to represent increase in nonspecific arousal and the latter sensory stimulation. The former has also been demonstrated to habituate upon repeated presentation of the stimulus (Risberg et al., 1977).

As Lader points out (this volume), the relationship between arousal and anxiety is somewhat unclear. Most investigators of this topic subscribe to the view that anxiety may be associated with hyperarousal. The research literature on the effect of anxiety on cerebral blood flow is scanty.

CEREBRAL BLOOD FLOW MEASURED BY THE NITROUS OXIDE TECHNIQUE IN ANXIOUS SUBJECTS

Kety and Schmidt (1948) developed a technique for measuring cerebral blood flow and cerebral oxygen consumption in human beings. In this procedure, the subject inhales nitrous oxide, and serial blood samples are drawn from the subject's internal jugular vein and femoral artery. Cerebral blood flow and oxygen consumption are calculated on the basis of the Fick Principle, using the arterial venous differences in nitrous oxide and oxygen and the blood brain partition coefficient for these substances. Values thus derived were shown to represent global cerebral blood flow with little contamination from extracranial circulation. The technique is invasive, however, and does not yield regional data.

Kety (1952) reported increased cerebral oxygen consumption in a patient who had an anxiety attack during cerebral blood flow measurement. Kety also investigated the effect of epinephrine and norepinephrine infusions on cerebral blood flow and cerebral oxygen consumption, finding that norepinephrine was not associated with significant changes, but epinephrine increased cerebral blood flow by 21 percent and cerebral oxygen consumption by 22 percent.

These changes are unlikely to be the result of direct action by epinephrine on the cerebral vessels, as intracarotid injections of epinephrine have been reported to have no effect on CBF (Olesen, 1972). The blood-brain barrier is likely to prevent most of the epinephrine from reaching the brain. Furthermore, brain blood vessels are known to contain enzymes capable of metabolizing epinephrine in their walls (Bertler et al., 1961, 1966). Pial capillaries are relatively insensitive to *in vivo* epinephrine application by micropipette; responses elicited by a large dose are vasoconstrictive (Wahl et al., 1972).

Epinephrine administered parenterally is known to induce anxiety in predisposed persons, probably via the peripheral symptoms of anxiety produced by the drug (Schildkraut and Kety, 1967; for full discussion, see Pitts and Allen, this volume). Thus, the increase in cerebral blood flow following epinephrine injection is likely to be secondary to increased arousal and not caused by the drug's direct action on cerebral blood vessels. Support for the hypothesis that epinephrine increases cerebral blood flow and oxygen consumption was provided by King et al. (1952) who showed that increases in CBF and cerebral oxygen consumption after epinephrine administration was not associated with changes in vascular resistance.

CEREBRAL BLOOD FLOW MEASURED VIA THE [133]XENON INHALATION TECHNIQUE—AND ANXIETY

The [133]Xenon inhalation technique is a relatively noninvasive method for accurate quantification of cerebral blood flow. [133]Xenon, a chemically inert and freely diffusible tracer gas, is mixed with ambient air and inhaled through a sterilized, close-fitting face mask. After one minute of inhalation, the desaturation activity of the isotope is monitored for 10 minutes by a system of 16 collimated probes mounted on a helmet and applied to the scalp. Values for regional cerebral blood flow are calculated by two-compartmental analysis of the recorded curves, based on a modification of the Fick Principle, by a minicomputer. Xenon recirculation to the brain is corrected using the end-tidal levels of the isotope which has been shown to be in equilibrium with arterial levels.

[133]Xenon emits gamma and x-rays whose desaturation curves derived from the brain are used for blood flow measurement. Previous reports have demonstrated the reliability and validity of blood flow values thus obtained. Blood pressure, pulse rate, respiratory rate, carbon dioxide and oxygen content of the expired air are monitored throughout the procedure. A comprehensive account of the procedural details and instrumentation may be found in Obrist et al. (1975), Meyer et al. (1978), and Deshmukh and Meyer (1978).

The [133]Xenon inhalation technique has the advantage of providing information on regional cerebral blood flow in a safe, relatively noninvasive manner. The technique, which uses radiation emitted from the brain registered by scintillation detectors applied to the scalp, measures cortical blood flow whereas the nitrous oxide inhalation technique, based on arterial venous (internal-jugular) differences, yields blood flow values for the entire brain (Kety and Schmidt, 1948).

Isocounts recorded by the collimated probes used in the Xenon inhalation technique were tested by moving a 1-mm-diameter point source of Xenon in a water-filled human skull and in the postmortem brain tissue from a baboon. The probes were found to view a truncated cone at the optimum depth of 4 to 8 cm with a maximum diameter of 4 cm (Juge et al., 1979; Sakai et al, 1979a and b).

Cerebral blood flow measurements were taken via the [133]Xenon inhalation technique in nine subjects who had been diagnosed as having generalized anxiety disorders, according to the *Diagnostic and Statistical Manual of Mental Disorders, Third Edition* of the American Psychiatric Association, and nine normal controls matched for age, sex, and hand preference. All subjects underwent a drug washout period of four weeks' duration and were expected to avoid coffee, tea, and tobacco for two hours before rCBF measurements. Degrees of anxiety experienced by the anxious patients during rCBF measurements were quantified by the state anxiety scale of the State Trait Anxiety Inventory(STAI) (Spielberger et al., 1970).

Gray matter flow was, in general, lower for the anxious subjects compared to the controls; however, the difference failed to reach statistical significance (patients: left hemisphere *81.61, S. D. 13.26, right hemisphere 83.35, S. D. 17.90; controls: left hemisphere 87.28, S. D. 13.16, right hemisphere 84.12, S. D. 9.22). The anxious patients and controls did not show significant differences on $PECO_2$, PEO_2 and the physiological indices. Next, state anxiety scores were correlated with rCBF values (Table 1).

Table 1

Correlations Between State Anxiety and Blood Flow (Patients n = 9)

Left	r	p	Right	r	p
Hemisphere	-.63	.03	Hemisphere	-.67	.02
Pre Frontal	-.46	.11	Pre Frontal	-.77	.008
Pre Central	-.90	.007	Pre Central	-.53	.07
Parietal	-.87	.002	Parietal	-.64	.04
Opercular	-.36	.17	Opercular	-.31	.20
Posterior Temporal	-.68	.02	Posterior Temporal	-.90	.001
Occipital	-.59	.04	Occipital	-.69	.02
Inferior Temporal	-.61	.04	Inferior Temporal	-.44	.11

*Graymatter blood flow expressed as millilitters/100 grams of brain tissue/minute.

These findings suggested that anxiety is associated with reduced cortical blood flow.

DISCUSSION

Cerebral blood flow measured by the nitrous oxide inhalation technique shows anxiety-related increases, while the [133]Xenon inhalation technique indicates anxiety-related reduction in blood flow.

Most experts agree that anxiety has two components, psychic and somatic (Lader, 1976; Tyrer, 1976). Psychic anxiety is characterized by such symptoms as apprehension, worry, inner tension, restlessness, and mental agitation, while symptoms of autonomic malfunctioning such as palpitations, increased perspiration, gastric discomfort, diarrhea, and frequent urination characterize somatic anxiety. That psychic anxiety is likely to be associated with an increase in cerebral blood flow is shown by the increases in blood flow that characterize other conditions of hyperarousal (Ingvar and Soderberg, 1956, 1958). An increase in sympathetic tone associated with somatic anxiety may, however, reduce blood flow to the cerebral cortex. Thus, the psychic and somatic components of anxiety are likely to have opposing influences on cerebral blood flow. It should be borne in mind that dense autonomic innervation exists in the more superficial cortical blood vessels only, with the vessels in deeper brain regions showing little or no such innervations.

Most anxious subjects manifest varying degrees of psychic and somatic anxiety. It is possible that the increase in cerebral blood flow and metabolism Kety reported (1950) is secondary to psychic anxiety and arousal, as the blood flow values measured with this technique represent blood flow of the entire brain. As the [133]Xenon inhalation technique we used measured mainly cortical blood flow, the lower blood flow levels found in anxious patients may be the result of cortical vasoconstriction secondary to increased sympathetic tone. Harper et al. (1972) suggested that a reciprocal relationship between blood flow to the superficial and deeper parts of the brain may exist.

The hypothesis that anxiety and cerebral blood flow are related should be regarded as preliminary because studies on which it is based suffer from several methodological shortcomings. Kety's studies on anxiety, for example, were limited in methodology and number of subjects, and the data are from normal subjects who experienced anxiety during blood flow measurement and after injection of epinephrine and norepinephrine. No information is available on the subjects' medication status and no attempts seem to have been made to quantify degrees of anxiety. Since the completion of our preliminary regional cerebral blood flow/anxiety study, we found that similar decreases in cerebral blood flow were associated with depression (Mathew et al., 1980). We had not carefully excluded depression in our anxious patients, which made the relationship we found between anxiety and cerebral blood flow uncertain. Our index group consisted of only nine subjects and we did not differentiate the psychic and somatic components of anxiety.

It is obvious that study of cerebral blood flow and metabolism would be of considerable significance to the study of anxiety. The [133]Xenon inhalation technique seems to be a promising approach to measuring cortical blood flow and functional activity. The nitrous oxide inhalation technique has become less popular because of its invasive nature. However, more recent techniques such as positron emission tomography, which provide information about cerebral blood flow and metabolism in deep brain, may increase our knowledge of subcortical activity in anxiety.

REFERENCES

ANTELMAN, S. M., and CAGGIULA, A. R. 1980. Stress induced behavior: Chemotherapy without drugs. In J. M. Davidson and R. J. Davidson (eds.), *The Psychobiology of Consciousness*, pp. 65-104. New York: Plenum.

BAMBRIDGE, R., and GIJSBERS, K. 1977. The role of tonic neural activity in motivational processes. *Exp. Neurol.*, 56:370-385.

BAPTISTA, A. G. 1976. Aspects of cerebral circulation. In H. E. Himwich (ed.), *Brain Metabolism and Cerebral Disorders*, pp. 129-161. New York: Spectrum.

BERNTMAN, L., CARLSSON, C., amd HAGERDAL, M. 1975. Circulatory and metabolic effects in the brain induced by amphetamine sulfate. *Acta Physiol. Scand.*, 102:310-323.

BERTLER, A., FALCK, B., and ROSENGREN, E. 1961. The direct demonstration of a barrier mechanism in the brain capillaries. *Acta Pharmacol. Toxicol.*, 20:317-321.

BERTLER, A., FALCK, B., OWMAN, C. H., and ROSENGREN, E. 1966. The localisation of monoaminergic blood brain barrier mechanisms. *Pharmacol. Rev.*, 18:369-385.

CHAN-PALAY, V. 1977. Innervation of cerebral blood vessels by norepinephrine, indoleamine, substance P and neurotensin fibres and the leptomeningeal indoleamine axons: Their role in vasomotor activity and local alterations of brain blood composition. *Neurogenic Control of Brain Circulation*. Wenner-Gren Center International Symposium Series, 30:39-53.

CHOROBSKI, J., and PENFIELD, W. 1932. Cerebral vasodilator nerves and their pathway from the medulla oblongata. *Arch. Neurol. Psychiatry*, 28:1257-1289.

DESHMUKH, V. D., and MEYER, J. S. 1978. *Noninvasive Measurement of Regional Cerebral Blood Flow in Man*, p. 121. New York: SP Medical and Scientific Books.

HARDEBO, J. E., NILSSON, B., and OWMAN, C. H. 1979. The effect of a short lasting intracarotid injection of sympathomimetic and serotonergic receptor stimulants upon cerebral blood flow as measured by a venous outflow method. *Acta Neurol. Scand.*, 60 (suppl 72):136-137.

HARPER, A. M., DESHMUKH, V. D., ROWAN, J. O., INST, P. F., and JENNETT, W. B. 1972. The influence of sympathetic nervous activity on cerebral blood flow. *Arch. Neurol.*, 27:1-6.

INGVAR, D. H. 1979. Hyperfrontal distribution of the cerebral grey matter flow in resting wakefulness; on the functional anatomy of the conscious state. *Acta Neurol. Scand.*, 60:12-25.

INGVAR, D. H., HAGGENDAL, E., NILSSON, E. J., SOURANDER, P., WICKBOM, I., and LASSEN, N. A. 1964. Cerebral circulation and metabolism in a comatose patient. *Arch. Neurol.*, 11:13-21.

INGVAR, D. H., and LASSEN, N. A. 1976. Regulation of cerebral blood flow. In H. E. Himwich (ed.), *Brain Metabolism and Cerebral Disorders*, pp. 181-206. New York: Spectrum.

INGVAR, D. H., SJOLUND, B., and ARDO, A. 1976. Correlation between dominant EEG frequency, cerebral oxygen uptake and blood flow. *Electroencephalogr. Clin. Neurophysiol.*, 11:268-276.

INGVAR, D. H., and SODERBERG, U. 1956. A new method for measuring cerebral blood flow in relation to the encephalogram. *Electroencephalography*, 8:403-412.

INGVAR, D. H., and SODERBERG, U. 1958. Cortical blood flow related to EEG patterns evoked by stimulation of the brain stem. *Acta Physiol. Scand.*, 42:130-143.

JUGE, O., MEYER, J. S., SAKAI, F., YAMAGUCHI, F., YAMAMOTO, M., and SHAW, T. 1979. Critical appraisal of cerebral blood flow measured from brain stem and cerebellar regions after [133]Xenon inhalation in humans. *Stroke*, 10:428-437.

KAWAMURA, Y., MEYER, J. S., and HIROMOTO, H. 1975. Neurogenic control of cerebral blood flow in the baboon. Effects of cholinergic inhibitory agent atropine on cerebral auto regulation and vasomotor reactivity to Pa CO_2. *J. Neurosurg.*, 43:676-688.

KELLY, D. 1976. Neurosurgical treatment of psychiatric disorders. In K. Granville-Grossman (ed.), *Recent Advances in Clinical Psychiatry*, pp. 227-262. London: Churchill Livingstone.

KETY, S. S. 1950. Circulation and metabolism in health and disease. *Am. J. Med.*, 8:205-217.

KETY, S. S. 1952. Consciousness and the metabolism of the brain. In H. A. Abramson (ed.), *Conference on Problems of Consciousness*, pp. 11-75. New York: Josiah Macy (Jr.) Foundation.

KETY, S. S., and SCHMIDT, C. F. 1948. The nitrous oxide method for the quantitative determination of cerebral blood flow in man: Theory, procedure and normal values. *J. Clin. Invest.*, 27:476-483.

KING, B. D., SOKOLOFF, L., and WECHSLER, R. L. 1952. The effects of 1-epinephrine and 1-norepinephrine upon cerebral circulation and metabolism in man. *J. Clin. Invest.*, 31:273-279.

KNOBLICH, O. E., GAAB, M., and WEBER, W. 1979. CBF, ICP and EEG in various forms of cerebral seizures. In F. Gotoh, H. Nagai, and Y. Tazaki (eds.), *Cerebral Blood Flow and Metabolism. Acta Neurol. Scand.* (Suppl. 72), 60:550-551.

LADER, M. H. 1976. The peripheral and central role of the catecholamines in the mechanisms of anxiety. In D. F. Klein and R. Gittelman-Klein (eds.), *Progress in Psychiatric Drug Treatment*, pp. 557-569. New York: Brunner/Mazel.

LAVYNE, M., WURTMAN, R. J., and MOSKOWITZ ZERVAS, N. 1975. Brain catecholamines and blood flow. *Life Sci.*, 16:476-486.

LURIA, A. R. 1973. *The Working Brain.* New York: Basic Books.

MACLEAN, P. 1973. Special award lecture: New findings on brain function and sociosexual behavior. In J. Zubin and J. Money (eds.), *Contemporary Sexual Behavior. Critical Issues in the 1970's*, pp. 53-74. Baltimore: Johns Hopkins.

MACLEAN, P. 1976. Sensory and perceptive factors in emotional functions of the triune brain. In R. G. Grenell and S. Gabay (eds.), *Biological Foundations of Psychiatry*, vol. 1, pp. 177-198. New York: Raven.

MATHEW, R. J., MEYER, J. S., FRANCIS, D. J., SEMCHUK, K. M., MORTEL, K., and CLAGHORN, J. L. 1980. Cerebral blood flow in depression. *Am. J. Psychiatry*, 137:1449-1450.

MEYER, J. S. 1978. Improved method for noninvasive measurement of regional cerebral blood flow by [133]Xenon inhalation. *Stroke*, 9:205-210.

MEYER, J. S., ISHIHARA, N., DESHMUKH, V. D., NARITOMI, H., SAKAI, F., HSU, M., and POLLACK, P. 1978. Improved method for non-invasive measurement of regional cerebral blood flow by [133]Xenon inhalation. Part I. Description of method and normal values obtained in healthy volunteers. *Stroke*, 9:195-205.

NAUTA, W. J. H. 1964. Some aberrant connections of the pre-frontal cortex in the monkey. In

J. M. Warren and K. Akert (eds.), *The Frontal Granular Cortex and Behavior*. New York: McGraw-Hill.

NAUTA, W. J. H. 1971. The problem of the frontal lobe: A reinterpretation. *J. Psychiatr. Res.*, 8:167-187.

OBRIST, W. D., THOMPSON, H. K., and WANG, H. S. 1975. Regional cerebral blood flow estimated by [133]Xenon inhalation. *Stroke*, 6:245-256.

OLDS, J. 1976. Behavioral studies of hypothalamic functions: Drives and reinforcements. In R. G. Grennel and S. Gabay (eds.), *Biological Foundations of Psychiatry*, vol. 1, pp. 322-448. New York: Raven.

OLESEN, J. 1972. The effect of intracarotid epinephrine, norepinephrine and angiotension on the regional cerebral blood flow in man. *Neurology*, 22:978-987.

OWMAN, C., EDVINSOON, L., and NIELSON, K. C. 1974. Autonomic neuroreceptor mechanisms in brain vessels. *Blood Vessels*, 11:2-31.

PHILIPS, M. I., and OLDS, J. 1969. Unit activity: Motivation dependent response from midbrain neurones. *Science*, 165:1269-1271.

POND, F. J., SINNAMON, H. M., and ADAMS, D. B. 1977. Single unit recording in the midbrain of rats during shock-elicited fighting behavior. *Brain Res.*, 120:469-484.

RAICHLE, M. E., HARTMAN, B. E., and EICHLING, J. O. 1975. Central noradrenergic regulation of cerebral blood flow and vascular permeability. *Proceedings of National Academy of Science*, 72:3726-3730.

RAICHLE, M., GRUBB, R. L., GADO, M. H., EICHLING, J. O., and TEN-POGOASSIAN, M. M. 1976. Correlation between regional cerebral blood flow and oxidative metabolism: In vivo studies in man. *Arch. Neurol.*, 33:523-526.

RENNELS, M. L., and NELSON, E. 1975. Capillary innervation in the cat brain. In A. M. Harper, W. B. Jennett, J. D. Miller and J. O. Rowan (eds.), *Blood Flow and Metabolism in the Brain*, pp. 1.10-1.11. London: Churchill Livingstone.

RISBERG, J. 1980. Regional cerebral blood flow measurements by [133]Xenon inhalation. Methodology and application in neuropsychology and psychiatry. *Brain and Language*, 9:9-34.

RISBERG, J., MAXIMILIAN, A. V., and PROHOVNIK, I. 1977. Changes of cortical activity patterns during habituation to a reasoning test. *Neuropsychologia*, 15:793-798.

ROSENBLUM, W. I. 1971. Neurogenic control of cerebral circulation. *Stroke*, 2:429-439.

ROUTTENBERG, A. 1968. The two-arousal hypothesis: Reticular formation and limbic system. *Psychol. Rev.*, 75:51-80.

SAKAI, F., MEYER, J. S., KARACAN, I., YAMAGUCHI, F., and YAMAMOTO, M. D. 1979a. Narcolepsy: Regional cerebral blood flow during sleep and wakefulness. *Neurology*, 29:61-67.

SAKAI, F., MEYER, J. S., YAMAGUCHI, F., YAMAMOTO, M., and SHAW, T. 1979b. [133]Xenon inhalation for measuring cerebral blood flow in conscious baboons. *Stroke*, 10:310-318.

SCHILDKRAUT, J. J., and KETY, S. S. 1967. Biogenic amines and emotion. *Science*, 156:21-30.

SIEGEL, J. M. 1979. Behavioral functions of the reticular formation. *Brain Research Reviews*, 1:69-105.

SKINHOJ, E. 1972. The sympathetic nervous system and the regulation of cerebral blood flow in man. *Stroke*, 3:711-716.

SOKOLOFF, L. 1959. The action of drugs on cerebral circulation. *Pharmacol. Rev.*, 11:1-85.

SPIELBERGER, C. D., GORSUCH, R. L., and LUSHENE, R. D. 1970. *STAI Manual*. Palo Alto, CA: Consulting Psychologists Press.

TAYLOR, S. P., and EPSTEIN, S. 1967. The measurement of autonomic arousal: Some basic issues illustrated by covariation of heart rate and skin conductance. *Psychosom. Med.*, 29:514-525.

TYRER, P. 1976. *The Role of Bodily Feelings in Anxiety*. New York: Oxford University Press.

VERTES, R. P., and MILLER, N. E. 1976. Brainstem neurones that fire selectively to a conditioned stimulus for shock. *Brain Res.*, 103:229-242.

WAHL, M., KUSCHINSKY, W., BOSSE, O., OLESEN, J., LASSEN, N. A., INGVAR, D. H., and THURAU, K. 1972. Effect of 1-norepinephrine on the diameter of pial arterioles and arteries in the cat. *Circ. Res.*, 21:248-258.

II.
THE ANXIETY–PRONE
PERSONALITY

4

GENETIC INFLUENCES ON ANXIETY NEUROSIS AND AGORAPHOBIA

GREGORY CAREY, Ph.D.

Anxiety has many different meanings for behavioral geneticists, ranging from scales on personality questionnaires to studies of benzodiazapine receptors in the brain. The literature is too vast to summarize succinctly, so this review will deal only with studies relating to human beings and psychopathology.

The recently revised edition of the *Diagnostic and Statistical Manual of Mental Disorders* (DSM-III) conceives anxiety disorder as a broad general category subsuming what was traditionally known as anxiety neurosis (panic disorder, generalized anxiety disorder, and atypical anxiety disorder), phobic neurosis and its subvarieties, and obsessional disorder. The genetic literature is best on anxiety neurosis; there are very few studies of the other two types of anxiety disorders. There is considerable difficulty, however, in aptly comparing results of one study of anxiety neurosis with those of another. The major difference seems to be diagnostic criteria. Earlier studies have often failed to mention the explicit operational criteria used for diagnoses, while the contemporary studies, as a rule, tend to make such criteria explicit.

ANXIETY DISORDER

Table 1 presents the results of all genetic and family studies of anxiety disorder. Most of the earlier studies used the family history method of investigation. That is, one interviews the proband (the initial anxiety neurotic ascertained) about the presence or absence of anxiety neurosis in family members. Occasionally, an additional informant, usually a relative, is used to confirm information given by the proband. This method of investigation has the advantage of ease in data collection, but many relatives may be

37

Table 1

Prevalence of Anxiety Neurosis Among Relatives of Anxiety Neurotics

Study	Type of Relative	Type of Investigation[1]	Prevalence in Relatives (%)		
			Males	Females	Total
Brown (1942)	Second degree	FH			3
Pauls et al. (1979)	Second degree	FH	5	14	10
McInnes (1937)	First degree	FH			15
Brown (1942)	First degree	FH			16
Cohen et al. (1951)	First degree	FH	12	20	16
Noyes et al. (1978)	First degree	FH	13	24	18
Wheeler et al. (1948)	First degree	FS			49
Crowe et al.[2] (1980)	First degree	FS	22	42	31
Cloninger et al.[3] (1981)	First degree	FS	2	13	8
Slater and Shields[2] (1969)	DZ twins	FS			4
Torgersen[2] (1978)	DZ twins	FS			9
Slater and Shields[2] (1969)	MZ twins	FS			41
Torgersen[2] (1978)	MZ twins	FS			30

[1]FH = Family history method; FS = Family study method
[2]Includes some relatives with only family history information
[3]Only definite cases included as probands and affected relatives

affected but not reported so by the informants. Thus, it is preferable also to have available *family study* methods in which the relatives are directly interviewed by a researcher about the presence or absence of psychopathology.

An important point to notice in Table 1 is the difference in prevalence by sex. Studies consistently show a higher prevalence among the female relatives of anxiety neurotics than among the male relatives. In general, slightly more than two women are affected for every affected man, although the Cloninger et al. (1981) preliminary report gives a slightly higher female-to-male ratio. Only those cases diagnosed as definite anxiety disorder in the Cloninger et al. study are included here. If one adds to these the questionable anxiety neurotics blindly diagnosed by the research team, figures become 19 percent females and 8 percent males affected, very close to the two-to-one females-to-male ratio shown in the other studies. In general the sex difference in prevalence among relatives is paralleled by a sex difference in prevalence among the general population (Carey et al., 1980). For example, Cloninger et al. estimate the prevalence of anxiety neurosis as 3.4 percent among women but 1.5 percent among men; if questionable cases are included in these figures, the prevalence estimates are raised to 10 percent and 4.2 percent respectively.

Another noteworthy point is that the prevalence in all relatives reported in Table 1 is greater than the prevalence reported for the general population or for control figures from studies which give them.

Table 1 also shows that the prevalence of anxiety disorder among second-degree relatives (grandparents, aunts, uncles, half-siblings) is lower than the prevalence among first-degree relatives (parents, siblings, or children). According to a genetic hypothesis, the risk for psychiatric illness should vary according to degree of genetic relationship to the proband. Second-degree relatives, on average, share one-quarter of their genes with the proband. First-degree relatives share one-half of their genes with the proband, this being exactly one-half in the case of parent to child and one-half on the average in the case of siblings. According to family history studies, the pooled risk for second-degree relatives (6 percent) is slightly less than half that for first-degree relatives (16 percent). According to some simple models of genetic transmission, the risk in second-degree relatives should be half that in first-degree relatives since the genetic correlation is exactly half that in first-degree relatives. The family history data are congruent with such a hypothesis but cannot, of course, confirm the hypothesis.

Generally, the family studies enumerated in Table 1 report a slightly higher prevalence of anxiety neurosis than do the family history investigations. This is not entirely unexpected as the same phenomenon occurs for affective disorders (Andreasen et al., 1977). It seems that there are many cases in the family that will go undetected when one is simply relying on one or two family members for information about psychiatric status. The main discrepancy from this observation seems to be the Cloninger et al. study (1981). The 8 percent prevalence among relatives is considerably lower than the 49 percent or 31 percent prevalence reported by Wheeler et al. (1948) and Crowe et al. (1980) respectively. I shall examine this discrepancy more fully later.

To have a heritable component, a disorder must run in families, but the observation that it does run in families does not necessarily imply heredity. To separate genetic from shared environmental effects, one must examine twins and assume that the environments of identical or monozygotic (MZ) twins are similar to those of fraternal or dizygotic (DZ) twins, or use an adoption study and assume that individuals who are adopted are a random sample of the general population and are placed in a random sample of adoptive environments. Many studies have addressed the issue of equal environments for MZ and DZ twin pairs. The twin method has thus far shown that these assumptions are robust (Loehlin and Nichols, 1976; Lytton, 1977; Scarr, 1969). Adoption studies need not concern us here for adoption data have yet to be gathered for any neurotic disorder.

The data in Table 1 show that there are only two twin investigations of anxiety neurosis. Slater and Shields (1969) studied a consecutive series of twins in the Maudsley Hospital in London, England. Case histories based on follow-up material, hospital notes, and general practitioner reports were prepared by Shields and then given to Slater who diagnosed the cases blindly with respect to zygosity and identification of the proband twin. As the data were collected in the 1950s and early 1960s, systematic structured interviews were not available, nor was criterion-oriented diagnosis. The Torgersen (1978) study is a preliminary report on a series of Norwegian twins ascertained by cross-matching the Norwegian Twin Register with the Norwegian Psychiatric Register. Torgersen had the advantage of using a structured interview (the Present State Examination), but the diagnostic criteria are not mentioned. Still, the results of the two twin investigations are congruent. Most studies demonstrate that MZ twins are more alike than DZ twins. Furthermore, the prevalence rates among DZ twins of the Slater and Shields and Torgersen studies are similar, 4 percent and 9 percent, and the MZ concordance rates for the two studies are also within sampling error of each other (41 percent and 30 percent). Thus, the data argue for some heritable component in anxiety disorder. Other data by Shields also suggest such a component: Shields (1962; in press) and Slater and Shields (1969) give the case histories of three identical pairs of twins raised apart, yet their anxiety symptoms are similar. Since these symptoms cannot be explained by common environmental influence or modeling, it is very likely that the assumptions of the twin method are met in these investigations and that a heritable influence on anxiety disorder is truly present.

Although data in Table 1 seem to implicate family and genetic factors in the etiology of anxiety neurosis, many of the family studies do not agree with one another. Specifically, the twin data and the Cloninger et al. family study do not agree at all with the two other family studies of first-degree relatives. Since all family studies are based on the personal investigation of relatives, the results should cohere, yet DZ twins who are as genetically similar as ordinary siblings seem to have a much lower rate of prevalence than the first-degree relatives studied by Wheeler et al. or Crowe et al. Although this difference may seem trivial, it is of contemporary importance when one considers that the analysis of one data set from the series concluded that panic disorder is caused by an autosomal dominant gene (Pauls et al., 1980).

Many possible discrepancies between the twin and family data have been addressed (Carey and Gottesman, 1981). The main differences seem to stem from two different sources—the threshold for calling an individual affected and the initial sample selection of the proband. These two aspects will be considered here.

Panic Disorder

Is panic disorder caused by an autosomal gene? Although the results of the Iowa investigations of panic disorders (Crowe et al., 1980; Noyes et al., 1978; Pauls et al., 1979, 1980) should be followed up with larger extended pedigrees, there are several reasons for caution before uncritically accepting autosomal dominant transmission as the "cause" for panic disorder. As already noted, there is a marked sex difference in the prevalence of panic disorder among family members. The sex difference is also found in many epidemiological studies (Carey et al., 1980). This does not invalidate dominant transmission—females and males may receive the gene with equal frequency but females may be more likely to exhibit the genetic effects (a phenomenon known as incomplete penetrance). Still, the sex difference indicates that something *in addition to* the hypothetical gene is also responsible for the onset of panic disorder.

Far more important, the prevalence reported in the Iowa research agrees with neither the twin data nor the family data of Cloninger et al. (1981). According to autosomal dominant transmission, MZ twins should show almost 100 percent concordance, DZ twins about 50 percent concordance, yet the observed rates are much lower. There are several reasons for this discrepancy, but two stand out: There may be diagnostic differences between the twin studies and the Iowa studies, and there may be a selection bias in the Iowa data.

The Iowa researchers did a record search on 1,024 charts of individuals with a hospital diagnosis of anxiety neurosis or a related diagnosis like hyperventilation syndrome. From these records only 155 cases met stringent diagnostic criteria given by Noyes et al. (1978). The 155 people were then followed up and 112 (72 percent) were given a research diagnosis of anxiety neurosis based on the follow-up information. The family study was based on 20 of these persons. It may well be that in the process of going from 1,024 records to 20 probands (only 2 percent of the original material), only the clear-cut, severe cases were selected as probands. If the disorder is actually transmitted as a polygenic system, then selecting severely affected individuals should yield a high rate of affected family members. The severity phenomenon is well documented in schizophrenia research in which MZ twin concordance is found to increase as the severity of the proband twin's illness increases (Gottesman, 1968).

Fortunately, one can explore these two competing hypotheses using the published data. Both Crowe et al. (1980) and Cloninger et al. (1981) used the Feighner diagnostic criteria (Feighner et al., 1972) for anxiety neurosis. Therefore, the two family studies should have had consistent results if there was no selection bias. Results from the control groups in both studies suggest this. The raw prevalence among the 90 control relatives in Crowe et al. is 3.3 percent; the lifetime risk among those control relatives who were personally interviewed was about 8 percent. In the Cloninger et al. study the raw prevalence among 1,082 relatives, all personally interviewed, was 2.8 percent when definite anxiety neurosis was diagnosed. When questionable cases are included, this figure increases to 7.5 percent.

The situation is very different when one looks at prevalence among relatives of affected probands, shown in the diagnostic portion of Table 2. In this table, I have given the raw prevalence data from the Crowe study for all relatives, both those interviewed and those not interviewed. Since all the relatives in the Cloninger study were personally interviewed, those cases undetected by relying only on family history information should make it more difficult to find differences between the two studies. Yet, as the chi squares show, there are still significant differences between the two rates of prevalence, even though both studies used similar diagnostic criteria.

The sampling portion of Table 2 shows the results of two studies which used similar sampling techniques to ascertain their probands. The Cloninger et al. (1981) study began with 500 randomly selected individuals attending an outpatient psychiatric clinic. They were not screened for severity or for clear-cut cases of psychopathology. Slater and Shields' (1969) sample group of twins was very similarly selected, although it did include some inpatients, because *all* twins entering their hospital were studied. Here the rates for first-degree relatives and dizygotic twins are within sampling error of each other. On the other hand, the rates for monozygotic twins, using either a narrow or broad definition, are considerably elevated. Thus, it would seem that the differences in sampling probands are the major reason for the discrepancy between the Iowa data and the rest of the literature, not differences in blind diagnostic criteria.

PHOBIC DISORDER—AGORAPHOBIA

Let us now consider other anxiety disorders closely related to what DSM-III calls panic disorder, namely agoraphobia and social phobias. Compared to the family and twin literature on anxiety neurosis, there are relatively few data for the phobic disorders. Of two family history studies, Solyom et al. (1974) reported a high rate of phobic disorders among mothers of agoraphobic women; Buglass et al. (1977), however, found little evidence for an increased familial prevalence.

Much of my own research is focused on the genetics of phobic disorders. With Irving I. Gottesman and the late James Shields, I recently followed

Table 2

Comparison of Sampling Versus Diagnostic Criteria as Reasons for Discrepancy Among Family Studies of Anxiety Neurosis

Similar Diagnostic Criteria

Study	N Relatives	% Affected
Crowe et al. (1981)	121	26
Cloninger et al. (1981) —definite anxiety neurosis	141	8
—definite and questionable anxiety neurosis	141	14

x^2 (Crowe vs. Cloninger definite) = 14.87, $p < 0.01$
x^2 (Crowe vs. Cloninger definite and questionable) = 5.10, $p < 0.01$

Similar Sampling

Study	MZ Twins N	% Affected	DZ Twins or First-Degree Relatives N	% Affected
Slater and Shields (1969) —definite anxiety neurosis	17	41	28	4
—definite & questionable anxiety neurosis	20	65	40	13
Cloninger et al. (1981) —definite anxiety neurosis			141	8
—definite & questionable anxiety neurosis			172	14

x^2: Cloninger vs. MZ, definite = 13.60, $p < 0.01$
Cloninger vs. DZ, definite = 0.15, NS
Cloninger vs. MZ. definite and questionable = 26.82, $p < 0.01$
Cloninger vs. DZ. definite and questionable = 0.002, NS

up phobic and obsessive twins who entered the Maudsley or Bethlem Hospitals from 1948 through 1979, a period of 31 years. We have completed the field work on all but one or two of these pairs, yet despite the long admission span there are relatively few of these pairs, especially when one wants to subdivide them into phobic and obsessional. Here, only the phobic pairs will be considered; however, a fuller report on both phobic and obsessive pairs appears elsewhere (Carey and Gottesman, 1981). Most phobic proband twins who enter either the inpatient or outpatient department of the hospital could be considered either agoraphobic or social-phobic; *no* individuals were admitted during this time period who were twins and also had only a specific animal phobia. (One such pair of identical twins entered after the cut-off date for the study and appears to be discordant, but we did not conduct a personal interview of the co-twin.) As a full work-up on the whole series has yet to be done, the results are preliminary, but we do not expect much change once the whole series is analyzed.

The first hint of genetic significance in this series, for both obsessives and phobics, came from a review of the case notes held at that time by James Shields. Notes on about one-quarter of the monozygotic and the dizygotic co-twins contained some record of the patients' having either a psychiatric referral or an Armed Forces discharge based on a psychiatric reason. These data seemed to indicate little heritability for these disorders. But further perusal of the notes showed something else: 74 percent of the 23 MZ twins were regarded in some way as psychiatrically noteworthy, either by psychiatrists, general practitioners, reports from other relatives, or from previous follow-up interviews that had been done with these twins. In contrast only 39 percent of the 28 DZ co-twins were regarded as having some noteworthy psychiatric phenomenon. This suggested that field work using modern methods of descriptive psychiatry might characterize types of potential disorders in the co-twins who had not received any psychiatric care.

An attempt was made to personally contact and interview all surviving probands and co-twins, using the Present State Examination, supplemented by additional questions on obsessions from the Leyton Obsessional Inventory (Cooper, 1970) and by a list of 20 common phobias. Family histories and Minnesota Multiphasic Personality Inventories (MMPI) also were administered. There were 21 phobic pairs among the 51 twins we have analyzed so far. Of these, on personal interview, 88 percent of the eight MZ pairs reported either phobic disorder or phobic features, all but one pair never having had any psychiatric referral for these particular phobias. Of the 13 DZ pairs, only 38 percent had phobic symptoms or phobic features, and only one had had psychiatric treatment for an episode involving phobias.

The term "phobic features" is deliberately used here to classify individuals with pronounced but very uncommon fears that did not lead to marked social incapacitation or interference in a normal lifestyle. The term may best be explained through a case history of a 58-year-old DZ co-twin who was raised apart from her agoraphobic twin sister. The case history is given fully in Carey (1978). During the interview, she reported that she did not "like" crowds, leaving her house on her own, being inside her home alone, and being in open places. She is very anxious on tube trains and as a passenger in a car. She dislikes these situations because they induce feelings of anxiety and fear in her, not because of any inconvenience they may cause. She avoids only open places, and will not enter alone an area such as an open field or even bleak landscapes not broken up by trees, forests, or buildings. She will encounter the other situations, although somewhat reluctantly. She recalled obsessional checking, beginning at about age 12, ". . . sort of posting a letter and going all the way back [from home] because I *knew* I put it in the box, but I had to go and make sure I put it in the box, that sort of silly thing, you know?" Because she lives in a semi-rural area, she reported no incapacitation from any of her fears and has never experienced a panic attack, as defined by Feighner et al. (1972) or DSM-III criteria, in any of these situations. One wonders whether her fear of crowds and tube trains would cause social incapacitation were she to live in a busy metropolis, or whether her fear of open places might cause her to be housebound if she were to live on an isolated farm. She reported that the checking compulsion causes only minor inconvenience—she might have to waste two or three minutes going back to recheck something—but it hardly dominated her life or made her miserable. She considered it a mere eccentricity. Because DSM-III criteria require that the fears be "pervasive" or "dominating individual's life," she would hardly qualify for a diagnosis of obsessive-compulsive neurosis according to the DSM-III definition. Hence, the term "features" is used to indicate mild symptoms (*not* phobic or obsessional *traits*) that are not severe or incapacitating enough to be of clinical significance.

Because of small sample size, these results do not firmly establish a heritable influence on the more severe forms of phobic disorders that come to the attention of psychiatrists. Small numbers, of course, reduce the power (Cohen, 1977) of statistical analysis, so it is not surprising that the difference in concordance rates between MZ and DZ twins does not reach significance. Furthermore, imitation or modeling has been proposed as one of the principal etiological factors in the acquisition of fears and phobias (Bandura, 1969), so it is possible that the higher MZ concordance rates reported here may actually reflect the greater tendency of identical twins to imitate each other, relative to fraternal twins or other family members.

Several observations argue against these criticisms. First, the case history given above demonstrates that there can be concordance even when twins are raised apart. Second, in at least two of the MZ pairs concordant for phobic features, the *type* of phobias exhibited by one twin was unknown to the other twin. Third, in one pair of female identical twins, both twins broke down while they were apart, one soon after she moved from Ireland to London, the other in Ireland. Fourth, in several of the pairs, there was concordance for agoraphobia-like features, yet there was discordance for the *same* phobic stimuli. In one DZ pair (not included in this series because they came to our attention independently), one twin was afraid of dark, enclosed places, especially traveling on underground trains throughout London and also riding on crowded buses. The co-twin, on the other hand, did not report either of these fears, but was afraid of leaving her house unaccompanied, walking down streets unaccompanied when there were no people on the streets, and especially of open places. Both pairs reported panic attacks in their own phobic situations and both may be regarded as showing agoraphobia-like syndromes. Yet, despite concordance on the syndrome level, there is a marked discordance on specific fears that each twin exhibits.

Because twins are rare, especially those who seek psychiatric assistance for agoraphobia, I chose to pursue the study of both common fears and phobias in families. Data were collected on 151 families of individuals attending a course in introductory psychology at the University of Minnesota. Although this was not strictly a random sample of the general population, it was not selected for the presence or absence of phobias as the student volunteers were not required to have phobias. The students who volunteered for the project were asked to have both parents and the sibling closest in age complete a questionnaire on fears, a personality inventory (the Differential Personality Questionnaire developed by Tellegen, 1978), and a short self-report questionnaire on the presence or absence of phobias. All participants were given the definition of a phobia presented in Table 3 and asked to indicate on the questionnaire whether or not they had a phobia and, if they did, what type of phobias they had. The responses from 654 persons who completed the questionnaire were coded by a graduate student who was blind with respect to sex, age, and family membership of an individual. A computer printout of these ratings detailed the type of phobia reported by each individual (e.g., insects, snakes, heights, enclosed places, driving a car, etc.). Random numbers were assigned to each person by sex, age, or family membership. Among all these respondents, only three reported types

Table 3

Phobia Criteria: Minnesota Family Study

1. A more intense fear than the object or situation merits.
2. Most other people would not be fearful in that situation or with that object.
3. The fear is beyond voluntary control, and the person cannot be reasoned out of the fear.
4. The fear leads to avoidance of the object or situation.

of fears that may be considered agoraphobic in nature; that is, they recorded a *multiphobic* condition that involved uncommon fears of spatial-type stimuli like enclosed places, driving over a bridge, and/or phobias like crowds, going out alone, being left alone by oneself. The central aspect of this diagnosis was a multiphobic condition, that is, having at least two fears, neither of which were specific animal phobias nor phobias commonly encountered among the general population, like heights and enclosed places. Another seven individuals reported phobias very similar to the types of phobias that had been reported by the MZ and DZ co-twins and would be considered concordant for phobic features as defined previously. Since these individuals were rated blindly, no criticism could be made of a contaminated rating as might apply to the clinical twin series reported above. Table 4 shows the prevalence of various classes of phobias among the relatives of these 10 agoraphobic-like individuals. On almost all measures, the prevalence of phobias is much greater among the family members of these agoraphobic-like individuals than in the whole group combined. The actual prevalence of any type of phobia in the whole population is high, almost one-third of the whole group reporting some type of phobia. This high prevalence may have been found because the criteria did not require the presence of social incapacitation or interference in lifestyle as a result of the phobia. Two respondents from the same family were blindly rated as having agoraphobic-like natures,

Table 4

Prevalence of Various Types of Phobias Among Relatives of Agoraphobic-like Probands and Among the General Population

Kind of Phobia	Relatives (N = 33)	General Population (N = 642)	p^*
Any phobia	66.7	33.2	.001
Specific animal phobia	33.3	14.5	.002
Non-animal phobia	48.5	26.0	.003
More than one phobia	33.3	13.7	.001
More than one non-animal phobia	24.2	8.1	.001
Agoraphobia-like	6.1	1.6	.03
Obsession-like	3.0	0.3	.02

*One-tailed significance based on the difference between two proportions

yielding a prevalence among these family members significantly higher than that of the whole group. Only two persons were rated as having obsession-like syndromes, one involving checking behavior, the other involving perfectionism and orderliness. One of these was the mother of an agoraphobic-like individual.

Differences between the relatives of these agoraphobic-like individuals and relatives in the rest of the sample are also apparent from their ratings on the different types of fears. Shown in Table 5 are mean scores, standardized for sex, of the relatives of these 10 agoraphobic-like individuals and the rest of the sample. The two cases in which no differences were detected involved fears of familiar animals like dogs, cats, horses, squirrels, etc. or fears of potential natural dangers like heights, storms, or deep water. It seems that the relatives of these blindly rated agoraphobic-like individuals are more fearful on average whether one considers the presence or absence of phobias or the mean rating of fear in a number of fearful situations.

One further bit of evidence suggests an important familial contribution among agoraphobics. The Cloninger et al. (1981) study had blindly diagnosed probands and their relatives. Although the prevalence of anxiety neurosis was relatively small among the relatives of anxiety neurotics, Cloninger et al. report a finding that is interesting, though not unexpected when one considers the twin family data reported here. The greatest familial aggregation of anxiety neurosis occurred in kindreds of six probands who had severe and long-lasting agoraphobic syndromes.

Table 5

Mean Fear Scale Scores in Relatives of Agoraphobic-like Probands and the Rest of the Sample

Scale	Relatives (N = 30)	Rest (N = 567)	Significance*
Nasty Animals	45	31	.0002
Normal Animals	4	4	.77
Physical Fears	42	38	.71
Orderliness	37	24	.0001
Health Fears	58	47	.03
Agoraphobic	19	12	.02
Social Fears	40	27	.002

Hotelling-Lawley Trace: $F(7,585) = 5.66$, $p < .0001$

*Based on ANOVA controlling for sex and possible response set (i.e., a tendency to "rate high" or "rate low")

In summary, then, it seems that there is some kind of significant relationship among family members of agoraphobic individuals. Exactly what characterizes them is not yet fully understood, partly because of small sample sizes in research and also because of unrefined methods of measurement and classification. Most therapists who deal with agoraphobic patients know the syndromal qualities of the disorder; the patients often report that they are nervous, high-strung, worrying types, the onset of panic attacks is often sudden, unexpected, and not attributable to any specific life event, and they often have associated symptoms like minor obsessions or compulsions or even frank episodes of depersonalization and derealization. Many of these individuals, particularly in later stages of the illness, also exhibit an overt depressive syndrome. It seems unlikely that all these events could be the result of simple, classical or instrumental conditioning, or even social learning. Both models should predict a simple phobia or possibly a few phobias caused by stimulus generalization. In addition, the overlap between agoraphobia and anxiety neurosis is wide. Many clinicians who deal with agoraphobic patients know the high anxiety levels of these individuals, both from subjective impressions derived from personal interviews and from psychophysiology (Lader, 1967). Obviously, much research has yet to be done on these individuals, particularly distinguishing the agoraphobia-like state from anxiety neurosis and differentiating the relatives of agoraphobics from the relatives of anxiety neurotics. No one has yet attempted such an exercise.

REFERENCES

ANDREASEN, N. C., ENDICOTT, J., SPITZER, R. L., and WINOKUR, G. 1977. The family history method using diagnostic criteria: Reliability and validity. *Arch. Gen. Psychiatry*, 34:1229-1235.

BANDURA, A. 1969. *Principles of Behavior Modification*. New York: Holt, Rinehart and Winston.

BUGLASS, D., CLARKE, J., HENDERSON, A. S., KREITMAN, N., and PRESLEY, A. S. 1977. A study of agoraphobic housewives. *Psychol. Med.*, 7:73-86.

BROWN, F. W. 1942. Heredity in the psychoneuroses (summary). *Proc. R. Soc. Med.*, 35:785-790.

CAREY, G. 1978. A clinical genetic twin study of obsessive and phobic states. Ph.D. thesis, University of Minnesota.

CAREY, G., and GOTTESMAN, I. I. 1981. Twin and family studies of anxiety, phobic and obsessive disorders. In D. F. Klein and J. Rabkin (eds.), *Anxiety: New Research and Changing Concepts*, pp. 117-135. New York: Raven Press.

CAREY, G., GOTTESMAN, I. I., and ROBINS, E. 1980. Prevalence rates for the neuroses: Pitfalls in the evaluation familiarity. *Psychol. Med.*, 10:437-443.

CLONINGER, C. R., MARTIN, R. L., CLAYTON, P., and GUZE, S. B. 1981. A blind follow-up and family study of anxiety neurosis: Preliminary analysis of the St. Louis 500. In D. F. Klein and J. Rabkin (eds.), *Anxiety: New Research and Changing Concepts*, pp. 137-148. New York: Raven Press.

COHEN, J. 1977. *Statistical Power Analysis for the Behavioral Sciences*, rev. ed. New York: Academic Press.

COHEN, J. E., BADAL, D. W., KILPATRICK, A., REED, E. W., and WHITE, P. D. 1951. The high familial prevalence of neurocirculatory asthenia (anxiety neurosis, effort syndrome). *Am. J. Hum. Genet.*, 3:126-158.

COOPER, J. 1970. The Leyton Obsessional Inventory. *Psychol. Med.*, 1:48-64.

CROWE, R. R., PAULS, D. L., SLYMEN, D. J., and NOYES, R. 1980. A family study of anxiety neurosis: Morbidity risk in families of patients with and without mitral valve prolapse. *Arch. Gen. Psychiatry*, 37:77-79.

FEIGHNER, J. P., ROBINS, E., GUZE, S. B., WOODRUFF, R. A., WINOKUR, G., and MUNOZ, R. 1972. Diagnostic criteria for use in psychiatric research. *Arch. Gen. Psychiatry*, 26:57-63.

GOTTESMAN, I. I. 1968. Severity/concordance and diagnostic refinement in the Maudsley-Bethlem schizophrenic twin study. In D. Rosenthal and S. S. Kety (eds.), *The Transmission of Schizophrenia*, pp. 37-48. New York: Pergamon.

LADER, M. H. 1967. Palmer skin conductance measures in anxiety and phobic states. *J. Psychosom. Res.*, 11:271-281.

LOEHLIN, J. C., and NICHOLS, R. C. 1976. *Heredity, Environment, and Personality.* Austin: University of Texas Press.

LYTTON, H. 1977. Do parents create, or respond to, differences in twins? *Developmental Psychology*, 13:456-459.

MCINNES, R. G. 1937. Observations on heredity in neurosis. *Proc. R. Soc. Med.*, 30:895-904.

NOYES, Jr., R., CLANCY, J., CROWE, R., HOENK, P. R., and SLYMEN, D. J. 1978. The familial prevalence of anxiety neurosis. *Arch. Gen. Psychiatry*, 35:1057-1059.

PAULS, D. L., NOYES, Jr., R., and CROWE, R. R. 1979. The familial prevalence in second-degree relatives of patients with anxiety neurosis (panic disorder). *Journal of Affective Disorders*, 1:279-285.

PAULS, D. L., BUCHER, K. D., CROWE, R. R., and NOYES, Jr., R. 1980. A genetic study of panic disorder pedigrees. *Am. J. Hum. Genet.*, 32:639-644.

SCARR, S. 1969. Environmental bias in twin studies. In M. Manosevitz, G. Lindzey, and D. D. Thiessen (eds.), *Behavioral Genetics: Methods and Research*, pp. 597-605. New York: Appleton-Century-Crofts.

SHIELDS, J. 1962. *Monozygotic Twins Brought Up Apart and Together.* London: University of Oxford Press.

SHIELDS, J. The genetics of neurosis: Facts or fiction. In *Facts About the Neuroses.* Ciba-Geigy Symposium, Stockholm (in press).

SLATER, E., and SHIELDS, J. 1969. Genetical aspects of anxiety. *Br. J. Psychiatry*, 3:62-71.

SOLYOM, L., BECK, P., SOLYOM, C., and HUGEL, R. 1974. Some etiological factors in phobic neurosis. *Can. Psychiatr. Assoc. J.*, 19:69-78.

TELLEGEN, A. 1978. *Manual for the Differential Personality Questionnaire.* Unpublished manuscript, University of Minnesota.

TORGERSEN, S. 1978. The contribution of twin studies to psychiatric nosology. In W. E. Nance (ed.), *Twin Research, Part A: Psychology and Methodology*, pp. 125-130. New York: Alan R. Liss.

WHEELER, E. O., WHITE, P. D., REED, D., and COHEN, M. E. 1948. Familial incidence of neurocirculatory asthenia ("anxiety neurosis," "effort syndrome"). *J. Clin. Invest.*, 27:562.

5

THE ANXIETY-PRONE PERSONALITY: EFFECTS OF PRENATAL STRESS ON THE INFANT

LORRAINE ROTH HERRENKOHL, Ph.D.

Stress and anxiety are common features of society today and have an impact on men and women facing the complex demands of work, career, and home. Stress and anxiety have been chronicled as being particularly debilitating features of the rapid social and technological changes which have taken place in the Western world in the past few decades. Stress and anxiety may affect the developing organism (men, women, laboratory animals) at any stage of the life cycle. At any stage in development, biological, psychological, and social factors influence behavior and make a person anxiety-prone. Intrapsychic, psychodynamic, interpersonal, psychosocial, and cognitive factors interact with each other and reciprocally affect the biological substrate. The theses of this chapter are twofold: (1) Stress has a particular impact on the developing organism during perinatal development, when the nervous system is differentiating and the neural circuitry underlying bio-chemical-behavioral events is laid down; and (2) perinatal stress therefore may have a permanent effect on behavior later in life. The goal of this review is to examine the prenatal stress literature representative of the past few decades in psychology and biology in order to learn from the past and set directions for future research.

For the purposes of this paper, we shall consider stress as any real or imagined trauma, of a physical or psychological sort, that leads to the release of stress hormones, particularly those associated with the adrenal glands. The range of stress-inducing stimuli is varied and differs considerably from person to person, and not uncommonly within the same person, depending on circumstance and time. The range of stressful stimuli examined in the psychological and biological literature has varied from a narrow molecular

51

focus employing the animal model (such as discrete changes in environmental temperature or discrete changes in dosages of stress hormones exogenously administered [e.g., Herrenkohl, 1979]) at one end of the continuum to the more molar orientation of social psychologists, for example, who have examined the effects of extreme life situational stress (such as death of a loved one, moving or marital discord on the health and behavior of men and women [e.g., Holmes and Rahe, 1967; Rahe et al., 1964]).

Now we shall consider anxiety. Anxiety is a consequence of exposure to real or imagined stress. It is a state that we all experience to a greater or lesser degree at any number of circumstances in our lives. According to the DSM-III (1980), there are two major classes of clinical anxiety. One class includes anxiety disorders of childhood or adolescence such as overanxious disorders or separation anxiety disorders, whereas the adult category (18 years or older) includes phobias, generalized anxiety reactions, panic anxiety reactions, posttraumatic stress disorders, and the like. The anxiety disorders of childhood and adolescence, according to the diagnostic criteria, include excessive anxiety concerning separation from those to whom the child is attached, as manifested by the presence of a group of symptoms including: unrealistic worry about possible harm befalling the attachment figure; unrealistic worry that a calamitous event will separate the child from the attachment figure; repeated nightmares involving the theme of separation; school phobias; and any other signs of distress upon separation from the attachment figure, including temper tantrums, crying, social withdrawal, apathy, or extreme sadness. The anxiety states or anxiety neuroses of adulthood include panic disorders with palpitations, chest pains, choking or smothering sensations, dizziness, tingling in hands and feet, sweating, faintness, and fear of dying. Generalized persistent anxiety states of adulthood are manifested by a cluster of symptoms which include: motor tension (shakiness, jitteriness, trembling, tension, muscle aches, fatigue, restlessness); autonomic hyperactivity (sweating, heart pounding or racing, cold clammy hands, dry mouth, lump in the throat); apprehensive expectation (excessive worrying, fears, ruminations or anticipation of misfortune); and vigilance and scanning (hyperattentiveness, difficulty in concentration, insomnia, feeling on edge, irritability). Anxiety disorders of adulthood also include obsessive-compulsive reactions and posttraumatic stress disorders associated with extreme life situational change (death of a loved one, moving, etc.). In a posttraumatic stress state, there is a numbing of responsiveness to or reduced involvement with the external world. Patients in this state have described themselves as being numb or walking around without feeling.

Several bodies of experimental literature have been drawn on to understand postnatal determinants of infantile anxiety. The comparative and phys-iological-psychological literature has employed the experimental strategies of scientists such as Denenberg et al. (1978), who have examined the effects of infantile stimulation on emotional reactivity in offspring. The develop-mental literature calls upon the animal ethological experimental strategy to gain understanding about the nature of attachment, and separation anxiety and stranger anxiety in infants. The voluminous work of John Bowlby (1969) pulls together the extensive animal findings in ethology and infant experi-ments in developmental psychology to explain functional impairments in institutionalized and socially deprived infants for whom there has been a loss of primary caretaker and attachment figure.

PRENATAL STRESS EFFECTS

What does the literature tell us about the effects of prenatal stress on the infant? We will focus on mammals and make an arbitrary division between lower animals and human beings. Generalizations will be limited, depending on the kind of mammal, as for example whether we are referring to an altricial or precocial mammal. The altricial mammal (laboratory rat, mouse, human infant) brings its offspring into the world in a much less advanced stage of development than does the precocial mammal (guinea pig, rabbit, horse); therefore, the impact of environmental or psychological factors during perinatal development would not be the same on the developing and dif-ferentiating nervous system of precocial offspring as it would be on the offspring of altricial mammals. Development occurs on a continuum. When we are talking about the postnatal organism, we must consider the impact of psychological or physical stress on the developing organism independent of a host-mediator. In the prenatal circumstance, the mother is the host-mediator between the fetus and the outside environment and there is an interplay between her system and that of the fetus she bears.

An adult under stress is exposed to an interplay of brain, pituitary and adrenal hormones, all of which interact in positive and negative feedback loops to modulate and regulate the amount of stress hormones which the mother produces (Krieger, 1980). In addition, the fetal system has a life and dynamic of its own. Its brain-pituitary-adrenal gland axis is active early in fetal development. The fetal system also undergoes positive and negative feedback influences unto itself. Because the mother hosts the fetus and because they share a common blood supply via the placenta, a dynamic interplay exists between them so that one can respond to the other. The fetus therefore can be a responder to changes in the mother's hormonal milieu. The fetus is exposed to maternal stress hormones as well as its own.

A complex feedback relationship exists within the mother and fetus individually and between the mother and fetus. On the one hand the maternal stress system has a stress stimulus which triggers the release of corticotropin-releasing factor (CRF) from her hypothalamus, which in turn triggers the release of adrenocorticotropin hormone (ACTH) from her anterior pituitary, which in turn leads to the release of glucocorticoid hormones (corticosteroids, or corticoids) from the adrenal cortex. A given tropic hormone may be released in response to a variety of stimuli. ACTH, for example, may be triggered by emotional stress, physical stress, low plasma corticosteroids and, independently of any of these, during the course of sleep. When the glucocorticoid hormones reach the brain and hypothalamus, their effect is inhibitory. The same feedback relationships exist in the fetal system. An interaction of a potential complex feedback relationship occurs when the fetus is *in utero*. It is possible, for example, for a stress stimulus such as increased epinephrine or norephinephrine or increased ACTH in the mother to be a stress stimulus which in turn triggers hypothalamic and pituitary secretions in the fetus.

Comparative and Physiological Psychology

In the past 20 to 25 years, the majority of studies on the effects of prenatal stress on offspring have come from two major disciplines—psychology and biology. In psychology, two foci have been important: experiments in comparative and physiological psychology, in which the animal model was used extensively to study the effects of stress during pregnancy, typically on emotionality and reactivity in offspring; and work in developmental psychology, which classically examined the effects of maternal anxiety and stress on the behavior of infants. The biological literature essentially concerned reproductive physiology and examined the effects of conditioned maternal anxiety on emotionality in offspring. See Table 1 for an outline of our review of the literature in comparative and physiological psychology. The implicit mechanism in most of the research involved the sharing of stress hormones by the maternal-fetal blood supply. Limitations of most of the research were that there was little or no direct examination of stress hormone changes in the mother or effects of stress on the central nervous system by either morphological, anatomical, or biochemical means. Admittedly gross, means were just becoming available to assess hormone or nervous system changes under stress (e.g., Glick et al., 1964; König and Klippel, 1963).

Thompson (1957) examined the hypothesis that emotional trauma during pregnancy could affect emotional characteristics in rat offspring. Studies from such diverse disciplines as teratology, pediatrics, experimental psychology, and population biology suggested to him that hormones such as cortisone, adrenaline, or ACTH injected into the mother during pregnancy could affect the fetus via the maternal-fetal blood exchange. Thompson hypothesized that strong maternal emotions may release stress hormones into the mother's blood, thereby affecting fetal behavioral development.

The 1957 experiment was done by training hooded rats in a double-compartment shuttle box first to expect strong shock at the sound of the buzzer and then to avoid the shock by opening the door between the compartments and running through to the safe side. When the rats had learned the task, they were mated. As soon as they were found to be pregnant, they were exposed to the buzzer three times daily in the shock side of the shuttle box but with the shock turned off and the door to the safe side locked. The procedure was terminated by the birth of the litter. Therefore, during gestation, the animals were exposed to "expected," not real, shock. Possible postnatal influences were controlled by cross-fostering the offspring in such a way as to generate six cells, each containing 10 offspring with two main variables—prenatal and postnatal treatment. Emotional characteristics were compared at 30 to 40 and 130 to 140 days. Experimental animals showed a much higher latency of activity than control animals at both ages of testing in an open field test in which amount and latency of activity were recorded. Also, experimental animals were slower to leave the home cage than controls at the first age of testing; no significant difference appeared at the later age. On the basis of his findings, Thompson believed that there was no question about the reliability of stress-produced behavioral differences but he did not yet know how stress exerted its effects.

Actually, one year before Thompson made this report, he collaborated with Lester Sontag of the Fels Research Institute in a study of prenatal audiogenic seizure on later behavior of offspring (Thompson and Sontag, 1956). Seizures were induced by placing the animal in a metal enclosure containing an electric bell which produced a sound level of high intensity and frequency. From the fifth day of pregnancy through the eighteenth day, females were exposed to two audiogenic seizures per day spaced about eight hours apart. Litters were weighed and culled at birth and the litter switches were made so that a significant proportion of control litters were reared by experimental mothers and experimental litters by control mothers. In some cases no switches were made. (Because the selection was nonsystematic, there is a serious limitation to this research.) Maze-learning was tested under stress conditions starting at 80 days of age. A Lashley patterned maze was used, with escape from water as the motivation. Water in the maze was deep and cold, forcing the animals to swim. In that circumstance, experimental

Table 1

Representative Past Studies in Comparative and Physiological Psychology

Study	Procedure	Results	Discussion
Thompson (1957)	Conditioned "anxiety" in rats prepregnancy, to "expect" shock while pregnant.	Higher latency to respond in open field, less activity in open field.	Fetal behavior affected by maternal emotions, probably through stress hormones.
Thompson and Sontag (1956)	Induced audiogenic seizures in pregnant rats.	Longer latencies and more errors in Lashley maze.	"Bloodborne anxieties" or changes in maternal blood chemistry. Also possible direct effect of sound on fetus.
Hockman (1961)	After Thompson (1957), conditioned "anxiety" in rats, but more rigorously.	Similar findings to Thompson (1957), but also observed practice and postnatal influences.	Generally, similar to Thompson (1957), but indicated role of potential confounding variables.
Keeley (1962)	Crowded pregnant mice.	Less activity and defecation in open field.	Behavioral stress during pregnancy alters offspring behavior.
Lieberman (1963)	Injected stress hormones into pregnant mice.	Altered activity and defecation in open field, but direction of change was a function of the particular hormone.	Different stress hormones may have different effects.

Morra (1965)	After Thompson (1957), conditioned "anxiety" in rats at 4 levels of stress and during 2 pregnancy periods.	Similar findings to Thompson (1957), but results were function of stress level; also second half of pregnancy.	"Bloodborne" anxieties.
DeFries et al, (1967)	Physically-stressed inbred and hybrid pregnant mice.	Less activity in open field, etc. but results were function of fetal-maternal genotype.	Experience interacts with genotype.
	Also injected adrenalin.	Some differences from above.	Stress hormones do not directly mimic behavioral stress. Therefore different hormones or quantities may be involved.
Ader and Plaut (1968)	Handled pregnant rats.	Fewer startle reactions, reduced corticosterone, more susceptibility to gastric erosions.	Physiological reactivity of offspring influenced by prenatal maternal stimulation. Also, psychophysiological changes in offspring mediated by maternal-fetal blood exchange. Postnatal conditions have some influence.
	Handled pregnant rats but housed some individually and others in groups.	Differences between prenatally handled and control rats more pronounced among individually housed.	

animals took significantly more average trials to reach criteria and produced significantly more errors to criteria than did the control animals. Switching litters produced no statistically significant differences, suggesting that the causal factor of the performance differences lay in the prenatal rather than the postnatal environment.

The question of the mechanism of the prenatal insult could not be answered in the Thompson and Sontag research. Since all animals used were seizure-prone, a genetic factor linked to seizure-proneness could be ruled out; other possibilities could include fetal asphyxia caused by spasmatic contractions of the uterine arteries, maternal blood chemistry changes due to shock, maternal endocrinological changes, or the direct effects of a sound stimulus on the fetus.

Thompson's (1957) study generated a great deal of research activity over the subsequent decade. Hockman (1961) replicated Thompson's study using similar apparatus and procedures, but with a larger sample of animals and litters and more rigid controls (i.e., litters were immediately cross-fostered at birth and not handled until testing). Hockman assumed on the basis of Thompson's findings that the offspring of the stressed mothers would show a lower activity than would the offspring of the controls. Indeed, the results of the first test series confirmed the hypothesis; however, the treatment effect did not appear as striking and as clear-cut. For example, the experimental animals raised by foster mothers were significantly less active than the controls in the early series. The experimental offspring raised by their own mothers were, however, comparable to the controls. There were no differences in activity between the control subgroups. It seemed to Hockman that the stress applied during gestation was not itself sufficient to affect the offspring noticeably but must be supplemented by a cross-fostering procedure. Moreover, Hockman attributed the big drop in activity from Test 1 to Test 2 to association with traumatic events of the first test. The animals had never been handled before the first test, so they were difficult to catch when removed from the open field. Also, they were separated for the first time from their mothers or foster mothers. It was not surprising, therefore, that a striking drop in activity occurred on the second test. The findings in Hockman's research tended to support Thompson's study, suggesting that prenatal maternal stress had an effect on emotional behavior of offspring; however, the effect was not a simple one. Hockman concluded that future research had to investigate the combined effects of both prenatal and postnatal treatments in terms of stress applied at distinct stages of fetal development. He also indicated that future research must inquire into possible mechanisms by which stressful events are transmitted from mother to fetus.

Keeley (1962) subjected pregnant albino mice to the stress of crowding.

Regardless of rearing conditions (whether by crowded or uncrowded mother), motivational state (hungry or not), or day of testing (30 or 100 days of age), crowded litters were significantly less active, slower to respond, and defecated less than control mice. One explanation Keeley offered for his results was that endocrine activity in the crowded pregnant female impaired development of the fetal response systems. Drawing from the observation that women with a hyperthyroid condition characteristically produce thyroxin-deficient children, Keeley concluded that high-population density stress must mobilize the endocrine defenses of the mother in such a way as to produce levels of circulating maternal hormones which "endanger the fetal glands."

Lieberman (1963) reported some preliminary work on the mechanism by which prenatal stress changes might occur. In one experiment he divided pregnant mice into five groups: saline-injected, epinephrine-injected, norepinephrine-injected, hydrocortisone-injected, and a group behaviorally stressed by overcrowding in a cage. Treatment was administered during the second trimester of pregnancy. Mothers gave birth in individual cages and were not disturbed until 18 days after parturition when cages were cleaned. There was no cross-fostering because of the small number of animals. At 35 days of age, offspring were tested in an open field for measurements of locomotion, defecation, escape jumps, and self-grooming. At 120 days, animals were killed and brain weight, body weight, gross brain serotonin and epinephrine were measured. Among the findings was that activity was increased and defecation decreased in the offspring of crowded and epinephrine-injected groups vs. offspring of the saline group. Activity was decreased and defecation increased, however, in offspring of hydrocortisone- and norepinephrine-injected mice compared with controls. These findings in general confirmed the previous findings that behavioral stress in pregnant rodents altered the behavior of offspring. Because epinephrine was found to mimic behavioral stressors in previous research (Thompson, 1957), Lieberman believed that epinephrine, which was known to cross the placental barrier, was the most likely hormonal mediator of behavioral stress to the offspring.

In a second experiment, Lieberman (1963) raised the question of how hormones alter offspring behavior. Do stress hormones alter the maternal or placental exchange systems, thus producing indirect effects on the embryo, or do they themselves cross the placenta and directly affect the developing system? One way to attack this problem was to inject chicken eggs and test the hatched animals. The results suggested that epinephrine could act directly on the developing embryo to produce changes in behavior. Lieberman concluded that, although more complex maternal and placental changes may be involved in producing behavioral changes in the mammal, at least part of the effect may be the result of direct hormonal action. It is possible, therefore, that severe emotional stress during pregnancy leaves its mark on the unborn through sympathetic activation of the stress syndrome and migration of hormones across the placental barrier.

Morra (1965) examined four levels of prenatal stress and two periods during pregnancy in a systematic attempt to investigate the varying influences of prenatal environment on postnatal offspring behavior. His prepregnancy avoidance training consisted of 0, 50, 100, and 120 conditioned stimulus (CS)-unconditioned stimulus (UCS) pairings in a shuttle box. Intense radiant heat instead of electric shock was the UCS during the prepregnancy avoidance training. Morra's data suggested that significant behavioral decrements occurred in offspring whose mothers were exposed to stress during the second, not the first, half of pregnancy. In addition, greater behavioral deficits were significantly associated with higher levels of stress. Morra also examined the rates of fertility and viability of offspring produced by stressed and nonstressed animals; stressed animals produced significantly fewer live young.

DeFries et al. (1967) reported that prenatal maternal stress in mice had differential effects on the behavior of offspring as a function of genotype and kind of stress. Two experiments were conducted. In the first, females carrying either inbred or hybrid litters were subjected daily to physical stress throughout the latter half of pregnancy. Stressors included daily exposure for three minutes to each of three stress conditions: swimming in a water tank, followed later in the day by excessive rocking in a motorized cage, followed later by exposure to a loud sound produced by a pure tone generated through a speaker mounted on a chamber. In a second experiment, a chemical stress was administered by injecting the female with adrenaline. Control females received placebo injections.

Beginning at about 40 days of age, offspring were given an open field test and the total number of grid portions crossed was used as each subject's activity score. From data on open field activity of the offspring, it was concluded that differential effects were a function of both fetal and maternal genotypes. A highly significant strain of male parent times treatment interaction, in the absence of a strain of female parent times treatment interaction, suggested that both fetal and maternal genotypes were involved in the differential response to prenatal physical stress. If mothers of the two inbred strains respond differently to physical stress (e.g., release different amounts of some hormone) and if hybrid fetuses are affected differently from inbreds, the result could be an interaction between strain of male parent and treatment. The significant second-order interaction between strain of male, strain of female parent, and treatment effects provided additional information that the fetal genotype was involved in the response.

The logic of DeFries et al. (1967) was similar to that of DeFries (1964). If the response to prenatal maternal stress was solely a function of the genotype of the mother, hybrid offspring would be expected to respond like inbred offspring carried by females of the same strain. If the response was solely a function of the genotype of the fetus, however, all hybrid offspring would be expected to respond alike regardless of the strain of the mother. If neither of these alternatives was observed, the possibility that the response to prenatal maternal stress is a function of some combination of the fetal and maternal genotypes would be indicated.

In a second experiment (DeFries et al., 1967), adrenal injections administered to females during days 10 and 11 of pregnancy as the stress condition were not found to mimic the effects of physical prenatal stress. Although highly significant effects of strain of male parent, strain of female parent, and their interaction were again found, the magnitude of the interaction was less than that of the physical stress experiment, and the treatment effects were in the opposite direction. Prenatal adrenaline injection to the mother did not mimic the psychological effects of prenatal maternal stress, suggesting either that different substances were involved in the two stressors or that quantities of the same or different substances were sufficiently different to bring different results. Nevertheless, a mechanism that alters development so that postnatal behavior is modified was of sufficient importance to warrant additional study.

Ader and Plaut (1968) studied the effects of prenatal maternal handling and differential housing on offspring emotionality, plasma corticosterone levels, and susceptibility to gastric erosions. The purpose of their first experiment was to examine the effects of prenatal maternal handling, including physiological reactivity and responses to stress (i.e., potentially pathogenic stimulation), by measuring plasma corticosterone levels and susceptibility to immobilization-produced erosions. Rats were held in the experimenter's hand twice daily for three minutes throughout gestation. At about two months of age, offspring were tested for differential plasma corticosterone response to electric-shock stimulation. Then they were given a reaction handling test in which the incidence of startle responses, vocalization, and resistance to being picked up were recorded. These behaviors were presumed to reflect emotional reactivity. One week after the reaction to handling tests all animals were deprived of food for about one day and immobilized in flexible wire mesh for six hours. The animals were then killed, their stomachs removed and inspected for gastric erosions. (Offspring of rats that

were either handled or unhandled during pregnancy were fostered to unhandled females at birth and group-housed at weaning.) Behavioral responses
to the handling tests indicated that the prenatally stressed animals had lower
scores than controls. The prenatally handled females had an attenuated
plasma corticosterone response to handling, and they were more susceptible
to immobilization-produced gastric erosions.

Ader and Plaut (1968) carried out a second experiment to investigate the
interaction between prenatal stimulation and subsequent housing conditions.
In this experiment, prenatally handled and control rats reared by unhandled
females were housed by groups or individually at weaning. The basic findings
of the first experiment were confirmed and an interaction between prenatal
treatment and housing was observed. The difference between prenatal handling and the control condition was more pronounced among the individually
housed groups. On the basis of both studies, the authors concluded that
physiological reactivity of offspring was influenced by the stimulation to
which the mother was exposed during pregnancy, and psychophysiological
changes in the offspring were mediated by physiological changes in the
mother transmitted to the developing fetus via the maternal fetal blood
exchange.

By the end of the decade of the Thompson-generated research, we saw
that:

1. A number of researchers provided evidence independent of each other
   that prenatal stress had long-term consequences for offspring behavior.
2. Agreement was growing that behavioral change in the offspring was a
   function of a general internal-chemical stress response and not a reaction
   to a specific kind of stress.
3. Although prenatal stress clearly was the predominant factor in later offspring behavior, it did interact with certain postnatal conditions (i.e.,
   individual housing) to maximize effects.
4. Prenatal stress not only affected later offspring behavior but also influenced resistance to disease.

There were several attempts in the decade to mimic the effects of prenatal
behavioral stress with stress hormone injections (adrenaline, epinephrine).
However, at the close of the 60s, a lull took place in prenatal stress research
in comparative and physiological psychology. This period of quiescence is
just beginning to end.

Developmental Psychology

Studies of the effects of maternal stress on infant development are summarized in Table 2. The developmental psychology literature of the past several decades has recognized that the mother's emotional state may influence the fetus through the release of hormones or other chemicals into the blood stream. Thus, emotional upset in the mother may "irritate" the fetus or "stimulate or depress the nervous system or its parts." Since the pioneering efforts of Lester Sontag, a number of researchers examined the effects of maternal stress on infant development, using some of the information that was already collected in the 1960s on feedback relationships in neuroendocrinology and possible maternal-fetal consequences. Limitations in the research include relative lack of consideration of the reciprocal interplay between the mother and her infant after birth. Mothers under stress during pregnancy may continue to be anxious and disturbed after they have given birth. Thus, at least in part, infant distress may reflect a tense mother-child interaction following birth. In addition, other factors (genetic) cannot be excluded in analyzing the adaptive and emotional difficulties experienced by the same parents with some children and not with others.

Sontag, long an important figure in child development, studied pregnant women undergoing stress. In a series of papers (Sontag, 1944; Sontag et al., 1944; Sontag, 1966), he presented the findings of work on human development carried on at the Fels Research Institute from 1932 to 1966. Essentially, the Sontag group explored the behavior of the human fetus, its developmental progress and individual differences, capabilities, perceptions and responses to stimuli during the last four months of pregnancy. The research was also designed to measure certain characteristics of fetal behavior in response to the environment as represented by the mother and its relationship to postnatal behavior and, the investigators hoped, to adolescent and adult behavior. The 1944 papers presented evidence on the relationship between pregnant maternal functions and "psychic and physiological" progress of the neonate. Sontag et al. (1944) acknowledged that the fetal and maternal endocrine systems complement each other and form what might be called an endocrine pool. The newborn infant's physiology and body structure could be modified, therefore, if endocrine functions were abnormal, as, for example, in thyroid dysfunction. The authors examined the status of infants at birth as related to basal metabolism of the mother during pregnancy. The infants of a normal group of mothers were divided into two

Table 2

Representative Past Studies in Developmental Psychology

Study	Procedure	Results	Discussion
Sontag (1944)	Pregnant mothers experienced emotional stress (incidental observations).	Increased fetal activity. Also increased crying, hyperactivity, irritability in neonates.	Pregnant maternal functions influence "psychic" and physiological progress in neonate.
Sontag et al. (1944)	Divided pregnant mothers into high basal metabolic rate (BMR) and low BMR groups.	Infants in high BMR group weighed more and were more "mature."	Effects due to common maternal-fetal endocrine pool.
Sontag (1966)	Pregnant mothers experienced emotional stress. Also presented with sound and other stimuli.	Increased fetal activity under emotional stress and with sound. Greater crying, hyperactivity, irritability in neonates.	Maternal emotional stress passed to offspring by virtue of common maternal-fetal endocrine pool. Fetal circumstance affects adaptation in the neonate.
Davids et al. (1963)	Interviewed and rated mothers on anxiety scale, considered high and low anxious groups.	Eight-month-old babies from highly anxious mothers had lower developmental quotients (Bailey Scale) and were less emotionally adjusted (clinical ratings).	Anxiety in mother affects fetus. Also possible carry-over into postnatal rearing.

Ottinger and Simmons (1964)	Rated pregnant mothers on anxiety.	Babies from highly anxious mothers during the first week of life were more active and cried more.	Positive relationship between maternal anxiety and neonatal crying.
Stott (1973)	Interviewed mothers for life situational stress during pregnancy.	Incidences of child morbidity were high (more physical illness, more functional abnormalities): more "fretfulness," "restlessness," "clinging," as observed by health nurses up through the fourth year of life.	Maternal stress during pregnancy negatively affects health and behavior of children.
McDonald (1968)	Reviewed literature on maternal emotional factors and obstetrical complications.	More problems during birth, pregnancy, and labor. Also anxious women with fewer repressive-defense mechanisms were more problem-prone.	Although not conclusive, some relationship exists between emotional factors and obstetrical difficulties.

groups according to basal metabolic rates (BMR) of the mothers during the ninth month of pregnancy. A similar division was made on the basis of the mother's BMR gain during pregnancy. In each case, the infants of the high BMR group were larger in skeletal structure and slightly more mature than infants in the low BMR group. Thus, Sontag et al. (1944) believed that a relationship existed between the mother's BMR rate and the birth weight of her infant. Moreover, maternal thyroid function seemed to affect the growth pattern of the fetus.

That behavior pattern alterations carry over into neonatal life or infancy was suggested by observations Sontag (1944) made of the infants of mothers who had undergone severe emotional stress during the latter part of these pregnancies. Sontag reported that infants of stressed mothers responded with large increases in sharp or irritable internal body movements, which presumably were the result of changes in the constituents of the mother's blood. After birth, these infants remained irritable and hyperactive for weeks or months. They cried a great deal and slept for short periods only. Most of these infants exhibited a food intolerance and frequent or often loose stools, suggesting an autonomic or psychosomatic component of prenatal stress exposure as expressed in gastrointestinal function. Moreover, they were the type of infants to regurgitate much of their food and frequently were switched from one formula to another without significant improvement. They failed to gain weight for a long time.

Sontag described the findings and procedures of the Fels Research Institute in greater detail in his 1966 report. Fetal movement was assessed by pressure changes recorded from inflated bags specially laid over quadrants of the mother's abdomen. At the same time, the mother was instructed to record her reactions by pressing a system of buttons which activated kymograph records during the period she felt fetal activity. It was possible therefore to establish a correlation between the mother's verbal reports of fetal movement and the mechanically recorded movements. Sontag (1966) described three differential types of fetal activity: sharp kicking or punching movement of the extremities which increased steadily from six months to birth; squirming or writhing slow movements which were at maximum frequency during the third to fourth month before birth and declined steadily until birth; and sharp, convulsive movements which could be described as fetal hiccups or spasms of the diaphragm. Differences in fetal activity seemed to be predictive of the degree of activity, restlessness, and sometimes resistance to handling of infants during the first year of life. Sontag also examined the reactions of fetuses to sound. In the 1920s a German investigator had reported a number of cases of expectant mothers who complained they could not go to symphony concerts because of greatly intensified activity level of the babies they were carrying. However, there had been no adequate explanation of the ability of the fetus to perceive sound. Sontag and his associates placed a small block of wood over the abdomen of eight-months pregnant women and struck a doorbell clapper at the rate of 120 vibrations per second. In 90 percent of the cases, there was an immediate convulsive response by the fetus, which Sontag believed was a startle response similar to the Moro reflex after birth. Sontag considered these findings additional evidence that maternal variations in endocrine function helped determine the psychic and physiological progress of the fetus and that it was self-evident that the physical and physiological adequacy of the fetus in turn were critical factors in its emotional and social adaptation after birth.

Sontag (1966) reported also that severe maternal emotions during the last trimester of pregnancy caused immediate and profound increases in the activity level of the fetus. He described a number of spontaneously occurring incidents:

> In one instance a young woman carrying her baby, which we had been studying weekly in terms of activity and heart rate level, took refuge at the Fels Institute building one evening because her husband had just suffered a psychotic break and was threatening to kill her. She was terrified, felt alone and did not know where to turn for help. She came to the Institute, and we gave her a bed and room for the night. When she complained after a few minutes conversation that the kicking of her fetus was so violent as to be painful, we proceeded to record the activity level. It was more than 10-fold what it had been in the weekly sessions prior to this incident. Another case came to our attention when a woman we had been studying lost her husband in an automobile accident. Again, the violence of the activity and the frequency of movement of the fetus increased by a factor of more than 10. During the period of 10 years, we managed to collect 8 such dramatic incidences, all showing the same phenomena of extreme increase of fetal activity in response to grief, fear and anxiety. Children of such mothers, who suffered their emotional trauma late in pregnancy and not early, showed, of course, no congenital defect. In general, they were, however, irritable, hyperactive, tended to have frequent stools and 3 of them had marked feeding problems (Sontag, 1966, p. 784).

Davids et al. (1963) reported that maternal anxiety during pregnancy influenced mother-child adjustment for eight months after childbirth. The study was an outgrowth of a national collaborative project by the then National Institute of Neurological Diseases and Blindness concerned with perinatal factors in child development. Fifty pregnant women were examined at the Providence Lying-In Hospital. They were given a psychological test battery during the third trimester of pregnancy and when the babies were eight months old. The pregnant women were examined individually by experienced clinical psychologists who administered intelligence tests, self-ratings, questionnaires on psychodynamics, and projective techniques designed to reveal unconscious motivations. Included was the Taylor Manifest Anxiety Scale (MAS). Eight months after birth, there was a psychological evaluation of the mother and the child. The emphasis was on the child's behavior and performance as judged by the Bailey Infant Mental Scale and Motor Test. The mother completed the Parental Attitude Research Instrument (PARI) which assessed 30 items of maternal attitudes regarding family relations and child-bearing practices. The examiner also observed the mother-child interaction. On the basis of the tests, pregnant women were dichotomized into high-anxiety and low-anxiety groups. Eight months later, the high-anxiety group evidenced significantly more negative child-rearing attitudes as measured by the PARI. They also received much less favorable ratings by the interviewers at eight months. In studying the children of the mothers, the researchers found that the children of low-anxiety mothers had significantly higher developmental quotients on the Infant Mental Scale and higher developmental quotients on the Motor Scale. Children from low-anxiety mothers also tended to receive a more favorable general emotional-tone score than did offspring of the high-anxiety mothers. In general, the findings were consistent with predictions that children reared by women who had been highly anxious during pregnancy would fare less well on tests of intellectual development and indices of emotional adjustment.

Ottinger and Simmons (1964) examined the relationship between the behavior of human neonates and prenatal maternal anxiety. A group of obstetrical patients were administered an anxiety scale during each trimester of pregnancy. Nineteen women representing extreme scores were selected to test the hypothesis that there would be a positive relationship between the mother's anxiety scores during gestation and neonatal behavior. Baby bodily activity, measured by a stabilimeter placed under the bassinet, and crying behavior, recorded on a microphone, were assessed on the second, third, and fourth day of life. Body weight was recorded at birth and on each day. The data tended to confirm the hypothesis of a positive relationship between the mother's anxiety level and the amount of the neonate's crying.

Stott (1973) conducted a follow-up study from birth of the effects of prenatal stress on 200 infants living in Glasgow. The sample was obtained by choosing every 200th live birth. Health nurses interviewed the mothers during the first month after birth and at the end of the first six months, and again at several intervals until the fourth year. During the first interview, the health nurse completed a form giving prenatal and birth schedules and information about the mother's health during pregnancy, her nervous and emotional condition, accidents, dental operations, conditions of employment and events or "happenings" calculated to produce stress, grief, harassment, or shock. Although the studies were retrospective, Stott believed there was little chance of unreliability because records were made during the first month after birth. There were 153 children (52 percent of the sample) followed up to their fourth year. Morbidity in the child was scored and related to prenatal factors. Morbidity was classified as follows: nonepidemic illness (failure to gain weight); neurological symptoms (convulsions, oversensitivity to noise, tremor); somatic abnormalities (small size, profuse sweating, uncontrolled salivation, choking when eating or drinking); malformations and physical defects; developmental retardation (sitting up, standing, walking, speech); behavioral disturbance (impaired affective responses and attachment behavior, overly active, passive, lack of constructive play, stereotypy, rage). Situational stresses without bad personal relationships which seemed to affect a child's morbidity score included death of mother's parent or sibling, serious illness or accident to the mother's husband, a witnessed accident or suicide attempt, and acute anxiety about a parent. Situational stresses with bad personal relationships (marital discord) produced extremely high child morbidity scores. A case involving extreme marital discord during pregnancy which produced a high child morbidity score is described:

> Marital relationship is not good. There has been frequent quarreling all through the marriage. The husband is reputed to be a heavy drinker, particularly at weekends when he is very abusive and often puts the wife out of the home. He is, however, a good worker (on constant night shift) and supports his wife and family fairly well. There are, nevertheless, signs that the family may break down completely. The night before the birth there had been a violent quarrel with husband (Stott, 1973, p. 776).

The types of child morbidity Stott associated with personal tensions in pregnancy included: physical illness (twice as much eczema and middle ear infection, somewhat more bronchitis and severe respiratory trouble); minor physical and functional abnormalities (small size, profuse sweating, flushing or choking); developmental difficulties (twice the incidence of late walking or poor walking such as flatfooted or clumsy, some speech defects); behavioral abnormalities (twice as many entries for fretful, whimpering, restless or clinging behaviors). Ten of the 14 cases had one or more indications of behavioral disturbances characteristically associated with congenital hyperactivity.

There is strong suggestive evidence that pregnant mothers under stress are more likely than other mothers to experience complications during birth, pregnancy, and labor. In reviewing the role of emotional factors in obstetrical complications, McDonald (1968) examined articles that had appeared in the preceding 15 years. He concluded that, when findings are presented psychodynamically (i.e., when pseudocyesis, or false pregnancy, is considered a hysterical symptom arising out of conflict between a fear of pregnancy and a wish for pregnancy so as not to be abandoned by the husband), there is virtually no correlation between emotional factors and obstetrical difficulties. The most consistent finding was, however, that women who subsequently experienced any of a variety of obstetric complications had higher anxiety levels and used fewer repressive types of defenses than did women who experienced normal pregnancies and deliveries. McDonald chronicled the numerous methodological shortcomings of the then-current literature. For example, case studies or random clinical observations lent themselves poorly to research purposes; a large bulk of the studies reviewed indicated small sample size and inadequate or total lack of controls; the experimental samples were heterogeneous; conclusions were based on retrospective data; and there was an even more fundamental failure to document sample characteristics or methods. In the light of such gross experimental inaccuracies, it is no wonder that McDonald found that the relationship between stress and obstetrical difficulties was not documented rigorously.

Contemporary experimental strategies are being developed that allow a more concise examination of the relationship between maternal attitudes and obstetrical difficulties (e.g., Laukaran and van den Berg, 1980); however, we can conclude the following about the state of the science in developmental psychology from 1944 to 1973:

1. A body of evidence was accumulating that indicated a relationship between prenatal stress and fetal reactivity.
2. The most parsimonious means by which to understand the transmission of maternal anxiety to the fetus involved "bloodborne" anxiety, or some physiological change in the central nervous system (CNS).
3. There was a continuum in development between fetal and infant reactivity. Behaviors developed during the fetal stage carried over into infancy.
4. Infant reactivity in turn affected emotional and social adaptation early in life, presumably by altering maternal behavior.

Reproductive Physiology

Summarized in Table 3 is a representative sample of the traditional body of reproductive physiological literature about the effects of prenatal stress on subsequent reproductive functions of offspring. The animal model is used to quantify more accurately than psychological studies have done the nature of the stimulus parameters associated with stress. Direct prenatal hormone administration is used to examine consequences on offspring fertility. These investigations pay little or no attention to behavioral consequences such as sexual behavior of offspring or maternal behavior.

Pennycuik (1966) examined factors affecting the survival and growth of young mice born and reared at extreme room temperatures. Mortality of pups born to mothers gestating at 36° was about 90 percent. In contrasting losses caused by maternal failure or poor viability of the pups themselves, Pennycuik concluded that maternal failure seemed to be more important. Judging from such indices as dissection of the mammary glands or the interval between birth and the first appearance of milk in the pups' stomach, maternal failure seemed to be the result of impairment of milk productivity. The impairment ranged from an almost total suppression of milk secretion before parturition to a delay in onset of copious milk secretion in the hours following birth. The incidence of glands which oozed milk was reduced, as judged by direct observation of dissected mammary glands.

Hensleigh and Johnson (1971a and b) showed that heat stress during pregnancy retarded fetal rat growth. They presented evidence for the view that the effects on the fetus are the result of a generalized stress response rather than of a specific stressor agent (1971a). They found that: Treatment of pregnant rats with epinephrine, ACTH, or corticosteroids produced similar fetal alteration; removal of the maternal adrenals before stress exposure prevented fetal changes; and animals conditioned to stressor agents showed decreased fetal alterations when exposed to the same agents during pregnancy. In a companion paper (1971b), Hensleigh and Johnson examined the effects of heat stress during pregnancy in intact, adrenalectomized and ovariectomized rats. Heat stress seemed to reduce the amount of pituitary gonadotropins but caused an increase in ACTH production, as manifested in increased adrenal size and serum corticosterone levels. Retarded fetal growth associated with heat stress could not be accounted for on the basis of reduced pituitary gonadotropin function alone. ACTH production seemed to interact with gonadotropin activity in some way so that these two anterior pituitary functions were not mutually independent.

Euker and Riegle (1973) described the effects of restraint stress at different stages of the rat reproductive life cycle including pregnancy. The greatest

Table 3

Representative Past Studies in Reproductive Physiology

Study	Procedure	Results	Discussion
Pennycuik (1966)	Cold-stressed pregnant mice and offspring.	Mortality of pups was high, due to maternal lactational deficiencies.	Extreme temperature reduces lactational success.
Hensleigh and Johnson (1971a)	Heat-stressed pregnant rats.	Retarded fetal growth.	Mechanism probably includes stress hormones. (ACTH production seemed to interact with gonadotropin activity.)
Hensleigh and Johnson (1972b)	Heat-stressed pregnant rats.	Fetal grown not affected when mothers ovariectomized and adrenalized.	Support for previous view (Hensleigh and Johnson, 1971a).
Euker and Riegle (1973)	Gave restraint-stress to rats at different stages, including pregnancy.	Greatest fetal loss when stressed during last trimester of pregnancy.	Because stress had effects at various reproductive stages, mechanism of stress probably is multifold (i.e., changes in uterine flow, maternal hormones, etc.).
Paris et al. (1973)	Applied short-term physical stressors to normal and infertile virgin mice.	Before puberty, stress had long-term effects on later conception.	Prepubertal stress therefore has a long-term effect on the developing CNS.
Paris and Ramaley (1973)	Applied short-term physical stressors to pregnant and neonatal mice.	Stress most reduced fertility and conception when present early in life.	Stress of heat exposure results in "partial masculinization" of the fetal female.

stress effect always occurred during the time of chronic stress administration. Embryonic mortality in stressed rats was characterized by an all-or-none effect; either the rats lost their entire litters after exposure to stress or they retained and gave birth to litters of normal size. The greatest fetal loss occurred in groups exposed to stress during the last trimester of pregnancy. Three rats produced normal litters, two delivered dead fetuses at term, and three rats reabsorbed their uterine contents. Two young from the group stressed at the end of pregnancy were hydrocephalic and did not survive beyond the first month or so after birth. Thus, some incidence of fetal malformation was associated with stress. Euker and Riegle were not able to say what the mechanism of action of stress on pregnancy might be. They reported that the ability of stress to interrupt reproductive processes at several stages of the life cycle suggests that the mechanism may in fact involve several components, including alterations in gonadotropin secretions, luteal or placental secretions, or uterine blood flow.

Paris et al. (1973) studied the effects of such short-term stresses as heat, ether, and immobilization on fertility of normal-cycling females and females rendered infertile by neonatal estrogen or hypothalamic lesion. In general, rats that were infertile before stress showed luteinization of the ovaries after stress, probably as a result of increased gonadotropin secretion, whereas the stress made normal-cycling females infertile. Fertility in immature mice was reduced by all kinds of stress as indicated by the reduction of the number of conceptions and an increase in time between exposure to a male and conception. If exposure to stress was done after puberty, however, there were no long-lasting effects on the female. Females were able to produce litters within a reasonable time after exposure to heat. Thus, Paris et al. contended that prepubertal stress has a long-term effect on the developing CNS.

A particularly interesting paper by Paris and Ramaley (1973) examined the effects of prenatal and early postnatal stress on female offspring; it was the first paper to hint at the use of the sexual differentiation model to explain reduction in fertility. Paris and Ramaley exposed pregnant mice to heat at different weeks during gestation and found that fewer mothers exposed during the third week of gestation survived to parturition when compared with others, and that litters born to those mothers showed a lower survival rate. Thus, the most vulnerable prenatal period for exposure to heat stress was the last week. The researchers also exposed newborn mice to heat stress during the first, second, or third postnatal week. On the basis of vaginal opening and percentage of conceptions produced, the most significant depression in fertility outcome occurred in mice that were exposed to heat stress at one week of age. It was part of their original intent to examine the effects of prenatal stress on fertility of female offspring but, ironically, Paris and Ramaley were not able to examine that result "due to failure of the air conditioning during the course of the experiment." Paris and Ramaley used the sexual differentiation hormone model to explain the effects of postnatal heat stress on reduced fertility in female offspring. In their words:

> The fact that heat exposure in neonatal mice has a greater effect than later exposure is reminiscent of the pattern of sexual differentiation of the hypothalamus reported in both mice and rats. It may be that the stress of heat exposure elicits adrenal secretions which result in a partial masculinization of the hypothalamus similar to that obtained with low doses of androgen, thus accounting for the irregular persistent estrus vaginal histology and the infertility after puberty (Paris and Ramaley, 1973, p. 544).

The work in psychology and biology reviewed above indicates that:

1. Severe behavioral and psychological stress during gestation such as conditioned anxiety, crowding, immobilization, and temperature extremes permanently modify structural or functional development of offspring in a variety of mammals.
2. Under certain conditions prenatal stress produces physical or behavioral abnormalities in offspring.
3. Prenatal influences on the offspring are believed to be mediated by a maternal response involving stress hormones such as epinephrine, corticosteroids from the adrenal glands, and ACTH from the anterior pituitary gland.
4. Although the mechanism of prenatal stress is unknown, it may in fact be quite varied to include sympathetic nervous system responses and vasoconstriction at one end of the continuum to gross and permanent alterations of the CNS as occurs in sexual differentiation of the brain.
5. Nevertheless, little doubt remains that the form and structure of the body, as well as later behavior, may be modified, sometimes adversely, by disadvantageous environmental conditions before birth.

CONTEMPORARY RESEARCH

Recent advances in prenatal stress research have been marked by a concerted quest for an underlying mechanism. In a truly interdisciplinary spirit, psychologists (researching hormones and behavior) have collaborated with biologists (endocrinologists, biochemists) to attempt a unified approach to understanding maternal stress effects on offspring (see Table 4). In contrast to that of previous decades, research in the 70s has been marked by: better quantification of stimulus parameters; a wider range of response measures; attempts to define experience directly, in terms of changes in maternal-fetal endocrinology; and a union of animal and human research even in the same laboratory. A major thrust has been to understand the human condition better so as to ameliorate problems and promote health.

Hormonal and Environmental Influences

The sexual differentiation model of the brain shows that the hormonal milieu, not the genome, determines sexual dimorphism in an inherently female brain (Gorski, 1980). Essentially, the principle says that normal patterns of sexual behavior and gonadotropin secretion are established by adulthood as a function of the presence or absence of androgens during critical perinatal sexual differentiation stages. Two lines of evidence have been called on to support this view. Chemical or surgical castration of genetic males during perinatal life feminizes and demasculinizes reproductive functions; and conversely, exposure of genetic females to androgens during a critical developmental stage masculinizes and defeminizes reproductive physiology, morphology, and behavior. Severity of the masculinizing and defeminizing action of perinatal androgens (more particularly the potent metabolite, estradial) depends on the amount and timing of the hormonal manipulation (Gorski, 1980).

The possibility that maternal stress may influence sexual differentiation was stimulated by Ward's discovery (1972) that prenatal stress feminizes and demasculinizes sexual behavior in males. She exposed late-pregnant rats to the stress of heat, restraint, and bright lights three times daily during the last trimester of gestation and reported that by adulthood there was a significant reduction in the percentage of stressed males that copulated and ejaculated compared to control males, and a significant increase in their lordotic performance. She believed that the prenatal stress syndrome in males, characterized by diminished copulatory patterns and increased lordotic behavior potentials, developed from diminished exposure of fetal males to gonadal androgens, presumably as a result of increased exposure to stress steroids.

In a later experiment with the endocrinologist Weisz, Ward presented direct evidence that maternal stress altered plasma testosterone in fetal males (Ward and Weisz, 1980). The investigators employed radioimmunoassay to measure plasma testosterone in Caesarean-delivered normal males and males stressed during the last trimester of pregnancy. Whereas in normal males

Table 4

Representative Contemporary Research

Study	Procedure	Results	Discussion
Ward (1972)	Subjected late-pregnant rats to heat-restraint stress.	Feminized and demasculinized sexual behavior of males (more lordotic responding, less copulation).	Maternal-fetal stress hormones reduce androgens in fetal males during a critical sexual differentiation stage.
Moyer et al. (1977)	Physical stress (Ward, 1972) applied to pregnant rats.	Altered catecholamine (CA) concentrations in discrete brain regions and nuclei (particularly, reduced norepinephrine [NE]).	Prenatal stress may alter hormones via CA. Reduced NE may set the stage for postpartum disorders.
Moyer et al. (1978)	Physical stress (Ward, 1972) applied to pregnant rats.	Altered CA concentrations in discrete brain region of offspring as adults (i.e., reduced NE in males, increased dopamine [DA] in females).	Reduced NE in males, particularly in brain regions associated with sexual behavior and gonadotropins. May be related to changes in sex behavior (Ward, 1972). DA changes in females were in brain regions associated with prolactin. May have consequences in pregnancy and lactation.

Herrenkohl (1979)	Physical stress (Ward, 1972) applied to pregnant rats.	Reduced fertility and fecundity in female offspring (estrous-cycle disorders, spontaneous abortions, high neonatal mortality).	Prenatal stress may partially masculinize CNS of the fetal female.
Ward and Weisz (1980)	Physical stress (Ward, 1972) applied to pregnant rats.	Exposed fetal males to a premature surge of plasma testosterone.	Feminization and demasculinization of CNS of fetal males may result from a desynchrony between level of CNS maturation and exposure to androgens.

a surge of plasma testosterone characteristically occurred on the 18th or 19th gestational day, this testosterone surge occurred prematurely in the stressed male, on gestational day 17. Ward and Weisz concluded that the CNS of the fetal male becomes demasculinized and feminized, not as a result of a decreased exposure in absolute amount of circulating testosterone during the late gestational stage, but because there is a desynchrony between the maturational stage of the CNS and patterns of testosterone secretion during fetal life. In other words, the fetal male under stress is exposed to the testosterone surge at a time in development when his CNS is not ready to manage it.

Herrenkohl (1979) presented the first evidence that maternal stress influences reproductive outcomes in female offspring. She exposed pregnant rats to repeated restraint-heat stress and observed that only a small percentage of their female offspring were able to bear young. Prenatal stress produced a syndrome in female offspring characterized by diminished reproductive capabilities in adulthood (estrous cycle disorders, spontaneous abortions and vaginal hemorrhaging, still births and neonatal mortality, low-birthweight young). Her cross-fostering experiments ruled out the possibility that pre-partal stress-induced disturbances in the behavior or lactational performance of the mother during the postnatal period were primary causes of the reproductive deficits in the offspring (Herrenkohl, 1979; Herrenkohl and Politch, 1978; Herrenkohl and Whitney, 1976; Politch et al., 1978). She concluded, therefore, that prenatal stress affected later reproduction in female offspring, not by disrupting postnatal rearing conditions, but by altering the fetus, possibly by changing the hormonal milieu.

Under severe environmental stress, sexual differentiation in some mammalian species is believed to take place in the presence of large amounts of steroids, some of which are secreted by the adrenal glands (Rose, 1969). Disturbances in gonadal or adrenal hormones during perinatal sexual differentiation may disrupt reproduction in female offspring by decreasing sexual receptivity or by inducing gonadotropic or ovarian irregularities (Harlan and Gorski, 1977a and b; Turner and Taylor, 1977). Therefore, it can be hypothesized that maternal stress may alter sexual differentiation in the fetal female by influencing the exchange of gonadal and adrenal hormones between the mother and the fetus (or the balance of these hormones in the fetus alone) during a critical hypothalamic sexual differentiation stage.

Evidence in our laboratory and in collaboration with David Jacobowitz at the Laboratory of Clinical Science, National Institutes of Mental Health, and John Moyer of Wyeth Laboratories, suggests that prenatal stress may modify the neuroanatomical and biochemical organization of the brains of both males and females and turn the direction of male fetal brain development toward that of the female sex. We reported (Moyer et al., 1977, 1978) that the stress of restraint and bright lights altered catecholamine (CA) concentrations in discrete brain regions of offspring as well as of the mothers under stress. We combined the microdissection technique of Palkovits (1973) for removing individual brain nuclei with a sensitive radioisotopic enzymatic assay for norepinephrine (NE) and dopamine (DA). With respect to the pregnant mothers we discovered (1977) that stress during pregnancy reduced steady-state NE levels by about the same amount in the medial preoptic nucleus, anterior hypothalamus, median forebrain bundle, and the nucleus interstitialis terminalus. Thus, of the two major noradrenergic pathways, regions innervated by the ventral ascending bundle showed the most changes in CA as a function of prepartal stress. Taken together, the correspondences suggested that prepartal stress-induced changes may operate through lymbic-hypothalamic CA-concentrating neurons to influence both sexual behavior and gonadotropin release from the pituitary gland.

The locations of CA decreases, as a function of prepartal stress, also overlapped with the brain regions in which CA depletion has been implicated in functional affective disorders. We noted that in humans anxiety and excessive emotional stress complicated pregnancy and birth. Further, we postulated that the relatively high incidence of certain mental disorders when sex steroids and CA fluctuate widely (as during diestrus, the postpartum period, and at menopause) suggests an interrelationship between female hormones, catecholamines, and psychological state. Stress during pregnancy with the corresponding changes in brain monoamines may set the stage for postpartum disorders.

Among the findings in stressed offspring as adults (Moyer et al., 1978), we observed reductions in NE levels in male offspring similar to those in stressed mothers. In female offspring, prenatal stress increased concentrations of the neurotransmitter dopamine (DA) in the hypothalamic arcuate nucleus. Because marked alterations in arcuate DA have been associated with abnormalities in the release of gonadotropic hormones from the anterior pituitary gland, we predicted and ultimately observed reproductive dysfunctions in female offspring (Herrenkohl, 1979; Herrenkohl and Politch, 1978).

DIRECTIONS FOR FUTURE RESEARCH

The experiments most likely to influence understanding in the future will build upon the strengths of the past. It seems probable, therefore, that the decade of the 80s will see more of us examining maternal stress effects on offspring by means of one of the following three essential strategies, or some combination thereof: 1) psychobiological studies of laboratory animals alone; 2) psychobiological experiments using both lower animals and human beings in the same study; and 3) studies with a human focus exclusively.

By way of illustrating the first proposition, current research in our laboratory is aimed at understanding the concomitant influence of maternal stress on morphological and behavioral development in the neonate. Experiments in the Neuropsychology Laboratory at Temple University are examining the relationship between maternal stress, neuroanatomical development in the fetus and neonate, and behavioral and reflex development over the first few weeks of life. A student, Susan Scott Carley, and I are administering perinatal stress and exogenous hormones to examine morphological changes in sexually dimorphic hypothalamic brain regions (medial preoptic nucleus, suprachiasmatic nucleus, ventromedial nucleus) in fetal and neonatal rats. Among Gorski's (1980) observations were that: It is possible with the naked eye (by gross histology) to observe that the medial preoptic nucleus (the sexually dimorphic nucleus) is five to eight times larger in male rats than in females; in males that are castrated neonatally, the sexually dimorphic nucleus is about the same size as that in intact females; and in androgenized females, the sexually dimorphic nucleus is about the same size as that of normal males. The morphology of the medial preoptic nucleus is, therefore, a function of perinatal androgen. Our working hypothesis is, in part, that prenatal stress will interact with exogenous androgen to maximize differences between experimental animals and controls. In concomitant research, we are examining locomotor and reflex reactivity between prenatally stressed and nonstressed offspring over the first few weeks of life.

As to the second strategy, Reinisch et al. (1978), in a pioneering and controversial report, united animal and human experiments in the same research to examine the effects of adrenocortical hormones administered during pregnancy on growth rates of fetal rats and babies. They noted that, although corticosteroid therapy has been used by obstetricians and gynecologists characteristically to induce ovulation and support pregnancy in women suffering from infertility, the deliberate exposure of large numbers of fetuses to augmented stress hormones has produced infants with high health risk and low birthweight. A sample of offspring of women who were treated with corticosteroids for infertility and for the maintenance of pregnancy were examined. To rule out maternal malfunction or disease as a confounding variable and to highlight the role of the stress hormone, Reinisch et al. undertook a simultaneous study of laboratory animals treated with corticosteroids in dosages proportional to those given to the women. The newborns of 119 women who had received prednisone during pregnancy at a private California infertility clinic between 1955 and 1975 served as the experimental group. A comparison group of 67 babies from women who did not receive hormone therapy was used. Birthweights were obtained from hospital and doctors' records at the time of delivery, and it was observed that babies exposed prenatally to prednisone weighed significantly less than control babies. In the animal laboratory, male and female mice were exposed to varying doses of the hormone at different stages during the third trimester of pregnancy and sacrificed at differing times after administration of the hormone. The growth of offspring exposed to prenatal prednisone administration was significantly retarded and resulted in diminished full-term birthweights. Three explanations were offered for the means by which prednisone affected fetal weight: Since corticosteroids cross the placental barrier, the lower weights may be an outcome of direct effect upon the fetus; the effects may be mediated by placental abnormalities resulting from the prednisone exposure; direct effects of exogenous corticoids on maternal physiology could lead to a subsequent indirect influence on placental or fetal growth (or both). These explanations should not be considered mutually exclusive as any or all could be possible theoretically.

Finally, we examined an exclusively human focus. In one kind of newly emerging research strategy, psychobiologists are adapting social and clinical psychological perspectives to understand stress and reproductive dysfunction in women. In one of these experiments, Herrenkohl (1981) examines the relationship between stress, personality, mood, and menstrual distress. Preliminary findings tend to support the hypothesis that prenatal stress may affect personality, mood, and menstrual activity. In a sample of 73 women questioned retrospectively about the incidence of life situational change (as measured by the Holmes-Rahe Social Stress Scale) over four stages of the reproductive life cycle (prenatal stage, early childhood, adolescence and young adulthood, adulthood), the following observations were made:

1. The higher the prenatal stress score (death of loved one, moving, marital discord), the higher the menstrual distress score (Moos Menstrual Distress Questionnaire) (Pearson product-moment $r = 0.92$, $p < 0.04$).
2. The higher the prenatal stress score, the more masculine the social self-perception (Bem Androgyny Scale) ($r = -0.94$, $p < 0.008$).
3. The higher the early childhood stress score, the more irregular the menses ($r = 0.75$, $p < 0.004$).
4. The higher the adolescence and young adulthood stress score, the more masculine the social self-perception ($r = -0.56$, $p < 0.023$).
5. The higher the premenstrual and intramenstrual distress, the higher the anxiety, depression and neurotic symptoms (Beck Anxiety Checklist, Beck Depression Inventory, Hopkins Self-Checklist) ($p < 0.005$).

A mechanism by which psychosocial stress may affect the developing re-productive substrate and later behavior is being explored.

The last series of experiments to be mentioned here represent dreams for the future more than present realities. Data banks and storehouses of information already exist which, if they were more fully utilized and more thoroughly reviewed, could provide large bodies of evidence on maternal stress and human development. One of these information banks is at the National Institute of Neurological Diseases and Stroke. Data are being compiled from a massive collaborative perinatal study of more than 10,000 women and their pregnancies which examined the relationship between numerous prenatal conditions (personal circumstances, drugs, health) and outcomes for the offspring (neonatal health, neurological development, school performance). From some of the findings to date (Niswander and Gordon, 1972), it is possible to note that important relationships exist between marital status during pregnancy and survival and health of offspring. The incidence of neonatal deaths and neurological impairment among infants is extraordinarily high among widows, suggesting that prenatal trauma associated with death of the husband had deleterious and far-reaching consequences for the offspring. Also, the incidence of low-birthweight young was high among non-married women. One wonders what the long-term developmental consequences of maternal stress during pregnancy might be like on offspring during their adolescence and adulthood. Would there be a relationship between prenatal maternal stress and reproductive dysfunction in the daughters, or with anxiety states in the offspring?

Tapping a data bank on 8,000 or so women at the Kaiser Foundation Health Plan in San Francisco, Laukaran and van den Berg (1980) have examined the relationship of maternal attitude to pregnancy outcomes and obstetrical complications. Because maternal health, nutritional and other factors were also examined, it was possible to focus in the report more prominently on maternal attitude as a contributing factor. And because the authors controlled for class, it was possible to see that the major factor associated with postpartum infection and hemorrhages in the mother, and deaths and congenital abnormalities in newborns, was a negative maternal attitude toward having the baby. The mechanism whereby the attitude of the mother affected the outcome of her pregnancy and the health and survival of her young is not known. The authors do, however, favor a "stress-mediated change in hormones" hypothesis.

A paper by Huttunen and Niskanen (1978) examined the relationship between prenatal loss of father and the incidence of psychiatric disorders. Using the epidemiological approach, the authors tested the hypothesis that maternal stress during pregnancy affects adult psychiatric disorders. They monitored a number of psychiatric patients, among whom were persons whose fathers had died before the patients were born. Death of the spouse has been postulated to be the most stressful single life event (Holmes and Rahe, 1967). A retrospective epidemiological study was conducted using the Finnish population register for persons born between 1925 and 1957. A sample of 167 persons was detected whose fathers had died before the subjects' birth. A control group was comprised of 168 persons whose fathers died during the first year of the control subjects' lives. The number of diagnosed schizophrenics treated in psychiatric hospitals and the number of persons committing crimes were significantly higher in the index than in the control group. There were no differences in age distribution among the two groups. The great majority of the fathers had died during the years of the Second World War. The distribution of the social classes of the parents was similar in both groups, as was the number of men and women. Although the authors favored the hypothesis of a direct biological effect of maternal stress during pregnancy on the fetus, it is possible that the effects of the prenatal loss of the father could be mediated (at least in part) through the "emotional insecurity of the widowed mother," or an altered mother-infant exchange. In any event, the actual possible mechanisms of action of maternal stress on the fetus require experimental research and can probably best be studied in animals.

A union of animal and human research possibly could reveal more direct evidence of a relationship between severe psychosocial stress during gestation and other psychiatric disorders, such as "anxiety." Observations over the past 30 years in both animal and human research that prenatal maternal stress is related to neonatal hyperactivity and irritability provides an intriguing clue. A mechanism for stress-induced changes in offspring behavior may lie in the maternal-fetal endocrine exchange and brain catecholamines. Such mechanism(s) may help explain "anxiety."

Summary and Conclusions

Severe physical and psychological stress during gestation (conditioned anxiety, crowding, immobilization, temperature extremes) permanently modify structural or functional development of offspring in a variety of mammals. Prenatal stress produces physical and behavioral abnormalities in offspring. Prenatal influences on offspring are believed to be mediated by a maternal response involving stress hormones such as epinephrine, corticosteroids from the adrenal glands, and adrenocorticotropin hormone (ACTH) from the anterior pituitary gland. The mechanism of prenatal stress is still unknown but it may be multifold. Nevertheless, little doubt remains that the form and structure of the body, as well as later behavior, may be modified, sometimes adversely, by disadvantageous environmental conditions before birth.

Contemporary animal research demonstrates that prenatal stress defeminizes and masculinizes sexual behavior of males and reduces fertility and fecundity in females (increases estrous cycle disorders, spontaneous abortions or vaginal hemorrhaging, neonatal mortality). Mechanisms of stress are being sought in the maternal-fetal blood exchange, secretory alterations in the hypothalamic-pituitary-gonadal/adrenal axes, and in brain catecholamines.

Contemporary human research employs epidemiological, psychological, and biomedical strategies to demonstrate that negative maternal attitudes toward pregnancy are related to high incidences of congenital abnormalities and infant deaths; and severe psychosocial stress (death of husband during the pregnancy) is related to high incidences of neonatal deaths and neurological impairments in infants and a high incidence of psychiatric disorders in adulthood. Mechanisms derived from animal research may help explain "anxiety."

REFERENCES

ADER, R., and PLAUT, S. M. 1968. Effects of prenatal maternal handling and differential housing on offspring emotionality, plasma corticosterone levels, and susceptibility to gastric erosions. *Psychosom. Med.*, 30:277-286.

AMERICAN PSYCHIATRIC ASSOCIATION, Task Force on Nomenclature and Statistics. *Diagnostic and Statistical Manual of Mental Disorders* (3rd Ed.), 1980. Washington, D.C.

BOWLBY, J. 1969. *Attachment*. New York: Basic Books.

DAVIDS, A., HOLDEN, R. H., and GRAY, G. B. 1963. Maternal anxiety during pregnancy and adequacy of mother and child adjustment eight months following childbirth. *Child Dev.*, 34:993-1002.

DEFRIES, J. C. 1964. Prenatal maternal stress in mice. *J. Hered.*, 55:289-295.

DEFRIES, J. C., WEIR, M. W., and HEGMANN, J. P. 1967. Differential effects of prenatal maternal stress on offspring behavior in mice as a function of genotype and stress. *J. Comp. Physiol. Psychol.*, 63:332-334.

DENENBERG, V. H., GARBANATI, J., SHERMAN, G., YUTZEY, D. A., and KAPLAN, R. 1978. Infantile stimulation induces brain lateralization in rats. *Science*, 201:1150-1152.

EUKER, J. S., and RIEGLE, G. D. 1973. Effects of stress on pregnancy in the rat. *J. Reprod. Fert.*, 34:343-346.

GLICK, D., VON REDLICH, D., and LEVINE, S. 1964. Fluorometric determination of corticosterone and cortisol in 0.02-0.05 milliliters of plasma or submilligram samples of adrenal tissue. *Endocrinology*, 74:653-655.

GORSKI, R. A. 1980. Sexual differentiation of the brain. In D. T. Krieger and J. C. Hughes (eds.), *Neuroendocrinology*, pp. 215–222. Sunderland, MA: Sinauer Associates.

HARLAN, R. E., and GORSKI, R. A. 1977a. Steroid regulation of luteinizing hormone secretion in normal and androgenized rats at different ages. *Endocrinology*, 101:741-749.

HARLAN, R. E., and GORSKI, R. A. 1977b. Correlations between ovarian sensitivity, vaginal cyclicity and luteinizing hormone and prolactin secretion in lightly androgenized rats. *Endocrinology*, 101:750-759.

HENSLEIGH, P. A., and JOHNSON, D. C. 1971a. Heat stress during pregnancy: I. Retardation of fetal rat growth. *Fertil. Steril.*, 22:522-527.
HENSLEIGH, P. A., and JOHNSON, D. C. 1971b. Heat stress during pregnancy: II. Pituitary gonadotropins in intact, adrenalectomized, and ovariectomized rats. *Fertil. Steril.*, 22:528-535.
HERRENKOHL, L. R. 1979. Prenatal stress reduces fertility and fecundity in female offspring. *Science*, 206:1097-1099.
HERRENKOHL, L. R. 1981. Stress, mood, personality and menstrual activity. Paper presented at annual American Assn. for the Advancement of Science meeting, Toronto.
HERRENKOHL, L. R., and POLITCH, J. A. 1978. Effects of prenatal stress on the estrous cycle of female offspring as adults. *Experientia*, 34:1240-1241.
HERRENKOHL, L. R., and WHITNEY, J. B. 1976. Effects of prepartal stress on postnatal nursing behavior, litter development and adult sexual behavior. *Physiol. Behav.*, 17:1019-1021.
HOCKMAN, C. H. 1961. Prenatal maternal stress in the rat: Its effects on emotional behavior in the offspring. *J. Comp. Physiol. Psychol.*, 54:679-684.
HOLMES, T. H., and RAHE, R. H. 1967. The social readjustment rating scale. *J. Psychosom. Res.*, 11:213-218.
HUTTUNEN, M. O., and NISKANEN, P. 1978. Prenatal loss of father and psychiatric disorders. *Arch. Gen. Psychiatry*, 35:429-431.
KEELEY, K. 1962. Prenatal influence on behavior of offspring of crowded mice. *Science*, 135:44-45.
KÖNIG, J. F. R., and KLIPPEL, R. A. 1963. *The Rat Brain: A Stereotaxic*. Baltimore: Williams & Wilkins.
KRIEGER, D. T. 1980. The hypothalamus and neuroendocrinology. In D. T. Krieger and J. C. Hughes (eds.), *Neuroendocrinology*, pp. 3-12. Sunderland, MA: Sinauer Associates.
LAUKARAN, V. H., and VAN DEN BERG, B. J. 1980. The relationship of maternal attitude to pregnancy outcomes and obstetric complications. *Am. J. Obstet. Gynecol.*, 136:374-379.
LIEBERMAN, M. W. 1963. Early developmental stress and later behavior. *Science*, 141:824-825.
MCDONALD, R. L. 1968. The role of emotional factors in obstetrics: A review. *Psychosom. Med.*, 30:222-237.
MORRA, M. 1965. Level of maternal stress during two pregnancy periods of rat offspring behaviors. *Psychonomic Science*, 3:7-9.
MOYER, J. A., HERRENKOHL, L. R., and JACOBOWITZ, D. M. 1977. Effects of stress during pregnancy on catecholamines in discrete brain regions. *Brain Res.*, 121:385-393.
MOYER, J. A., HERRENKOHL, L. R., and JACOBOWITZ, D. M. 1978. Stress during pregnancy: Effect on catecholamines in discrete brain regions of offspring as adults. *Brain Res.*, 144:173-178.
NISWANDER, K. R., and GORDON, M. 1972. *The Women and Their Pregnancies*. Washington, DC: U.S. Department of Health, Education and Welfare.
OTTINGER, D. R., and SIMMONS, J. E. 1964. Behavior of human neonates and prenatal maternal anxiety. *Psychol. Rep.*, 14:391-394.
PALKOVITS, M. 1973. Isolated removal of hypothalamic and other brain nuclei of the rat. *Brain Res.*, 59:449-450.
PARIS, A., and RAMALEY, J. A. 1973. Effects of short-term stress upon fertility. I. Before puberty. *Fertil. Steril.*, 24:540-545.
PARIS, A., KELLY, P., and RAMALEY, J. A. 1973. Effects of short-term stress upon fertility. II. After puberty. *Fertil. Steril.*, 24:546-552.
PENNYCUIK, P. R. 1966. Factors affecting the survival and growth of young mice born and reared at 36°. *Aust. J. Exp. Biol. Med. Sci.*, 44:405-418.
POLITCH, J. A., HERRENKOHL, L. R., and GALA, R. R. 1978. Effects of ether stress on prolactin and corticosterone levels in prenatally-stressed male rats as adults. *Physiol. Behav.*, 20:91-93.
RAHE, R. H., MEYER, M., SMITH, M. KJAER, G., and HOLMES, T. H. 1964. Social stress and illness onset. *J. Psychosom. Res.*, 8:34-44.
REINISCH, J. M., SIMON, N. G., KAROW, W. G., and GANDELMAN, R. 1978. Prenatal exposure

to prednisone in humans and animals retards intrauterine growth. *Science*, 202:436-438.

ROSE, R. M. 1969. Androgen responses to stress: I. Psychoendocrine relationships and assessment of androgen activity. *Psychosom. Med.*, 31:405-417.

SONTAG, L. W. 1944. Differences in modifiability of fetal behavior and physiology. *Psychosom. Med.*, 6:151-154.

SONTAG, L. W. 1966. Implications of fetal behavior and environment for adult personalities. *Ann. N.Y. Acad. Sci.*, 134:782-786.

SONTAG, L. W., REYNOLDS, E. L., and TORBET, V. 1944. Status of infant at birth as related to basal metabolism of mothers in pregnancy. *Am. J. Obstet. Gynecol.*, 48:208-214.

STOTT, D. H. 1973. Follow-up study from birth of the effects of prenatal stresses. *Dev. Med. Child. Neurol.*, 15:770-787.

THOMPSON, W. R. 1957. Influence of prenatal maternal anxiety on emotionality in young rats. *Science*, 125:698-699.

THOMPSON, W. R., and SONTAG, L. W. 1956. Behavioral effects in the offspring of rats subjected to audiogenic seizure during the gestational period. *J. Comp. Physiol. Psychol.*, 49:454-456.

TURNER, B. B., and TAYLOR, A. N. 1977. Effects of postnatal corticosterone treatment on reproductive development in the rat. *J. Reprod. Fert.*, 51:309-314.

WARD, I. L. 1972. Prenatal stress feminizes and demasculinizes the behavior of males. *Science*, 175:82-84.

WARD, I. L., and WEISZ, J. 1980. Maternal stress alters plasma testosterone in fetal males. *Science*, 207:328-329.

6

POSTNATAL STIMULATION, BRAIN LATERALIZATION, AND EMOTIONAL REACTIVITY

VICTOR H. DENENBERG, Ph.D.

By titling this volume the *Biology of Anxiety*, the editors immediately established several important principles. First, they assumed that the psychological phenomenon of anxiety has relevant biological underpinnings, and that an understanding of these biological processes will aid in understanding the nature of anxiety. Next, grounding the construct of anxiety in the biological world broadens its theoretical structure and empirical data base. Third, since human beings and other animals often have similar biological processes, animal research becomes part of the discourse.

Animals have, of course, been used for many years to study the effects of drugs on behavior. This is the field of psychopharmacology and its findings are directly relevant to those interested in anxiety. There is another field of animal research, of very recent origin, that is also relevant to the study of the biology of anxiety. This is the field of brain laterality in animals (Denenberg, 1981; Walker, 1980).

The study of lateralization of behavioral functions in animals was initiated by Nottebohm's (1970) paper which showed that the left hypoglossal nerve controlled song production in the chaffinch. Nottebohm followed this with an extensive series of elegant studies showing that the left side of the brain controlled song output (Nottebohm, 1971, 1972, 1977, 1979; Nottebohm and Nottebohm, 1976).

A major aspect of Nottebohm's work was that he showed a *population* effect for song production. That is, the vast majority of birds had left-hemispheric dominance for this behavior. Evidence for lateralization at the level of the *individual* had been found by many researchers working with a variety of species (see Harnad et al., 1977), but it was not until 1978 that papers

87

began appearing in the literature showing that rats, chicks, and nonhuman primates also had lateralized brains at the population level for the key behavioral functions of communication, affect, and spatial orientation (Denenberg, 1981). The distinction between individual and population lateralization is important. If the population is lateralized, this is evidence that evolutionary processes have been active, and thus there is a strong biological basis for the behavior. If the population is not lateralized even though individual animals are, this may or may not have evolutionary significance, making it more difficult to establish a biological substrate for the behavior.

Recent evidence has shown that the brains of chicks and rats are lateralized for emotional functions (Andrew et al., 1980; Denenberg et al., 1978, 1980; Garbanati et al., 1981; Howard et al., 1980; Rogers, in press). The differences in emotional reactivity of the two hemispheres in these species seem to parallel what we know about emotional reactivity of the human brain, and I will comment on this later. The important point to note here is that cerebral hemispheric differences in emotional responses are probably critical to an understanding of the biology of anxiety. Wexler (1980) made a similar point with respect to cerebral laterality and psychiatric illness.

Our own research on brain laterality in animals has added another dimension to this complex and intriguing field, namely, the effects of early experiences. I will review several of our studies on this topic and then comment on the implications for the central theme of this volume.

Early Experiences, Emotional Behavior, and Brain Laterality in the Rat

Background

Before describing the main findings on laterality, I will describe briefly our previous studies on infantile stimulation and early experiences in the rat (see Denenberg, 1969, 1977). Our experimental intervention starts at birth with a procedure called "handling." Maternity cages are inspected every morning. When a litter is found, we remove the tray containing the pups, leaving the mother in the cage, and cull the litter to eight. Typically we keep four males and four females per litter, but this will vary according to our experimental design. Litters are randomly assigned to the handling or nonhandling treatment conditions. A nonhandled litter is returned to the maternity cage immediately after sexing and culling and is not disturbed thereafter for 21 days when the pups are weaned. Cages are arranged so that food and water are available from external sources, so there is no need to open the cage door.

The handled pups are placed singly for three minutes into one-gallon cans with shaving-covered bottoms and then returned to the maternity cage. This is repeated daily from day 1 through day 20 of life. The procedure, which appears to be rather innocuous, has significant immediate and long-term consequences. For example, handling causes an increased adrenocortical response in two-day-old pups (Denenberg et al., 1967). In addition, when handled pups are returned to their cage, the mother becomes very active, carrying a pup around in her mouth, dropping it, picking up another pup, repeating this, and then gathering the young together into a nest. Thus, maternal activity is another significant source of early-experience stimulation for the pups.

On a long-term basis a number of behavioral and biological processes are significantly changed by the handling experience. We have found that both male and female handled rats are sexually precocious (Morton et al., 1963). We have found that handling in infancy reduces emotional reactivity in adulthood both behaviorally and physiologically (Levine et al., 1967; Whimbey and Denenberg, 1967a and b). In addition, handled rats engage in more exploratory behavior than do nonhandled animals (DeNelsky and Denenberg, 1967a and b; Whimbey and Denenberg, 1967a and b). Finally, as one would anticipate from the adrenocortical data, handling also modifies the hypothalamic-pituitary-adrenal axis (Campbell et al., 1973; Denenberg and Zarrow, 1971; Levine, 1969; Levine and Mullins, 1966; Zarrow et al., 1972).

Handling has been the major variable manipulated between birth and weaning. When we have intervened experimentally after weaning, the procedure most often used is to place animals into an enriched environment. This environment, first described by Hebb (1949), consists of a large cage in which 12 rat weanlings are placed. The cage contains a shelf to climb upon, various "toys" to play with, and food and water sources (Rosenzweig et al., 1972). Animals reared in such an environment are known to do better on problem-solving and perceptual tasks; there are also changes in brain chemistry and brain anatomy (Rosenzweig, 1971). In addition, exposure to an enriched environment after weaning reduces the rats' emotional reactivity (Denenberg, 1969).

To summarize: Handling between birth and weaning reduces emotional reactivity of rats in adulthood, increases their exploratory behavior, and modifies the hypothalamic-pituitary-adrenal axis. Environmental enrichment, introduced at the time of weaning, will also modify emotional reactivity. The question we asked in our current research is whether there is any evidence of brain lateralization for these behavioral functions. The answer is yes, and I will describe three studies showing that early experiences modify emotional behavior via brain lateralization.

Open-Field Activity

Our initial hypothesis was that the effects of early experience would be asymmetrically distributed between the two hemispheres (Denenberg et al., 1978). Two lines of thought led to this hypothesis. First, there is the evidence, summarized above, that early stimulation reduces emotionality and increases exploratory behavior. The second line of evidence comes from clinical observations of human patients. Psychoanalytic theory explicitly implicates experiences during infancy as influencing affective behavior. In many forms of psychotherapy early emotional experiences are considered to be quite important; the difficulty of expressing one's emotional problems in words suggests that the nonverbal right hemisphere is significantly involved. Combining these rather disparate lines of evidence leads to the suggestion that the right hemisphere may be more heavily involved in emotional reactivity in animals, and that early stimulation may act to modify that reactivity.

To test the hypothesis of an asymmetrical distribution of the effects of early experiences, we formed four experimental groups by the following procedure. At birth litters were sexed and reduced to eight pups with at least four males. Litters were then randomly assigned to the handling or nonhandling procedure as described above. When weaned at day 21, half the litters in the two infant-treatment conditions were randomly assigned to enriched environment cages while the remaining litters were placed into standard laboratory cages, with two or three litter mates per cage. The enrichment animals remained in the complex environments until day 50 when they were removed and also placed into standard laboratory cages, with two or three per cage. When 70 days old, they were each placed singly into laboratory cages. At approximately 135 days of age, four males from a litter were randomly assigned to one of four surgical conditions: right or left neocortical ablation, a sham operation, or no surgery. They were given one month to recover from the effects of surgery and then were tested for four days in the open field. Table 1 summarizes the mean activity score summed over four days. The nonsurgical and the sham-operation groups did not differ, and their data were pooled into one intact brain group.

The results confirmed our hypothesis, but in a somewhat more complex way than we had anticipated. First, there is no evidence that nonhandled rats have lateralized brain functions, whether they get enrichment after weaning or not. In sharp contrast, the handling procedure does induce brain lateralization, but two distinctly different patterns occur, depending on whether laboratory cage experience or enriched environment experience follows the handling. When handling is combined with subsequent laboratory cage experience, the most active group is animals with isolated left hemi-

Table 1

Open-field Activity as a Function of Early Experience and Adult Brain Lesion (from Denenberg et al., 1978)

Days 1-20	Days 21-50	Intact Controls	Right Brain Intact	Left Brain Intact
NH	LC	8.90	27.64	22.33
		N = 20	N = 11	N = 12
NH	EE	9.91	27.08	32.89
		N = 22	N = 12	N = 9
H	LC	12.51	17.91	36.27
		N = 23	N = 11	N = 11
H	EE	17.52	20.42	3.00
		N = 20	N = 12	N = 10

NH: nonhandled; LC: laboratory cage; H: handled; EE: enriched environment.

spheres (activity score of 36.27 units). When one adds enrichment after the handling experience, however, the left hemisphere group has the lowest activity score of any in that table (3.00 units).

The interpretation of these data is as follows (see Denenberg, 1980, for an extended discussion of the model on which these interpretations are based): For both nonhandled groups, the removal of a hemisphere results in an increase in activity, but the increase is equivalent whether the right or the left hemisphere is removed. Since the animals with intact brains are less active, we conclude that each hemisphere inhibits the activity level of the opposite one when the two are coupled in the normal brain. In the handled, lab cage condition, animals with intact brains and those with an isolated right hemisphere have equivalent activity scores, while those with an isolated left hemisphere are more active. Thus, we conclude that the left hemisphere has greater activity than the right, but in the intact animal this greater activity is overridden by the right hemisphere's inhibition of the left. Combining handling plus enrichment, one finds again that the intact and the right hemisphere group have similar scores, but the left hemisphere group has a markedly reduced activity level. The most parsimonious interpretation is that the right hemisphere is dominant for this behavior under this particular combination of rearing circumstances.

The following conclusions are derived from these findings and interpretations: First, the hypothesis that the effects of early experiences are asymmetrically distributed was confirmed in the two handled groups. Next, since the two nonhandled groups showed no evidence of brain laterality, while both handled groups did, we infer that early stimulation is capable of bringing about brain reorganization which results in asymmetrical cortices. Third, the right hemisphere is heavily involved in these brain dynamics via inhibition of the left hemisphere (handled, laboratory cage group) or by simple dominance (handled, enriched environment group). Finally, it is not possible to state unequivocally that emotional functions have been lateralized because previous research, using factor-analytic techniques, has found that open-field activity loads both on an emotionality factor as well as on an exploratory factor (Whimbey and Denenberg, 1967a and b). For that reason, it was necessary to conduct other tests of emotional behavior.

Taste Aversion

One difficulty of the open-field test is that it uses activity as an index of emotionality, and activity also is involved in exploratory behavior. Therefore, we chose a procedure that did not require locomotor behavior on the part of the animal, yet would give us a clear-cut index of an emotional response—the taste aversion paradigm (Garcia et al., 1974). It is known that if an animal eats a novel food followed by gastric upset, the animal will form a strong aversion to that food and avoid it in the future. Wild animals will generally not eat that food again, but the domestic rat will usually extinguish the avoidance response over a series of trials. Two other attractive features of this procedure are that it is not necessary to remove the animal from its home cage to test it, nor is the animal handled during the testing.

Our procedure was as follows: Adult male rats, handled or not disturbed in infancy, were trained to drink from a bottle containing sweetened milk. After the second day of milk consumption, they were injected with lithium chloride which induces a strong visceral disturbance, or with saline as a control of the effects of the injection and the stomach loading. After this one association of stomach upset with the taste of milk, the rats were placed back onto a 24-hour water regimen. All this took place while animals had intact brains. We waited 25 days after the conditioned association and then did brain surgery, removing the right or left neocortex, doing a sham operation, or no surgery. We then waited four weeks to be certain the animal was fully recovered before testing for retention of taste aversion. Note that these animals had only one association between the sweetened milk and the stomach poisoning while their brains were intact, and were not exposed to the sweetened milk again until more than 50 days later after neocortical ablations. The question asked by this design is: If handled and nonhandled rats learn a conditioned fear response with an intact brain, and one hemisphere is subsequently destroyed, what is the nature of the retention of the remaining hemisphere? The key findings are shown in Figures 1 and 2 (Denenberg et al., 1980).

Figure 1 shows extinction curves for handled and nonhandled animals that receive a lithium chloride. Preliminary tests found that the no-surgery and sham-operation groups did not differ and their data were pooled into one whole-brain group (designated by the letter W). The initial low levels of milk consumption establish that the groups remembered the poisoning. The increase in consumption reflects varying degrees of extinction of the learned fear response. Within the nonhandled group, there were no differences in extinction among the three brain conditions. In contrast, all three of the handled curves differ significantly from each other, the isolated right-hemisphere group consuming the least amount of milk, followed by the left-hemisphere group, while those with an intact brain consumed the greatest amount. Since greater milk consumption indicates a lesser conditioned fear, the isolated right-hemisphere group had the greatest amount of fear, while the intact-brain group had the least, with the left-hemisphere group being

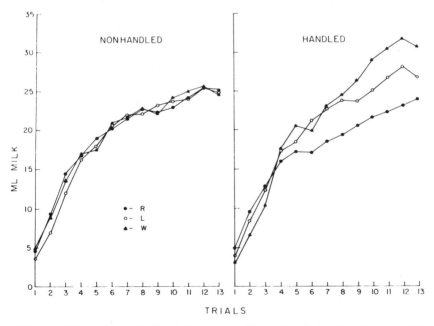

Figure 1. Mean amount of milk solution consumed by nonhandled and handled rats which had received a lithium chloride injection. W = whole brain; L = left hemisphere intact; R = right hemisphere intact (from Denenberg et al., 1980).

intermediate. However, it is necessary to examine the data of the saline controls (Figure 2) before a final interpretation can be made of these findings.

In Figure 2, the first thing to note is that the amount of milk consumed on the first extinction trial is much higher than was the case in Figure 1, thereby demonstrating that the lithium injection and the attendant stomach poisoning engendered a learned conditioned avoidance response. The statistical analysis of the data in Figure 2 found only one effect: The groups with only a right hemisphere consumed less milk than the other two groups. This was true regardless of early experience condition.

The interpretations are as follows. First, the saline data show that the brain of the laboratory rat is lateralized for some functions independent of early experiences. Thus, the right hemisphere is sufficiently sensitive so that even the relatively mild procedure of injecting saline into the stomach is enough to bring about a long-term conditioned avoidance response. Next, in Figure 1 we see that the more powerful lithium poisoning eliminates the differences among the nonhandled groups. Lithium drops their asymptote to the level of the nonhandled saline-injected group with an intact right hemisphere in Figure 2. Thus, the laterality differences seen with the mild

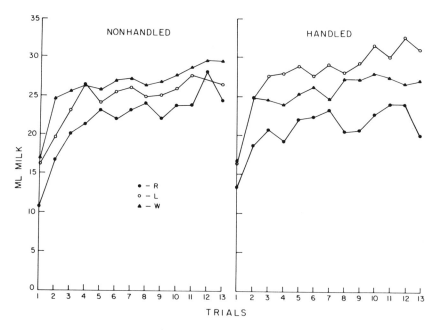

Figure 2. Mean amount of milk solution consumed by nonhandled and handled rats which had received an injection of physiological saline (from Denenberg et al., 1980).

saline treatment are masked in nonhandled animals by the strong lithium treatment. Turning to the handled groups (Figure 1), the asymptote of the right-brain intact group is equivalent to that of the right-brain intact, saline-injected group in Figure 2. In other words, lithium was no more powerful than a saline injection for animals with only a right hemisphere. Figure 1 shows that the intact left-hemisphere group and the group with a fully intact brain both consumed more milk than the right-hemisphere group. We conclude that handled rats with an intact left hemisphere are less emotional than handled rats with an right intact hemisphere, and that handled animals with an intact brain are the least emotional of all.

One general conclusion is that the right hemisphere is more heavily implicated in emotional behavior for both handled and nonhandled animals. A second is that handling acts upon the left hemisphere to reduce its emotional reactivity. This latter conclusion is consistent with the data on open-field performance (Table 1), in which we found that handled animals with an intact left brain were more active in the open field than were those with an intact right brain.

The data also offer an interesting speculation. Recall that the intact handled group showed less fear than either of the other groups. This leads to the conclusion that each hemisphere acts to inhibit the fear response of the other one. Might this offer a useful model of repression?

The next experiment describes a very different approach to the study of emotional behavior.

Muricide (Mouse Killing)

Mouse killing by rats is a species-typical behavior pattern. Food or water deprivation are not required to trigger the response. This is a form of affective behavior quite different from the previous paradigm, as this occurs spontaneously while the other involves a conditioning procedure. If similar results could be obtained across such different measures, this would strongly substantiate our conclusions concerning early stimulation and brain laterality for emotional processes.

In this experiment, we handled or did not disturb rats between birth and weaning. After weaning, half the litters went into an enriched environment, while the other half went into standard laboratory cages. This design, then, is identical to the one we used when studying open-field behavior. When about 115 days old, males were given a right or left neocortical ablation, a sham operation, or no surgery. The test for mouse killing was done when the animals were between 9 and 12 months old. Thus, the effects obtained are relatively permanent consequences of the early stimulation in combination with brain surgery. As in previous experiments, a preliminary test found no difference between the sham surgery and nonoperated group and their data were pooled. Table 2 presents the incidence of killing for the 12 groups in the experiment (Garbanati et al., 1981).

The data for intact controls show that both handling and enrichment act independently and additively to reduce the incidence of mouse killing. To understand the brain dynamics involved, it is necessary to examine the data of the lesion groups. For the nonhandled laboratory cage group, removing a hemisphere reduced the incidence of killing, but there is no evidence of a laterality effect. We conclude that when the two hemispheres are coupled, they act to facilitate killing behavior of the intact brain. For the nonhandled enriched group, there are no significant differences among the three surgical conditions, even though the means suggest that the left-hemisphere group is more likely to kill than the right. There is a significant laterality effect within the handled laboratory cage group: Rats with an intact isolated right hemisphere have a higher killing incidence than those with an isolated left hemisphere. Finally, there are no differences among the surgical conditions for the handled and enriched combination.

The data of the handled laboratory cage group are particularly pertinent. Since the isolated right-hemisphere group kills more than either the left-hemisphere or the intact group (which do not differ from each other), the conclusion is that the left hemisphere inhibits the killing response of the right when the two are coupled in the intact brain. Thus, the right hemisphere of the handled animal is more emotional than is the left hemisphere, and the left hemisphere exerts inhibitory control over the right. This is essentially the same conclusion we came to with respect to the taste aversion

Table 2

Incidence of Muricide as a Function of Early Experiences and Adult Brain Lesion (from Garbanati et al., 1981)

Days 1-20	Days 21-50	Intact Controls	Right Brain Intact	Left Brain Intact
NH	LC	96.0	75.0	68.8
		N = 50	N = 32	N = 32
NH	EE	79.4	73.7	94.7
		N = 34	N = 19	N = 19
H	LC	78.0	94.6	67.6
		N = 50	N = 37	N = 37
H	EE	62.9	61.1	57.1
		N = 35	N = 18	N = 21

data, namely, that the handled group with an isolated right hemisphere is more emotional than the group with the isolated left hemisphere and that the left hemisphere inhibits the right in the intact brain.

General Conclusions

We may now make some general summary statements from the research described above.

1. The brain of the laboratory rat (independent of early experience) is lateralized for some emotional processes, as indicated by the taste aversion experiment using saline injection. The right hemisphere has greater retention of a conditioned fear response than does the left hemisphere.
2. The hypothesis that the effects of early experiences are asymmetrically distributed has been confirmed in all three experiments, since laterality effects were obtained in all instances among handled animals.
3. The right hemisphere has stronger emotional responses than does the left. This is seen for open-field activity, in which animals in the handled laboratory cage group with an intact right brain were less active than those with an intact left brain; in the taste aversion experiment, in which the handled right-brain group consumed less milk after lithium poisoning than did their litter mates with an intact left brain; and in the mouse-killing study, in which handled animals with an intact right brain killed more mice than did their litter mates with an intact left brain.
4. Early handling reduces the emotional reactivity of the left hemisphere. This follows from the statements made in #3 above, as in all instances the left-hemisphere group was less emotional than the right-hemisphere group.
5. In most instances (but not all), the brain dynamics underlying emotional activity involve activation of one hemisphere and inhibition by the other hemisphere. Thus, the two hemispheres interact in maintaining emotional balance. The inhibition can go in either direction. For the open-field study, the more emotional right hemisphere inhibited the left (see handled laboratory cage condition in Table 1), while in both the taste aversion and mouse-killing studies, the less emotional left hemisphere inhibited the right.
6. One broad conclusion from these findings is that the brain of the rat is already lateralized for some processes and is sufficiently plastic that extra stimulation in early life may lateralize the brain for even more emotional functions. Thus, early experiences are capable of bringing about significant reorganization of the brain of the rat.

LATERALITY AND EMOTIONAL BEHAVIOR IN HUMAN BEINGS

There is now a considerable body of evidence showing that the right and left hemispheres have different emotional response patterns. This evidence is based on clinical data, the use of amytal before neurosurgery, and experimental investigations.

In 1972, Gainotti reported on 80 patients with right-hemisphere lesions and 80 with left-side damage. While receiving a standard neuropsychological examination, the patients' verbal expressions were transcribed verbatim and a record was made of any behavior considered indicative of emotional reaction and mood. Those with left-brain damage were more likely to show anxiety reactions, tears, swearing, depressed renouncements, and sharp refusals; those with damage of the right hemisphere joked more, were indifferent, denied their illness, or minimized the impact of their paralysis. The pattern of findings associated with damage to the left hemisphere has been called a "catastrophic reaction" or a depressive response, while the pattern involved with right-hemisphere damage has been called an "indifference reaction" (Gainotti, 1972; Perria et al., 1961; Rossi and Rosadini, 1967).

Another opportunity to study the relationship between hemisphere and emotional response occurs when patients are scheduled for neurosurgery. It is necessary to establish unequivocally which brain hemisphere controls speech. The only certain way to do so is to inject a barbiturate, on separate occasions, into the right and left carotid arteries (Wada, 1949). This will anesthetize the hemisphere ipsilateral to the injection. The cessation of speech determines the hemisphere containing the speech area. Different emotional responses often accompany this procedure. Terzian and Cecotto (1959, as cited by Gainotti, 1972) reported that a "depressive-catastrophic" reaction followed the pharmacological inactivation of the left hemisphere, and a "euphoric-maniacal" reaction followed inactivation of the right hemisphere. These findings have been confirmed by others (Perria et al., 1961; Rossi and Rosadini, 1967). Rossi and Rosadini describe the depressive and euphoric reactions as follows:

The depressive type is characterized by a sad attitude of the patient and by his tendency to pessimism; the patient complains of almost anything . . . he often starts weeping. The euphoric reaction is characterized at first by a relaxed attitude and then by the extremely optimistic view he takes of everything, by his smiling and making jokes, and by his breaking into actual laughter . . . Both emotional states may have a duration of several minutes. After their disappearance, the patient, questioned on the cause of the peculiar behavior, is not capable of giving an explanation (p. 171).

The studies of brain-damaged patients and of the intracarotid artery test both conclude that inactivation of the left hemisphere brings about a catastrophic-depressive response. However, the euphoric-maniacal pattern, reported when the right hemisphere is immobilized by a barbiturate injection, is not found when brain-damaged patients are observed. There is agreement, though, that such patients do joke and express indifference to their condition. From his extensive neurological observations, Geschwind (1980) agrees with the indifference classification for those with right-hemisphere damage, but states that depression is seen much more frequently than catastrophic reactions following left-hemisphere damage.

It should be noted that Milner (1967) did not report emotional differences in subjects who were given intracarotid injections. There is a considerable body of other observations, however, which support the conclusion that two hemispheres have different emotional patterns (Gainotti, 1979; Wexler, 1980). As an example, Dimond et al. (1976) reported that subjects viewing a movie of a surgical operation with their right hemispheres (via specially designed contact lenses) scored the film as more "horrific" than another group who saw the film with their left hemisphere.

In a recent paper, Sackeim et al. (1980) analyzed case reports in the literature of patients with uncontrollable emotional outbursts. They examined cases of pathological laughing and crying, hemispherectomy, and the presence of uncontrollable laughing or crying in epileptic patients. They concluded that there is a significant degree of brain lateralization in the regulation of emotion and that the left side of the brain subserves positive emotional states to a greater extent than the right side, whereas the reverse holds for negative emotional states. They suggest that the emotional changes observed following predominantly unilateral destructive lesions are most often caused by disinhibition of contralateral brain centers.

To summarize: Damage or inactivation of the left hemisphere is associated with strong negative emotions that involve crying, depression, anxiety reactions, and swearing; inactivating or injuring the right hemisphere results in the expression of positive emotions that are exemplified by laughing or joking, or by an indifference reaction that involves denial of illness or minimizing its impact. The lesion or the anesthetic drug seems to remove inhibitory control of the hemisphere, thus releasing the emotional responses from the other side of the brain.

A situation in which contrasting affective responses alternate is seen in the emotional adjustment to death and dying (Kübler-Ross, 1969). From her studies Kübler-Ross reports that five stages are involved in this process: denial, anger, bargaining, grief, and acceptance. Denial and bargaining are left-hemisphere responses while anger and grief are associated with the right side of the brain. Thus, the emotional expression seems to alternate between the hemispheres until there is final integration by both when acceptance of death occurs. It would be of interest to know the sequence of emotional responses to death and dying by those with right- or left-hemisphere damage.

Finally, in terms of the biology of anxiety, Gainotti's (1972) findings seem pertinent. He reports that patients with right-hemisphere lesions had a significantly higher incidence of anxiety reactions than those with left-side lesions. This leads to the conclusion that anxiety is associated with the right hemisphere and is typically under inhibitory control by the left.

CONCLUSIONS AND IMPLICATIONS

The animal studies found that, for certain tests, rats have lateralized brains, independent of their early rearing histories. Handling pups in infancy will exaggerate already present laterality differences or will induce laterality in symmetrical brains. The strong negative emotions involved in taste aversion and mouse killing were associated with the right hemisphere, while the left hemisphere acted to inhibit those responses. The clinical research finds that strong negative emotions are associated with the right hemisphere, while the left side of the brain acts in an inhibitory capacity. The parallel between these two conclusions is quite striking and suggests a similarity in brain organization across species (Denenberg, 1981). Several implications follow from these conclusions.

1. Experiences in early life have a significant impact on organization of emotional behaviors and, in the rat at least, act to lateralize the brain with respect to emotions.
2. The finding that rats have a similar lateralization pattern to human beings means that animal models of brain laterality can now be set up to investigate emotional processes. This should lead to significant advancements in our understanding of emotions, including anxiety.
3. The conclusion reached from both the animal and the human studies is that the strong negative emotions are in the right hemisphere and are under left-hemispheric inhibition. Thus, there are two mechanisms whereby one can prevent these negative emotions from expressing themselves: Reduce the emotional reactivity of the right hemisphere, or increase the inhibitory control of the left hemisphere.

4. From #3 above, it follows that one can devise therapeutic procedures for either the right or the left hemisphere. One wonders which of these routes is involved in psychotherapy and drug therapy.

5. Finally, in keeping with the title and the spirit of this volume, the finding that early experiences influence emotion via brain lateralization broadens the biological base of the construct of anxiety and offers new directions for research.

REFERENCES

ANDREW, R. J., MENCH, J., and RAINEY, C. Right-left asymmetry of response to visual stimuli in the domestic chick. In D. J. Ingle, R. J. W. Mansfield, and M. A. Goodale (eds.), *Advances in the Analysis of Visual Behavior.* Cambridge, MA: MIT Press, in press.

CAMPBELL, P. S., ZARROW, M. X., and DENENBERG, V. H. 1973. The effect of infantile stimulation upon hypothalamic CRF levels following adrenalectomy in the adult rat. *Proc. Soc. Exp. Biol. Med.,* 142:781-783.

DeNELSKY, G. Y., and DENENBERG, V. H. 1967a. Infantile stimulation and adult exploratory behaviour in the rat: Effects of handling upon visual variation-seeking. *Anim. Behav.,* 15:568-573.

DeNELSKY, G. Y., and DENENBERG, V. H. 1967b. Infantile stimulation and adult exploratory behavior: Effects of handling upon tactual variation seeking. *J. Comp. Physiol. Psychol.,* 63:309-312.

DENENBERG, V. H. 1969. The effects of early experience. In E. S. E. Hafez (ed.), *The Behaviour of Domestic Animals,* pp. 96-130. London: Baillière, Tindall & Cassell.

DENENBERG, V. H. 1977. Assessing the effects of early experience. In R. D. Myers (ed.), *Methods in Psychobiology,* vol. 3, pp. 127-147. New York: Academic Press.

DENENBERG, V. H. 1980. General systems theory, brain organization, and early experiences. *Am. J. Physiol.,* 238: R3-R13; or *Am. J. Physiol.: Regulatory Integrative Comparative Physiology,* 7: R3-R13.

DENENBERG, V. H. 1981. Hemispheric laterality in animals and the effects of early experience. *Behavioral and Brain Sciences,* 4:1-49.

DENENBERG, V. H., and ZARROW, M. X. 1971. Effects of handling in infancy upon adult behavior and adrenocortical activity: Suggestions for a neuroendocrine mechanism. In D. N. Walcher and D. L. Peters (eds.), *Early Childhood: The Development of Self Regulatory Mechanisms,* pp. 39-64. New York: Academic Press.

DENENBERG, V. H., BRUMAGHIM, J. T., HALTMEYER, G. C., and ZARROW, M. X. 1967. Increased adrenocortical activity in the neonatal rat following handling. *Endocrinology,* 81:1047-1052.

DENENBERG, V. H., GARBANATI, J., SHERMAN, G., YUTZEY, D. A., and KAPLAN, R. 1978. Infantile stimulation induces brain lateralization in rats. *Science,* 201:1150-1152.

DENENBERG, V. H., HOFMANN, M., GARBANATI, J. A., SHERMAN, G. F., ROSEN, G. D., and YUTZEY, D. A. 1980. Handling in infancy, taste aversion, and brain laterality in rats. *Brain Res.,* 200:123-133.

DIMOND, S. J., FARRINGTON, L., and JOHNSON, P. 1976. Differing emotional response from right and left hemispheres. *Nature,* 261:690-692.

GAINOTTI, G. 1972. Emotional behavior and hemispheric side of the lesion. *Cortex,* 8:41-55.

GAINOTTI, G. 1979. Affectivity and brain dominance: A survey. In J. Obiols, C. Ballus, E. Gonzalez Monclus, and J. Pujol (eds.), *Biological Psychiatry Today,* pp. 1271-1276. New York: Elsevier/North-Holland Press.

GARBANATI, J. A., SHERMAN, G. F., ROSEN, G. D., HOFMANN, M., YUTZEY, D. A., and

DENENBERG, V. H. 1981. Handling in infancy, brain laterality, and muricide in rats. Unpublished manuscript.

GARCIA, J., HANKIN, W. G., and RUSINIAK, K. 1974. Behavioral regulation of the milieu interne in man and rat. *Science*, 185:824-831.

GESCHWIND, N. 1980. Personal communication.

HARNAD, S., DOTY, R. W., GOLDSTEIN, L., JAYNES, J., and KRAUTHAMER, G. 1977. *Lateralization in the Nervous System*. New York: Academic Press.

HEBB, D. O. 1949. *The Organization of Behavior*. New York: Wiley.

HOWARD, K. J., ROGERS, L. J., and BOURA, A. L. A. 1980. Functional lateralisation of the chicken forebrain revealed by use of intracranial glutamate. *Brain Res.*, 188:369-382.

KÜBLER-ROSS, E. 1969. *On Death and Dying*. New York: Macmillan.

LEVINE, S. 1969. An endocrine theory of infantile stimulation. In A. Ambrose (ed.), *Stimulation in Early Infancy*, pp. 45-55. New York: Academic Press.

LEVINE, S., HALTMEYER, G. C., KARAS, G. G., and DENENBERG, V. H. 1967. Physiological and behavioral effects of infantile stimulation. *Physiol. Behav.*, 2:55-59.

LEVINE, S., and MULLINS, R. F., Jr. 1966. Hormonal influence on brain organization in infant rats. *Science*, 152:1585-1592.

MILNER, B. 1967. Discussion of experimental analysis of cerebral dominance in man. In G. H. Millikan and F. L. Darley (eds.), *Brain Mechanisms Underlying Speech and Language*, pp. 177-179. New York: Grune & Stratton.

MORTON, J. R. C., DENENBERG, V. H., and ZARROW, M. X. 1963. Modification of sexual development through stimulation in infancy. *Endocrinology*, 72:439-442.

NOTTEBOHM, F. 1970. Ontogeny of bird song. *Science*, 167:950-956.

NOTTEBOHM, F. 1971. Neural lateralization of vocal control in a passerine bird. I. Song. *J. Exp. Zool.*, 177:229-262.

NOTTEBOHM, F. 1972. Neural lateralization of vocal control in a passerine bird. II. Subsong, calls, and a theory of vocal learning. *J. Exp. Zool.*, 179:35-50.

NOTTEBOHM, F. 1977. Asymmetries in neural control of vocalization in the canary. In S. Harnad, R. W. Doty, L. Goldstein, J. Jaynes, and G. Krauthamer (eds.), *Lateralization in the Nervous System*, pp. 23-44. New York: Academic Press.

NOTTEBOHM, F. 1979. Origins and mechanisms in the establishment of cerebral dominance. In M. S. Gazzaniga (ed.), *Handbook of Behavioral Neurobiology*, vol. 2, pp. 295-344. New York: Plenum.

NOTTEBOHM, F., and NOTTEBOHM, M. E. 1976. Left hypoglossal dominance in the control of canary and white-crowned sparrow song. *J. Comp. Physiol.*, 108:171-192.

PERRIA, L., ROSADINI, G., and ROSSI, G. F. 1961. Determination of side of cerebral dominance with amobarbital. *Arch. Neurol.*, 4:173-181.

ROGERS, L. J. Functional lateralisation in the chicken fore-brain revealed by cycloheximide treatment. *Proceedings 17th International Ornithology Congress*, West Berlin, in press.

ROSENZWEIG, M. R. 1971. Effects of environment on development of brain and behavior. In E. Tobach, L. R. Aronson, and E. Shaw (eds.), *The Biopsychology of Development*, pp. 303-342. New York: Academic Press.

ROSENZWEIG, M. R., BENNETT, E. L., and DIAMOND, M. C. 1972. Brain changes in response to experience. *Scientific American*, 226:22-29.

ROSSI, G. F., and ROSADINI, G. 1967. Experimental analysis of cerebral dominance in man. In C. H. Millikan and F. L. Darley (eds.), *Brain Mechanisms Underlying Speech and Language*, pp. 167-175. New York: Grune & Stratton.

SACKHEIM, H. A., GREENBERG, M. S., WEIMAN, A. L., GUR, R. C., HUNGERBUHLER, J. P., and GESCHWIND, N. 1980. Functional brain asymmetry in the expression of positive and negative emotions. Lateralization of insult in cases of uncontrollable emotional outbursts. Paper presented to the International Neuropsychological Society, Chianciano, Italy.

TERZIAN, H., and CECOTTO, D. 1959. Su un nuovo metodo per la determinazione e lo studio della dominanza emisferica. *Giornale di Psichiatria Neuropatologica*, 87:889-924.

WADA, J. 1949. A new method for the determination of the side of cerebral speech dominance:

A preliminary report on the intracarotid injection of sodium amytal in man. *Med. Biol.* (Tokyo), 14:221-222.

WALKER, S. F. 1980. Lateralization of function in the vertebrate brain: A review. *Br.J.Psychol.*, 71:329-367.

WEXLER, B. E. 1980. Cerebral laterality and psychiatry: A review of the literature. *Am. J. Psychiatry*, 137:279-291.

WHIMBEY, A. E., and DENENBERG, V. H. 1967a. Experimental programming of life histories: The factor structure underlying experimentally created individual differences. *Behaviour*, 29:296-314.

WHIMBEY, A. E., and DENENBERG, V. H. 1967b. Two independent behavioral dimensions in open-field performance. *J. Comp. Physiol. Psychol.*, 63:500-504.

ZARROW, M. X., CAMPBELL, P. S., and DENENBERG, V. H. 1972. Handling in infancy: Increased levels of the hypothalamic corticotropin releasing factor (CRF) following exposure to a novel situation. *Proc. Soc. Exp. Biol. Med.*, 141:356-358.

III.
TREATMENT OF ANXIETY

7

THE ROLE OF NEUROTRANSMITTERS IN THE PHARMACOLOGIC ACTIONS OF BENZODIAZEPINES

S. J. ENNA, Ph.D.

The development of the benzodiazepines represented a major advance in therapeutics. These drugs were rapidly accepted by the medical community because of their efficacy and the fact that their margin of safety greatly exceeds that of barbiturates and related sedative-hypnotic agents. Indeed, the lethal dose of benzodiazepines is unknown as there have been no recorded deaths resulting from an overdose of these compounds alone (Greenblatt et al., 1977).

Another reason for their popularity is their broad spectrum of activity. In addition to their anxiolytic action, these compounds are, like other central nervous system depressants, effective as sedatives, hypnotics, anticonvulsants, and muscle relaxants. Unlike other depressants, however, the benzodiazepines do not induce anesthesia, though they are used as a preanesthetic medication (Greenblatt and Shader, 1974; Haefely, 1977).

With regard to basic pharmacology, the advent of the benzodiazepines stimulated a reassessment of theories relating to the biochemical and physiological processes important for central nervous system activity. Before the development of benzodiazepines, drugs used to treat anxiety states, such as the barbiturates, had limited usefulness because they were also highly sedating. This duality of action was so characteristic of minor tranquilizers that many clinicians believed that a certain amount of sedation was essential to abolish the symptoms of anxiety. This theory implied that the biochemical

Preparation of this manuscript was facilitated by the support of USPHS grants NS-13803 and NS-00335, a Research Career Development Award, and by the excellent secretarial assistance of Ms. Doris Rayford.

substrate for the two actions is the same, suggesting that the anxiolytic and sedative effects differ only quantitatively rather than qualitatively. This thinking was radically altered by the benzodiazepines as clinical experience indicated that for most people the dosage necessary to relieve anxiety differs from that necessary to induce a significant degree of sedation. Although this finding did not conclusively disprove the theory that these actions were only quantitatively different, it reopened the possibility that the two effects may be mediated, at least in part, by different processes. This represented an important conceptual breakthrough because, if the latter hypothesis is correct, it becomes theoretically possible to develop even more specific pharmacological agents.

The ineffectiveness of the benzodiazepines as general anesthetics was also taken as proof for the validity of this theory. That is, all other central nervous system depressants, from alcohol to the barbiturates, were known to induce a progressively greater degree of depression with increasing dosage. Thus, as larger quantities were taken, individuals experienced sedation, hypnosis, anesthesia, and finally death as a result of depression of the vasomotor and respiratory control centers in the brain. Accordingly, these various stages were thought of as part of a continuum. The fact that the benzodiazepines are incapable of causing anesthesia suggests, however, that the progression is not necessarily inexorable. Although it is conceivable that the benzodiazepines might induce anesthesia if sufficient quantities could be ingested, some investigators took these findings as further proof for the theory that the stages of central nervous system depression may be mediated by different biochemical substrates.

To address these issues it was important to define the molecular mechanism of action of the benzodiazepines. Investigators turned their attention to studying the effect of benzodiazepines on neurotransmitter substances. As acetylcholine, norepinephrine, dopamine, and serotonin were the most popular neurotransmitters during this period, hundreds of studies attempted to link the action of the benzodiazepines with one or more of these substances. These studies failed to reveal the precise mode of action of these drugs, although they provided some insights.

In more recent years the number of possible neurotransmitters has greatly multiplied, opening up new avenues of investigation. These studies have generated even greater amounts of data and, because of this activity, significant advances have been made in understanding the biochemical basis of benzodiazepine action. There appears to be a link between benzodiazepines and the neuronal receptors for γ-aminobutyric acid (GABA), an amino acid neurotransmitter candidate (Enna, 1981; Krogsgaard-Larsen et al., 1979). In addition, investigators have discovered the existence in the brain of highly specific binding sites for the benzodiazepines themselves (Braestrup and Squires, 1977; Mohler and Okada, 1977). Since these sites do not appear to be receptors for any known neurotransmitter, this finding opens up the possibility that there may be some endogenous anxiolytic or anxiogenic substance in the brain. Identification of such a substance would have an impact equal to that generated by the recent discovery of endogenous opiates.

In this report, research relating to the interaction of the benzodiazepines with brain neurotransmitters will be briefly reviewed and discussed. Because of the enormous amount of literature on this topic it will be impossible to examine every aspect. Readers interested in obtaining more detailed information may consult any of the excellent books and reviews on this subject (Costa and Greengard, 1975; Costa et al., 1980; Haefely, 1977; Haefely, 1978a and b; Schallek et al., 1972; Yamamura et al., 1980).

The Effect of Benzodiazepines on Neurotransmitter Systems

Early studies on the interactions between the benzodiazepines and brain neurotransmitters focused on the influence of these drugs on steady-state levels of monoamines. Most of these studies proved negative. Steady-state concentrations of biogenic amines are, however, a poor index of activity because neurotransmission is a dynamic process. That is, neurotransmitter activity could be dramatically altered without changing steady-state values if the increased neurotransmitter release were balanced by an increase in synthesis. Because of this possibility, workers turned to studying the influence of benzodiazepines on monoamine turnover rates (Costa and Greengard, 1975). From this line of investigation came the finding that these agents could, to a greater or lesser extent, significantly modify the rates of transmitter turnover. But the results were somewhat disappointing because, in all cases, the rate of turnover declined (Table 1). The observation that this

Table 1

The Effect of Benzodiazepines on Neurotransmitter Turnover in Brain

Neurotransmitter	Turnover Rate	Reference
Acetylcholine	Decreased	Cheney et al., 1973; Consolo et al., 1975
Norepinephrine	Decreased	Corrodi et al., 1971; Fuxe et al., 1975
Dopamine	Decreased	Corrodi et al., 1968; Fuxe et al., 1975
Serotonin	Decreased	Stein et al., 1975
γ-Aminobutyric Acid	Decreased	Mao et al., 1977; Bertilsson, 1978

effect occurred with all neurotransmitters studied and that the direction of change was identical suggested that these alterations were not primary. Indeed, it could be argued that the decreased turnover of neurotransmitters was simply secondary to central nervous system depression. Nevertheless, attempts were made to link alterations in specific monoamine systems to particular actions of the drugs. For example, Stein and his colleagues (1975) performed a number of elegant biochemical and behavioral studies which indicated that the decrease in serotoninergic transmission may be an important mediator of anxiolytic activity. These workers went on to show that, in contrast, alterations in noradrenergic activity may be more important for the depressant action of these drugs. It is known, for example, that although a tolerance develops to the sedative effects of benzodiazepines, anxiolytic activity remains unchanged during chronic therapy (Goldberg et al., 1967; Margules and Stein, 1968). After administering oxazepam chronically to rats, these investigators found that tolerance developed to the decrease in norepinephrine turnover but the decline in serotonin turnover remained unaffected. The authors concluded that these neurochemical effects probably are secondary to another biochemical action of the drug.

As for norepinephrine and serotonin, some evidence indicates that dopamine turnover is attenuated in most brain areas after administration of a benzodiazepine (Fuxe et al., 1975; Keller et al., 1976). Using microspectrofluorometry, Fuxe and his collaborators demonstrated that both diazepam and chlordiazepoxide reduce dopamine turnover in several brain areas including the nucleus accumbens and caudate nucleus. They found the effects in limbic regions particularly intriguing since they occurred at a dose (0.6 mg/kg) that is minimally effective in modifying animal behavior and as an anticonvulsant, which suggests that the modification of dopaminergic activity may be important in mediating these responses.

Other evidence that the benzodiazepines may alter dopamine function was provided by the finding that these drugs are capable of counteracting the elevation of homovanillic acid, a dopamine metabolite, that follows the administration of a neuroleptic (Keller et al., 1976). These data suggested that benzodiazepines are capable of enhancing inhibitory influences on dopaminergic neurons. In both studies the authors speculated that the effects observed could be secondary to some other effect of the benzodiazepine, which in turn causes inhibition of dopaminergic neuron activity.

Consolo and co-workers (1975) reported that benzodiazepines are capable of increasing the steady-state levels of acetylcholine in selected areas of rat brain. This finding could be explained by an earlier study which indicated that diazepam decreases the turnover of this neurotransmitter in the brain (Cheney et al., 1973). Interestingly, a correlation was found between the increase in striatal acetylcholine content and the benzodiazepine-induced muscle relaxation, suggesting that these two phenomena may be closely related.

With the development of relatively simple biochemical procedures for studying neurotransmitter receptor binding (Yamamura et al., 1978), other workers focused their attention on the interaction of benzodiazepines with postsynaptic sites. One of the first studies using this approach suggested that the benzodiazepines may exert their anxiolytic and muscle-relaxing effects by directly activating glycine receptors in the spinal cord and brain (Snyder and Enna, 1975; Young et al., 1974). This conclusion was based on the finding that benzodiazepines are capable of inhibiting radioligand (^{3}H-strychnine) binding to glycine receptors in rat spinal cord membrane preparations with relative potencies that correlate in a highly significant fashion with their relative potencies as anxiolytics and skeletal muscle relaxants. A major difficulty with this hypothesis was the fact that electrophysiological studies failed to find any evidence for the contention that benzodiazepines enhance postsynaptic inhibition in the spinal cord, a glycine-mediated phenomenon, and that the benzodiazepines are ineffective in antagonizing strychnine-induced seizures (Curtis et al., 1976a; Haefely, 1978b). The theory became even more untenable when a specific benzodiazepine receptor site was discovered (see below) which has an affinity in the low nanomolar range, whereas the potency of these compounds to inhibit glycine receptor binding is in the micromolar range.

In trying to assign a particular neurotransmitter system as the primary site of action of benzodiazepines, the most recent evidence would seem to implicate GABA for such a role. As is true for other neurotransmitter systems, benzodiazepine administration decreases GABA turnover in the brain (Bertilsson, 1978; Mao et al., 1977). Unlike other systems, however, there is a wealth of electrophysiological, biochemical, and behavioral data to indicate that benzodiazepines activate GABAergic pathways (Costa and Greengard, 1975; Enna and DeFrance, 1980; Haefely, 1977). Schmidt and his collaborators (1967) probably were the first to suggest such a possibility when they found that diazepam enhances presynaptic, but not postsynaptic, inhibition in the spinal cord, a GABA-mediated process. Many other workers have confirmed and extended this finding to other GABA-mediated systems in the brain. For example, benzodiazepines reduce the firing rate of cerebellar Purkinje fibers, neurons that are under the direct inhibitory control of the GABAergic basket cells (Curtis et al., 1976b; Pieri and Haefely, 1976).

Other evidence suggesting that the benzodiazepines act, at least in part, through the GABAergic system includes the fact that these drugs are potent inhibitors of bicuculline-induced seizures and that most, if not all, of the electrophysiological and biochemical responses to benzodiazepines are specifically blocked by bicuculline or picrotoxin, GABA receptor antagonists (Costa et al., 1975; Haefely, 1977; Stratten and Barnes, 1971). The distinct absence of peripheral side effects associated with the use of benzodiazepines also makes the GABA hypothesis attractive, for, unlike acetylcholine and the catecholamines, GABA seems to be a neurotransmitter only in the central nervous system.

Once the weight of evidence favored a GABA hypothesis for the action of benzodiazepines, studies were undertaken to define the manner in which these drugs activate the GABAergic system. There were several possibilities. It was conceivable that benzodiazepines increase GABAergic transmission by inhibiting high-affinity GABA transport, enhancing GABA release, or delaying the degradation of this amino acid.

Studies exploring these possibilities were inconclusive because the concentration of benzodiazepines necessary to perturb these processes was substantially higher than could be expected following systemic administration. The inability to link benzodiazepines with presynaptic or enzymatic processes was partially responsible for directing attention to GABA receptor interactions.

BENZODIAZEPINES AND THE GABA RECEPTOR

The development of an *in vitro* biochemical assay for studying brain GABA receptors made it possible to examine the influence of various drugs on this site (Enna and Snyder, 1975, 1977; Zukin et al., 1974). For this assay, membranes prepared from a variety of animal species, including man, are incubated with ^{3}H-GABA and, under proper conditions, the number of GABA receptors in the tissue can be quantified by measuring the amount isotope bound. When added to the incubation mixture, drugs capable of interacting with this receptor site will inhibit the binding of ^{3}H-GABA. The potency of a drug to inhibit radioligand binding may be taken as an index of its potency to activate, or inhibit, the receptor site following systemic administration (Enna et al., 1979).

The possibility that benzodiazepines are direct-acting GABA receptor agonists was examined by studying their ability to inhibit ^{3}H-GABA binding (Snyder and Enna, 1975). Although some potency was noted, as a group the benzodiazepines were found to be rather weak in this regard, and the rank order of potencies did not correlate with their known biological activity. This finding suggested that benzodiazepines do not activate the GABAergic system by directly stimulating the receptor recognition site for this neurotransmitter.

These biochemical data lent support to physiological findings that, although the benzodiazepines potentiate GABAergic processes in the spinal cord, this action is greatly diminished if the animal is pretreated with an agent that inhibits GABA synthesis (Polc et al., 1974). Accordingly, benzodiazepines are capable of activating the GABA receptor system only indirectly as GABA itself must be present to elicit the response. More recent studies to define the biochemical properties of GABA receptors may have revealed the manner in which this would occur.

If brain membranes are incubated with a low concentration of Triton X-100, a nonionic detergent, the amount of ^{3}H-GABA bound to the membranes increases dramatically (Enna and Snyder, 1977) because the affinity of the receptor for GABA is significantly increased in Triton-treated tissue. Indeed, treatment with Triton revealed the presence of a second GABA receptor site with an affinity for the neurotransmitter some ten times greater than the site observed in tissue not treated with the detergent (Enna and Snyder, 1977). Numerous workers interpreted this finding as indicating that, on or near the GABA receptor recognition site, there is a substance or substances which normally mask the higher affinity site (Guidotti et al., 1978; Johnston and Kennedy, 1978; Toffano et al., 1978). Removal of these substances leads to a more sensitive receptor since a higher affinity site will be activated by a lower concentration of ligand. Guidotti and his collaborators (1979) found that, if membranes are incubated with benzodiazepines rather than Triton, a similar phenomenon occurs (Table 2). Thus, without benzodiazepine treat-

Table 2

The Influence of Benzodiazepines on GABA Receptor Binding in Rat
Brain Cerebral Cortex[a]

Drug	Concentration (M)	GABA Receptor Affinity Constant (nM)	
		High	Low
Control	—	—	210
Diazepam	5×10^{-9}	—	190
	5×10^{-7}	61	200
	5×10^{-6}	34	321
	5×10^{-5}	26	285
Clonazepam	5×10^{-7}	35	265
Nitrazepam	5×10^{-7}	26	290
Flunitrazepam	5×10^{-7}	31	295

[a]Adapted from Guidotti et al., 1979.

ment, only a single, low affinity (210 nM) GABA receptor binding site can be detected in brain membranes. If the tissue is preincubated with increasing concentrations of diazepam, however, a second, higher affinity site becomes apparent. At maximal concentrations of diazepam this high affinity site has approximately tenfold greater attraction for GABA than the low affinity component (Table 2). Similar results were obtained with other clinically effective benzodiazepines such as clonazepam, nitrazepam, and flunitrazepam. Clinically inactive benzodiazepines were ineffective in this regard (Guidotti et al., 1979).

These findings are quite provocative and, if confirmed by others, may represent a breakthrough in understanding the mechanism of action of benzodiazepines. Thus, administration of these compounds results in the removal of an endogenous modulator of GABA receptor binding. Displacement of these substances reveals a higher affinity receptor site, making the postsynaptic membrane more sensitive to activation by GABA. In this way, benzodiazepines can potentiate GABAergic activity, which may in turn influence the activity of other neurotransmitter systems.

THE BENZODIAZEPINE RECEPTOR

Another significant advance made in understanding the molecular basis of benzodiazepine action was the discovery of a specific receptor site for these drugs in brain tissue (Braestrup and Squires, 1977; Mohler and Okada, 1977; Speth et al., 1978). These studies showed that radiolabeled diazepam or flunitrazepam binds to brain membranes with high affinity and specificity. That is, only other benzodiazepines are capable of interfering with the binding to this receptor site and the order of potency of these compounds is virtually identical to their order of potency in clinical and animal studies. Neither GABA nor any other putative neurotransmitter substance has any significant potency in inhibiting ^{3}H-benzodiazepine receptor binding.

If the benzodiazepine site in the brain is affiliated with GABA receptors, then the regional distribution of these two receptor sites should be similar. Regional distribution studies in human brain have revealed, in fact, that both binding sites are widely distributed throughout the central nervous system and that the relative densities of the two sites are quite similar though not identical (Table 3). For example, GABA receptor binding is highest in the cerebellum, followed by the hippocampus and frontal cortex. These latter two regions have about one-half the number of receptors as that found in cerebellar tissue. In contrast, benzodiazepine binding is highest in the cerebral cortex, followed by the amygdala and hippocampus. The cerebellum ranks fourth in density of benzodiazepine receptors. These findings suggest

Table 3

Regional Distribution of Benzodiazepine and GABA Receptors in Human Brain

Brain Region	Receptor Binding (fmoles/mg protein)	
	Benzodiazepine[a]	GABA[b]
Frontal cortex	105	63
Hippocampus	64	76
Amygdala	80	30
Thalamus	26	34
Caudate	32	36
Putamen	34	16
Globus pallidus	16	14
Substantia nigra	33	10
Cerebellar vermi	58	132
Dentate nucleus	9	11
Inferior olivary nucleus	14	23
Pons (base)	6	25
Pontine tegmentum	9	12
Medullary tegmentum	6	<9

[a]Adapted from Speth et al., 1978
[b]Adapted from Enna et al., 1977

that perhaps not all GABA receptors are linked to the benzodiazepine receptor system, or vice versa. On the other hand, it may be possible that all GABA and benzodiazepine receptors are associated, but that the ratio of sites differs in different regions of the brain. In any event, the data are consistent with the notion that there may be a functional link between the two receptor systems.

More direct proof of a relationship between GABA and benzodiazepine receptors was provided by the discovery that benzodiazepine receptor binding is altered in the presence of GABA (Karobath and Sperk, 1979; Maggi et al., 1980; Tallman et al., 1978). As illustrated in Table 4, when brain membranes are incubated with ^{3}H-diazepam in the presence of 100 μM muscimol, a direct-acting GABA receptor agonist (Enna and Snyder, 1977), there is a substantial increase in the amount of isotope bound. Similar results are found when GABA or other GABA receptor agonists are used. This activation phenomenon is dose-dependent and is blocked by bicuculline, a GABA receptor antagonist (Tallman et al., 1978). The increase in binding is caused primarily by an increase in the affinity of the benzodiazepine receptor for its ligand. In human brain, the maximal activation observed is between 70 and 100 percent in all areas examined, suggesting that the

Table 4

The Activation of Benzodiazepine Receptor Binding by Muscimol in
Various Areas of the Human Brain[a]

Brain Region	Specifically Bound ^{3}H-Diazepam (fmoles/mg protein)		
	Basal	Activated[b]	% Increase
Inferior frontal gyrus	45	85	90
Amygdala	36	66	83
Hippocampal gyrus	32	56	76
Caudate (head)	12	25	108
Globus pallidus	5	9	80
Substantia nigra	8	15	88
Cerebellar cortex	23	44	91

[a]Adapted from Maggi et al., 1980
[b]To study activation, ^{3}H-diazepam binding was examined in the presence of 100 μM muscimol

proportion of benzodiazepines linked to GABA receptors is similar through-out the brain. In contrast, however, the potency of muscimol to activate ^{3}H-diazepam binding varies among the different brain regions, being greatest in the cerebellum and lowest in the amygdala (Maggi et al., 1980). Thus, based on the potency data, it would be predicted that the cerebellar benzodiazepine receptors will respond to lower doses of GABA agonists than will those located in the amygdala.

If benzodiazepines act by enhancing GABA receptor binding (see above), what is the meaning of a GABA-activated benzodiazepine receptor site? The answer must await the discovery of the biological function of benzodiazepine receptors in the brain. The fact that such receptors exist indicates that there may be some endogenous agent, be it a neurotransmitter or neuromodulator, that normally interacts with this site. Since the benzodiazepines can affect central nervous system function, this theoretical substance must play a role in controlling anxiety, wakefulness, and possibly seizure threshold. The possibility of such an endogenous substance has stimulated studies aimed at proving its existence.

ENDOGENOUS INHIBITORS OF BENZODIAZEPINE RECEPTOR BINDING

Using the benzodiazepine receptor binding assay as an analytical procedure, several groups have attempted to identify endogenous compounds which have an appreciable affinity for this receptor site. For these studies, extracts of tissue or biological fluids are placed into incubation tubes along with brain membranes and a ^{3}H-benzodiazepine. If radioligand binding is significantly reduced in the presence of a given extract, this indicates the presence of some substance that has an affinity for the benzodiazepine receptor. Attempts are then made to identify the constituents of the extract and to test each separately in the binding assay. If a particular chemical is identified as having some potency, it is then analyzed by other procedures such as electrophysiological or behavioral tests.

Using this approach, four endogenous compounds have been described as having some potency at the benzodiazepine receptor site (Table 5). Two of these agents, inosine and hypoxanthine, are purines which, although they inhibit benzodiazepine receptor binding, do so relatively weakly, with inhibitory constants in the micromolar range (Paul et al., 1980, 1981; Skolnick et al., 1978). However, the neurophysiological effects of these compounds are similar to the benzodiazepines and, like the benzodiazepines, these agents prolong the latency of metrazole-induced convulsions. In addition, the structure-activity relationship of the benzodiazepines and purines is similar. Although these data are certainly not conclusive, they do suggest that, while the purines may not be the endogenous benzodiazepine, they may act in some way to modulate this receptor site.

Another compound isolated from brain tissue that has been found to possess "benzodiazepine-like" activity is nicotinamide (Mohler et al., 1979). Like inosine and hypoxanthine, nicotinamide is only a weak inhibitor of benzodiazepine receptor binding. However, the neuropharmacological profile of nicotinamide is more characteristic of the benzodiazepines than are those associated with the purines. Like the benzodiazepines, nicotinamide enhances presynaptic inhibition in the spinal cord, is active in the anticonflict test in rats, and has significant anticonvulsant activity. Furthermore, this compound is also a muscle relaxant and has hypnotic activity. Once again, however, because of its low potency as an inhibitor of benzodiazepine receptor binding, Mohler et al. (1979) concluded that nicotinamide may not

Table 5

Endogenous Inhibitors of Benzodiazepine Receptor Binding

Substance	Reference
Inosine	Skolnick et al., 1978
Hypoxanthine	Paul et al., 1981
Nicotinamide	Mohler et al., 1979
Ethyl-β-carboline-3-carboxylate	Braestrup et al., 1981

act directly on the benzodiazepine receptor recognition site, but rather may influence some other portion of the receptor complex.

Potency at this receptor site is not a problem for ethyl-β-carboline-3-carboxylate (β-CCE), the fourth substance proposed as an endogenous inhibitor of benzodiazepine binding (Braestrup et al., 1981). This compound, initially identified in extracts of human urine, is capable of displacing ^{3}H-benzodiazepine binding from its receptor in the low nanomolar range. Like the benzodiazepines, a radiolabeled derivative of β-CCE, ^{3}H-propyl-β-carboline-3-carboxylate, binds to brain membranes and the binding is enhanced in the presence of GABA receptor agonists (Braestrup et al., 1981). Interestingly, however, the ability of β-CCE to displace ^{3}H-benzodiazepine binding is somewhat region-selective, being more potent in the cerebellum than in the hippocampus, hypothalamus, or cerebral cortex. This regional selectivity may suggest a certain amount of heterogeneity for benzodiazepine receptor sites.

With regard to the possibility that β-CCE is the endogenous ligand for the benzodiazepine site, present evidence makes this seem unlikely as ethyl esters are not commonly found in the brain, and no one has yet been able to identify β-CCE or other β-carboline esters in this tissue. The potency of these compounds raises the possibility, however, that other derivatives of β-CCE, such as an amide or some small peptide, may be the naturally occurring form in the brain.

SUMMARY AND CONCLUSIONS

The potency, safety, and activity spectrum of the benzodiazepines are sufficiently different from other sedative-hypnotics to suggest that their mode of action differs at the molecular level. As modifications in neurotransmitter activity are known to underlie the action of a variety of psychopharmacological agents, studies were undertaken to identify which of the known neurotransmitters in the brain are influenced by the benzodiazepines. The results of these investigations revealed that virtually every transmitter system is modified by these drugs, suggesting that these effects are secondary to some other action. More recent results indicate that the primary site of action of benzodiazepines is the synaptic receptor site for GABA, an inhibitory amino acid neurotransmitter which influences most transmitter systems in the brain. Although the precise manner in which benzodiazepines activate the GABA system is still unknown, data suggest that they may do so by removing an endogenous modulator of GABA receptor binding. Removal of this substance reveals a higher affinity receptor site for this neurotransmitter, making the system more responsive to GABA.

That the benzodiazepines act at a site different from that of other sedatives is further shown by the discovery of a specific benzodiazepine receptor in the brain. This site does not seem to be influenced directly by other sedative-hypnotic agents, or by any known neurotransmitter substance. GABA, however, is capable of enhancing the affinity of this benzodiazepine site for the drug, indicating that this amino acid is not acting directly at the recognition site, but rather alters the conformation of this site by attaching to some other portion of the receptor. The biological function of the benzodiazepine receptor in the brain is unknown, though its presence suggests the existence of an endogenous agent that normally interacts at this site. Attempts to find such an agent have been undertaken and, although several compounds have been proposed, none have yet been shown unequivocally to be the endogenous substrate for this receptor. Since it is unknown whether the benzodiazepines are agonists or antagonists, it is equally possible that the endogenous substance could be an anxiolytic or an anxiogenic agent. The isolation, identification, and characterization of this endogenous substance will greatly enhance the probability of developing even more potent, specific, and perhaps less toxic, anxiolytic and anticonvulsant drugs.

REFERENCES

BERTILSSON, L. 1978. Mechanism of action of benzodiazepines—The GABA hypothesis. *Acta Psychiat. Scand.*, 274:19-26.
BRAESTRUP, C., NIELSEN, M., SKOVBJERG, H., and GREDAL, O. 1981. β-Carboline-3-carboxylates and benzodiazepine receptors. In E. Costa, G. Di Chiara, and G. Gessa (eds.), *GABA and Benzodiazepine Receptors*, pp. 147-155. New York: Raven Press.
BRAESTRUP, C., and SQUIRES, R. F. 1977. Specific benzodiazepine receptors in rat brain characterized by high affinity ³H-diazepam binding. *Proc. Natl. Acad. Sci. U.S.A.*, 74:3805-3809.
CHENEY, D. L., TRABUCCHI, M., HANIN, I., and COSTA, E. 1973. Effect of several benzodiazepines on concentrations and specific activities of choline and acetylcholine in mouse brain. *Pharmacologist*, 15:162.
CONSOLO, S., GARATTINI, S., and LADINSKY, H. 1975. Action of the benzodiazepines on the cholinergic system. In E. Costa and P. Greengard (eds.), *Mechanism of Action of Benzodiazepines*, pp. 63-80. New York: Raven Press.
CORRODI, H., FUXE, K., and HOKFELT, T. 1968. The effect of immobilization stress on the activity of central monoamine neurons. *Life Sci.*, 7:107-112.
CORRODI, H., FUXE, K., LIDBRINK, P., and OLSEN, L. 1971. Minor tranquilizers, stress and central catecholamine neurons. *Brain Res.*, 29:1-16.
COSTA, E., DI CHIARA, G., and GESSA, G. L. (eds.) 1980. *GABA and Benzodiazepine Receptors*. New York: Raven Press.
COSTA, E., and GREENGARD, P. (eds.) 1975. *Mechanism of Action of Benzodiazepines*. New York: Raven Press.
COSTA, E., GUIDOTTI, A., and MAO, C. C. 1975. Evidence for involvement of GABA in the action of benzodiazepines: Studies on rat cerebellum. In E. Costa and P. Greengard (eds.), *Mechanism of Action of Benzodiazepines*, pp. 113-130. New Yor4k: Raven Press.
CURTIS, D. R., GAME, C. J. A., and LODGE, D. 1976a. Benzodiazepines and central glycine

receptors. *Br. J. Pharmacol.*, 56:307-311.

CURTIS, D. R., LODGE, D., JOHNSTON, G. A. R., and BRAND, S. J. 1976b. Central actions of benzodiazepines. *Brain Res.*, 118:344-347.

ENNA, S. J. 1981. Neuropharmacological and clinical aspects of γ-aminobutyric acid (GABA). In G. Palmer (ed.), *Neuropharmacology of Central Nervous System and Behavioral Disorders*, pp. 507-537. New York: Academic Press.

ENNA, S. J., BENNETT, J. P., BYLUND, D. B., CREESE, I., BURT, D. R., CHARNESS, M. E., YAMAMURA, H. I., SIMANTOV, R., and SNYDER, S. H. 1977. Neurotransmitter receptor binding: Regional distribution in human brain. *J. Neurochem.* 28:233-236.

ENNA, S. J., and DEFRANCE, J. F. 1980. Glycine, GABA and benzodiazepine receptors. In S. J. Enna and H. I. Yamamura (eds.), *Neurotransmitter Receptors, Part 1*, pp. 41-70. London: Chapman and Hall.

ENNA, S. J., FERKANY, J. W., and KROGSGAARD-LARSEN, P. 1979. Pharmacological characteristics of GABA receptors in different brain regions. In P. Krogsgaard-Larsen, J. Scheel-Kruger, and H. Kofod (eds.), *GABA-Neurotransmitters*, pp. 191-200. New York: Academic Press.

ENNA, S. J., and SNYDER, S. H. 1975. Properties of γ-aminobutyric acid (GABA) receptor binding in rat brain synaptic membrane functions. *Brain Res.*, 100:81-97.

ENNA, S. J., and SNYDER, S. H. 1977. Influences of ions, enzymes, and detergents on γ-aminobutyric acid receptor binding in synaptic membranes of rat brain. *Mol. Pharmacol.*, 13:442-453.

FUXE, K., AGNATI, L. F., BOLME, P., HOKFELT, T., LIDBRINK, O., LJUNGDAHL, A., PEREZ DE LA MORA, M., and OGREN, S. 1975. The possible involvement of GABA mechanisms in the action of benzodiazepines on central catecholamine neurons. In E. Costa and P. Greengard (eds.), *Mechanism of Action of Benzodiazepines*, pp. 45-61. New York: Raven Press.

GOLDBERG, M. E., MANIAN, A. A., and EFRON, D. H. 1967. A comparative study of certain pharmacological responses following acute and chronic administration of chlordiazepoxide. *Life Sci.*, 6:481-491.

GREENBLATT, D. J., and SHADER, R. I. 1974. Benzodiazepines. *N. Engl. J. Med.*, 291:1011-1015, and 1239-1243.

GREENBLATT, D. J., ALLEN, M. D., NOEL, B. J., and SHADER, R. I. 1977. Acute overdosage with benzodiazepine derivatives. *Clin. Pharmacol. Ther.*, 21:497-513.

GUIDOTTI, A., TOFFANO, G., BARALDI, M., SCHWARZ, J., and COSTA, E. 1979. A molecular mechanism for the facilitation of GABA receptor function by benzodiazepines. In P. Krogsgaard-Larsen, J. Scheel-Kruger, and H. Kofod (eds.), *GABA-Neurotransmitters*, pp. 406-415. New York: Academic Press.

GUIDOTTI, A., TOFFANO, G., and COSTA, E. 1978. An endogenous protein modulates the affinity of GABA and benzodiazepine receptors in rat brain. *Nature*, 275:353-355.

HAEFELY, W. E. 1977. Synaptic pharmacology of barbiturates and benzodiazepines. *Agents and Actions*, 713:353-359.

HAEFELY, W. E. 1978a. Central actions of benzodiazepines: General introduction. *Br. J. Psychiatry*, 133:231-238.

HAEFELY, W. E. 1978b. Behavioral and neuropharmacological aspects of drugs used in anxiety and related studies. In M. A. Lipton, A. DiMascio, and K. F. Killam (eds.), *Psychopharmacology: A Generation of Progress*, pp. 1359-1374. New York: Raven Press.

JOHNSTON, G. A. R., and KENNEDY, S. M. E. 1978. GABA receptors and phospholipids. In F. Fonnum (ed.), *Amino Acids as Chemical Transmitters*, pp. 507-516. New York: Plenum Press.

KAROBATH, M., and SPERK, G. 1979. Stimulation of benzodiazepine receptor binding by γ-aminobutyric acid. *Proc. Natl. Acad. Sci. U.S.A.*, 76:1004-1006.

KELLER, H. H., SCHAFFNER, R., and HAEFELY, W. E. 1976. Interaction of benzodiazepines with neuroleptics at central dopamine neurons. *Naunyn Schmiedebergs Arch. Pharmacol.*, 294:1-7.

KROGSGAARD-LARSEN, P., SCHEEL-KRUGER, J., and KOFOD, H. (eds.) 1979. *GABA-Neurotransmitters*. New York: Academic Press.

MAGGI, A., SATINOVER, J., OBERDOFER, M., MANN, E., and ENNA, S. J. 1980. Phylogenetic characteristics of muscimol-activated benzodiazepine receptor binding. *Brain Res. Bull.*, 5:167-171.

MAO, C. C., MARCO, E., REVUELTA, A., BERTILSSON, L., and COSTA, E. 1977. The turnover rate of γ-aminobutyric acid in the nuclei of telencephalon: Implications in the pharmacology of antipsychotics and of a minor tranquilizer. *Biol. Psychiatry*, 12:359-371.

MARGULES, D. L., and STEIN, L. 1968. Increase of "antianxiety" activity and tolerance of behavioral depression during chronic administration of oxazepam. *Psychopharmacologia*, 13:74-80.

MOHLER, H., and OKADA, T. 1977. Benzodiazepine receptor: Demonstration in the central nervous system. *Science*, 198:849-851.

MOHLER, H., POLC, P., CUMIN, R., PIERI, L., and KETTLER, R. 1979. Nicotinamide, a brain constituent with benzodiazepine-like actions. *Nature*, 278:563-565.

PAUL, S., MARANGOS, P., BROWNSTEIN, M., and SKOLNICK, P. 1981. Demonstration and characterization of an endogenous inhibitor of GABA-enhanced ^{3}H-diazepam binding from bovine cerebral cortex. In E. Costa, G. Di Chiara, and G. L. Gessa (eds.), *GABA and Benzodiazepine Receptors*, pp. 103-110. New York: Raven Press.

PAUL, S., MARANGOS, P., and SKOLNICK, P. 1980. CNS benzodiazepine receptors: Is there an endogenous ligand? In H. I. Yamamura, R. Olson, and E. Usdin (eds.), *Psychopharmacology and Biochemistry of Neurotransmitter Receptors*, pp. 661-676. New York: Elsevier/North Holland.

PIERI, L., and HAEFELY, W. E. 1976. The effect of diphenylhydantoin, diazepam and clonazepam on the activity of Purkinje cells in the rat cerebellum. *Naunyn-Schmiedebergs Arch. Pharmacol.*, 296:1-4.

POLC, P., MOHLER, H., and HAEFELY, W., 1974. The effect of diazepam on spinal cord activities: Possible sites and mechanisms of action. *Naunyn Schmiedebergs Arch. Pharmacol.*, 284:319-337.

SCHALLEK, W., SCHLOSSER, W., and RANDALL, L. O. 1972. Recent developments in the pharmacology of the benzodiazepines. *Adv. Pharmacol. Chemother.*, 10:119-183.

SCHMIDT, R. F., VOGEL, E., and ZIMMERMANN, M. 1967. Die Wirkung von Diazepam auf die prasynaptische Hemmung und andere Rückenmarksreflexe. *Naunyn Schmiedebergs Arch. Pharmacol.*, 258:69-82.

SKOLNICK, P., MARANGOS, P. J., GOODWIN, F. K., EDWARDS, M., and PAUL, S. 1978. Identification of inosine and hypoxanthine as endogenous inhibitors of ^{3}H-diazepam binding in the central nervous system. *Life Sci.*, 23:1473-1480.

SNYDER, S. H., and ENNA, S. J. 1975. The role of central glycine receptors in the pharmacologic actions of benzodiazepines. In E. Costa and P. Greengard (eds.), *Mechanism of Action of Benzodiazepines*, pp. 81-91. New York: Raven Press.

SPETH, R. C., WASTEK, G. J., JOHNSON, P. C., and YAMAMURA, H. I. 1978. Benzodiazepine binding in human brain: Characterization using ^{3}H-flunitrazepam. *Life Sci.*, 22:859-866.

STEIN, L., WISE, C. D., and BELLUZZI, J. 1975. Effects of benzodiazepines on central serotonergic mechanisms. In E. Costa and P. Greengard (eds.), *Mechanism of Action of Benzodiazepines*, pp. 29-44. New York: Raven Press.

STRATTEN, W. P., and BARNES, C. D., 1971. Diazepam and presynaptic inhibition. *Neuropharmacology*, 10:685-696.

TALLMAN, J. F., THOMAS, J. W., and GALLAGER, D. W. 1978. GABAergic modulation of benzodiazepine binding site sensitivity. *Nature*, 27:383-385.

TOFFANO, G., GUIDOTTI, A., and COSTA, E. 1978. Purification of an endogenous protein inhibitor for the high affinity binding of gamma-aminobutyric acid to synaptic membranes of rat brain. *Proc. Natl. Acad. Sci. U.S.A.*, 75:4024-4028.

YAMAMURA, H. I., ENNA, S. J., and KUHAR, M. J. (eds.) 1978. *Neurotransmitter Receptor Binding*. New York: Raven Press.

YAMAMURA, H. I., OLSEN, R. W., and USDIN, E. (eds.) 1980. *Psychopharmacology and Biochemistry of Neurotransmitter Receptors*. New York: Elsevier/North Holland.

YOUNG, A. B., ZUKIN, S. R., and SNYDER, S. H. 1974. Interactions of benzodiazepines with central nervous system receptors: Possible mechanism of action. *Proc. Natl. Acad. Sci. U.S.A.*, 71:2241-2250.

ZUKIN, S. R., YOUNG, A. B., and SNYDER, S. H. 1974. Gamma-aminobutyric acid binding to receptor sites in the rat central nervous system. *Proc. Natl. Acad. Sci. U.S.A.*, 71:4802-4807.

8

ANTIANXIETY EFFECTS OF MAO INHIBITORS

ALEXANDER NIES, M.D., DIANTHA HOWARD, M.Sc.,
and DONALD S. ROBINSON, M.D.

Soon after their introduction more than 20 years ago, the monoamine oxidase inhibitors (MAOIs) were noted to exhibit significant antianxiety effects, although they remain classified primarily as antidepressants. In their delineation of an MAOI responsive syndrome, West and Dally (1959) stated, "We have started to recognize a group of patients showing somewhat atypical depressive states, sometimes resembling anxiety hysteria with secondary depression, who seem to be specifically and almost completely relieved of their disabling symptoms by iproniazid after the failure of all other forms of treatment." "Atypical depression," a dysphoric disorder characterized by the relative absence of classical endogenous features, the presence of "reverse" endogenous vegetative symptoms and/or neurotic symptoms such as phobias, panic episodes, and depersonalization, has become recognized as one indication for MAOI treatment (Nies and Robinson, 1981). As noted, some MAOI responders resembled patients with "anxiety hysteria with secondary depression," and MAOI use was soon extended to the treatment of anxiety states with or without depression (Sargant and Dally, 1962).

In the last 10 years the efficacy of the MAOIs has been rediscovered and active efforts at more precisely defining their optimum clinical spectrum continue. It was noted that phenelzine (PH) was particularly effective in relieving anxiety symptoms in depressed outpatients (Robinson et al., 1973) and in relieving general anxiety, panic episodes, and social fears in agoraphobic patients (Sheehan et al., 1980; Solyom et al., 1973; Tyrer et al., 1973,

The authors thank John Corcella, M.D., John O. Ives, M.D., and C. L. Ravaris, M.D., for assistance in selecting and managing patients, and Lorraine Korson, M.Sc., Elizabeth Hill, R.N., Mary Varese, R.N., and Sally Roberts, R.N., for invaluable research assistance.

123

1980). Studies in which the significant antianxiety effects of MAOI treatment, particularly with PH, were established are summarized in Table 1. We will concentrate on the evidence of antianxiety properties of PH obtained in our studies of PH treatment of outpatients including those with mixed anxiety-depressive states, atypical depression, and nonendogenous depression following phobic disorders (Nies et al., 1975; Ravaris et al., 1976; Robinson et al., 1973). These and other studies have recently been reviewed along with a presentation of guidelines for safe and effective MAOI treatment (Nies and Robinson, 1981).

METHODS

The results were obtained in a series of outpatient studies of PH treatment using virtually identical protocols. The patients were selected from referrals by primary care practitioners to a small research clinic which provided a general psychiatry private practice setting. Selection criteria were the presence of a depressive episode of at least four weeks' duration meeting Research Diagnostic Criteria for primary depressive disorder in the absence of alcoholism, drug abuse, schizophrenia, organic mental syndromes, epilepsy, or significant physical illness. Persons with long-standing and/or intermittent phobic and anxiety symptoms were accepted if the index episode met the criteria for primary depression. After evaluation and selection by clinical interview, patients were rated after a one-week drug-free washout by a nurse trained in the use of a Standard Depression Interview (SDI), a structured interview developed by the senior author for systematically eliciting and rating symptoms and signs of classical endogenous depression and atypical symptoms considered potentially useful as predictors of MAOI response at the beginning of our studies. The SDI allows ratings to be made of symptoms such as anxiety and depressed mood, and requires that judgments be made of the presence or absence of a number of such "marker" variables as retained psychomotor activity, terminal insomnia, and long-standing phobias (beginning before the present episode) or phobias of recent onset.

In the first two studies, PH 60 mg/day and 30 mg/day were compared to placebo (PL), and in the third study PH 60 mg/day was compared to 150 mg/day of amitriptyline (AT). In each of these clinical experiments the dosage was rapidly increased to the fixed levels over five to seven days and maintained for the remainder of the six-week total treatment period. Serial determinations of platelet MAO activity were made on blood samples obtained at two-week intervals in all studies. In the third study, plasma AT and nortriptyline (NT) and PH were measured at the same times. Clinical biweekly assessments were made at interview and by means of the Beck scale and the Hopkins Symptom Check List (SCL-90 version); the SDI was completed before and after the six weeks of treatment. Double-blind conditions were maintained throughout. We ascertained the acetylator phenotype in a group of PH-60 patients from the second and third studies.

RESULTS

The results of our first two studies showed that in both instances 60 mg/day of phenelzine (PH) was significantly superior to placebo, and in the second study 30 mg/day of PH did not differ from placebo. These results occurred with the subject-rated scales (Beck or SCL-90), SDI scales, and blind global clinical evaluation. At the conclusion of treatment and before breaking the code, the treating psychiatrists guessed which drug the patient had received. Contrary to our preconceptions, we were correct no more often than chance, which, while demolishing notions of clinical omniscience, provides assurance that these experiments were carried out under conditions of blind, objective evaluation. Not only did patients improve overall and improve on measures of depression, but PH-60 patients showed particularly good improvement in symptoms of phobic, somatic, and total anxiety. There was also a relationship to platelet MAO inhibition. PH-60 patients with more than 80 percent inhibition of the platelet enzyme showed 60 percent relative improvement on the somatic and total anxiety scales of the SDI, whereas those with less than 80 percent of MAOI showed only 20 percent and 40 percent improvement on these scales. For comparison, improvement on the HDS was respectively 52 and 38 percent for patients with more and less than 80 percent platelet MAO inhibition. When patients are stratified by level of platelet MAO inhibition into groups with less than 30 percent, 30 to 79 percent, and higher than 80 percent MAOI, the proportion of patients with more improvement in total anxiety than the median improvement of the whole group in the three MAOI strata is respectively 40, 40, and 70 percent. (If there were no MAOI effect, the proportion of patients in each stratum would be 50 percent.) This relationship of outcome to platelet MAOI applies to enzyme assay at two weeks and clinical assessment at six weeks, that is, it is predictive.

These results, revealing a significant antianxiety effect of the MAOI phenelzine in depressed outpatients, complement findings of controlled trials of phenelzine in patients selected primarily on the basis of the presence of anxiety, as in agoraphobia. The three placebo-controlled trials of Tyrer et al. (1980), Solyom et al. (1973), and Sheehan et al. (1980) summarized in Table 1 provide unequivocal evidence of a primary antianxiety effect of MAOI treatment. The Sheehan study is particularly significant because it

Table 1

Antianxiety Effects of MAO Inhibitors

Investigators	Study Type	Patients	Daily Dosage	Outcome
West and Dally, 1959	Retrospective analysis	101, depression	Variable, most 100-150 mg iproniazid	58 MAOI responders more phobia, tremor, g.i. and cardiovascular symptoms.
Sargant and Dally, 1962	Open trial, MAOI vs. MAOI and benzodiazepine	48, neuroses	Variable, 3 drugs	Better antianxiety effect than benzodiazepine alone.
Nies and Robinson, 1980; Robinson et al., 1973; Ravaris et al., 1976	Controlled trials, two doses phenelzine, placebo, and amitriptyline	Mixed anx.-depression (1) 33 PH-60 vs. 27 PL (2) 14 PH-60, 14 PH-30, 19 PL (3) 89 PH-60 vs. 89 AT-150	Fixed PH 60 mg or 30 mg; AT 150 mg; 6 weeks	PH very effective for anxiety; dose effect PH superior to AT for anxiety; PH more anxiolytic in chronic patients
Tyrer et al., 1973	Controlled phenelzine vs. placebo	Agoraphobia, social phobia and mixed; 14 PH and 14 PL pts. matched	Fixed, 45 mg; 8 weeks	PH better for "secondary phobias" and in overall improvement

Study	Design	Patients	Dose	Results
Solyom et al., 1973	Controlled, four behavior groups, two with phenelzine and placebo	Small numbers in each group, agoraphobics	Fixed, 45 mg	More rapid improvement with PH than best behavior therapy and more economical
Sheehan et al., 1980	Controlled, phenelzine, imipramine, and placebo	Panic with agora- and social phobia; 17 PH, 18 IMI, 22 PL	Fixed, 45 mg; IMI 150 mg; 12 weeks	PH, IMI both better than PL; PH pts. less disabled and avoidant
Tyrer et al., 1980	Controlled, high vs. low dose phenelzine	Depression, anxiety, and phobic neuroses; 14 high, 16 low dose	Fixed, 45 mg, 90 mg; 4 weeks	Greater and more rapid improvement on high dosage

is a direct comparison of phenelzine with a tricyclic antidepressant. Although the only statistically significant differences between treatments with the two drugs were reductions in social and work disability and in avoidance, it should be noted that phenelzine dosage was only 45 mg/day. One could expect quantitatively greater improvement with 60 mg/day, or perhaps at least more rapid improvement with the more optimal dosage. As the dosage of imipramine (IMI) was 150 mg/day, more certainly an adequate dosage, particularly for outpatients, the comparison was, if anything, biased against PH. For this reason it is especially noteworthy that PH produced greater improvement than IMI on almost all individual rating scales. The three studies provide systematic evidence for a fact well known to clinicians who have not abandoned the MAOIs, namely, that these agents are potent and exceedingly effective for treating agoraphobia and other anxiety syndromes.

Because amitriptyline (AT), with its sedative effects, had been touted as a useful, even relatively specific, agent for depression complicated by anxiety and agitation, a logical extension of our studies of phenelzine was a direct comparison of these two antidepressant drugs. The data in Table 2 were obtained from an outpatient study with the same protocol used earlier in our investigations of PH alone. This time we compared 60 mg/day of PH with 150 mg/day of AT for six weeks. Eighty-nine patients began each treatment; 18 AT and 14 PH patients dropped out. PH and AT patients showed

Table 2

Antianxiety Effects of Phenelzine and Amitriptyline

Item		Drug		2 wk	4 wk	6 wk	n
				Percentage Improvement			
SCL-90	Anxiety	Amitriptyline		23 ± 5	36 ± 5	46 ± 5	71
		Phenelzine		34 ± 5	51 ± 5	62 ± 4	74
			p	.06	.01	.004	
SCL-90	Interpersonal	Amitriptyline		40 ± 4	50 ± 3	55 ± 4	71
	Sensitivity	Phenelzine		34 ± 5	57 ± 5	64 ± 4	74
			p	NS	.04	.05	
SCL-90	Phobia	Amitriptyline		29 ± 7	37 ± 9	49 ± 6	71
		Phenelzine		22 ± 8	45 ± 7	52 ± 7	74
			p	NS	NS	NS	
SDI	Total	Amitriptyline		—	—	44 ± 3	71
	Anxiety	Phenelzine		—	—	52 ± 4	74
			p			.07	

equal improvement on the Total Depression scale of the Standard Depression Interview, the AT patients showing slightly greater (not statistically significant) improvement on the Hamilton Depression Scale (predominantly endogenous symptoms). A significant antianxiety effect of PH compared to AT is shown in Table 2 for the SCL-90 (general) Anxiety scale at two, four, and six weeks and for the Interpersonal Sensitivity scale (which contains items measuring social fears) at four and six weeks. There was no effect on the SCL-90 Phobia scale; however, relatively few patients had highly elevated pretreatment phobic anxiety scores. There was also a trend for the observer-rated SDI Total Anxiety scale to show greater improvement with PH compared to AT.

The SDI is constructed so that at one point the interviewer is required to ask about phobic symptoms. If at least one phobic symptom leads to relatively strenuous efforts at avoidance and/or causes significant subjective distress, the response is rated positive. In addition, the interviewer determines whether the phobic symptoms, if present, occurred before the onset of the depressive symptoms for which the patient was selected for treatment or whether they occurred secondary to the index depressive episode. Patients with phobic symptoms can, therefore, be classified as long-standing phobics (LSP) or recent phobics (RP), and the former designation may serve as a marker for chronic neurotic anxiety. Of the 178 patients who entered the protocol, 140 (78 percent) had phobic symptoms, and of these 81 (45 percent) were in the LSP and 59 (33 percent) in the RP categories. The outcomes of PH and AT treatment were analyzed with respect to LSP and RP status (Table 3). The RP group showed more improvement than the LSP group with either drug, and PH had significantly more benefit on SCL-90-rated Anxiety and a trend for more improvement on SDI-measured Total Anxiety. In the more chronically anxious LSP group, more improvement occurred with PH than AT on five of the six scales, a difference which is statistically significant for Anxiety and Interpersonal Sensitivity (social fears) and approaches significance for Phobia and Depression on the SCL-90 scale and Total Anxiety on the SDI. In the RP group there was also a tendency for PH to have better antianxiety effects than AT. Although not at all statistically significant, both LSP and RP groups taking AT showed slightly more improvement in endogenous depressive items measured by the HDS.

To examine the influence on outcome of depressive illness typology, the presence of "marker" symptoms, retained reactivity of mood (nonendogenous) and terminal (endogenous) insomnia (early-morning waking, trouble returning to sleep) before treatment were used to divide patients into groups. As the results in Table 4 show, when the nonendogenous characteristic, intact reactivity of mood, was present, PH had greater antianxiety effect,

Table 3

Drug Effects in Chronic and Recent Phobic Patients

| | | | | Percentage Improvement | |
				Long-Standing Phobics	Recent Phobics
Item	Drug				
SCL-90	Anxiety	Amitriptyline		41 ± 7	52 ± 8
		Phenelzine		58 ± 6	69 ± 6
			p	.04	.05
SCL-90	Interpersonal Sensitivity	Amitriptyline Phenelzine		48 ± 5 67 ± 4	60 ± 6 65 ± 6
			p	.01	NS
SCL-90	Phobia	Amitriptyline		45 ± 11	66 ± 8
		Phenelzine		59 ± 10	61 ± 9
			p	.10	NS
SCL-90	Depression	Amitriptyline		50 ± 6	63 ± 5
		Phenelzine		61 ± 4	66 ± 7
			p	.10	NS
SDI	Total Anxiety	Amitriptyline Phenelzine		42 ± 4 50 ± 4	50 ± 5 61 ± 6
			p	.10	.10
SDI	Hamilton Depression Scale	Amitriptyline Phenelzine		46 ± 4 41 ± 4	55 ± 4 48 ± 5
			p	NS	NS

Table 4

Indicators of Phenelzine and Amitriptyline Response

Pretreatment Symptom		Outcome
Mood Reactivity:	Present SCL-90 Anxiety	$PH(n = 41) > AT(n = 27) \, p = .02$
	Absent	$PH(n = 33) = AT(n = 44)$
Terminal Insomnia:	Present SCL-90 Anxiety	$PH(n = 24) = AT(n = 32)$
	Absent	$PH(n = 50) > AT(n = 39) \, p < .01$

and when there was impaired reactivity (psychomotor retardation) PH and AT did not differ. Conversely, in patients without the classical endogenous terminal insomnia, PH had a significantly greater antianxiety effect, which was absent in patients with terminal insomnia.

Because the genetically governed capacity to acetylate hydrazine drugs may influence their therapeutic and toxic effects, we examined the relationship of acetylator status as determined by sulfamethazine acetylation to therapeutic effects of phenelzine. The results in a relatively small number of patients for whom both acetylation and SCL-90 data are available are given in Table 5. There was no statistically significant difference but, contrary to expectation, the fast acetylators showed more improvement, particularly earlier in treatment. The fast acetylators also had greater inhibition of platelet MAO, which raises the possibility that the production of an intermediate such as acetylhydrazine plays a role in the therapeutic action of PH (Timbrell, 1979). These findings are supported by the data of Davidson et al. (1978), which show greater clinical and MAOI effects of PH in fast acetylators, and by Tyrer et al. (1980) who also found more improvement with PH in fast acetylators. The possibility of greater improvement in fast acetylators seems to have been overlooked because the differences were not statistically significant and the investigators assumed that hydrazine drugs are inactivated by acetylation. As Timbrell pointed out, the effects of acetylation seemingly can depend on the metabolic products of competing acetylation paths, so that some drug effects are more pronounced in rapid acetylators.

DISCUSSION AND CONCLUSIONS

An examination of the literature, clinical experience, and the results of controlled trials provide unequivocal evidence that monoamine oxidase-in-

Table 5

Phenelzine Improvement in Slow and Fast Acetylators

SCL-90 Scale	Percentage Improvement	
	Slow Acetylators (n = 17)	Fast Acetylators (n = 12)
Two-Week Treatment		
Depression	24 ± 9	42 ± 9
Anxiety	28 ± 9	45 ± 8
Interpersonal Sensitivity	26 ± 13	44 ± 10
Phobia	25 ± 30	43 ± 13
Six-Week Treatment		
Depression	64 ± 7	69 ± 6
Anxiety	63 ± 9	67 ± 7
Interpersonal Sensitivity	63 ± 8	72 ± 7
Phobia	30 ± 29	87 ± 6

hibiting drugs have significant antianxiety effects. Indeed, they can be agents of choice for syndromes of severe and persistent pathological anxiety like agoraphobia and its variants (Quitkin et al., 1979). Although other antidepressants such as imipramine also "block" spontaneous panic attacks, the MAOIs seem more useful in lowering secondary anxiety and allowing the patient to reduce avoidant behavior. They are certainly to be preferred to the benzodiazepines for severe and disabling anxiety because, not only do minor tranquilizers have little lasting effectiveness, but in the doses required for symptom suppression, they are more likely to cause pharmacological dependence.

How is it that drugs considered to be antidepressants can have such significant antianxiety effects? First, anxiety and depression are not mutually exclusive conditions and neither occurs in a pure state. Second, although both classes of antidepressants increase the concentrations of neurotransmitters whose deficit is presumed to play a role in depression, some of these amine transmitters (norepinephrine, epinephrine) are known to have inhibitory effects at locations such as the locus coeruleus. Hydrazine drugs such as phenelzine are known to affect other enzyme systems and, as has been shown by Manyam et al. (1980), at least one such drug raises central nervous system levels of the inhibitory neurotransmitter gamma aminobutyric acid (GABA), which is believed to play a role in central mediation of anxiety.

In summary, there is excellent evidence that the MAOIs are effective (and safe) agents for the treatment of pathological anxiety, particularly in patients with agoraphobia and atypical depression who are resistant to more conventional therapies.

REFERENCES

DAVIDSON, J., McLEOD, M. N., and BLUM, R. 1978. Acetylation phenotype, platelet monoamine oxidase inhibition, and the effectiveness of phenelzine in depression. *Am. J. Psychiatry*, 135:467-469.

MANYAM, N. V. B., HARE, T. A., and KATZ, L. 1980. Effect of isoniazid on cerebrospinal fluid and plasma GABA levels in Huntington's disease. *Life Sci.*, 26:1303-1308.

NIES, A., ROBINSON, D. S., and LAMBORN, K. R. 1975. The efficacy of the MAO inhibitor, phenelzine, dose effects and prediction of response. In J. R. Boissier, H. Hippius, and P. Pichot (eds.), *Neuropsychopharmacology*. Proceedings, Collegium Internationale Neuropsychopharmacologicum. 1974. New York: Elsevier/North Holland.

NIES, A., and ROBINSON, D. S. 1981. The monoamine oxidase inhibitors. In E. S. Paykel (ed.), *Handbook of Affective Disorders*. Edinburgh: Churchill Livingstone, in press.

QUITKIN, F., RIFKIN, A., and KLEIN, D. F. 1979. Monoamine oxidase inhibitors. A review of antidepressant effectiveness. *Arch. Gen. Psychiatry*, 36:749-760.

RAVARIS, C. L., NIES, A., ROBINSON, D. S., IVES, J. O., and BARTLETT, D. 1976. A multiple-dose controlled study of phenelzine in depressive-anxiety states. *Arch. Gen. Psychiatry*, 33:347-350.

ROBINSON, D. S., NIES, A., RAVARIS, C. L., and LAMBORN, K. R. 1973. The monoamine oxidase inhibitor, phenelzine, in the treatment of depressive-anxiety states. *Arch. Gen. Psychiatry*, 29:407-413.

SARGANT, W., and DALLY, P. J. 1962. Treatment of anxiety states by antidepressant drugs. *Br. Med. J.*, 1:6-9.

SHEEHAN, D. V., BALLENGER, J., and JACOBSEN, G. 1980. Treatment of endogenous anxiety with phobic, hysterical, and hypochondriacal symptoms. *Arch. Gen. Psychiatry*, 37:51-59.

SOLYOM, L., HESELTINE, G., MCCLURE, D. J., and SOLYOM, J. 1973. Behavior therapy versus drug therapy in the treatment of phobic neuroses. *Can. Psychiatr. Assoc. J.*, 18:25-32.

TIMBRELL, J. A. 1979. The role of metabolism in the hepatotoxicity of isoniazid and iproniazid. *Drug. Metab. Rev.*, 10:125-147.

TYRER, P., CANDY, J., and KELLY, D. 1973. A study of the clinical effects of phenelzine and placebo in the treatment of phobic anxiety. *Psychopharmacologia*, 32:237-254.

TYRER, P., GARDNER, M., LAMBOURN, J., and WHITFORD, M. 1980. Clinical and pharmacokinetic factors affecting response to phenelzine. *Br. J. Psychiatry*, 136:359-365.

WEST, E. D., and DALLY, P. J. 1959. Effects of iproniazid in depressive syndromes. *Br. Med. J.* 1:1491-1494.

9

BETA-ADRENERGIC BLOCKADE IN THE TREATMENT OF ANXIETY

FERRIS N. PITTS, JR., M.D., and ROBERT E. ALLEN, M.D.

A large body of experimental data supports the concept that one cause of pathological somatic anxiety in human beings is hyperactivity (or hypersensitivity) in one or more of the complex chain of events triggered by beta-adrenergic, but not by alpha-adrenergic, agonists. Another substantial amount of experimental data demonstrates that beta-adrenergic blocking agents are effective in the treatment-control of a wide range of anxiety symptoms in various clinical circumstances. In this review we shall examine the data on these obviously related topics and consider the implications for the directions of further research. The agonist research started decades before the first beta-blocker was developed; both beta-agonist and beta-blocker research have apparently been discontinued for the present; it is our opinion that both should be restarted and expanded.

BETA-ADRENERGIC AGONISTS AND EXPERIMENTAL ANXIETY

Tompkins et al. (1919) reported that 5 mg of intramuscularly administered adrenaline (mostly epinephrine, some norepinephrine) produced marked exacerbation of anxiety symptoms in neurotic soldiers who had "irritable heart syndrome" (DaCosta's syndrome, neurocirculatory asthenia), but not in normal control soldiers, although both groups manifested adrenergic physiologic changes with the injection. Many others have confirmed that epinephrine injection regularly produces anxiety symptoms in neurotic patients, who generally manifest their specific anxiety symptom pattern with the injection (Basowitz et al., 1956; Cameron, 1945, 1947; Cantril and Hunt, 1932; Darrow and Gellhorn, 1939; Dynes and Tod, 1940; Frankenhauser et al., 1961; Frankenhauser and Jarpe, 1962, 1963; Funkenstein, 1955; Funkenstein and Meade, 1954; Gantt and Freile, 1944; Hawkins et al., 1960; Jersild and Thomas, 1931; Kraines and Sherman, 1940; Landis and Hunt, 1932; Lindemann and Finesinger, 1938, 1940; Maranon, 1924; Pollin and Goldin, 1961; Rothballer, 1959; Rudolph, 1938; Thorley, 1942). Normal subjects respond less regularly to epinephrine injections and with many fewer symptoms. Neither group responds with anxiety symptoms to electrolyte infusions.

Much of the later literature consisted of argumentation about the role of the investigator and previously learned associations of the subjects in evoking anxiety symptoms; a careful reading of these papers reveals that the topics discussed at such great length varied more in clinical condition than did the role of the investigator in the experiments conducted. Lindemann and Finesinger (1938, 1940), among the later investigators, *were* able to make the critical distinctions and reported that markedly anxious patients with known histories of sympathomimetic symptoms responded to intramuscularly administered adrenaline with anxiety symptoms, but other subjects did not.

Mendlowitz and co-workers (Vlachakis et al., 1974) gave intravenous infusions of norepinephrine and epinephrine to mildly hypertensive patients already under ganglionic blockade. These researchers found no anxiety responses to norepinephrine, but marked anxiety responses to epinephrine infusions *only in patients with histories of anxiety symptoms*. Patients with little or no naturally occurring previous anxiety symptoms had little or no anxiety response to epinephrine infusion. An additional correlation of natural previous and experimental-epinephrine-evoked anxiety symptoms was of digital vascular reactivity (DVR) to epinephrine, but not to norepinephrine. Patients with high DVR to epinephrine had both histories of anxiety symptoms and developed anxiety with infusion of epinephrine (but not with saline or norepinephrine). None of many other cardiovascular variables correlated with natural or experimental anxiety. The authors concluded that this work tended to demonstrate *increased reactivity to epinephrine in anxious patients*.

Epinephrine has both alpha- and beta-adrenergic actions, although the latter predominate. Isoproterenol, a pure beta-adrenergic agonist with no alpha-adrenergic action, was used by Frohlich et al. (1966) in defining the hyperdynamic beta-adrenergic circulatory state. This is a labile hypertensive state with multiple anxiety symptoms, hypersensitivity to isoproterenol infusion, and relief of both hypertension and anxiety symptoms with beta-adrenergic blocking medications such as propranolol. Hypertensive (and nonhypertensive) anxious patients responded to isoproterenol infusion with marked anxiety symptoms and anxiety attacks; normal controls and nonanxious hypertensives developed many fewer and much less severe anxiety symptoms with isoproterenol infusion. These results resemble those of Mendlowitz's group with epinephrine infusions under ganglionic blockade. Others have reported anxiety symptoms and attacks in anxious subjects with isoproterenol infusions (Combs and Martin, 1974; Easton and Sherman, 1976; Frohlich et al., 1969), but to date no psychiatrically sophisticated investigator has systematically infused isoproterenol (and saline for control) into patients with anxiety neuroses and normal controls in natural and beta-blocked states using a double-blind design to determine individual and group differences in psychologic, psychiatric, and physiologic responses. This should not be difficult and should yield much important information.

Gershon and his associates (Garfield et al., 1967) gave separate epinephrine and yohimbine infusions to seven schizophrenic and five nonschizophrenic inpatients and found that both evoked the same sort of cardiovascular changes, epinephrine immediately and yohimbine in a somewhat delayed manner. Subjects manifested "anxiety" to some psychologic testing after each drug but not after saline infusion. No patients with anxiety neurosis have been reported to have been given yohimbine, although this alpha-adrenergic blocker might well produce anxiety symptoms in such susceptible persons by producing relative beta-adrenergic accentuations. Systematic administration of yohimbine and/or other alpha-adrenergic blockers to such persons is another experiment yet to be done, which promises to yield important information.

What does an epinephrine infusion do to the volunteer research participant? The epinephrine molecule directly activates beta-adrenergic receptors throughout the body. Epinephrine displaces or, more precisely, removes by chelation a calcium molecule from the receptor site and initiates a series of biochemical steps which result in: increased heart rate; constriction of splanchnic blood vessels; dilatation of blood vessels in the major muscles, the skin, and the brain; and an activation of the Embden-Meyerhof (anaerobic glycolytic) Pathway which results in a manifold increase in lactate production from muscles and other tissue. The effect of epinephrine infusion on blood pressure is highly variable and depends on the relative responses of heart rate, vascular constriction, and vascular dilatation. The subject is always aware, however, of increased heart rate (palpitations) and physiologic changes that result in a variable degree of tension, tremulousness, apprehension, and paresthesias. An essential concomitant is marked lactate production. Persons subject to anxiety experience severe anxiety with epinephrine infusion (and marked lactate production) but persons not subject to anxiety usually do not experience anxiety with epinephrine infusion (and marked lactate production). Control solutions do not produce anxiety symptoms in any subjects. The relationship between epinephrine action and great changes in lactate production is absolute; therefore, anxiety symptoms secondary to epinephrine infusion cannot occur in the absence of increased lactate production. What about the relationship between anxiety symptoms (and anxiety neurosis) and lactic acid in the human? A great deal of information is available on such a seemingly esoteric question.

Investigations in four countries have shown that the rise in blood lactate with exercise is excessive in anxiety neurotics (Cohen and White, 1950; Holmgren et al., 1959; Holmgren and Strom, 1959; Jones and Mellersh, 1946; Kelly and Walter, 1968; Levander-Lindgren and Ek, 1962; Linko, 1950; Tournaire et al., 1961). The appearance of anxiety symptoms evoked in patients by exercise was concomitant with the extremely rapid rise in lactate; nonpatients serving as controls did not develop anxiety symptoms with exercise and showed only the expected normal lactate increase. In the anxiety neurotics, the excessive rise in lactate (per unit of work per unit of time) was approximately that seen in patients with such serious medical conditions as arteriosclerotic or rheumatic heart disease.

It occurred to us that perhaps the lactate itself could produce anxiety attacks in susceptible people. We conducted a pilot study of nine patients, with nine nonpatients as controls. All patients and two controls developed typical anxiety attacks with lactate infusions that were sufficient to raise the venous lactate level to between 10 and 15 millimoles per liter, a range that is normally attained only with maximum muscular exertion or after adrenalin administration. Such attacks did not develop in patients or controls with either of two control infusions.

Next we conducted a double-blind experiment of lactate infusion into anxiety neurotics and normal controls (Pitts and McClure, 1967). On the basis of rigid criteria we selected 14 patients who could be classified as anxiety neurotics and picked a carefully matched group of 10 normal subjects to serve as controls. Each subject received 10 milliliters per kilogram of body weight of each of three experimental solutions by intravenous infusion at three experimental sessions 5-10 days apart, with the solutions administered in carefully randomized order. The physician who conducted the procedure was unaware of any infusion's content, the subjects' medical history, or the purpose of the experiment. He gave the infusion, recorded the subject's behavior and comments, and took blood and urine samples in a location away from the blind investigator. Then the subjects were questioned systematically about their symptoms.

The three infusions were solutions of 500 millimolar sodium lactate, 500 millimolar sodium lactate with 20 millimolar calcium chloride added, and 555 millimolar glucose with 167 millimolar sodium chloride. The calcium in the control infusion was approximately enough to saturate the binding capacity of the added lactate, so the lactate would presumably leave the ionized calcium level in the subject's blood and tissue fluids unaltered. The second control solution, glucose-in-saline, was chosen because its concentration was in the range of that of the lactate solutions (hypertonic) and its metabolism would not differ from that of the glucose formed in the liver from intravenously administered lactate.

After the third session each subject was asked to rate the three infusions in order of the severity of their effects. The blind observer did the same thing for each subject. All 24 subjects were able to "identify" the three solutions, reporting that sodium lactate had caused the most symptoms, glucose very few symptoms or none, and sodium lactate with added calcium an intermediate number of symptoms. This result had a high statistical significance. The probability that the 24 subjects would correctly rank all three solutions by chance was one in 10,000. The blind investigator did almost as well. He correctly ranked all three solutions for 11 of the 14 patients and for seven of the controls, a performance that would be achieved by chance only five times in 10,000 trials.

The most striking outcome of the experiments was that the infusion produced anxiety attacks. This was the first time, to our knowledge, that such a result had been systematically achieved with a chemical, physiological, or psychological stimulus. Thirteen of the 14 patients and two of the 10 controls had typical acute anxiety attacks during the lactate infusion. No subject in either group had such attacks with either of the control infusions. Thus, the addition of calcium markedly reduced the effect of lactate on the anxiety neurotics, and the infusion of another hypertonic solution did not *per se* cause anxiety attacks in susceptible individuals.

When individual anxiety symptoms are considered, the results show a strong effect of lactate, a mitigating effect of calcium, and a difference in the response of patients and controls to lactate (Table 1). It is noteworthy that with the lactate infusion all subjects in both patient and control groups experienced paresthesias. With the lactate plus calcium infusion, only a small minority of the subjects reported paresthesias, and none of them did with glucose infusion. Significantly more patients than controls reported nearly all the other symptoms with lactate, but with the two control infusions there was no significant difference in the extent to which each symptom was reported by the two groups (Table 1). These observations hold true for the cumulative total of symptoms as well as for individual reports. Of the 294 possible symptoms (21 symptoms for each of 14 subjects), the patients with anxiety neurosis reported experiencing 190, or 64.6 percent, during lactate infusion, 25.5 percent with lactate plus calcium, and 4.4 percent with glucose. Of 210 possible symptoms, the control subjects reported experiencing

Table 1
Symptoms During Infusions*

Symptom	14 Patients with Anxiety Neurosis			10 Normal Controls		
	Lactate	Lactate with Calcium	Glucose in Saline Infusion	Lactate	Lactate with Calcium	Glucose in Saline Infusion
Paresthesia	14	3	0	10	1	0
Tremor	14	7	2	5	4	0
Shakiness	14	7	2	8	4	0
Dizziness	13	4	0	4	3	0
Palpitation	13	8	2	5	4	2
Giddiness	13	5	0	5	2	0
Cold	11	8	1	3	3	1
Nervousness	11	7	3	6	4	1
Dyspnea	10	4	0	3	2	1
Chest pain	9	2	0	0	1	0
Blurred vision	9	3	0	3	0	0
Nervous chill	9	2	0	1	0	0
Weakness	8	4	1	5	1	1
Lump in throat	7	0	0	1	0	0
Headache	7	5	0	5	4	0
Smothering	6	1	0	1	0	0
Sighing	6	2	1	1	2	0
Faintness	5	1	0	2	1	0
Irritability	5	0	1	1	0	0
Nausea, Choking	4	2	0	3	0	0
	2	0	0	0	0	0
Total symptoms	190	75	13	72	36	6

*Number of subjects having symptoms during infusions

34.3 percent during lactate infusion, 17.1 percent with lactate plus calcium, and 2.9 percent with glucose. These figures show that the anxiety neurotics developed significantly more symptoms than the controls did with lactate but not with the control infusions ($p < 0.00001$). No symptoms other than those listed developed in any subject with any infusion.

The reported *intensity of symptoms* (on a 0-4 scale) was high with lactate infusion in the patient group, the mean being 1.5 or higher for 11 of the 21 symptoms (Table 2). The mean scores for the anxiety neurosis group were markedly reduced when lactate with added calcium was infused, 1.5 for only two symptoms. The mean scores were 0.0 for 11 of the 21 symptoms with glucose infusion in the patient group, and 0.5 or below for the remaining 10 symptoms. The patients' mean symptom scores during infusion of lactate with added calcium were significantly lower than those during lactate infusion for 15 of the 21 symptoms ($p < 0.025$); those during glucose infusion were significantly lower in 20 of 21 ($p < 0.025$).

Table 2
Intensity of Symptoms During Infusions*

Symptom	Mean Score of 14 Patients with Anxiety Neurosis			Mean Score of 10 Normal Controls		
	Lactate	Lactate with Calcium	Glucose in Saline Infusion	Lactate	Lactate with Calcium	Glucose in Saline Infusion
Paresthesia	3.0	0.5	0.0	2.4	0.2	0.0
Tremor	2.9	1.5	0.2	0.8	0.7	0.2
Shakiness	3.3	1.2	0.2	1.7	0.7	0.0
Dizziness	2.8	0.7	0.0	0.4	0.7	0.0
Palpitation	3.1	1.2	0.2	1.0	0.5	0.2
Giddiness	2.9	1.0	0.1	1.1	0.2	0.0
Cold	2.5	1.5	0.3	0.6	0.7	0.2
Nervousness	2.5	1.0	0.5	1.2	0.6	0.1
Dyspnea	2.0	0.7	0.0	0.3	0.2	0.1
Chest pain	1.4	0.5	0.0	0.0	0.3	0.0
Blurred vision	1.6	0.5	0.0	0.4	0.2	0.0
Nervous chill	1.9	0.2	0.0	0.1	0.0	0.0
Weakness	1.4	0.7	0.1	1.1	0.1	0.1
Lump in throat	1.4	0.0	0.0	0.2	0.0	0.0
Headache	1.2	1.0	0.0	1.0	0.8	0.0
Smothering	1.1	0.2	0.0	0.1	0.0	0.0
Sighing	1.3	0.4	0.1	0.1	0.2	0.0
Faintness	0.7	0.2	0.1	0.2	0.1	0.0
Irritability	1.2	0.0	0.1	0.1	0.0	0.0
Nausea, choking	0.7	0.2	0.0	0.7	0.0	0.0
	0.1	0.0	0.0	0.0	0.0	0.0

*Mean scores for each symptom on 0-4 scale (see text for experimental detail and results of statistical analyses of these data)

Lactate infusion produced a mean score of 1.5 or above in the normal group of control subjects for only two symptoms, paresthesias and "inward shakiness." These two symptoms (in addition to weakness) were significantly reduced ($p < 0.025$) by the addition of calcium. Scores for glucose infusion were significantly lower than those for lactate for eight symptoms in the normal control group.

The mean scores for 12 of the 21 symptoms were significantly lower in the control group than in the patient group with lactate infusion. None of the score differences between the patient and the control groups was statistically significant for either the lactate with added calcium or the glucose infusions. The data on intensity scores in Table 2, then, demonstrate that lactate infusion causes significant symptoms of anxiety in both normal controls and patients with anxiety neurosis, that the addition of calcium largely prevents these effects, that glucose infusion results in no significant anxiety symptoms, and that lactate infusion produces significantly more intense symptoms in patients with anxiety neurosis than in normal control subjects.

There were marked aftereffects (significant symptoms lasting more than 24 hours) from the lactate infusion in patients but not in controls; there were no marked aftereffects for either group from either of the two control infusions. The anxiety-exhaustion aftereffects occurred in 10 patients but in none of the controls following lactate infusion.

In summary, a 20-minute infusion of lactate into a patient with anxiety neurosis reliably produced an anxiety attack that began within a minute or two after the infusion was started, decreased rapidly after the infusion, but was often followed by from one to three days of exhaustion and heightened anxiety symptoms. Such patients did not have anxiety attacks and had many fewer individual symptoms when calcium was added to the lactate. Patients had almost no symptoms when they were infused with glucose solution. Nonpatient controls had many fewer and less severe symptoms in response to lactate; they had only a few symptoms in response to lactate with calcium and almost none with glucose. The patient group differed from the controls significantly only in the case of the lactate infusion. Clearly the patients were responding to a specific effect of the lactate, not to any psychological effects of intravenous infusion (Pitts, 1969, 1971; Pitts and McClure, 1967).

Fink et al. (1969) completed a double-blind replication of the work described above in five patients and four controls. Their results were essentially identical to those Pitts and McClure (1967) had described. Additionally, "in concurrent scalp-recorded electroencephalograms (EEG), we observed changes with lactate in the patients but not in the controls, nor in either group after dextrose-in-saline and lactate-with-calcium solutions. The EEG exhibited increased beta and decreased alpha abundances and a decreased alpha amplitude. These findings are consistent with EEG changes usually seen in anxiety states" (Fink et al., 1969). Fink and co-workers, then, had found that an objective, independent measure—the EEG—could determine that an anxiety attack was occurring in the double-blind infusion experiment.

Grosz and Farmer (1969) apparently repeated the lactate infusions in some manner, for they wrote that "this is not to say that the infusion of sodium lactate into certain susceptible individuals does not induce anxiety symptoms. It certainly does, as we have been able to replicate. But as we have shown, it hardly does so for the reasons, and by the means of mechanisms, proposed by Pitts and McClure." They said nothing more than this about replication and the main body of their communication consisted of lengthy scholastic argumentation attacking Pitts and McClure. Especially prominent in Grosz and Farmer's arguments were criticisms of Pitts and McClure for measurements not yet made and experiments not yet done, even though the original report (Pitts and McClure, 1967) had specified that the exact mechanism of the differential production of anxiety symptoms and anxiety attacks by lactate infusion in anxiety neurotics as compared to controls was *not yet established.* The substance of Grosz and Farmer's disputations seems to be that, since Pitts and McClure had not paid enough attention to the alkalinizing action of sodium lactate in their original report, the finding of the production of anxiety attacks with lactate infusion in anxiety neurotics but not in normal controls was invalid. This, we feel, is an illogical conclusion.

In a second paper, Grosz and Farmer (1972) asserted that "Pitts and McClure have recently suggested that all symptoms of anxiety and anxiety neurosis are caused by a raised blood and body fluids lactate level" and then proceeded to destroy that straw man. They reported that the infusion in 30 minutes of 8 milliliters per kilogram of 500 millimolar sodium lactate into 10 normal young men caused 52 of 100 possible anxiety symptoms; 500 millimolar sodium bicarbonate caused 42 of 100 possible anxiety symptoms, and 555 millimolar glucose in 155 millimolar sodium chloride produced only three of 100 possible anxiety symptoms. Both sodium lactate and sodium bicarbonate produced anxiety; both did this with statistically greater potency than glucose in saline and with similar reliability. Grosz and Farmer had shown that the complexation of ionized calcium by infusion of alkalinizing solutions into normal subjects is followed by paresthesias and other hypocalcemic symptoms. Grosz and Farmer failed to demonstrate that sodium bicarbonate infusions cause anxiety attacks in anxiety neurotics but not in normals because they failed to infuse lactate and bicarbonate into anxiety neurotics. It is probable that sodium bicarbonate and sodium lactate have similar actions in causing anxiety attacks in susceptible individuals but not in normal controls. After failing to make the significant finding that sodium bicarbonate (like sodium lactate) infusions cause anxiety attacks in anxiety neurotics but not in normal controls because it "seemed unnecessary to expose patients with anxiety neurosis to the distressing experience of this experiment," Grosz and Farmer ended their summary with the assertion that, because sodium lactate and sodium bicarbonate infusions are roughly equivalent in normals, "neither their [Pitts and McClure's] study nor their theory is soundly based."

Friedhoff (1972) pointed out that Grosz and Farmer's demonstration that anxiety hypocalcemic symptoms could be produced in normals by sodium bicarbonate infusions was an extension of Pitts and McClure's work, not a refutation.

Disagreeing with Friedhoff's suggestion that "these newer findings should be viewed simply as an extension and refinement of the hypothesis of Pitts and McClure," Grosz (1973) claimed that the reason his findings were presented as a "refutation of Pitts and McClure's conclusions is first, that the kind of study we did should have been carried out by Pitts and McClure as a necessary control experiment, and secondly, that we do not believe that the results of our study impart any substantially new knowledge. . . ." Grosz then asserted that "the common denominator seems to be some deviation from the norm in the patient's internal biophysical environment. This leads us to believe that *anxiety-prone subjects, and perhaps anxiety neurotics, may essentially suffer from an excessive sensitivity or intolerance to disturbances in their internal bio-physical homeostasis*" (italics Grosz's). "*Viewed in this light Pitts and McClure's experiment does little more than illustrate what happens when anxiety-prone subjects are suddenly exposed to major perturbation of homeostasis—in this case to major electrolyte and acid-base disturbances*" (italics ours). Not only is the "Grosz theory of anxiety and anxiety neurosis" quoted here a more general and vague restatement of our speculations and others', but it is stated as truth without any evidence other than Grosz's assertions that the same people would manifest anxiety with a wide variety of very different fluid and electrolyte disturbances. (Ackerman and Sachar added another argument emphasizing central-psychologic causes of anxiety in 1974.)

There is at present no systematic evidence that patients with anxiety neurosis reliably develop anxiety attacks (and normal controls do not) with anything other than the infusion of beta-adrenergic agonists, sodium lactate, or sodium bicarbonate. (The infusion of sodium bicarbonate inseparably causes a manifold increase of lactate production like that resulting from epinephrine.) In fact, the infusion of more powerful complexing (chelating) agents for ionized calcium such as sodium ethylenediamine-tetracetic acid (EDTA) produces profound and painfully severe hypocalcemic symptoms but no anxiety attacks in either anxiety neurotics or controls (Pitts, unpublished data). These results with EDTA tend to disprove Grosz's general theories of anxiety being evoked in "nonspecific disequilibrium of internal biophysical homeostasis" and tend, rather, to support a less general theory that somatic anxiety symptoms in anxiety neurotics are caused by hyperactivity and/or hypersensitivity somewhere in the complex chain of events triggered by beta-adrenergic agonists. Certainly Mendlowitz and co-workers (see above) have demonstrated specific psychologic and physiologic *increased reactivity to epinephrine but not to norepinephrine in anxious patients* (Vlachakis et al., 1974), so that the theory of "nonspecific bio-physical disequilibrium of homeostasis" as a cause of anxiety is disproved unless one chooses to believe that norepinephrine infusions do not affect homeostatic equilibrium.

Kelly et al. (1971) replicated the effects of sodium lactate infusion in anxiety neurotics in a careful, detailed study, adding measurements of forearm blood flow (FBF) and heart rate (HR), which reflect arousal. Twenty patients were selected who satisfied Pitts and McClure's criteria for anxiety neurosis; they and 10 matched normals were subjected to double-blind experimental infusions after completing numerous psychometric and anxiety ratings. The anxiety neurotics had higher mean scores on the Taylor Manifest Anxiety scale for anxiety ($p < 0.001$), neuroticism ($p < 0.001$), free-floating anxiety ($p < 0.001$), phobia ($p < 0.001$), obsession ($p < 0.001$), somatic complaints ($p < 0.001$), observer depressive rating ($p < 0.05$), and depressive self-rating ($p < 0.05$). On the hysteria scale the anxiety neurotics did not differ from controls. Kelly et al. made a large number of controlled observations. Before injection and during cannulation and saline infusion, several of the anxiety measures and arousal measures were higher in anxiety neurotics than in controls. During the sodium lactate infusions, anxiety neurotics developed anxiety attacks but controls did not; during the sodium lactate infusion, observer ratings and self-ratings of anxiety were significantly higher in anxiety neurotics, as were FBF and HR. The sodium lactate infusions were stopped immediately when an anxiety attack began so that the average amount of lactate given was 79 percent of the Pitts and McClure amount for anxiety neurotics and 99 percent for controls; nevertheless, the 20 anxiety neurotic patients reported 249 of 420 possible symptoms, and the 10 normal controls reported 72 of 210 possible symptoms ($p < 0.001$). Neither group experienced symptoms with saline infusion, so that sodium lactate produced significantly more symptoms in anxiety neurotics than in controls and significantly more symptoms than did saline in all subjects.

Kelly et al. (1971) treated eight anxiety neurotic patients who had experienced anxiety attacks during sodium lactate infusion with monoamine ox-idase-inhibiting antidepressants for a mean period of 10 weeks (range 5 to 17 weeks) and then repeated the sodium lactate infusion experiments. The five "much improved" patients experienced fewer and less severe symptoms with lactate infusion; the two "improved" patients experienced similar symptoms with repeated infusion; and the one "unimproved" patient had an anxiety attack during saline infusion. Kelly et al. concluded that they had confirmed Pitts and McClure's 1967 observations, that "sodium lactate provides a biochemical means of producing anxiety in the laboratory which may prove useful for testing the anti-anxiety effect of various types of treatment"; and "the Pitts and McClure hypothesis for explaining the relationship between anxiety and sodium lactate may not be correct, but more information about the biochemical changes involved may further our understanding of the aetiology and treatment of anxiety."

In summary, beta-adrenergic agonists (epinephrine, isoproterenol) or metabolic products of their action (lactate) will reliably produce (with dose-response qualification) anxiety symptoms and anxiety attacks in susceptible subjects (anxiety neurotics) but not in matched normal controls. A host of experiments dealing with production of anxiety symptoms await the energetic psychiatrist. Systematic use of beta-adrenergic agonists and/or blockade in groups of patients compared to matched normal controls will be the general experimental approach. Anxiety requiring such study occurs secondarily and/or concomitantly to large numbers of patients with unipolar and bipolar affective disorders, with schizophrenia, with obsessive-compulsive disease, with nearly every other psychiatric disorder, with many diseases of the liver, and with many infectious and endocrinological diseases. Are all these anxiety states similarly evoked by beta-adrenergic agonists and modulated by beta-adrenergic blockade, or are there many different types of anxiety states? Only further clinical experimentation can provide reasonable answers to these questions.

Other experimental techniques that result in an outpouring of lactate from muscles have produced more anxiety symptoms in susceptible individuals compared to controls: hyperventilation, hypoxia, exercise, and infusion of bicarbonate are measures that can result in both very large increases in lactate production and anxiety symptoms in anxiety neurotics. Clinically and experimentally, the infusion of calcium ion or the production of respiratory acidosis or the administration of competitive beta-adrenergic blocking drugs tends to reduce or prevent naturally occurring (or experimentally produced) anxiety symptoms in susceptible individuals. In contrast, such alpha-adrenergic agonists as norepinephrine and phenylephrine and others do *not* produce anxiety symptoms in susceptible persons. Alpha-adrenergic *blockade* with yohimbine has been shown, perhaps, to produce some of the symptoms of anxiety.

BETA-ADRENERGIC BLOCKADE IN THE TREATMENT OF ANXIETY

There are many reports that beta-adrenergic blockade is effective in treatment of a wide range of anxiety symptoms. Some of these reports are anecdotal case studies, some are reports of groups of patients treated in open trials, and others are results of various types of blind clinical pharmacological investigations. These studies differ so much in experimental design, patients studied, definitions of anxiety, types and dosages of beta-adrenergic blockers, and other variables that no two are comparable. Most will be summarized in the following pages. The essential point is that these studies have been reported from at least seven countries over a period of 15 years and *no negative report has ever been made*—every study of beta-adrenergic blockade in the treatment of anxiety has found considerable improvement in symptoms consequent to the medication.

In 1965, there were three reports of symptomatic benefit in anxiety from the use of propranolol. Besterman and Friedlander (1965) described the alleviation of palpitations and tachycardia by propranolol in four patients with effort syndrome and sinus tachycardia. In spite of sedation, their casual pulse rates had averaged 130, 130, 110, and 100 respectively. After treatment with propranolol the patients' pulse rates slowed and averaged 85, 80, 87, and 70 respectively. Only one of the patients still noticed palpitation, and she found the symptom greatly reduced. When one patient's treatment was stopped, heart rate increased from 78 to 130 with recurrence of anxiety and palpitations. The slower rate and symptom relief was restored by restarting propranolol.

Nordenfelt (1965) reported testing 12 patients with 5 mg of propranolol given intravenously (i.v.); of these, "the remaining 3 patients sought medical advice for palpitations and were nervous and uneasy. Physical examinations and x-rays did not reveal any heart disease." The tachycardia before propranolol (pulses, respectively, 100, 95, and 110 recumbent; and 115, 110, and 130 erect) was corrected (pulses, respectively, 75, 70, and 80 recumbent; and 80, 85, and 95 erect) after 5-mg propranolol administration. The very slight T-wave depressions while recumbent, to which were added biphasic or negative T-deflection (only in leads III, II, and/or V_4) in the erect posture (which was the clinical reason for testing these three neurotic patients), were completely cleared in all three after the intravenous propranolol. The "patients stated unanimously that they became calmer and experienced far less cardiac disturbance after the injection." Nordenfelt then suggested that the neurotic manifestations and the slight EKG-cardiac changes resulted from increased sympathetic tone, and he speculated that carefully selected neurotic patients would benefit from treatment with oral beta-receptor blocking agents.

Turner et al. (1965) reported that 5 mg of intravenous propranolol (but not i.v. saline or 62.5 mg i.v. amytal) produced a significant reduction in tachycardia and discomfort in eight patients with thyrotoxicosis and in eight patients with anxiety neurosis.

In 1966, Granville-Grossman and Turner reported a systematic double-blind comparison of one week each on placebo and propranolol (with an Armitage closed sequential design) in the treatment of anxiety neurotics free of severe depression, schizophrenia, organic brain disease, heart disease, bronchial asthma, and others. Twenty milligrams of propranolol four times per day were found to be significantly more effective than placebo in this short-term therapeutic design. "Only autonomically mediated symptoms were found to be significantly affected, suggesting that improvement was related to the known adrenergic beta-receptor peripheral action of the drug," the investigators stated.

In 1968, Suzman gave a preliminary report of an extensive systematic long-term therapeutic trial of propranolol in treatment of anxiety neurosis. Forty patients presenting with symptoms of anxiety of one month to 35 years' duration were studied before and during the administration of propranolol in the total daily dose of 40 to 160 mg as well as during placebo substitution, for periods varying from one to 40 months. The report said that during propranolol therapy tachycardia was controlled, and the patients' multiform somatic symptoms were completely or partially relieved. Feelings of anxiety were allayed, particularly when they were primarily attributable to somatic symptoms, but to a lesser extent when obsessive, phobic, or depressive features were prominent. The patients' compelling tendency to overbreathe spontaneously under emotional stress was subdued, and the cerebral and peripheral effects of hypocapnea, formerly readily induced by voluntary hyperventilation, were prevented or greatly lessened. During periods of placebo substitution (in all but five of the 40 cases) the somatic symptoms recurred, accompanied by a recrudescence of the anxiety and the reappearance of the electrocardiographic changes. The relapse occurred within hours of stopping propranolol with the same intensity as formerly in some patients, but to a lesser extent in others. Suzman seemed to indicate a delayed resolution of central-psychologic-apprehensive anxiety and an immediate resolution of the cardiac and other somatic symptoms of anxiety.

Suzman has reported continued treatment of anxiety neurotics with propranolol—in 1976 he published a study of 725 patients treated for one to 12 years. All other studies have been of short-term administration of propranolol, have found immediate improvement in somatic symptoms of anxiety, and have usually been interpreted to show that propranolol has no effect on central-psychological anxiety, rather than (more precisely) *little immediate effect on psychological anxiety*. Suzman's 1976 report suggests that psychological (central, apprehensive) anxiety improves with continued beta-blockade in the treatment of anxiety neurosis. Kabes and Dostal (1976) reported that propranolol, which crosses the blood-brain barrier and has significant central action, was significantly superior to practolol, which does not enter the brain, in the treatment of anxiety.

In 1969, Wheatley reported a cooperative blind comparative treatment study conducted by general practitioners; the subjects were patients with acute and chronic anxiety neurosis (but no hypertension, asthma, hay fever, bronchitis, or pregnancy). Thirty-five general practitioners treated 105 patients for six weeks with either 30 mg of propranolol or 10 mg of chlordiazepoxide three times a day, in double-blind randomized fashion. Fifty-four patients received chlordiazepoxide and 51 propranolol; there were very similar degrees of improvement in anxiety in the two groups. There were fewer side effects among those receiving propranolol, and there was more improvement of depression and sleep disturbance among those receiving chlordiazepoxide.

Nordenfelt et al. (1968) reported on a randomized double-blind crossover trial of alprenolol, a propranolol analogue, and placebo in 14 patients with "nervous heart complaints." Heart disease, asthma, and other diseases had been ruled out. Complex exercise and cardiovascular function tests and interviews for symptom tabulation were done before drug administration, after two weeks on 80 mg of alprenolol four times daily, and after two weeks on placebo. The authors considered their patient study group a heterogeneous one; consequently, they were careful to avoid making general conclusions. The symptoms tabulated, however, were those of anxiety neurosis (palpitations, chest pain, oppression, breathlessness, sweating, tremor, nervousness, dizziness, fatigue, headache, mild depression, gastrointestinal symptoms), and all were cleared or greatly improved (compared to placebo) with alprenolol ($p < 0.00001$ according to our X^2 assessment of their tabulated data). All 14 patients had relief of palpitations with alprenolol, compared to five on placebo. In a global blind assessment, 12 of the 14 had greatly preferred the alprenolol to placebo because of the marked reduction of symptoms. Of the two patients who preferred the placebo, one had experienced nausea with alprenolol but had also noted clearing of tremor, vertigo, and palpitations. Another patient preferred placebo because of nausea with alprenolol but had complete relief of symptoms and no side effects when, still blind, he received a smaller dosage of alprenolol. (Nordenfelt et al. scrupulously counted as preferring placebo a third patient who felt better during alprenolol therapy but attributed this to resuming smoking.) The probability of this blind drug preference occurring by chance alone is less than 0.01 (our X^2 calculation). Additionally, heart rate during exercise and physical working capacity tended to improve to normal on alprenolol as compared to prestudy and placebo assessments. Nordenfelt et al., cautious to the end, stated "it seems reasonable to assume that Beta-blocking agents can be valuable in the treatment of patients with nervous heart complaints."

In 1969, Frohlich et al. reported the effectiveness of propranolol in the short-term treatment of "hyperdynamic Beta-adrenergic circulatory state," a condition they had described and defined in two patients in 1966. In brief, they characterized patients with hyperdynamic beta-adrenergic circulatory state by: (a) symptoms characteristic of anxiety neurosis—"disturbing palpitations, chest discomfort . . . rapid heart action associated with varying degrees of physical limitations, and . . . these symptoms persisted inordinately long following exertion"; (b) systolic and/or diastolic hypertension in most cases although two of 14 were normotensive at all times and four others of the 14 had only labile or episodic hypertension; (c) marked reported and observed activation of cardiac and other symptoms at times of great anxiety and/or physical exercise; (d) extraordinary sensitivity to infusion of the beta-adrenergic agonist isoproterenol (but not to alpha-adrenergic agonists or control solutions) with excessive increase of heart rate and cardiac index as compared to both normal control subjects and other hypertensives, and with production of anxiety attacks ("almost uncontrollable hysterical outbursts"); (e) instantaneous response of isoproterenol-evoked signs and symptoms to the infusion of the beta-adrenergic blocker propranolol (but not to placebo infusions); and (f) clearing or marked improvement of all symptoms and signs with daily ingestion of propranolol in individualized dosages (varying between 20 and 80 mg four times daily, usual dosage 40 mg four times daily) but not to placebo.

Some of the comments of Frohlich et al. at the end of their 1969 report are of interest. Patients with such diseases as thyrotoxicosis, pheochromocytoma, and porphyria were excluded. Increased sympathetic vasomotor outflow was one possible explanation for the patients' increased heart rate and emotional responses, and even for the hypertension, *"but the arterial pressure or vascular resistance responses to upright tilt, cold, Valsalva maneuver, levarterenol and tyramine were normal and seemed to exclude this mechanism"* (italics ours) *of increased sympathetic activity.* Pressure responses following tyramine *indicated normal catecholamine stores and re-*

lease. Diminished parasympathetic activity seemed to be excluded by normal response of heart rate during the overshoot phase of the Valsalva maneuver, and to carotid sinus stimulation and ocular pressure. Tachycardia followed atropine administration. The investigators state that "until a short-acting parasympatholytic agent is available for more precise dose-response measurements and until more exact responses to atropine in the normotensive and hypertensive subject have been established, the interrelationship of parasympathetic and beta-adrenergic functions remains speculative." They go on to say that, although several other groups noted amelioration of cardiac symptoms and anxiety with inhibition of beta-adrenergic receptor activity and suggested that beta-adrenergic stimulation may be the mechanism producing cardiac symptoms in certain anxious individuals, no attempt was made to aggravate anxiety and cardiac symptoms pharmacologically by beta-stimulation. Frohlich and associates believed that there was evidence for a syndrome of *increased beta-adrenergic activity, or responsivity*, but that afflicted patients did not constitute a homogeneous group presenting with a single disease. Included among these patients were those who were normotensive or whose blood pressure elevation was sustained, labile, or episodic. Some were classified as "hypertensive" even though at the time of the hemodynamic study their arterial pressures were normal. Others considered to be hypertensive had pretreatment control blood pressure averages within the normal range, although at times the pressure was significantly elevated. The investigators said that "the fact that most of these patients were hypertensive does not necessarily indicate that this syndrome occurs predominantly in hypertensive individuals; rather it probably reflects our investigative interest."

Bonn and Turner (1971) demonstrated that D-propranolol, the unnatural isomer which has little or no beta-blocking action, had no antianxiety action in a dosage of 40 mg four times a day given in a double-blind sequential crossover design to 15 patients who had marked anxiety symptoms in various psychiatric conditions.

Bonn et al. (1972) then used the Armitage closed sequential design in a double-blind drug-placebo study of practolol in a mixed group of outpatients whose "most prominent symptoms were attributable to anxiety. Patients whose symptoms were associated with severe depression, organic brain disease, or schizophrenia, or who had heart disease were excluded." Two anxiety rating scales were obtained before and after each of the two 14-day experimental treatment periods. Patients received either 200 mg of practolol or placebo twice daily for two weeks and then the other for a second 14 days. Plasma practolol levels demonstrated patient compliance. Some patients had side effects with practolol but not placebo: Five patients experienced slight

BETA-ADRENERGIC BLOCKADE IN TREATMENT OF ANXIETY

nausea; one patient noted reduced exercise tolerance but marked alleviation of anxiety symptoms; another patient (who had originally denied that she had a history of asthma as a child and who had actually had no attacks for 16 years) had an asthmatic attack on the practolol experimental sequence. After the first eight patients had completed the trial, investigators' blind preferences for practolol over placebo were statistically significant ($p < 0.05$), and when the 15 subjects already in the study had completed the blind therapeutic sequences, all 15 patients preferred practolol to placebo ($p < 0.01$). The authors noted that practolol appeared to block autonomic anxiety symptoms (palpitations, etc.) but not the psychological-apprehensive anxiety in the two-week trial. They noted that little practolol enters the central nervous system, further supporting their notion that beta-adrenergic blocking agents act primarily on somatic (as opposed to psychic) aspects of anxiety.

Carlsson (1971) noted "hyperkinetic circulation" in alcoholics in the initial abstinence phase and reported "normal conditions were restored by 40 mg propranolol; even tension symptoms decreased." As a consequence of these findings Carlsson and Johansson (1971) devised a propranolol-placebo comparison of the effects of propranolol on anxiety and other symptoms during the first 10 to 12 days of alcohol withdrawal. Patients were given an eight-day trial of 40 mg of propranolol or placebo four times a day; before and after the trial psychological questionnaires for tension (anxiety), depression, and dysphoria scales were obtained. The 18 propranolol subjects had significantly fewer anxiety-tension symptoms during treatment than did the 18 placebo patients; depression symptoms were not quite statistically significantly less in the propranolol group; dysphoric symptoms were not at all different between the two groups.

Gallant et al. (1973) reported a double-blind random trial of propranolol in 10 patients and placebo in 10 patients. All were "hospitalized volunteer chronic alcoholic patients with the target syndrome of 'anxiety and tension.' All subjects were free of significant disabilities of the cardiovascular, renal, and hepatic systems. Psychotherapeutic drugs were discontinued for five days prior to initial doses of study drugs, and most recent exposure to alcohol was a minimum period of 10 days prior to initiation of the study medication." Thus, all subjects presumably had completed alcohol withdrawal before the study. Patients were given propranolol (or equivalent placebo tablets) according to an incremental dosage schedule: 20 mg twice daily for seven days; then 20 mg four times daily for seven days; and finally, 40 mg three times daily for two weeks. Dosage was not increased if marked therapeutic and/or side effects appeared. A number of physiological, serological, and psychological assessments were done. By the end of four weeks of treatment, both the placebo and propranolol groups showed considerable improvement; no covariance measure of improvement of anxiety showed propranolol to be statistically more effective than placebo plus ward programs, but the blind investigator's global assessment of change showed the propranolol group to be significantly ($p < 0.05$) more improved than the placebo group. The investigators pointed out that their study groups would have to be much larger than 10 subjects to show clear superiority of propranolol over placebo in a circumstance in which all subjects are improving considerably as a result of the natural history of maintained abstinence from alcohol abuse.

Linken (1971) reported clinical success with three patients treated with small amounts of propranolol (30 to 40 mg per day) for severe anxiety symptoms consequent to LSD ingestion.

McMillin (1973) performed a double-blind crossover, one-week drug comparison of 80 mg of practolol and 5 mg of diazepam three times a day in tense, anxious, and frightened Belfast citizens caught in the Irish Civil War. He found that both treatments resulted in considerable and similar improvement in the target symptoms, which recurred after medications were discontinued. In competitive ski jumpers, 40 mg of oxprenolol given before a competition effectively inhibited the athletes' emotional tachycardia and excessive tension (Imhof et al., 1969). Similarly, Brewer (1972) reported such beta-adrenergic blockade to alleviate or prevent the anxiety-tension state noted by many students (Pitts et al., 1961) before major examinations.

Taggart et al. (1973) reported that, in susceptible individuals, multiple cardiac manifestations and apprehensive anxiety associated with public speaking were prevented or markedly alleviated by a single oral dose of 40 mg of oxprenolol one hour before speaking; the researchers concluded "that beta-blockade could be used to alleviate the unpleasant symptoms associated with speaking before an audience." Their data were obtained from 23 normal subjects and seven subjects with coronary artery disease.

In two further clinical studies of Belfast citizens, McMillin (1975) described treatment with oxprenolol beta-adrenergic blockade for anxiety and tension states. In the first, 10 patients completed a double-blind crossover comparison of 20 and 80 mg of oxprenolol three times a day for a week; half of the patients were given 20 mg capsules the first week and half received the (identical in appearance) 80 mg capsules the first week. "The results from trial 1 showed a significant improvement with 80 mg of oxprenolol in tension ($p < 0.05$), depression ($p < 0.05$), and well-being ($p < 0.01$) and a patient preference for the larger dose (8 patients vs. 1 patient; $p < 0.04$). One patient in trial 1 had no preference. On all the items except sleep, treatment was significantly more effective than pretreatment (anxiety and tension, $p < 0.001$; concentration and depression, $< p\ 0.05$; well-being, $p < 0.01$)." In the second double-blind crossover trial, McMillin compared 80 mg of oxprenolol to 5 mg of diazepam three times a day for one week each. Half of the subjects received one drug during the first week, the other half began treatment with the other drug; again, the capsules were indistinguishable. "The results from trial 2 showed no significant difference between 5 mg of diazepam and 80 mg of oxprenolol; this may be due to the small number of patients in the study. However, 5 mg diazepam seemed to give better results in improving sleep while 80 mg of oxprenolol seemed to give better results in improving concentration. Treatment was significantly more effective than pretreatment states on all items (anxiety and tension, p < 0.001); sleep, concentration, depression, and well-being, p < 0.01)." McMillin stated that he believed beta-adrenergic medications were useful in the treatment of anxiety and tension states in response to such mental stresses as speaking in public, driving in traffic, race car driving, or living in the midst of civil disorder.

In 1973, Tyrer and Lader reported on a double-blind crossover drug-placebo study of sotalol in the treatment of chronic anxiety of at least six months' duration in psychiatric outpatients free of other disease. Fourteen of 16 patients completed the Armitage closed sequential design of two weeks of placebo and two weeks of beta-blockade. Sotalol was given in individualized dosages of 20 to 100 mg four times a day. "Significant drug-placebo differences were found for a number of clinical ratings, but for many of these there was discrepancy between patient and therapist." Investigator ratings produced more significant differences between sotalol and placebo than did subject ratings, apparently because of a greater effect on somatic than psychological symptoms of anxiety during the two-week trial.

Ramsey et al. (1973) described a double-blind attempt to assess the matter of somatic and/or psychologic-subjective-"central" anxiety symptom relief with propranolol. A two-week crossover drug-placebo design was used; propranolol dosage was 160 mg per day in four divided doses; by randomization, seven anxious neurotic and seven thyrotoxic patients received propranolol first, and seven anxious neurotic and five thyrotoxic patients received placebo first; clinical ratings of anxiety, IPAT Anxiety Scale Questionnaire scores, and several physiological measures of palmar skin conductance provided the pretrial, intertrial, and endtrial data. The authors were unable to solve the peripheral and/or central anxiety dilemma because of the uniformly good results and the small experimental samples. Their conclusions were "(1) Among patients with anxiety states, a significant reduction in anxiety, as measured by clinical ratings and by IPAT Scale scores, had occurred at the end of the trial irrespective of the order of administration of propranolol or placebo. (2) In patients with thyrotoxicosis, the administration of propranolol was significantly associated with a decrease in palmar skin conductance. (3)

No significant differences between propranolol and placebo were found with respect to clinical ratings or IPAT scores of anxiety in either diagnostic group."

Kellner and co-workers (1974) compared one week of propranolol therapy to one week of placebo after a "practice week" on amobarbital, using a double-blind crossover design for 22 chronically anxious outpatients. Amobarbital, 30 mg, was given three times a day; the dosage of propranolol was self-selected, beginning at 20 mg four times a day and increasing daily to symptom relief or a maximum of 50 mg four times a day; placebo dosage was similarly self-selected, starting with one tablet four times a day and increasing to complete symptom relief on eight tablets per day. Several observer and subjective rating scales were completed before and after each week of experimental treatment. When propranolol was compared to placebo, all measures of anxiety and somatic symptoms favored propranolol, with the differences reaching statistical significance for the Symptom Questionnaire. All measures of depression and inadequacy either were not different or tended toward negative correlation (placebo produced better results in depression than did propranolol). Kellner et al. felt that their results were not conclusive but stated "there was a trend and consistency of results which suggests that propranolol has short-term anti-anxiety effects."

Tyrer and Lader (1974) also used a one-week trial, double-blind balanced crossover design to compare response to placebo, diazepam, and propranolol in 12 chronically anxious psychiatric outpatients. Six patients had predominantly somatic and six had predominantly psychic (psychological) anxiety symptoms. Clinical ratings of anxiety were made separately by patient and psychiatrist after each week of experimental treatment. The dosages varied from 3 to 9 capsules per day (1 to 3 times per day). Patients received between 6 and 18 mg of diazepam daily, and between 120 and 360 mg of propranolol daily. Both diazepam and propranolol produced equal and marked improvement in the six patients with predominantly somatic anxiety as compared to placebo. Diazepam also produced marked relief of anxiety in the six patients with predominantly psychic anxiety (as compared to placebo), but propranolol apparently did not. From these results, Tyrer and Lader concluded that diazepam is superior to propranolol in treatment of morbid anxiety, presumably because of its more general usefulness. They did not comment on the limitation their one-week trial might place on their conclusions, but stated, "Nevertheless propranolol does have important clinical effects in somatically anxious patients. Its efficacy in this group is comparable to diazepam and its use is preferable because it rarely produces sedation, is very safe, and not prone to abuse."

In a double-blind study, Krishman (1975) gave diazepam and oxprenolol to university students with pronounced preexamination and examination anxiety symptoms. Seventeen students received 2 mg of diazepam twice a day, and 15 students took 40 mg of oxprenolol twice daily for several days. Self-rating scales for anxiety and tension revealed improvement in symptoms in both groups, but neither drug was superior to the other. Six of 17 students on diazepam overestimated the mark they would achieve on the exam and none did better than predicted. On oxprenolol, five students exceeded their predicted exam grade, eight equaled it, and only two did worse than predicted. Krishman believed his results to show that diazepam increased confidence, perhaps unwarrantedly, while reducing anxiety. He concluded further that the more accurate predictions of achievement accompanying anxiety symptoms-relief with oxprenolol indicated that beta-adrenergic blockade does not interfere with the student's critical faculties. An alternative hypothesis that beta-adrenergic blockade may enhance the concentration powers of the severely anxious student was not considered by Krishman in this report.

Hawkings (1975) reported treating 88 patients with various forms of severe anxiety with individualized dosages of beta-adrenergic blocking drugs for at least three months in a consultant psychiatric practice. He subdivided these morbidly anxious patients into those with mental anxiety (16), phobic anxiety (17), anxiety with depression (13), and physical-somatic anxiety (42). Although individualized dosages ranged from 30 to 480 mg daily, in the majority of patients the dosage was 120 mg per day of propranolol or oxprenolol. Twenty-three of the patients did not benefit, and the medication was stopped after three months; 18 benefited markedly and recovered, so that symptoms did not recur when the beta-blockade was stopped; 41 continued beta-blockade after three months because of clinical benefits. Improvement was assessed clinically and by statistical improvements in Hamilton Anxiety Scales. Diagnostic subclassification of anxiety had predictive value only for those with physical-somatic anxiety; 93 percent (39 of 42) of these patients responded satisfactorily to treatment. Satisfactory responses to treatment with beta-adrenergic blockade occurred regularly but less frequently in the other anxiety subgroups after three months. Fifty-six percent (9 of 16) of those with mental anxiety, 65 percent (11 of 17) of those with phobic anxiety, and 46 percent (6 of 13) of those with anxiety and depression responded satisfactorily to beta-adrenergic blockade. Hawkings' experience seems to support the notion that propranolol and other beta-blocking medications work well in a high percentage of patients with anxiety states, whatever the predominance of somatic and/or mental-psychic-psychological symptoms, if the treatment is given for more than a week or two and the dosages are individualized to the point of clinical response. Hawkings' experience seems to parallel that of Suzman (1976) (see above) in that, after continued use of propranolol, central-apprehensive anxiety also responds to beta-blockade.

Johnson et al. (1976) used an interesting and unusual double-blind research design to compare diazepam, oxprenolol, and placebo in the treatment of anxiety states. In an anxiety specialty outpatient clinic, patients with primary clinical anxiety for not less than three weeks nor longer than two years, between the ages of 18 and 65, free of all other medical and psychiatric states, were given a week's trial on placebo. The placebo responders (5 of 38) were eliminated, and the remaining patients were blindly and randomly assigned to a three-week individualized dosage treatment schedule with placebo, oxprenolol (80 mg capsules), or diazepam (5 mg capsules). The first week the dosage was one capsule three times a day; during the second and third weeks the dosage was individualized, with a minimum of one and a maximum of seven capsules per day. The Hamilton Anxiety Scale and the Rapid Symptoms Checklist were used to evaluate changes in symptoms. Blood specimens were drawn weekly to measure diazepam and oxprenolol. Twenty-nine patients completed the protocol properly and were available for statistical analyses of covariance of group data. Thirteen patients received diazepam, 11 oxprenolol, and five placebo. After one week of treatment, diazepam had significantly reduced anxiety, as compared to both placebo and oxprenolol (which did not differ statistically although the direction of change was for improvement with oxprenolol). At the end of the three-week individualized trial, both diazepam and oxprenolol were associated with significantly reduced anxiety, as compared to placebo, and at this point diazepam and oxprenolol did not differ from one another. This interesting and difficult study indicates that beta-blockade takes somewhat longer to produce maximum relief of anxiety symptoms than does benzodiazepine therapy.

Burrows et al., (1976) used both the Hamilton Anxiety Scale and an individualized Target Symptom Improvement Scale to measure improvement in a double-blind study design that was nearly identical to that of Johnson et al. (1976). Sixty-two patients completed the three-week individualized treatment schedules; 20 received placebo, 22 received oxprenolol, and 20 received diazepam; all three treatment groups were subdivided into the predominantly psychic and the predominantly somatic symptom anxiety groups. At the end of the three-week trial, improvement was significantly greater in both the diazepam- and oxprenolol-treated groups than in the placebo group; there was no difference between diazepam- and oxprenolol-group improvements (except for observer-investigator preference) and there was no different group response to any of the treatments by the psychic and somatic subgroups.

Easton and Sherman (1976) wrote of their experience in evaluating and treating patients with anxiety states for the "hyperdynamic beta-adrenergic circulatory state" described by Frohlich and associates (1966, 1969). Easton and Sherman describe the production of severe anxiety attacks in six patients with such anxiety states by infusion of the pure beta-adrenergic agonist, isoproterenol. The isoproterenol-induced anxiety attacks could be prevented and/or aborted by propranolol; treatment of these six patients with individualized daily doses of 60 to 320 mg per day virtually eliminated anxiety symptoms during a four- to 24-month follow-up period.

Tanna et al. (1977) conducted a double-blind controlled trial comparison of placebo and two dosages of propranolol (40 mg/day and 120 mg/day) given one week each in a three-week randomized design (after one week of placebo for all). The 28 patients were moderately to severely ill chronic anxiety neurotics diagnosed according to rigorous criteria after systematic, structured psychiatric interviews. The placebo and the lower dosage (40 mg/day) of propranolol were ineffective; the larger dosage (120 mg/day) of propranolol was safe and effective in controlling the symptoms of anxiety neurosis. Tanna and co-workers demonstrated with elegant statistical analysis of the data from this study that 12 of the 14 chief symptoms of anxiety neurosis were significantly ($p < 0.01$) reduced by the larger propranolol dosage after one week's therapy. Symptoms alleviated were headache, dizziness, blurred vision, sighing, tiredness, easy fatigability, paresthesias, trembling, shakiness, weakness, initial insomnia, and palpitations. The two symptoms that failed to clear up after one week, fears and chest pain, were symptoms that cleared later in the experiences reported by Suzman (1976) and Hawkings (1975)—and in the reviewers' experience. Tanna and co-workers said they encountered no side effects of any importance; the two patients who dropped out were unable to complete the initial week on placebo because of severe, recurrent anxiety symptoms. Tanna et al. suggested longer treatment studies monitored by frequent plasma propranolol levels. Their study demonstrates that beta-blocker dosage is a critical variable in the short-term study of anxiety symptom relief.

The studies summarized indicate that adequate beta-adrenergic blockade is an effective treatment for symptoms of anxiety. Beta-adrenergic blockers were consistently noted to be effective in relieving palpitations, tachycardia, and other symptoms. In most reports these drugs were significantly superior to placebo. Only in some instances when beta-adrenergic blocking agents were given for two weeks or less (and in smaller dosages) was there little superiority to placebo. Studies comparing beta-adrenergic blockers to benzodiazepines most often indicated equal efficacy. Studies that found benzodiazepines superior to beta-blockade were either based on a psychic anxiety versus somatic anxiety dichotomy, or on a finding of differences after one week of treatment which disappeared after three weeks. Two reports indicated problems in concentration associated with benzodiazepines but not with beta-adrenergic blockade, and others noted that fewer side effects are associated with beta-adrenergic blockade than with benzodiazepines.

Since beta-adrenergic blocking agents specifically reduce the somatic symptoms of anxiety, produce little or no sedation, cause few side effects, and have little or no potential for abuse, they should be considered the treatment of choice for somatic anxiety. Moreover, the distinction between psychologic and somatic anxiety may be an artificial and unfortunate one. Anxiety neurosis, a syndrome which affects about 5 percent of the adult population, is characterized by cardiorespiratory and other somatic anxiety symptoms as well as subjective apprehensive (central) anxiety. Our clinical experience, supported by this literature review, is that adequate beta-adrenergic blockade not only controls somatic anxiety immediately, but also relieves psychologic anxiety after three to six weeks' continued therapy.

Although dosages must be individualized, the usual therapeutic range of propranolol (the beta-adrenergic blocking agent most used in the United States) is between 40 and 160 mg/day. Dosage schedule is usually four times a day since the biologic half-life of propranolol is two to three hours. Because of the time lag before subjective anxiety symptoms diminish, small dosages of benzodiazepines may be useful in the early phases of treatment (for the first one to three weeks). There is a scientific need for double-blind comparison of adequate beta-blockade, adequate benzodiazepine therapy, and combinations of the two in treating various anxiety states. Adequate dosages should allow two-week double-blind crossover trials. "States of anxiety" which should be studied separately include chronic anxiety neurosis and secondary anxiety states. Other conditions with frequent secondary anxiety worthy of study include primary affective disorder, alcoholism, schizophrenia, hysteria (Briquet's Syndrome), obsessive-compulsive neurosis, and a number of endocrinological and neurological disorders.

REFERENCES

ACKERMAN, S. H., and SACHAR, E. J. 1974. The lactate theory of anxiety: A review and re-evaluation. *Psychosom. Med.*, 36:69-81.
BASOWITZ, H., KORCHIN, S. J., OKEN, D., GOLDSTEIN, M. D., and GUSSACK, H. 1956. Anxiety and performance changes with minimal doses of epinephrine. *Arch. Neurol. Psychiatry*, 76:98-106.
BESTERMAN, E. M. M., and FRIEDLANDER, D. H. 1965. Clinical experiences with propranolol. *Postgrad. Med. J.*, 41:526-535.
BONN, J. A., and TURNER, P. 1971. D-propranolol and anxiety. *Lancet*, 1:1355-1356.

BONN, J. A., TURNER, P., and HICKS, D. 1972. Beta-adrenergic-receptor blockade with practolol in treatment of anxiety. *Lancet*, 1:814-815.

BREWER, C. 1972. Beneficial effect of Beta-adrenergic blockade on "exam nerves." *Lancet*, 2:435.

BURROWS, G. D., DAVIES, B., FAIL, L., POYNTON, C., and STEVENSON, H. 1976. A placebo controlled trial of diazepam and oxprenolol for anxiety. *Psychopharmacology*, 50:177-179.

CAMERON, D. E. 1945. Adrenalin administration in resistant anxiety states. *Am. J. Med. Sci.*, 210:281-288.

CAMERON, D. E. 1947. Behavioral changes produced in patients suffering with chronic tensional anxiety states, by long-continued adrenalin administration. *Psychiatric Quarterly*, 21:261-273.

CANTRIL, H., and HUNT, W. A. 1932. Emotional effects produced by injection of adrenalin. *Am. J. Psychol.*, 44:300-307.

CARLSSON, C. 1971. Haemodynamic studies in alcoholics in the withdrawal phase. *Int. J. Clin. Pharmacol. Therap. Toxicol.*, 3(supp.):61-63.

CARLSSON, C., and JOHANSSON, T. 1971. The psychological effects of propranolol in the abstinence phase of chronic alcoholics. *Br. J. Psychiatry*, 119:605-606.

COHEN, M. E., and WHITE, P. D. 1950. Life situations, emotions, and neurocirculatory asthenia (anxiety neurosis, neurasthenia, effort syndrome). *Trans. Assoc. Res. Nerv. Ment. Dis.*, 29:832-869.

COMBS, D. T., and MARTIN, C. M. 1974. Evaluation of isoproterenol as a method of stress testing. *Am. Heart J.*, 87:711-715.

DARROW, C. W., and GELLHORN, E. 1939. The effects of adrenaline on reflex excitability of the autonomic nervous system. *Am. J. Physiol.*, 127:243-251.

DYNES, J. G., and TOD, J. 1940. Emotional and somatic responses of schizophrenic patients and normal controls to adrenaline and doryl. *J. Neurol. Psychiatry*, 3:1-9.

EASTON, J. D., and SHERMAN, D. G. 1976. Somatic anxiety attacks and propranolol. *Arch. Neurol.*, 33:689-691.

FINK, M., TAYLOR, M. A., and VOLAVKA, J. 1969. Anxiety precipitated by lactate. *N. Engl. J. Med.*, 281:1429.

FRANKENHAUSER, M., JARPE, G., and MATTEL, G. 1961. Effects of intravenous infusions of adrenaline and noradrenaline on certain psychological and physiological functions. *Acta Physiol. Scand.*, 51:175-186.

FRANKENHAUSER, M., and JARPE, G. 1962. Psychophysiological reactions to infusions of a mixture of adrenaline and noradrenaline. *Scand. J. Psychol.*, 3:21-29.

FRANKENHAUSER, M., and JARPE, G. 1963. Psychological changes during infusions of adrenaline in various doses. *Psychopharmacology*, 4:424-432.

FRIEDHOFF, A. J. 1972. Pitts' and McClure's lactate-anxiety study revisited. *Br. J. Psychiatry*, 121:338.

FROHLICH, E. D., DUSTAN, H. P., and PAGE, I. H. 1966. Hyperdynamic Beta-adrenergic circulatory state. *Arch. Int. Med.*, 117:614-619.

FROHLICH, E. D., TARAZI, R. C., and DUSTAN, H. P. 1969. Hyperdynamic Beta-adrenergic circulatory state. *Arch. Int. Med.*, 123:1-7.

FUNKENSTEIN, D. H. 1955. The physiology of fear and anger. *Scientific American*, 192:74-80.

FUNKENSTEIN, D. H., and MEADE, L. W. 1954. Norepinephrine-like and epinephrine-like substances and the elevation of blood pressure during acute stress. *J. Nerv. Ment. Dis.*, 119:380-397.

GALLANT, D. M., SWANSON, W. C., and GUERRERO-FIGUEROA, R. 1973. A controlled evaluation of propranolol in chronic alcoholic patients presenting the symptomatology of anxiety and tension. *J. Clin. Pharmacol.*, 13:41-43.

GANTT, W. H., and FREILE, M. 1944. The effect of adrenaline and acetylcholine in excitation, inhibition, and neurosis. *Trans. Am. Neurol. Assoc.*, 70:180-181.

GARFIELD, S. L., GERSHON, S., SLETTEN, I., SUNDLAND, D. M., and BALLOU, S. 1967. Chemically induced anxiety. *International Journal of Neuropsychiatry*, 3:426-433.

GRANVILLE-GROSSMAN, K. L., and TURNER, P. 1966. The effect of propranolol on anxiety. *Lancet*, 1:788-790.

GROSZ, H. J. 1973. Pitts' and McClure's lactate-anxiety study revisited. *Br. J. Psychiatry*, 122:116-117.

GROSZ, H. J., and FARMER, B. B. 1969. Blood lactate in the development of anxiety symptoms. A critical examination of Pitts and McClure's hypothesis and experimental study. *Arch. Gen. Psychiatry*, 21:611-619.

GROSZ, H. J., and FARMER, B. B. 1972. Pitts' and McClure's lactate-anxiety study revisited. *Br. J. Psychiatry*, 120:415-418.

HAWKINGS, J. R. 1975. Clinical experience with Beta-blockers in consultant psychiatric practice. *Scott. Med. J.*, 20:294-297.

HAWKINS, E. R., MONROE, J. T., SANDIFER, M. G., and VERNON, C. R. 1960. Psychological and physiological responses to continuous epinephrine infusion. *Psychiatric Research Reports American Psychiatric Association*, 12:40-52.

HOLMGREN, A., JONSSON, G., LEVANDER-LINDGREN, M., LINDERHOLM, H., SJOSTRAND, T., and STROM, G. 1959. Low physical working capacity in suspected heart cases due to the inadequate adjustment of peripheral blood flow (vasoregulatory asthenia). *Acta Med. Scand.*, 163:158-184.

HOLMGREN, A., and STROM, G. 1959. Blood lactate concentrations in relation to absolute and relative work load in normal men, and in mitral stenosis, atrial septal defect, and vasoregulatory asthenia. *Acta Med. Scand.*, 163:185-193.

IMHOF, P. R., BLATTER, K., FUCCELLA, L. M., and TURRI, M. 1969. Beta-blockade and emotional tachycardia, radiotelemetric investigations in ski jumpers. *J. Appl. Physiol.*, 27:366-369.

JERSILD, A. T., and THOMAS, W. 1931. Influence of adrenal extract on behavior and mental efficiency. *Am. J. Physiol.*, 43:447-456.

JOHNSON, G., SINGH, B., and LEEMAN, M. 1976. Controlled evaluation of the Beta-adrenoceptor blocking drug oxprenolol in anxiety. *Med. J. Aust.*, 1:909-921.

JONES, M., and MELLERSH, V. 1946. Comparison of exercise response in anxiety states and normal controls. *Psychosom. Med.*, 8:180-187.

KABES, J., and DOSTAL, T. 1976. Therapeutic use of beta-adrenergic blockers in psychiatry (Czech.). *C. S. Psychiatr.*, 72:124-132.

KELLNER, R., COLLINS, A. C., SHULMAN, R. S., and PATHAK, D. 1974. The short-term antianxiety effects of propranolol HCl. *J. Clin. Pharmacol.*, 5:301-304.

KELLY, D. H., and WALTER, C. J. S. 1968. The relationship between clinical diagnosis and anxiety assessed by forearm blood flow and other measurements. *Br. J. Psychiatry*, 114:611-626.

KELLY, D. H., MITCHELL-HEGGS, N., and SHERMAN, D. 1971. Anxiety and the effects of sodium lactate assessed clinically and physiologically. *Br. J. Psychiatry*, 119:129-141.

KRAINES, S. H., and SHERMAN, C. 1940. Neurotic symptoms and changes in the blood pressure and pulse following injection of epinephrine. *JAMA*, 114:843-845.

KRISHMAN, G. 1975. Oxprenolol in the treatment of examination nerves. *Scott. Med. J.*, 20:288-289.

LANDIS, C., and HUNT, W. A. 1932. Adrenalin and emotion. *Psychol. Rev.*, 39:467-485.

LEVANDER-LINDGREN, M., and EK, S. 1962. Studies in neurocirculatory asthenia (Da Costa's Syndrome). *Acta Med. Scand.*, 172:665-676.

LINDEMANN, E., and FINESINGER, J. E. 1938. The effect of adrenaline and mecholyl in states of anxiety in psychoneurotic patients. *Am. J. Psychiatry*, 95:353-370.

LINDEMANN, E., and FINESINGER, J. E. 1940. Subjective responses of psychoneurotic patients to adrenaline and mecholyl. *Psychosom. Med.*, 2:231-248.

LINKEN, A. 1971. Propranolol for L.S.D.-induced anxiety states. *Lancet*, 2:1039-1040.

LINKO, E. 1950. Lactic acid response to muscular exercise in neurocirculatory asthenia. *Ann. Med. Internae Fenniae*, 39:161-176.

MARANON, G. 1924. Emotive action of epinephrine. *Revue Française d'Endocrinologie*, 2:301. Cited by Cantril and Hunt, 1932.

MCMILLIN, W. P. 1973. Oxprenolol in anxiety. *Lancet*, 1:1193.

MCMILLIN, W. P. 1975. Oxprenolol in the treatment of anxiety due to environmental stress. *Am. J. Psychiatry*, 132:965-968.

NORDENFELT, O. 1965. Orthostatic ECG changes and the adrenergic Beta-receptor blocking agent, propranolol (Inderal). *Acta Med. Scand.*, 178:393-401.

NORDENFELT, O., PERSSON, S., and REDFORS, A. 1968. Effect of a new Beta-blocking agent, H 56/28, on nervous heart complaints. *Acta Med. Scand.*, 184:465-471.

PITTS, F. N. 1969. The biochemistry of anxiety. *Sci. Am.*, 220:69-75.

PITTS, F. N. 1971. Biochemical factors in anxiety neurosis. *Behav. Sci.*, 16:82-91.

PITTS, F. N., and MCCLURE, J. N. 1967. Lactate metabolism in anxiety neurosis. *N. Engl. J. Med.*, 227:1329-1336.

PITTS, F. N., WINOKUR, G., and STEWART, M. A. 1961. Psychiatric syndromes, anxiety symptoms and responses to stress in medical students. *Am. J. Psychiatry*, 118:333-340.

POLLIN, W., and GOLDIN, S. 1961. The physiological and psychological effects of intravenously administered epinephrine and its metabolism in normal and schizophrenic men. II: Psychiatric observations. *J. Psychiatr. Res.*, 1:50-66.

RAMSEY, I., GREER, S., and BAGLEY, C. 1973. Propranolol in neurotic and thyrotoxic anxiety. *Br. J. Psychiatry*, 122:555-560.

RICHTER, D. 1940. The action of adrenaline in anxiety. *Proc. R. Soc. Med.*, 33:615-618.

ROTHBALLER, A. B. 1959. The effect of catecholamines on the central nervous system. *Pharmacol. Rev.*, 11:494-544.

RUDOLPH, G. DE M. 1938. Unusual results following the injection of epinephrine. *Endocrinology*, 23:366-367.

SUZMAN, M. M. 1968. An evaluation of the effects of propranolol on the symptoms and electrocardiographic changes in patients with anxiety and the hyperventilation syndrome. *Ann. Int. Med.*, 68:1194.

SUZMAN, M. M. 1976. Propranolol in the treatment of anxiety. *Postgrad. Med. J.*, 52 (suppl. 4):168-174.

TAGGART, P., CARRUTHERS, M., and SOMERVILLE, W. 1973. Electrocardiogram, plasma catecholamines and lipids, and their modification by oxprenolol when speaking before an audience. *Lancet*, 2:341-346.

TANNA, V. T., PENNINGROTH, R. P., and WOOLSON, R. F. 1977. Propranolol in the treatment of anxiety neurosis. *Compr. Psychiatry*, 18:319-326.

THORLEY, A. S. 1942. Action of adrenalin in neurotics. *J. Neurol. Psychiatry*, 5:14-21.

TOMPKINS, E. H., STURGIS, C. C., and WEARN, J. T. 1919. Studies in epinephrine. II. *Arch. Int. Med.*, 24:247-268.

TOURNAIRE, A., TARTULIER, M., BLUM, J., and DEYRIEUX, F. 1961. Dans les nevroses tachycardiques et chez les sportifs. *Presse Medicale*, 69:721-723.

TURNER, P., GRANVILLE-GROSSMAN, K. L., and SMART, J. V. 1965. Effect of adrenergic receptor blockade on the tachycardia of thyrotoxicosis and anxiety state. *Lancet*, 2:1316-1318.

TYRER, P. J., and LADER, M. H. 1973. Effects of beta-adrenergic blockade with sotalol in chronic anxiety. *Clin. Pharmacol. Ther.*, 14:418-426.

TYRER, P. J., and LADER, M. H. 1974. Response to propranolol and diazepam in somatic and psychic anxiety. *Br. Med. J.*, 2:14-16.

VLACHAKIS, N. D., DEGUIA, D., MENDLOWITZ, M., ANTRAM, S., and WOLF, R. L. 1974. Hypertension and anxiety. A trial with epinephrine and norepinephrine infusion. *Mt. Sinai J. Med. N.Y.*, 41:1615-1625.

WHEATLEY, D. 1969. Comparative effects of propranolol and chlordiazepoxide in anxiety states. *Br. J. Psychiatry*, 115:1411-1412.

10

BIOFEEDBACK IN THE TREATMENT OF ANXIETY DISORDERS

KATHLEEN M. RICE and EDWARD B. BLANCHARD, Ph.D.

In the last decade, biofeedback has come to be accepted as a viable therapeutic technique in the treatment of many psychophysiological and physical disorders (Orne, 1979). Moreover, speculation continues about the potential of biofeedback in treating psychological or psychiatric disorders (Blanchard and Epstein, 1978). This article will summarize and critically review the literature on the treatment of one category of psychological disorders, the *anxiety disorders* (as defined by DSM-III, panic disorder, generalized anxiety disorder, phobic disorders, obsessive compulsive disorder, and fears), by some form of biofeedback training.

The rationale for the use of biofeedback in the treatment of anxiety disorders follows in part from Lang's (1968) model of fear and anxiety. He argued that three partially correlated response systems are involved in the defining operations for anxiety: subjective report, overt motor behavior, and physiological arousal responses. These different response systems may be influenced by different treatment procedures; moreover, change in one response system may or may not lead to change in another response modality.

Biofeedback has been shown to be an effective means of changing various physiological responses (Blanchard and Epstein, 1978). Thus the use of biofeedback in the treatment of anxiety disorders arises from the idea that, if the autonomically mediated physiological arousal associated with anxiety can be reduced or controlled, the motoric-behavioral manifestations and subjective reports of anxiety may subsequently decrease.

Since the physiological component of arousal is manifested in numerous response systems (e.g., cardiovascular, musculoskeletal, gastrointestinal), and since attempts have been made to reduce anxiety through modifying some response in each of these systems, we will summarize the research according to the specific physiological response studied.

This review will examine studies that have used biofeedback techniques for the treatment of anxiety from the explicit perspective of these questions: (1) Was there significant anxiety reduction associated with biofeedback training? (2) Was there evidence that biofeedback training led to a reliable change in the target physiological response? (3) What evidence is there that biofeedback-mediated physiological changes *per se* account for anxiety reductions? (4) What evidence is there that some *other* variables account for anxiety reductions, and if so, what are these variables?

HEART RATE

Cardiovascular effects, especially noticeable increases in heart rate (HR) and stroke volume, are the hallmark of anxiety (Goodwin and Guze, 1979). Moreover, as noted by Blanchard and Epstein (1978), control of HR through biofeedback has been the subject of more research than any other response system. Thus it followed fairly naturally that investigators would seek to test the efficacy of HR biofeedback training as a treatment for anxiety disorders.

Tables 1 and 2 summarize the single group outcome studies and/or single subject experiments and controlled group outcome studies, respectively, in which biofeedback of heart rate has been used in the treatment of anxiety disorders.

The results in Tables 1 and 2 show several differences between the studies listed in the two tables. The less well-controlled studies in Table 1 tended to be conducted with clinically disabled patients, whereas most of the controlled studies in Table 2 were analog studies conducted with mildly fearful volunteers. The exceptions to this were the two studies by Rupert and her associates (Rupert and Holmes, 1978; Schroeder and Rupert, *in press*). The less well controlled studies generally showed clinical improvement in the patients who received biofeedback training, whereas clinical improvement was much more variable in the controlled studies tabulated in Table 2. The studies in Table 1 tend to show some evidence for heart rate control as a result of biofeedback training, whereas the evidence for a specific biofeedback training effect on heart rate is generally absent in the controlled studies. Only the study by Gatchel and Proctor (1976) showed a specific feedback training effect on heart rate among the studies in Table 2.

Referring back to our initial evaluation questions and to the last point in the paragraph above, it seems that in controlled studies there generally is little evidence for a specific biofeedback training effect on heart rate. When HR biofeedback training is compared to relaxation (Gatchel et al., 1977; Schroeder and Rupert, *in press*), one cannot show a specific effect on HR. This failure to find a biofeedback training effect could be due, in part, to the very brief training regimens. In the two case reports, biofeedback training

Table 1

Single Subject Experiments and Single Group Outcome Studies Involving Biofeedback of Heart Rate as a Treatment for Anxiety Disorders

Authors	Subjects and Type of Anxiety Problem	Treatment and Training	Physiological Response	Clinical Response	Follow-up
Nunes and Marks (1975)	Female clinical population. Therapist ratings of moderate to severe animal phobias (n = 10).	2, 3, or 4 HR reduction training sessions combined with graded in vivo exposure to phobic stimulus. Sessions included 2 FB, 2 no-FB epochs.	HR significantly reduced during FB epochs ($\Delta = -4.5$ BPM).	Steady reduction in subjective anxiety and increase in approach behavior during sessions. No difference between FB and no-FB epochs.	No data
Blanchard and Abel (1976)	Female psychiatric patient. Episodic sinus tachycardia elicited by stimuli involving rape.	Controlled single-subject design Subject trained to lower HR during audio description of rape.	HR significantly lowered during FB training (8 sessions) $\Delta = -4.$ BPM. HR lowered during FB + audiotape (25) sessions $\Delta = -4.1$ BPM reduction in HR maintained in absence of feedback (6) sessions $\Delta = -3.3$ BPM.	Tachycardia episodes disappear and patient reports sustained reduction in anxiety at end of treatment.	No return of symptoms at 4 mos.
Nunes and Marks (1976)	Female, clinical population. Therapist ratings of moderate to severe animal phobias (n = 10).	1-hr HR FB training session followed by 1-4 2-hr sessions combined with graded in vivo exposure. All sessions included FB epochs and instructions to reduce HR with no-FB epochs.	HR reduced significantly during FB epochs only (Δ HR not given).	Subjective anxiety declined and approach behavior increased at same rate across blocks of FB and no-FB trials.	No data.
Gatchel (1977)	Volunteer subject. Claustrophobia with anxiety attacks.	14 1-hr sessions of HR training with home practice and high expectancy manipulation.	Average decrease in HR of 7.6 BPM.	Significant reduction in number and severity of anxiety attacks.	Maintenance of improvement at 6 mos.

Table 2

Controlled Group Outcome Experiments Involving Biofeedback of Heart Rate as a Treatment for Anxiety Disorders

Authors	Subjects and Type of Anxiety	Treatment and Training	Physiological Response	Clinical Response	Follow-up
Prigatano and Johnson (1972)	Volunteer undergrads. Severe spider fear assessed by Fear Survey Schedule (FSS) and Spider Questionnaire.	Two groups: (n = 13 per cell) 1) treatment condition (TC)—trained to hold HR constant while viewing pictures of spiders; 2) placebo control condition (PCC)—told that attention to extraneous stimuli (visual FB of TC group) could reduce fear of spiders. All Ss received two 1-hr training sessions and one 45-min test session.	TC group did not learn HR control.	TC and PCC groups show decreases in fear on FSS and decreases in avoidance behavior at posttest. No difference between groups.	No data.
Gatchel and Proctor (1976)	Undergrad volunteers. High scores in public speaking anxiety on FSS.	Four groups: (n = 9 per cell) 1) FB/high expectancy; 2) FB/neutral expectancy; 3) tracking task/high expectancy; 4) tracking task/neutral expectancy. Two 15-min FB or tracking sessions with expectancy manipulation. Pre- and posttraining assessments of public speaking anxiety.	Both FB groups able to significantly control HR but do not differ (Δ = −5 BPM).	FB groups lower in subjective anxiety and therapist ratings of anxiety in posttraining, speech-giving situation. High expectancy also contributes to reduction in self-reported anxiety.	FB groups report greater improvement than tracking groups at 4 wks. Biofeedback perceived as more credible treatment. No HR data collected at follow-up.
Gatchel et al. (1977)	Undergrad volunteers. High scores in public speaking anxiety on FSS (n = 50).	Four groups: 1) HR FB; 2) muscular relaxation (MR); 3) HR FB plus MR; 4) false FB control. All Ss receive four 25-min training assessments of public speaking anxiety.	Three experimental groups significantly reduce HR (Δ = approximately −4 BPM).	Experimental and control groups report decrease in anxiety from pre- to posttest. No difference between 4 groups.	No differences between groups on satisfaction with treatment at 4-8 wks. No HR data collected.

Table 2 (Continued)

Authors	Subjects and Type of Anxiety	Treatment and Training	Physiological Response	Clinical Response	Follow-up
Gatchel et al. (1979)	Undergrad volunteers. High scores in public speaking anxiety on FSS (n = 26).	Three groups: 1) HR FB/MR; 2) false FB; 3) systematic desensitization. All Ss receive 4 training sessions. Pre- and posttraining measures of anxiety.	HR FB/MR group produces significantly greater HR slowing than other groups.	All groups report comparable reductions in subjective anxiety at posttest.	Improvement in subjective anxiety maintained at 1 mo.
Rupert and Holmes (1978)	Hospitalized adult males. Physician ratings of high degree of anxiety.	Seven conditions (n = 8 per cell) formed by 2 (instructions to increase HR, instructions to decrease HR) X 3 (true FB, placebo FB, No FB) plus 1 (No treatment control) design. Four HR training/recording sessions followed by 1 transfer-test session.	No difference in HR among any groups instructed to decrease HR (true FB, placebo FB, No FB).	No differences in anxiety at posttest reported by any groups.	No data.
Schroeder and Rupert (in press)	Hospitalized adult male volunteers. Physician ratings of high degree of anxiety.	Three groups; (n = 8 per cell) 1) HR FB; 2) no FB (both groups practiced increasing and decreasing HR); 3) no treatment control with instructions to rest. Four 25-min sessions. Pre and post self-ratings of anxiety.	HRs of all Ss decreased over trials in each session. No difference in HR decrease among 3 groups ($\Delta = -2.8$ BPM.)	HR training had no effect on subjective anxiety.	No data.

lasted for 14 or 33 sessions, whereas in the other studies it was more typically two to four sessions. In summary, at least one of the initial conditions, evidence of control of the physiological response through biofeedback training, is missing in most of the controlled studies.

With regard to the issue of clinical improvement associated with biofeedback training, evidence for this is in all uncontrolled studies listed in Table 1. Moreover, in all controlled studies by Gatchel and colleagues listed in Table 2, clinical improvement was associated with biofeedback training. This is also the case in the study by Prigatano and Johnson (1972) but not in Rupert's two studies (Rupert and Holmes, 1978; Schroeder and Rupert, *in press*).

As to the more crucial issue of whether the clinical improvement is differentially associated with biofeedback training rather than other conditions, the evidence is more mixed. In the two studies by Nunes and Marks (1975, 1976) the same degree of improvement occurred with and without biofeedback training during the exposure treatment. Gatchel et al. (1977, 1979) found comparable clinical improvement among subjects receiving HR biofeedback training and various other active treatments *and control conditions.* Only the Gatchel and Proctor (1976) study showed evidence for differential improvement associated with HR biofeedback training. This study is the only one to associate HR control as a result of biofeedback training with differential evidence of clinical improvement. As Gatchel and his colleagues failed to replicate their initial result in the two later studies, some question must be raised about the generality of the earlier results achieved by Gatchel and Proctor (1976).

Thus, research to date on HR biofeedback training and the reduction of fear and anxiety offers only minimal support for the idea that HR biofeedback may be effective in facilitating anxiety reduction; moreover, it has not been shown that HR reduction, per se, is the crucial influence on treatment outcome. For example, Gatchel and his associates (Gatchel and Proctor, 1976; Gatchel et al., 1977, 1979) have found that such factors as expectation and motivation may be more important than actual HR control in determining the outcome of treatment. The case reports by Blanchard and Abel (1976) and Gatchel (1977), while demonstrating that controlling the cardiac component of arousal leads to reduction in subjective anxiety and distress, suggest that in some limited cases HR biofeedback training may be a valuable tool. It certainly does not seem to be a powerful enough and general enough tool to warrant its wholesale adoption, however. Moreover, the precise means of its action remain unclear. Finally, what would be valuable in this area would be a well-controlled group outcome study of clinical populations who receive adequate HR biofeedback training so that HR control is manifested as a reliable test of the technique's efficacy.

Electromyogram

A second organ system greatly involved in the physiological aspects of anxiety disorders is the musculoskeletal system. The principal response which has been monitored from this organ system is the electromyogram (EMG). It is well known that some degree of muscle tension frequently occurs in stressful situations (Jacobson, 1938). Further, the hypothesis is that, when an individual repeatedly mobilizes physiological defensive reactions with their concomitant elevation in general muscle tension, he or she is likely to lose the ability to relax and thus be continually in a state of elevated muscle tension. The idea that deep relaxation of muscles should be a prominent component of treatment for anxiety-related disorders has a long history: Jacobson's (1938) progressive relaxation and Luthe's (1963) autogenic training both use muscle-relaxing techniques to help reduce anxiety.

Most anxiolytic applications of EMG biofeedback follow from the empirical work and theories of two investigators, Budzynski and Stoyva. In a pioneering set of studies (Budzynski et al., 1970, 1973), they showed that frontal EMG biofeedback training combined with regular relaxation practice at home greatly benefited sufferers of tension headaches. The researchers went on to theorize that this same treatment could lead to profound states of relaxation, which they termed "cultivated low arousal," that seemed to have general anxiolytic properties (Stoyva and Budzynski, 1974). Their preliminary data supported this hypothesis (Budzynski, 1973).

Table 3 lists the controlled group outcome studies of frontal EMG biofeedback training as a treatment for persons with anxiety disorders. One single group outcome study is also included.

Unlike the previously reviewed work on HR biofeedback, the studies with frontal EMG biofeedback on patient populations and analog volunteer groups are quite adequate. With regard to the criterion of evaluation, all eight studies showed a significant reduction on the various indices of anxiety used. As to the second criterion, evidence of biofeedback-mediated physiological change, there was significant reduction in frontal EMG between pre- and posttraining in the reports that contained this information. An absence of such data seems to us a serious fault of the Counts et al. (1978) study.

Four of the studies in which frontal EMG biofeedback training led to significant EMG reductions reported significant differential reduction in frontal EMG associated with biofeedback training as contrasted with other treatment and control conditions. In the three studies that compared frontal EMG biofeedback training to some other form of relaxation training, however, there was a discrepancy in two of the three: Raskin et al. (1980) and Miller et al. (1978) found no greater reduction in frontal EMG from bio-

Table 3

Treatment of Anxiety Disorders by Frontal Electromyography

Authors	Subjects and Type of Anxiety	Treatment and Training	Physiological Response	Clinical Response	Follow-up
Raskin et al. (1973)	Chronically anxious subjects who had remained symptomatic despite 2 yrs of psychotherapy and medication.	All Ss (n = 10) trained to sustain deep muscle relaxation with and without FB—followed by 8 wks of at-home practice with periodic laboratory monitoring.	All Ss maintained deep muscle relaxation with and without FB (2.5 μv/min or less averaged over 25 min).	40% subjects report decrease in subjective anxiety. 60% report no change in anxiety. 5/6 Ss with insomnia report improvement in symptoms. 4 Ss with headaches report reduction in frequency and intensity of headaches.	No data.
Townsend et al. (1975)	Psychiatric patients judged by psychiatrist, self-ratings, and scores on STAI to be suffering from chronic anxiety.	Two groups: 1) EMG FB (n = 13)—received nine 20-min training sessions in muscle tension reduction, followed by 2 wks home practice; 2) group psychotherapy comparison group (n = 8)—received 16 1-hr group psychotherapy sessions with EMG monitoring on 5 days of treatment.	EMG significantly reduced in FB group. No change in EMG in group psychotherapy subjects.	Significant reductions in mood disturbance and trait anxiety in EMG FB group. No changes in comparison group.	2 subjects report improved adjustment to stress at 6 mos follow-up. No EMG data available.
Canter et al. (1975)	Psychiatric patients with diagnosis of anxiety neurosis.	Two groups: (n = 14 per cell) 1) EMG FB—received 10-25 20-min sessions of muscle relaxation; 2) progressive relaxation (PR)—10-25 sessions of modified Jacobsonian PR. EMG recorded but no FB given.	By final session, FB group shows significantly lower muscle tension than PR group (FB: 12.8 μv, PR: 24.4μv).	85% of patients in FB group and 50% of PR subjects report decrease in subjective anxiety. Samples too small to determine significance of these differences.	No data.

Table 3 (Continued)

Authors	Subjects and Type of Anxiety	Treatment and Training	Physiological Response	Clinical Response	Follow-up
Raskin et al. (1980)	Volunteers satisfying criteria for anxiety neurosis and scoring above 80th percentile on Taylor Manifest Anxiety Scale (TMAS). Majority of Ss had prior psychiatric therapy for anxiety.	Three groups: 1) EMG FB (n = 11)—FB trials interspersed with No-FB trials; 2) relaxation training (n = 10)—modified progressive relaxation and visual imagery; 3) transcendental meditation (n = 10). 6 wk baseline, 6 wk treatment, 6 wk posttreatment observation, follow-up.	Frontalis tension decreases from baseline to treatment and post-treatment measures in all groups.	No difference in groups reported at posttest. All treatments significantly reduce anxiety.	Posttreatment gains are maintained if subject continues to practice (mean follow-up time = 9 mos).
Kappes and Michaud (1978)	Undergraduate volunteers scoring high on Suinn Test Anxiety Behavior Scale (STABS).	Two groups: (n = 6 per cell) 1) Five sessions contingent EMG FB followed by 5 sessions noncontingent FB; 2) noncontingent FB followed by contingent FB.	Group 1 subjects produce low EMG levels during contingent FB and maintain these levels during noncontingent FB.	Group 1 STABS scores decrease following contingent and noncontingent FB. Group 2 STABS scores increase following noncontingent FB and decrease following contingent FB.	No data.
Miller et al. (1978)	Volunteers with serious anxiety reactions to dental treatment (self-reports and dentist ratings). Anxiety also assessed by Dental Anxiety Scale (DAS) and STAI.	Three groups: (n = 7 per cell) 1) EMG FB—10 20-min sessions; 2) progressive relaxation—10 10-40 min sessions; 3) relaxation control—10 20-min sessions.	Comparable decrease in EMG levels for FB and PR groups. No change in control group EMG.	Significant decrease in DAS and state anxiety in all groups at posttest. Decreases in FB and PR groups significantly greater than control group decreases.	Authors report 1-yr follow-up but give no data.

Table 3 (Continued)

Authors	Subjects and Type of Anxiety	Treatment and Training	Physiological Response	Clinical Response	Follow-up
Gatchel et al. (1978)	Volunteer undergrads reporting great difficulty managing everyday anxiety and stress.	Two groups: (n = 6 per cell) 1) EMG FB/relaxation—muscle relaxation and standard FB instructions; 2) false FB—received FB indicating decrease in muscle tension. Physiological measures and self-ratings of anxiety taken in stressful pre- and posttreatment situations.	Significant EMG reductions in FB group during training and posttraining stress test. (Pre-post changes = 11.1 μv/sec—5.7 μv/sec).	Both groups report reduction in anxiety at post-test. No difference between groups in self-ratings.	No data.
Counts et al. (1978)	Undergrad volunteers scoring high on Test Anxiety Scale.	Four groups: (n = 10 per cell) 1) EMG assisted cue-controlled relaxation; 2) cue-controlled relaxation; 3) attention-placebo; 4) no treatment control. Ss received six 45-min sessions.	No data.	Posttreatment measures of test anxiety and state anxiety indicated superiority of Groups 1 and 2 for anxiety reduction. EMG assisted cue-controlled relaxation was not superior to cue-controlled relaxation alone.	No data.

feedback training than was achieved by training in progressive relaxation. Moreover, Raskin et al. found no differential EMG reduction for the biofeedback training over that achieved through a passive, meditative form of relaxation, transcendental meditation. This issue requires further clarification. It is evident, however, that frontal EMG biofeedback training is superior to group therapy and to false feedback training in bringing about physiological change.

With regard to our third criterion, evidence for biofeedback-mediated physiological change accounting for anxiety reductions, in only two studies (Kappes and Michaud, 1978; Townsend et al., 1975) did the subjects receiving frontal EMG biofeedback show a differential advantage in terms of reduced anxiety. What is even more puzzling is that, in two of the four studies which showed a significant reduction in frontal EMG as a result of biofeedback training, as opposed to EMG reductions using other relaxation techniques, there was no differential effect on anxiety reduction (Canter et al., 1975; Gatchel et al., 1978). One finds, by and large, equal clinical benefits from frontal EMG biofeedback training and from such other relaxation training procedures as brief progressive relaxation, transcendental meditation, or cue-controlled relaxation. Finally, except for the recent study by Raskin et al. (1980), follow-up data are lacking.

What, then, can be concluded from the research on EMG biofeedback as a treatment for anxiety disorders? Taken as a whole, these studies suggest that EMG biofeedback training may be an effective treatment for anxiety, but that its exact mechanism of action remains unclear at this time. Obviously, frontalis-muscle tension reduction is not a necessary condition for the experience of relaxation, nor is muscle relaxation a necessary condition for subjective anxiety reduction. A reduction in EMG activity may be sufficient to decrease subjective anxiety levels, but the learning of EMG control does not seem to be the crucial component of the anxiety treatment package. It is becoming increasingly obvious that other factors in the biofeedback context (or in any treatment context) may be responsible for reducing anxiety in a specific group of subjects.

As muscle relaxation does not seem to facilitate anxiety reduction, the wisdom of relying strictly on this technique as an anxiety treatment is questionable. As Raskin and her associates (1980) point out, relaxation treatments seem to be insufficient in treating persons for chronic anxiety; one must incorporate other interventions in treatment (e.g., cognitive restructuring).

One problem in EMG research that may contribute to the absence of a strong relationship between EMG levels and subjective anxiety is the almost exclusive use of the frontalis as the target muscle. Originally, it was believed that, since the frontalis is one of the most difficult muscles in the body to relax voluntarily, a lack of muscle tension in the frontalis would necessarily indicate relaxation of other major muscle groups. Basmajian (1976) stated that frontalis EMG scores, as measured in the typical clinical application, do not indicate frontalis activity only but reflect muscle activity from the first rib upward. Because of this lack of specificity, therefore, training in frontalis tension reduction would be especially useful in inducing general muscle relaxation. As stated previously, Stoyva and Budzynski (1974) also reported that training in frontalis EMG feedback may be a means of bringing about a state of cultivated low arousal. The reported results have, however, cast a serious doubt on the value of this technique. Alexander (1975) questioned the generalizability of relaxation from the frontalis to other muscle groups and presented evidence for his claim. However, one cannot conclude, as Alexander does, that "EMG biofeedback cannot yet be accepted as a viable general relaxation technique" (p. 656). The fact remains that EMG biofeedback may be equivalent (or superior) in effectiveness (e.g., Canter et al., 1975; Miller et al., 1978; Townsend et al., 1975) to traditional relaxation procedures and psychotherapeutic techniques in facilitating relaxation.

ELECTROENCEPHALOGRAM

Early researchers of electroencephalographic (EEG) biofeedback reported that persons often entered a quasimeditational state of consciousness during EEG alpha enhancement training (Brown, 1970; Kamiya, 1968). This state was described by subjects as pleasant, relaxed, and serene. It was also observed that the EEGs of experienced meditators often showed increases in alpha strength during meditation (e.g., Kasamatsu and Hirai, 1969). The possibility of directly influencing experience through voluntary control of the electrical activity of the brain was an exciting notion and fostered the speculation that EEG alpha biofeedback training was potentially a powerful alternative to traditional anxiolytic techniques such as relaxation and meditation.

The few studies which have experimentally tested this speculation are summarized in Table 4.

The results in Table 4 are highly conflicting. In the analog studies, Garrett and Silver (1976) and Hardt and Kamiya (1978) found significant changes in alpha as a result of the alpha biofeedback training, but Rice and Plotkin (1980), using a similar population, did not. The studies which showed significant differential changes in alpha as a result of biofeedback training also reported improvement on the anxiety measures. This is somewhat clouded by the fact that all three studies reported significant reductions in anxiety: that is, Rice and Plotkin found significant reductions in anxiety in both the

Table 4

Treatment of Anxiety Disorders by Alpha EEG Biofeedback Training

Authors	Subjects and Type of Anxiety	Treatment and Training	Physiological Response	Clinical Response	Follow-up
Mills and Solyom (1974)	Five volunteer outpatients diagnosed as obsessives with marked ruminations.	20 1-hr sessions in which Ss were instructed to increase EEG alpha activity.	2/5 Ss increase alpha (22% and 51% increase over baseline). 3/5 Ss do not change alpha from baseline levels.	All Ss report decline in ruminative activity during EEG training regardless of alpha levels.	No data.
Glueck and Stroebel (1975)	Psychiatric inpatients. Anxiety measures obtained through self-report, MMPI, psychiatrist reports, nursing notes.	Three groups: 1) autogenic training (n = 12); 2) EEG alpha FB (n = 26); 3) transcendental meditation (n = 187).	Persons in alpha FB group learned some control over 15 sessions (no specification of mean alpha increase).	All persons in autogenic training group drop out of study. Alpha FB group reports increase in tension and anxiety. Only TM group improves significantly.	Follow-up of discharged TM patients indicates majority still meditating with improved daily functioning.
Garrett and Silver (1976)	Undergrad volunteers scoring above median on test-anxiety questionnaire and giving self-reports of test anxiety.	Five groups: 1) EEG alpha FB (n = 10); 2) EMG FB (n = 10); 3) both EEG and EMG FB (n = 9); 4) relaxation training—no-FB (n = 10); 5) no training control (n = 10). Ss receive 10 training sessions over 10 wks. Instructions for practice outside laboratory	Alpha group increases % alpha (33.2% baseline). EMG group reduces muscle tension (49.55%). Combined group successful at both EEG and EMG tasks (alpha; 44.85% increase; EMG: 41.37% decrease). Relaxation training Ss showed a smaller increase in alpha but comparable reductions in EMG levels to FB groups (18.37%; 41.37%).	EEG, EMG, and combined EEG and EMG groups decrease significantly in test anxiety; control groups do not.	No data

Table 4 (Continued)

Authors	Subjects and Type of Anxiety	Treatment and Training	Physiological Response	Clinical Response	Follow-up
Hardt and Kamiya (1978)	Volunteers either high or low in trait anxiety—assessed by Welsh Anxiety Scale.	Subjects high or low in trait anxiety trained to increase and decrease alpha levels in 7 48-min sessions.	Low trait anxiety subjects superior at both alpha enhancement and suppression training.	Anxiety changes were inversely related to alpha levels, but only in high trait anxious persons.	No data
Rice and Plotkin (1980)	Volunteer undergrads reporting chronic anxiety and scoring high in anxiety on STAI, TMAS, and Welsh Anxiety Scales.	Two groups: 1) alpha enhancement training (n = 5); 2) alpha suppression training (n = 5); 3) waiting-list control (n = 3). Ss receive five 40-min training sessions with home practice instructions.	No change in alpha levels in alpha-enhance group. Reductions in alpha-levels in alpha suppress group.	Both EEG groups report significant decrease in anxiety at posttreatment assessment. No change in anxiety in waiting-list control Ss.	No data

alpha-enhancement and alpha-suppression groups; Garrett and Silver found significant reductions in test anxiety for all three biofeedback groups but not for their no-treatment or relaxation groups; finally, Hardt and Kamiya found a direct relationship between increase in alpha levels and decreases in anxiety for high trait-anxious individuals.

Among the clinical researchers, Mills and Solyom (1974) reported that only two of the five obsessive ruminators showed significant changes in EEG alpha as a result of biofeedback training, yet all five patients reported decreases in ruminative activity during the actual feedback training, regardless of alpha level. This lends more support to a nonspecific treatment effect than to any effect specifically related to changes in the alpha portion of the EEG. Moreover, the reductions in rumination did not generalize for patients outside the actual feedback training situation.

By far the most ambitious study in this area is that of Glueck and Stroebel (1975). They tested the relative efficacy of alpha training, transcendental meditation (TM), and autogenic training in alleviating the symptoms of a group of psychiatric inpatients. The results of this study are surprising. Patients assigned to the alpha training group were able to learn some (the authors do not specify how much) alpha control after 15 training sessions; however, they were not able to transfer their ability to situations outside of the laboratory. Subsequently, attempts to produce alpha in the absence of the biofeedback signals resulted in an increase in tension and anxiety because of the patients' uncertainty about the results. Those in the autogenic training group rapidly lost interest in the procedure and did not experience any of the desired positive subjective effects. All patients in this group had asked to stop or be switched to one of the other two treatment groups by the fourth week of the study. On the other hand, the TM group had a low attrition rate; moreover, persons in this group showed a significantly greater level of clinical improvement than a matched sample of psychiatric inpatients. Interestingly, subjects who regularly practiced TM showed a spontaneous increase in GSR, a slight decrease in HR, and a rapid increase in EEG alpha density. Apparently, EEG alpha increases may be a reflection of a generalized relaxed state, but an increase in alpha is not a necessary prerequisite for the experience of relaxation.

SKIN RESISTANCE LEVEL

Although various aspects of electrodermal activity have been used frequently as dependent measures in studies of anxiety disorders (Gelder et al., 1973; Marks et al., 1971), to the best of our knowledge only one study has been conducted using biofeedback of an electrodermal response. Javel and Denholtz (1975) treated volunteer female spider phobics with a combination of systematic desensitization followed by eight one-hour sessions in which patients received feedback of skin-resistance level (erroneously called GSR by the authors) to help them relax while they were exposed to live spiders. Results showed significant reduction in skin resistance during the exposure, marked increase in approach behavior, and marked decrease in self-reported fear and anxiety. Because of the absence of controls, no strong conclusions can be drawn from this study. However, it does fulfill the criteria of showing a change in physiological response as a result of biofeedback training, as well as reduced anxiety associated with the physiological change.

SKIN TEMPERATURE

The use of finger temperature (or finger blood volume) biofeedback as a technique in treatment of anxiety disorders has been suggested by several researchers. Sargent et al. (1973), for example, showed that learning to increase one's finger temperature may promote general relaxation. The rationale for this line of research is that anxiety leads to vasoconstriction of peripheral blood vessels and an increase in blood flow to those parts of the body that will be needed to cope with the stressful situation. The decrease in blood flow to the periphery of the body results in a subsequent temperature reduction in the periphery (Mathews and Lader, 1971).

Although no clinical studies have been conducted on the use of temperature training for anxiety disorders, several investigations of the parameters and correlates of finger temperature and blood volume indicate that this is a promising question to pursue.

Boudewyns (1976) measured the finger temperature of normal adult subjects under both relaxed and stressful conditions. He found that finger temperature increased significantly from initial levels to a first relaxation phase, decreased significantly during the stressful phase, and again increased significantly during a second relaxation phase. Self-reports of arousal level correlated significantly with the finger temperature response.

Bloom et al. (1976), in a similar study, measured the finger pulse volume, pulse rate, and subjective anxiety levels of normal adults exposed to threatening and nonthreatening situations. Their results indicated that finger pulse volume was significantly correlated with both pulse rate and with subjective reports of anxiety.

Burish and Horn (1979), investigating frontal EMG as an index of arousal, found that while frontal EMG levels were *not* related to subjective reports of anxiety, finger tip temperature clearly decreased in subjects in stressful situations. Pulse rate and finger pulse volume were also significantly correlated with self-reports of arousal.

Taken together, the three studies suggest that temperature and finger pulse volume biofeedback may have potential as treatment procedures. Given that temperature and pulse volume seem to be reliable indicators of emotional arousal, and that they may, in fact, be superior to other physiological measures as arousal indices, it would be worthwhile to study the efficacy of these types of biofeedback with clinically anxious subjects and to compare temperature and pulse volume feedback with the other, more commonly used types of feedback.

DISCUSSION

Two major conclusions emerge from the data we have summarized. First, for HR and EEG alpha biofeedback training, there is no consistent evidence, either from studies with patients or from analog studies, that these forms of treatment are useful for the anxiety disorders. Although a few scattered studies show differential physiological change as a result of biofeedback training and a concomitant differential reduction in some measure or measures of anxiety, the bulk of the evidence is disappointing.

Second, for frontal EMG biofeedback, the evidence is more consistent that biofeedback training results in differential physiological change and that fairly consistent clinical improvement is associated with the treatment. Clinical improvement is not, however, clearly associated with physiological change. The evidence, with two exceptions (Kappes and Michaud, 1978; Townsend et al., 1975), fails to meet the crucial test for demonstrating the specific value of frontal EMG biofeedback training for treatment of the anxiety disorders. Moreover, other forms of relaxation training tend to yield comparable clinical effects.

Thus, although the actual learning to control a specific physiological function or process *per se* does not seem to be the decisive factor in the efficacy of biofeedback techniques for treatment of anxiety, biofeedback, nevertheless, *has* been shown to be an effective treatment for certain individuals, in some cases succeeding where drugs, psychotherapy, and traditional relaxation techniques have failed. What factors, then, are responsible for the effectiveness of biofeedback in these cases?

Plotkin (in press) discussed several features of the biofeedback context that may render it an "ultimate placebo" or a mobilizer of a person's own self-healing powers. First, the dual attribution of responsibility (internal and external) present in the biofeedback setting may be important in determining what is ultimately experienced. During biofeedback training, trainees attribute the therapeutic outcomes primarily to themselves, not to an external agent. Nevertheless, they may attribute success partially to the biofeedback signal that serves as a guide to achieving control over a specific physiological process. The biofeedback context does share features with an inactive drug placebo treatment in that trainees may experience a suggested psychological effect that, in fact, has no significant physiological basis (or a clinically insignificant effect, or a physiological effect comparable to that induced by traditional treatments). The effects generated in the biofeedback setting, however, may be more powerful than the typical drug placebo. Biofeedback treatment offers a unique contribution to therapeutic intervention in that patients become active and responsible agents in the therapeutic process (Stroebel and Glueck, 1973). Whereas recipients of a drug placebo are led to attribute the physiological, behavioral, and psychological transformations entirely to the drug, biofeedback trainees will attribute the outcome, at least in part, to themselves, thereby enhancing their sense of competence, mastery, and self-control. The experience of success in the feedback task may contribute to the therapeutic outcome even if the actual physiological change is negligible or irrelevant to the symptoms. Legewie (1977) noted, "Especially when biofeedback techniques are used for relaxation, e.g., in the treatment of tension headache, anxiety, hypertension or insomnia, but also when used for neuromuscular reeducation, similar mechanisms can be hypothesized: Through successful biofeedback training a certain functional control is attained, which by itself is minimal or clinically irrelevant (e.g., in the case of heart rate deceleration), but which nevertheless can lead to an increased susceptibility to further suggestion relating to relaxation and therapy" (p. 478).

It seems that, for biofeedback to be successful, certain features of the biofeedback context must be actively exploited: dual attribution of responsibility, objective and flexible indices of success, enhancing feelings of personal mastery, capitalizing on demand characteristics, etc. In addition, biofeedback, as a treatment, generates strong appraisals of credibility—perhaps because of its air of modern medical technology and its impersonal array of electronic equipment. As Plotkin has stated, there is no reason biofeedback therapists should not take advantage of the credibility and reputation for effectiveness that the general population attributes to biofeedback training.

It would appear that if the therapist using biofeedback is careful to capitalize on all the beneficial features of the biofeedback context, then it may, as Stroebel and Glueck point out, be the "ultimate placebo." But, it also seems that this has not been the case in the majority of studies that have used various forms of biofeedback in the treatment of anxiety. What are some of the common pitfalls that have prevented biofeedback treatments from being more effective?

Biofeedback has often been used in a physiologically naive manner (Surwit and Keefe, 1978). It is unreasonable to expect that merely teaching a person control of a single specific physiological response will result in total physical and psychological relaxation. A number of studies have demonstrated that physiological arousal systems are not necessarily correlated, so it is even more amazing to believe that a single physiological change will lead to alterations in the subjective and motoric components of anxiety. Also, technical difficulties and misunderstandings may have undermined much research. For example, the controversy over the generalizability of frontalis muscle tension reduction, the fact that EEG is subject to orienting responses and visual processes, the fact that the GSR is subject to changes in movement—all these may have adversely affected results.

Another problem in biofeedback research is that individuals vary in terms of which response system plays the primary role in maintaining their fear responses. In most cases, individuals are not questioned about their awareness of various physiological responses, and the treatment is not geared to the most salient response systems. The experiments that *have* focused on the most prominent physiological component of the anxiety (Blanchard and Abel, 1976; Gatchel, 1977) have resulted in clinically significant improvements in anxiety. Borkovec (1973) has stated that persons who display significant increases in physiological arousal, which they can perceive, may be good candidates for biofeedback methods that focus on the perceivable system. When there are no strong physiological cues, a different method with strong demand characteristics may prove more effective. In those persons for whom a strong physiological cue is the overriding component of the anxiety response, it seems essential that the intensity of the physiological cue be decreased before treatment techniques aimed at other response systems (i.e., behavioral) can be effective. Biofeedback is a means to do this. The absence of strong physiological cues implies, however, that biofeedback treatment may be worthless, or that one must use a feedback method that relies solely on the beneficial features of the biofeedback context. For this reason we believe that EEG biofeedback may be closest to what Stroebel and Glueck term the "ultimate placebo." During EEG biofeedback, there are almost no physiological cues available to the subject about his or her brain wave activity, and it is easy for the therapist to structure the situation so that the subject feels successful. The subject may, therefore, be instilled with a sense of competence and control (assuming that the subject is motivated and has faith in the treatment). The EEG biofeedback setting is the perfect opportunity for the subject to begin exercising his or her powers of self-control, which may then generalize to other aspects of his or her life.

Although biofeedback holds great potential as a therapeutic technique, its powers have yet to be fully realized in most situations in which it has been used. When one considers all the information available at this time, one is forced to conclude that there is strong support only for the use of frontal EMG biofeedback in treatment for anxiety. Unless, as previously stated, the therapist capitalizes on specific features of the biofeedback context, *and* the client possesses certain beliefs and cognitions that will render him/her susceptible to biofeedback treatment, the use of even EMG biofeedback as the primary treatment is questionable. Biofeedback, however, may be useful as an adjunct treatment for anxiety, especially when there is a strong physiological cue associated with the anxiety. (For example, biofeedback may be used to supplement a behavioral treatment.) Given the often present desynchrony among the three systems that comprise the anxiety response, it is becoming evident that an approach geared toward *one* of these systems is insufficient. As Lang (1968) has stated and the research has borne out, these response systems are only partially correlated; therefore, to ensure success, a treatment program should include features aimed at these three different systems. Biofeedback may be the treatment of choice for altering the physiological component of the anxiety response. It may be superior to drug treatment in this respect, as there are no risks or side-effects from biofeedback training. Because there is at present no evidence for a clear, specific effect of biofeedback over and above relaxation and attention-placebo controls, one may be more likely to choose one of these latter treatments simply because of the prohibitive cost of biofeedback.

Further research is needed to define clearly the role and importance of biofeedback in the treatment of anxiety. Until that time, the question should not be "Is biofeedback effective in the treatment of anxiety?", but "What combination of cognitive, behavioral and biofeedback approaches would benefit which patients, with which symptoms, under what circumstances, and at what expense?"

REFERENCES

ALEXANDER, A. B. 1975. An experimental test of assumptions related to the use of electromyogram biofeedback as a general relaxation training technique. *Psychophysiology*, 12:656-662.

BASMAJIAN, J. V. 1976. Facts vs. myths in EMG biofeedback. *Biofeedback and Self-Regulation*, 1:369-371.

BLANCHARD, E. B., and ABEL, G. G. 1976. An experimental case study of the biofeedback treatment of a rape-induced psychophysiological cardiovascular disorder. *Behavior Therapy*, 7:113-119.

BLANCHARD, E. B., and EPSTEIN, L. H. 1978. *A Biofeedback Primer*. Reading, MA: Addison-Wesley.

BLOOM, L. J., HOUSTON, B. K., and BURISH, T. G. 1976. An evaluation of finger pulse as a psychophysiological measure of anxiety. *Psychophysiology*, 13:40-42.

BORKOVEC, T. D. 1973. The role of expectancy and physiological feedback in fear research: A review with special reference to subject characteristics. *Behavior Therapy*, 4:491-505.

BOUDEWYNS, P. A. 1976. A comparison of effects of stress vs. relaxation instruction on the finger temperature response. *Behavior Therapy*, 7:54-67.

BROWN, B. B. 1970. Recognition aspects of consciousness through association with EEG alpha activity represented by a light signal. *Psychophysiology*, 6:442-452.

BUDZYNSKI, T. H. 1973. Biofeedback procedures in the clinic. *Seminars in Psychiatry*, 5:537-547.

BUDZYNSKI, T., STOYVA, J., and ADLER, C. 1970. Feedback-induced muscle relaxation: Application to tension headache. *Journal of Behavior Therapy and Experimental Psychiatry*, 1:205-211.

BUDZYNSKI, T. H., STOYVA, J. M., ADLER, C. S., and MULLANEY, D. J. 1973. EMG biofeedback and tension headache: A controlled outcome study. *Psychosom. Med.*, 6:509-514.

BURISH, T. G., and HORN, P. W. 1979. An evaluation of frontal EMG as an index of general arousal. *Behavior Therapy*, 10:137-147.

CANTER, A., KONDO, C. Y., and KNOTT, J. R. 1975. A comparison of EMG feedback and progressive muscle relaxation training in anxiety neurosis. *Br. J. Psychiatry*, 127:470-477.

COUNTS, D. K., HOLLANDSWORTH, J. G., and ALCORN, J. D. 1978. Use of electromyographic feedback and cue-controlled relaxation in the treatment of test anxiety. *J. Consult. Clin. Psychol.* 46:990-996.

GARRETT, B. L., and SILVER, M. P. 1976. The use of EMG and alpha biofeedback to relieve test anxiety in college students. In I. Wickramasekera (ed.), *Biofeedback, Behavior Therapy, & Hypnosis*. Chicago: Nelson-Hall.

GATCHEL, R. J. 1977. Therapeutic effectiveness of voluntary heart rate control in reducing anxiety. *J. Consult. Clin. Psychol.*, 45:689-691.

GATCHEL, R. J., HATCH, J. P., MAYNARD, A., TURNS, R., and TAUNTON-BLACKWOOD, A. 1979. A comparison of heart rate feedback, false biofeedback, and systematic desensitization in reducing speech anxiety: Short and long-term effectiveness. *J. Consult. Clin. Psychol.*, 47:620-622.

GATCHEL, R. J., HATCH, J. P., WATSON, P. J., SMITH, D., and GAAS, E. 1977. Comparative effectiveness of voluntary heart rate control and muscular relaxation as active coping skills for reducing speech anxiety. *J. Consult. Clin. Psychol.*, 45:1093-1100.

GATCHEL, R. J., KORMAN, M., WEIS, C. B., SMITH, D., and CLARKE, L. 1978. A multi-response evaluation of EMG biofeedback performance during training and stress-induction conditions. *Psychophysiology*, 15:253-258.

GATCHEL, R. J., and PROCTOR, J. D. 1976. Effectiveness of voluntary heart rate control in reducing speech anxiety. *J. Consult. Clin. Psychol.*, 44:381-389.

GELDER, M. G., BANCROFT, J. H. J., GATH, D. H., JOHNSTON, B. W., MATHEWS, A. N., and SHAW, P. M. 1973. Specific and non-specific factors in behaviour therapy. *Br. J. Psychiatry*, 123:455-462.

GLUECK, B. C., and STROEBEL, C. F. 1975. Biofeedback and meditation in the treatment of psychiatric illnesses. *Compr. Psychiatry*, 16:303-321.

GOODWIN, D. W., and GUZE, S. B. 1979. *Psychiatric Diagnosis*, 2nd Ed. New York: Oxford University Press.

HARDT, J. V., and KAMIYA, J. 1978. Anxiety change through electroencephalographic alpha feedback seen only in high anxiety subjects. *Science*, 201:79-81.

JACOBSON, E. 1938. *Progressive Relaxation*. Chicago: University of Chicago Press.

JAVEL, A. F., and DENHOLTZ, M. S. 1975. Audible GSR feedback and systematic desensitization: A case report. *Behavior Therapy*, 6:251-253.

KAMIYA, J. 1968. Conscious control of brain waves. *Psychology Today*, 1 (1):57-60.

KAPPES, B., and MICHAUD, J. 1978. Contingent vs. noncontingent EMG feedback and hand temperature in relation to anxiety and locus of control. *Biofeedback and Self-Regulation*, 3:51-59.

KASAMATSU, A., and HIRAI, T. 1969. An electroencephalographic study of Zen meditation (Zazen). In C. T. Tart (ed.), *Altered States of Consciousness*. New York: Wiley.

LANG, P. J. 1968. Fear reduction and fear behavior: Problems in treating a construct. In J. M. Shlien (ed.), *Research in Psychotherapy*, vol. 3. Washington, DC: American Psychological Association.

LEGEWIE, H. 1977. Clinical implications of biofeedback. In J. Beatty and H. Legewie (eds.), *Biofeedback and Behavior*. New York: Plenum.

LUTHE, W. 1963. Autogenic training: Method, research, and application in medicine. *Am. J. Psychother.*, 17:174.

MARKS, I. N., BOULOUGOURIS, J. C., and MARSET, P. 1971. Flooding versus desensitization in the treatment of phobic patients: A crossover study. *Br. J. Psychiatry*, 119:353-375.

MATHEWS, A. M., and LADER, M. H. 1971. An evaluation of forearm blood flow as a physiological measure. *Psychophysiology*, 8:509-524.

MILLER, M. P., MURPHY, P. J., and MILLER, T. P. 1978. A comparison of electromyographic feedback and progressive relaxation training in treating circumscribed anxiety stress reactions. *J. Consult. Clin. Psychol.*, 46:1291-1298.

MILLS, G. K., and SOLYOM, L. 1974. Biofeedback of EEG alpha in the treatment of obsessive ruminations: An exploration. *J. Behav. Ther. Exper. Psychiatry*, 5:37-41.

NUNES, J. S., and MARKS, I. M. 1975. Feedback of true heart rate during exposure in vivo. *Arch. Gen. Psychiatry*, 32:933-936.

NUNES, J. S., and MARKS, I. M. 1976. Feedback of true heart rate during exposure in vivo: Partial replication with methodological improvement. *Arch. Gen. Psychiatry*, 33:1346-1350.

ORNE, M. T. 1979. The efficacy of biofeedback therapy. *Ann. Rev. Med.*, 30:489-503.

PLOTKIN, W. B. in press. The placebo effect, self-healing, and biofeedback: The role of faith in therapy. *Am. Psychol.*

PRIGATANO, G. P., and JOHNSON, H. J. 1972. Biofeedback control of heart rate variability to phobic stimuli: A new approach to treating spider phobia. In *Proceedings, Annual Convention, American Psychological Assn.*, pp. 403-404.

RASKIN, M., BALI, L. R., and PEEKE, H. V. 1980. Muscle biofeedback and transcendental meditation. *Arch. Gen. Psychiatry*, 37:83-97.

RASKIN, M., JOHNSON, G., and RONDESTVEDT, J. W. 1973. Chronic anxiety treated by feedback-induced muscle relaxation. *Arch. Gen. Psychiatry*, 28:263-267.

RICE, K. M., and PLOTKIN, W. B. 1980. Biofeedback as a placebo: Anxiety reduction facilitated by training in either suppression or enhancement of alpha brainwaves. Presented to American Psychological Assn., Montreal.

RUPERT, P. A., and HOLMES, D. S. 1978. Effects of multiple sessions of true and placebo heart rate biofeedback training on the heart rates and anxiety levels of anxious patients during and following treatment. *Psychophysiology*, 15:582-590.

SARGENT, J. D., WALTERS, E. D., and GREEN, E. E. 1973. Psychosomatic self-regulation of migraine headaches. *Seminars in Psychiatry*, 5:415-428.

SCHROEDER, D. J., and RUPERT, P. A. in press. Effects of bi-directional heart rate biofeedback training on the heart rates and anxiety levels of anxious psychiatric patients. *Psychophysiology*.

STOYVA, J., and BUDZYNSKI, T. 1974. Cultivated low arousal—An antistress response? In L. V. DiCara (ed.), *Limbic and Autonomic Nervous Systems Research*. New York: Plenum.

STROEBEL, C. F., and GLUECK, B. C. 1973. Biofeedback treatment in medicine and psychiatry: An ultimate placebo? In L. Birk (ed.), *Biofeedback: Behavioral Medicine*. New York: Grune & Stratton.

SURWIT, R. S., and KEEFE, F. J. 1978. Frontalis EMG feedback training: An electronic panacea? *Behavior Therapy*, 9:779-792.

TOWNSEND, R. E., HOUSE, J. F., and ADDARIO, D. 1975. A comparison of biofeedback-mediated relaxation and group therapy in the treatment of chronic anxiety. *Am. J. Psychiatry*, 132:598-601.

IV.
PSYCHOSOMATIC MANIFESTATIONS
OF ANXIETY

11

STRESS, EMOTIONS, AND ILLNESS: A PROBLEM IN BIOPSYCHOSOCIAL MEDICINE

CHASE PATTERSON KIMBALL, M.D.

This paper seeks first to explore and define the concepts of anxiety, stress, and illness as they are used in clinical medicine and research.

Anxiety will be explored by positing the following questions: What is angst, anxiety, fear? What is trait anxiety, state anxiety? To what extent is anxiety stimulus-bound? What is an emotion? Can an emotion be expressed without some sense of or identification of physiologic alteration? Should an emotion be defined as an attitude and its physiologic correlates? What is the relationship of anxiety to conservation-withdrawal, depression, or other emotions or states? What is adaptive and/or maladaptive about anxiety?

Secondly, we will consider the definition of stress. What makes a stress stressful? What is the relationship between stress and strain? Is a stress a stress if there is no observable or recordable response? To what extent is a stress defined by the stress response? What are the external modifiers of a potential stress-stimulus, the environmental adjuvants, facilitators, agents, or vectors? What are the internal modifiers: previous experience; learned, perceptual, cognitive and psychological defenses; conative and genetic markers? Why has stress research focused so exclusively on somatic symptoms and signs as opposed to psychological and social symptoms and signs? What are some of the other criticisms of the stress-illness onset model?

Third, we need to define illness. As behavior, what are its characteristics? How does it relate to dis-ease? Does one kind of deviance correlate with or diminish its manifestation in a somatic as opposed to a psychological and/or social process? What do we mean by psychophysiologic processes? What relationship do these have to psychosomatic processes?

The development of psychosomatic medicine has attempted to interrelate

187

those aspects of behavior described in pathophysiologic, psychological, and social (environmental) terms. Initially, physical behavior was associated (conversion) with hysterical personality. The theory of conversion has been extended to include such processes as pain, and a physiologic mechanism has been postulated. Then came a preoccupation with emotions and physiologic variables. Subsequently, an interest developed in the relationship of personality factors to specific pathophysiologic patterns. This formulation fell into disrepute, but it has recently been resurrected in terms of behavior pattern Type A, infantile personality, Alexithymia, and *la pensée opératoire* (Marty and de'Uzan, 1963). Next, the concept of personality specificity was exchanged for one of conflict specificity and vulnerable organ specificity. This gave rise to the idea of genetic or constitutional markers, biological and/or psychological, that put the individual at risk for subsequent organic pathology. A fourth factor was (re-)introduced into this formula, that of the environment. Great attention has been given to the illness-onset situation and the relationship of illness to the environmental factors proximal to the onset. Other investigators have focused on reactions to illness, viewing illness itself as stressful for the individual. This has come to include addressing the environments of illness and the procedures and processes occurring within these.

More recent developments in psychophysiologic and biochemical research have suggested that autonomic learning occurs and can be taught. Symptoms and perhaps their associated signs may be learned through mechanisms identified in classic conditioning terms. As the environments of illness were explored, tacit rules governing patient and professional behavior were noted. The idea of the sick role was developed (Kasl and Cobb, 1966a and b). The patient progressed through stages of illness with different behaviors expected at each stage. In the acute stage, anxiety, sadness, and delirium were noted. During the convalescent stage, conservation-withdrawal and grieving are frequently noted. A later stage, rehabilitation, is seen as one in which active tasks of coping and adaptation occur.

These ideas and investigations have led us not only to consider etiological and causal relationships, but also to seek out points and methods of intervention, using several therapeutic approaches simultaneously.

As a technologic society, we are preoccupied with the idea of stress. I suppose that our elders in the present or the past would be much amused at this preoccupation. I can recall my grandfather in the year of his death at age 97 saying with vigor and optimism, "Don't give me the good old days. There was nothing good about them. Everything was work, work, work. Why, just harnessing the horses and hooking up the carriages to go to work was hard work." Perhaps, to be able to discuss such things as stress requires both the luxury of freedom from manual labor and time for such concern.

ANXIETY

The latter years of the previous century saw the birth of Freudian developmental psychology and its identification of the German term *angst* (usually interpreted as anxiety) as being a primordial feeling under which we are all conceived, born, and live. Angst may be seen as a generative phenomenon, without which few would work, play, create. It is also a force that generates activity that would keep angst at least at bay until death brings deliverance and respite. War has frequently replaced the free-floating amorphous angst of our unconscious with objective fear, mobilizing ourselves and our societies into directive forces galvanized around one objective, the overcoming of the enemy. Franklin D. Roosevelt best identified the difference between objectified fear and angst by his fourth freedom, freedom from fear, in the words, "The only fear we have (to fear) is fear itself." After World War II, the Western world fell into a malaise of lost objectives and questioned values. This gave way to anxiety, which was indeed an angst. The period became known as the "Age of Anxiety," and books were written on the meaning of anxiety (May, 1977; Wheelis, 1966) to objectify it, get hold of it, tame it, make it bend to our control. We sought to give its amorphous form a definitive shape so as to confront and overcome it. The songs and literature of the period testify to these attempts. Angst, while basic to Freudian psychology, also became basic to the philosophy and derivative psychology of existentialism articulated so well by Jean Paul Sartre (1947) and Albert Camus (1946). We even have sketchy historical roots of angst going back at least to the Judeo-Christian tradition and the expulsion of Adam from the Garden of Eden. It seems to be a basic human condition, perhaps common to all organisms. For human beings, the artifacts of culture may be seen as structures to overcome basic angst, confrontations with anxiety that arise from smaller bits and pieces of life with which we can indeed learn to cope and frequently overcome. We overcome by looking for certainty, for causes or at least correlations of events and situations that lead to the experience of anxiety. We call these *stresses*, more specifically life stresses. We are preoccupied with identifying these in order to address them, modify them, and overcome them. In these efforts, we are plagued by definitions.

STRESS

Stress gained stature as a major factor in the sociopsychobiology of our time by the careful physiological models of Hans Selye (1976). Selye identified the adrenal cortical response in laboratory animals as a nonspecific response to exogenous and endogenous stressors that make a nonspecific demand for readjustment to a new situation. He called this response the general adaptation syndrome and regarded it as an initial and nonspecific, generalized defense directed at stabilizing the organism in the face of an internal or external assault. As part of the hypothalamic-pituitary-adrenal-cortical axis, this generalized response had repercussions in other parts of the system. Selye further observed that, in addition to this generalized response, there was often a continued response or a continued activation of a part of the response system long after the provoking organism or situation was gone. It was as though a process, once set in motion, became independent of the stimulus and continued autonomously. Was the process kept going because of failure in feedback mechanisms, or the presence of new, functional processes, or encoded stressors in the body similar to the provoking stimuli? The persistence of this stereotyped systemic manifestation, the general adaptation syndrome, led to diseases of adaptation and was explained as an insufficient, excessive, or faulty reaction to stressors—not ascribable to any one pathogen, but to "pathogenic constellations." Included were many diseases that Franz Alexander (1950) had called the psychosomatic diseases: rheumatoid arthritis, hyperthyroidism, neurodermatitis, ulcerative colitis, essential hypertension, peptic ulcer disease, bronchial asthma. It remains for consideration that each of these processes is either exacerbated or ameliorated by cortisone and its derivatives.

For Selye the definition of stress was quite simple. It was the nonspecific response of the body to any demand. It identified stressors as exogenous or endogenous agents, as the initiators of the response in the organism. Included as agents were such conditioning factors as genetic predisposition, age, gender, and exogenous hormones, drugs, nutritional agents. To a large extent, this concept of stress prevails, although others define stress as the stimulus, response, the interaction between, and all intervening factors. Selye's early model was temporally and directly linked to a generalized response, which could be initiated by an indiscriminate number of stressors. While Selye originally gave little acknowledgment to "psychogenic stress," others, such as Mason (1968), postulated an "emotional arousal system." Much of the subsequent stress research has followed these models; however, a number of problems can be raised about them. For example, is emotion or stress a stimulus if it does not produce an identifiable response in one organism, although it usually does in similar organisms?

The Cornell school, founded by Harold Wolff and Stewart Wolf (1960) in the fifties on the basis of social and behavioral theories, emphasized the relationship of life situational factors and the development of symptoms relating to illness and disease. Using ingenious designs for experimental research, they introduced material from previously recorded anamnestic interviews, while a subject was connected to instruments that recorded physiologic responses. The material introduced was taken from life situations which the subject had reported as disturbing. The researchers correlated the introduction of such material with fluctuations in the subject's physiologic variables. In these experiments, they were able to correlate the response of organ systems with events the subject had previously identified as stressful. In addition, they were able to identify more precisely the feeling states and defensive maneuvers (touching on a psychological model) associated with these events. Stress was seen in terms of an internal response associated with an external stimulus. The researchers also demonstrated, however, that a similar response could be elicited by *recall* of a previous stimulus not currently present. Thus, memory (encoded stress) became an important factor. The model suggested that a pattern of stress and response could be explained on the basis of learning theory: that the initial stimulus-response association was a chance occurrence that was subsequently reinforced by spontaneously repeated associations. However, similar situations could also serve as stimuli of the same general response. Such a notion could be called "stimulus contamination" (Table 1).

Holmes and Rahe (1967), coming from the Cornell school, subsequently developed studies which resulted in tables of stress that have come to dominate much of the thinking and research on the relationships of stress and illness. They worked on the basis of what amount of effort individuals thought would be required to readjust to varying projected life events such as the death of a spouse, a promotion, a job loss, marriage. They arranged a scale

Table 1

Model of Learned Stress Response and Modifiers

(Modifiers)

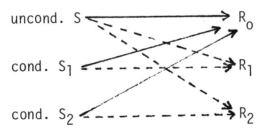

Theory of stimulus contamination
Theory of modifiers, adjuvants, and contingency factors

of 43 items called The Social Readjustment Rating Scale, to which they assigned numerical values called life event units. They followed groups of individuals over six months and two years, recording life events and illnesses, and then correlated these with one another. Results showed that those who accumulated the most life crisis units experienced the most illness. Furthermore, there was a correlation between more severe illness with higher totals of life event units.

The Stress Process

Holmes and Rahe's studies have given rise to stress-illness research and its criticism. Similar scales have been adapted for different cultures and age groups. Among the criticisms are: (a) the correlations are nonspecific because life crisis units and illness accumulate independently with age (which could be controlled for); (b) the association of life events with illness is limited to somatic illness and ignores social and psychological states that may be modifiers of and/or correlates in their own right with life crisis (independent studies for psychiatric illness have been done by Paykel and Uhlenhuth, 1971); (c) life events alone are often not specific enough to be useful in identifying discrete relationships; (d) there may be little relationship between what one would anticipate as a response to a life crisis and what one actually experiences; (e) the researchers most often use cumulative life crises rather than specific life crises in their correlations, increasing the degree of nonspecificity. There is little question that these relationships have some significance. Few of us would argue that serious life situations would not adversely affect our social and interpersonal functioning or that our physical health would not in some way be affected. We are reminded of John Hunter, the famous English cardiologist of the 18th century, who, knowing the status of his own cardiac condition, stated that his life rested in the hands of him who would vex him (Home, 1796). And indeed, this was so. He was vexed exceedingly and roused to anger which he contained, whereupon he died in what was called a cataplectic fit. The issue is the specificity of these relationships. The problem is trying to get each part of the formula into particular enough terms and proximal enough relationships to validate specificity as opposed to global relationships. Obviously, the degrees of vexation, grief, anxiety, or sadness experienced secondary to a catastrophic event will vary from individual to individual and will depend on that person's experience. The modifying factors in this relationship rest more likely in the individual than outside.

Several investigators have identified a three-phase response of alarm, resistance, and depletion, each with its corresponding physiologic relationship. The state of depletion is suggested as relating to psychosomatic diseases, possibly exhaustion. Ursin and colleagues (1978), staying within physiologic definitions, call these the idiographic factors that modify individual coping and adaptation (Table 2). These factors may be explained in terms derived from research in perception, cognition, learning theory, and developmental psychology, involving concepts such as optimal and suboptimal activation, tonic and phasic (chronic) activation, motivation, performance, memory, attention, tolerance, habituation and other terms, many of which allow physiologic identification and measurement. To these may be added genetic makeup, temperament, past experience, defense mechanisms, emotions, perception of control, circadian rhythm arousal, anticipation, and expectancy. Chronic activation results in the loss of physiologic resilience in the autonomic nervous system, an idea relevant to psychosomatic disease.

The question relating to the stress ⟷ illness formulation, then, is one of the individual factor(s): the extent to which these can be discretely identified as facilitating, inhibiting, protecting, ameliorating, putting at risk the individual's response to an environmental situation. When that response is either a hypo-response or an overcompensating one, a hyper-response, the provoking environmental event or situation may be stressful for that individual. When there is no response or an adequate response that does not stress the individual's capacity in untoward or secondary ways, then, at least for that person, the situation is not stressful. Hence, we have returned to the world of individual processes.

To date, much of the value of stress research, such as that of Holmes and Rahe, has been one of sensitization. It has made us aware of these global relationships, focusing our attention on the illness-onset situation and the

Table 2

Modifiers of Stress

Perception and defenses against
               impaired
Cognition   and defenses against
               impaired
Memory
Learning of what is stressful
Learning of coping strategies
Intelligence
Motivation
Role identification
Performance

environmental events that occur proximal to the experience of illness. We have found in our practices that patients who become ill at a time when other catastrophic events have occurred or are occurring in their lives frequently have a subsequent course of illness that is rocky and untoward. Often, we attend patients in the coronary care units who are more preoccupied with a recent separation, death, or loss of job than with this most recent catastrophe of illness. In this setting, our own preoccupation is not with the dilemma of causal relationships, but rather with identifying the source of the preoccupation and attempting to defuse it so that we can work more effectively with the patient's newest problem. Attention to the illness-onset situation has become imperative to our understanding of patients' reactions to illness.

In our efforts to define relationships between stress and illness, we are still left with a clinical analysis of the patient, his or her vulnerability or lack of vulnerability to a potentially stressful environmental event.

Psychological Reactions to Stress

Engel and Schmale (1967), among others, have presented us with such paradigms. They call this the Giving-up–Given-up State (GU²). It is one which frequently follows a catastrophic environmental event, less frequently the anticipation of an imminent one, and even less frequently, the fantasy of one (Tables 3 and 4). The individual responds with an affect of helpless-

Table 3

Models of Stress Anxiety—Illness

A.   General:

Stress ⟶ Psychological State ⟶ Behavior

B.   Engel-Schmale Model:

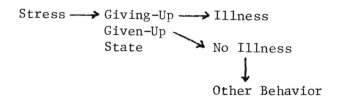

Table 4

Engel and Schmale's Giving-up–Given-up (GU²) State

1. Catastrophic environmental situation
   (real, imminent, fantasied)
2. Sense of inadequacy, inability to cope
3. Affect of helplessness or hopelessness
4. Preoccupation with tragedies of the past
5. Diminished concern regarding the future
6. Withdrawal, inability to act

ness or hopelessness, finding it difficult to move or act without assistance, or, less often, being unable to act even with assistance. The verbal expression of this is: "I can no longer cope; it is all too much; there isn't any use; there is nothing any more that I can do." Such individuals become preoccupied with the past and frequently the tragedies of the past. It is as if all of the unpleasantness of the past returns and is heaped upon them, overwhelming and suffocating them. It is difficult for them to envision a future or a way out. They turn away from others, withdrawing further into themselves, preoccupied with the past. Engel and Schmale view this state as an *in limbo* one, a pivotal one, which puts individuals at risk of and vulnerable to illness. The biology of this phase may coincide with the interphase of resistance and exhaustion. With external help or the girding together of internal resources, individuals may be able to overcome this state, rise up from it, make the necessary internal and external adjustments, thereby climbing out of the abyss, returning to the market place and averting further disaster and illness.

We are left the task of identifying the biology of this state. Are there physiologic correlates to be found in the adrenal-cortical-pituitary axis and/or epinephrine-norepinephrine activity that identify hypo- or hyper-responses, that protect, protect too much or not enough, making the individual vulnerable to infection, a myocardial insult or other disease? It is probable that the GU² state is similar to an avoidance, conservation-withdrawal resistant state associated with an adrenal-cortical pituitary response and its depletion, especially in states clinically requiring cortisone, whereas epinephrine and norepinephrine relate to arousal, the alarm reaction. GU² is a clinically useful concept, an identifiable state. It does occur frequently in the face of catastrophic events. As such, it occurs both before and after illness. Illness itself is a potentially catastrophic event leading to the arousal of feelings initially of anxiety, and subsequently, of despair, hopelessness and helplessness. Recognition of the state leads us to look around both at what preceded illness and what follows it. Without this recognition and subsequent attention we may overlook the critical social and psychological factors circling in the life space of our patient and whose resolution or its failure determine the future course of the patient.

Feelings and Physiologic Reactions

The problem remains of the relationship between the specific feelings induced by stress and illness. This returns us to earlier psychosomatic and psychophysiologic concepts. Earlier in the century, workers in this field sought to identify specific feelings with specific physiologic and hormonal systems. Some workers are still attempting this, although it is fraught with difficulty. Findings that were established were soon challenged; they do not seem to cross over between species or individuals. Walter Cannon (1920) was especially interested in the relationship of epinephrine and norepinephrine to anxiety and other states related to arousal. He was also aware of feedback pathways that attended these states of arousal, attenuating and modifying them. Others, following Selye, were interested in cortisol and its correlation with states of withdrawal, conservation, and possibly depression and susceptibility to infection and other disease. The problem is more complex than this and probably more idiographic and specific for the individual, as Ursin et al. (1978) and Mason (1968) have suggested. Thus far, efforts have not clearly resulted in the correlation of specific hormones, physiologic systems, or even neurotransmitters with specific affects or emotional and behavioral states. Whereas such relationships may indeed be characteristic of an individual, they are less likely to extend to all individuals in a larger group.

Returning to Franz Alexander's (1950) concepts regarding psychosomatic processes, we can review his three criteria for the onset and/or exacerbation of an illness state (Table 5). He gave considerable emphasis to the illness-onset situation, turning attention again to the *milieu externa*, and away from the *milieu interna* of Claude Bernard (1957) and Sigmund Freud (1926).

Table 5

Franz Alexander's Conditions

1. Catastrophic environmental situation (real conflict)
2. Reevokes unconscious unresolved earlier conflict
3. Is manifested through:
    a. most vulnerable organ system
    b. organ system sensitized by earlier conflict

Alexander suggested that what became, and why something was, stressful in the environment depended on the unique psychological experience of the individual and related specifically to a repressed, unresolved trauma (perhaps an encoded stressor) that had occurred at an earlier stage of development. Because of the overwhelming anxiety related to this repressed trauma, an anxiety so great as to be tantamount to annihilating the integrity of the individual, the attempted resolution of the reevoked trauma and its resulting anxiety was through an organ system. The organ system selected for this was the one most vulnerable, the weakest and/or most sensitive one. Garma (1960) and Grinker (1967) suggested that this was the organ system that was in the process of most active development at the time of the original trauma. Thus, anxiety and other emotions, their feeling and expression, have no specific hold on any one organ system but may be manifested by and through one or more organ systems depending on experience, learning, conditioning, genetics, and other factors.

The work of Waggoner Bridger (1962) suggests that individuals are born with one organ system more responsive to a nonspecific stimulus than another organ system. Using a bell stimulus shortly after birth, he recorded responses in heart beat, respiration, and gastrointestinal motility. A neonate responded with an increase or decrease in the activity of one system, not the others. When repeated over time, the initial organ system of response and the direction of response remained the same. One might question as to whether he was eliciting a Pavlovian conditioning response or not. One wonders whether this organ system of response was the product of *in utero* sensitizing and became the organ system of wear and tear and the eventual organ system of disease for that individual.

These and other works have led to the idea of biological markers that identify factors that put an individual at risk for one illness as opposed to another. Herbert Weiner addressed this subject in *Psychobiology and Human Disease* (1977), the penultimate outgrowth so far of his earlier study of pepsinogen and peptic ulcer disease. He emphasizes that the marker is but one variable, albeit a necessary one, that presumably depends for expression on other specific social and psychological variables' coming together at a specific time and place. Following Johns Hopkins medical students over a period of 40 years, C. B. Thomas (Thomas and Greenstreet, 1973) identified biological and psychological markers which correlate with subsequent illness. David Graham and colleagues (1962) identified what might be called "verbal markers" that correlated with an individual's somatic complaints and disease. They noted that patients who complained that others were "a pain in the neck," "made them sick," "got under their skin" came to suffer and/or suffered from arthritis, peptic ulcers, and neurodermatitis, respectively. Gottschalk and Gleser (1969) identified speech patterns that correlate with emotions and behavioral patterns.

Other states may be seen as containing anxiety and other affects. The grief state, following a major loss, contains elements of anxiety and anger, as well as sadness (Engel, 1961). This is also a state that puts the individual at risk and may go through the triphasic sequence identified earlier. Whether or not illness follows depends again on the person and his or her internal and external resources for coping. We might hypothesize hyper- or hypo-activity states as transient, altering internal processes which, if prolonged or un-modulated, place the individual at risk for transient pathophysiological and more enduring pathoanatomic processes.

It would seem that there is not a single biological factor in the formation of psychosomatic illness. Rather, there are variable phases of reactivity, not necessarily always in the same sequence, each with its biological process. The multiple social, psychological, and biological determinants coalesce, in time and place, to result in a somatic expression which may be called psychosomatic disease. The latter may be conceptualized as the channeling and processing of the expression of psychosocial events, by a persistence of autonomic nervous system activity, through the vulnerable organ system. Depending on the stage of the psychosomatic illness, one may identify the following phases: arousal—a tonic response—alarm (epinephrine, norepinephrine); resistance—a phasic or chronic response—resistance (hypothalamic-pituitary-adrenal cortical); depletion—loss of physiologic resilience in the autonomic nervous system.

CLINICAL APPROACHES TO STATES OF RISK

The single most important factor in interceding in life crisis situations that place individuals at risk is their identification. This is accomplished by an extended therapeutic interview which addresses not only the symptom but the patient who has the symptom (Kimball, 1969). It is as important to know something about who the patient is, where he or she is in terms of life phase and situation, what has been going on in life in proximity to experiencing the symptom, and how he or she has been coping with events, as it is to find out the what, where, when, why, and how of the symptom. If we give the patient enough time to give us his or her feelings about these events and what he or she is currently trying to do to cope with them, we will have a better idea of how we, as physicians or other health professionals, might help the patient. If we know a little bit more about what kind of person he or she is, how he or she has coped in the past, his or her usual approaches to life, we will know a bit more about how to help the patient (and ourselves) to anticipate his or her response in the present situation. Is the patient likely to overreact, to minimize the crisis and its consequences, to deny and ignore, to exaggerate and protest? To what extent are these helpful in maintaining an equilibrium? What facilitates and what gets in the way of optimal adjustment? What are the available family and social resources? To what extent are the patient's symptoms and signs related to states of acute or chronic anxiety or depression? To what extent are they related to attempts to defend against these affective states? What are the patient's familial and individual biological markers? An interview process in which we listen, explore, and hear helps us to identify relationships between vulnerability factors, stresses, emotional and defensive reactions, and symptoms and signs.

The evaluation of the patient through the therapeutic interview identifies not only the individual's complaint in the here-and-now, the life setting and situations in which it has developed, but also the past somatic and psychosocial history of the patient and his or her family. This can be obtained best not in a mechanical or perfunctory manner, but when the information comes through the natural flow of an interview which moves back and forth at the patient's lead. Frequent, short summaries at salient points during the interview can help the physician and the patient encapsulate and order events into a chronology. In this way, the physician may put together in his or her mind a life chart for the individual (Table 6), beginning with the genetic history and following through with significant epigenetic events of biological and psychosocial development, past illnesses, the present illness-onset situation, and the phases of illness, acute, convalescent, and rehabilitative. Sometime during this examination, the physician needs to evaluate the patient's mental status, formally or informally, in terms of the specific cognitive functions of orientation, memory, attention, and judgment-abstraction (Table 7), which are also measures of arousal. These aspects of examination are overlooked as often as the deficits are present.

The interview conducted in this fashion is essentially the major vehicle of the therapeutic relationship and of therapy (Table 8). It allows the individual to put into words what is bothering him or her, thereby giving concrete objectification to the complaint. The complaint becomes an object, somewhat apart from the patient, that can be gotten hold of by both patient and physician. Something can be done with it. It can be looked at, turned upside down, looked at again, turned sideways, looked at again, and so on. The therapeutic interview gives the patient an opportunity to express his or her feelings about the pain, through words and nonverbal behavior. The physician assists in structuring and ordering the patient's report of the complaint, its onset in relationship to other events, what the patient has done about it so far, and, most of all, what meaning its presence has for the patient here

Table 6

The Stages of Illness

Genetic	Developmental	Pre-illness Situation	Illness Onset	Acute (ICU)	Convalescent	Rehabilitative
Family history Aroused patterns (Precursors of disease)	Personality Behavior patterns (Associates of disease)	Stresses and strains (Immediate correlates)	Experience of symptoms Response to symptoms	Anxiety Sadness Delirium	Grief Restitutive	Adaptation and coping

Pre-Illness

Hospital

Altered Organism

Table 7

Assessment of Cognitive Status

Orientation
Attention/concentration
Memory
Abstraction/Judgment
Affective Lability
Motor Agitation/Retardation

Table 8

Therapeutic Aspects of the Interview

1. Objectification of problem
2. Ventilation of feelings
3. Clarification
4. Binding with helping individual
   (contract)
5. Structure/ordering
6. Matching relationships
7. Interpretation
8. Education
9. Abreaction (coming together)

and now. During the interview, the physician and the patient get to size each other up as individuals, to develop feelings about one another that facilitate or impede the communication. Acknowledgment of this relationship is implicitly important and sometimes requires explicit attention. Education is an important aspect of the communication. The physician is the teacher helping the patient understand the nature of his or her complaint, making it rational, objective, something that can be "gotten ahold of" and, consequently, tackled and alleviated. Thus the interview serves to objectify, clarify, structure, support, facilitate verbal and nonverbal expression, teach, and reassure the patient.

As the affects consequent to illness or the illness-onset situation are identified, they will need to be brought out and objectified more vigorously. How much anxiety, how much anger, how much depression? Are these such significant aspects of the complaint to deserve attention in their own right? Is the complaint secondary to an acute anxiety or depressive reaction? Is the anger a manifestation of a more serious depression? Does the affective disorder deserve further investigation in its own right? If so, what modalities of treatment—pharmacological, behavioral, group, family—will best address it, in addition to the psychotherapeutic process that has begun? In conclusion, I suggest that there is still room for the single case study as its own control as a model for correlating physiologic factors with social, psychological, and behavioral events (Garrick, 1981).

REFERENCES

ALEXANDER, F. 1950. *Psychosomatic Medicine.* New York: W. W. Norton.
BERNARD, C. 1957. *Introduction to the Study of Experimental Medicine.* New York: Dover Press.
BRIDGER, W. H. 1962. Sensory discrimination and autonomic function in the newborn. *J. Am. Acad. Child Psychiatry,* 1:67-82.
CAMUS, A. 1946. *Stranger.* New York: Knopf.
CANNON, W. B. 1920. *Bodily Changes in Pain, Hunger, Fear and Rage.* New York: Appleton.
ENGEL, G. L. 1961. Is grief a disease? A challenge for medical research. *Psychosom. Med.,* 23:18-22.
ENGEL, G. L., and SCHMALE, A. 1967. Psychoanalytic theory of somatic disorder: Conversion, specificity and the disease-onset situation. *J. Am. Psychoanal. Assoc.,* 15:344.
FREUD, S. 1926. Inhibition, symptoms and anxiety. In *The Standard Edition of the Complete Psychological Works of Sigmund Freud,* vol. 20, pp. 77-174. London: Hogarth Press, 1959.
GARMA, A. 1960. The unconscious images in the genesis of peptic ulcer. *Int. J. Psychoanal.,* 41:444.
GARRICK, T. R. 1981. Behavioral therapy for irritable bowel syndrome: A case report. *Gen. Hosp. Psychiatry,* 3:48-51.
GOTTSCHALK, L. A., and GLESER, G. C. 1969. *The Measurement of Psychological States Through the Content Analysis of Verbal Behavior.* Berkeley: University of California Press.
GRAHAM, D. T., LUNDY, R. M., and BENJAMIN, L. S. 1962. Specific attitudes in initial interviews with patients having different psychosomatic diseases. *Psychosom. Med.,* 24:257-266.
GRINKER, R. R. (ed.) 1967. *Toward a Unified Theory of Human Behavior: An Introduction to General Systems Theory,* 2nd Ed. New York: Basic Books.
HOLMES, T. H., and RAHE, R. H. 1967. The social readjustment rating scale. *J. Psychosom. Res.,* 11:213-218.
HOME, E. 1796. John Hunter's treatise on the blood inflammation and gun-shot wounds. In *Life of John Hunter.* Philadelphia: Bradford.
KASL, S. V., and COBB, S. 1966a. Health behavior, illness behavior, and sick role behavior. I. Health and illness behavior. *Arch. Environ. Health,* 12:246-266.
KASL, S. V., and COBB, S. 1966b. II. Sick role behavior. *Arch. Environ. Health,* 12:531-542.
KIMBALL, C. P. 1969. Techniques of interviewing. I. Interviewing and the meaning of the symptom. *Ann. Int. Med.,* 71:147-153.
MARTY, P., and DE'UZAN, M. 1963. La "pensée opératoire." *Rev. Franc. Psychoanal.,* vol. 27, suppl. 1345.
MASON, J. W. 1968. The scope of psychoendocrine research. *Psychosom. Med.,* 30(5, part 2):565-575.
MAY, R. 1977. *The Meaning of Anxiety.* New York: W. W. Norton.
PAYKEL, E. S., and UHLENHUTH, E. 1971. Scaling of life events. *Arch. Gen. Psychiatry,* 25:340-347.
SARTRE, J. P. 1947. *Existentialism and Human Emotions.* New York: Citadel Press.
SELYE, H. 1976. *Stress in Health and Disease.* Boston: Butterworths.
THOMAS, C. B., and GREENSTREET, R. L. 1973. Psychological characteristics in youth as predictors of five disease states: suicide, mental illness, hypertension, coronary heart disease, and tumor. *Journal of Johns Hopkins Medical School,* 132:16-43.

URSIN, H., BOADE, E., and LEVINE, S. 1978. *Psychobiology of Stress: A Study of Coping Man.* New York: Academic Press.

WEINER, H. 1977. *Psychobiology and Human Disease.* New York: Elsevier/North-Holland.

WHEELIS, A. 1966. *Quest for Identity.* New York: Harper & Row.

WOLFF, H., and WOLF, S. 1960. Stressors as a cause of disease in man. In J. M. Tanner (ed.), *Stress and Psychiatric Disorder*, vol. 2, pp. 17-31. Oxford: Blackwell.

12

PSYCHOBIOLOGY OF ESSENTIAL HYPERTENSION

HERBERT WEINER, M.D.

Of all the ills that afflict humankind in our part of the globe, none is commoner, more prevalent, or paradigmatic than essential hypertension (EH). It is the scourge of 40 percent of the U.S. population over the age of 60 years. It is particularly common in black citizens; this fact alone suggests that EH is a mirror held up to our society. EH also reflects the poverty of our usual models of disease. As Ader (1980) stated in a memorable address, there may be alternative views of disease to Koch's postulates. To quote Ader:

> One simple, universal observation underlies psychosomatic research. It is that when a population is exposed to the same environmental pathogens only some individuals manifest disease (p. 307).

Koch enunciated his postulates clearly after overwhelming the host by massive challenges. Individual differences seemed not to matter to him: He simply proved a point. Cataclysmic events—fighting in Stalingrad (Miasnikov, 1961) or in the North African desert (Graham, 1945)—do indeed produce high blood pressure (BP) in *some*, but not all, persons. One cannot recover a pathogen from the unfortunate people exposed to such an extreme situation, however; one can only learn about its effects.

ENVIRONMENTAL FACTORS IN ESSENTIAL HYPERTENSION

Fortunately, many of us have never been exposed to such extreme situations, but some of our fellow citizens have been. Harburg and his co-workers (1973) have demonstrated that poor, black Americans living in crowded conditions, exposed to crime and violence and police brutality, and subjected to social and marital disruption suffer higher blood pressure levels than do middle-class black or white persons. Deeply resentful of their oppressive living conditions, they feel that they must keep a rein on expressing their resentment. In these studies multiple social (environmental) factors played a role in raising blood pressure levels. D'Atri and Ostfeld (1975) reported that prisoners forced to live in crowded—not single—cells had higher blood pressure levels.

When a society is stable, when its customs, traditions, and institutions are well-established and well-structured and its members respond to a predictable sociocultural environment with integrated patterns of psychological adaptation, blood pressure levels do not become elevated with age. Those who live in a social milieu that is rapidly changing, is unpredictable, dangerous, or unfamiliar—so that psychological adaptation to it is difficult or impossible—tend to develop increasing blood pressure levels with age. Not everyone who lives in such a social milieu develops high blood pressure levels or EH—probably only the predisposed do (Henry and Cassel, 1969).

Cultural change or social chaos may impose adaptive psychological burdens that become intolerable if they also disrupt a person's habitual patterns of coping. Patterns of coping are usually established in childhood; if successful, they become habitual. If changing conditions make them no longer effective, especially during early middle life, blood pressure levels may rise. Studies have indicated that participants in rapid social change and migrants to an urban environment or to another culture are likely to develop high blood pressure levels (Cruz-Coke, 1960; Stamler et al., 1967; Syme et al., 1964). New roles that have to be assumed in a new setting may be stressful (Scotch, 1961). A change in social or professional status may impose strains on psychological adaptation (Christenson and Hinkle, 1961) and elevations in blood pressure have been found in men after they lost their jobs (Kasl and Cobb, 1970). However, not all persons develop EH (even after their blood pressure levels have risen) in new settings or after job loss; additional factors must play a pathogenetic role. Not everyone meets and overcomes the challenge of change, migration, a new job, or new relationships in a different setting, in the same way.

We do not know why some do and some do not develop EH in new settings or when exposed to social disruption; all the risk factors in EH have not been explicated. Yet we know that there is a genetic tendency to EH that accounts for about 30 percent of the etiological variance. Additionally, obesity, a high salt intake, and other dietary factors play an etiological role (for reviews see Genest et al., 1978; Weiner, 1977, 1979). Since oral contraceptive pills produce elevations of blood pressure only in women with a family history of high blood pressure (Shapiro, 1973), they presumably elicit a genetically determined tendency to high blood pressure.

We do not know how the risk factors manifest themselves physiologically—for example, as an increased vascular reactivity to many stimuli (Doyle and Fraser, 1961; Sokolow and Harris, 1961), or as an increased heart rate at rest (Gorlin, 1962). Therefore, we cannot do predictive studies to test many of the hypotheses about the etiology or pathogenesis of EH. Furthermore, it is increasingly clear that EH is not a uniform disease entity —several different subforms have been identified (Julius and Esler, 1975; Rose and Levin, 1979; Weiner, 1977, 1979), and different risk factors may be associated with the various subforms of the disease.

Studies of the psychosocial onset conditions of essential hypertension—unless some dramatic event occurs, like an explosion (Ruskin et al., 1948), or persons are exposed to noise (Simonson and Brozek, 1959), or engaged in such occupations as controlling air traffic (Cobb and Rose, 1973)—are fraught with the insuperable problem that the onset of EH is not usually associated with any symptoms. All studies of the context in which blood pressure levels rise must therefore be retrospective.

Onset Conditions of Essential Hypertension and Its Exacerbations

Although not every hypertensive patient is exposed to extreme situations, for the reasons just stated there have been few studies of the usual (everyday) settings in which EH begins. Observational studies have been carried out, however, with the avowed purpose of uncovering the conditions that alter its course. These observations have not identified any specific feature of the human environment with which the onset or course of EH can be associated. It is presumed, therefore, that some property or feature of the hypertensive person, and how that person responds psychophysiologically to environmental events, is responsible for the onset or exacerbation of the hypertensive process.

Psychological Features of Hypertensive Persons

The onset of hypertension may occur in the course of everyday events and situations. Similar events may also suddenly alter the course of EH, so that the disease changes from its benign to its malignant form. Weiss (1942) found that it begins in stressful situations. Fischer (1961) reported that its onset could be correlated in time with the anniversary of an important relative's death. The personal relationship of the patient to the dead relative was "primitive," close, dependent, and ambivalent.

Such formulations about the personal relationship of patients appear and reappear in the psychosomatic literature, not only with respect to patients with hypertension but also with respect to persons who have other diseases or no diseases at all. Despite the absence of apparent specificity of these life events for hypertension, they play a "necessary," if not "sufficient," role in the onset of EH. Other predisposing factors, including genetic ones, may play additional roles. However, these assertions need be verified with much greater rigor and validated with more than one patient. Reiser and co-workers (1950, 1951a) did so. They found that in 40 of 80 patients significant and palpable life events could be identified that preceded or corresponded in time with the known onset of EH. Because of the patients' psychological make-up, the events had particular meanings for the patients.

The psychosocial factors that modify the course of the disease were studied by Reiser et al. (1951b). The onset of the malignant phase of primary and secondary hypertension in 12 patients, in whom the disease had previously had a benign course, was precipitated by interpersonal conflicts about dependency and hostility expressed in sadomasochistic fears. Moreover, these conflicts were very much like those with which the onset of the disease had been correlated. In 76 percent of the patients studied by Chambers and Reiser (1953), the occurrence of cardiac failure in patients with limited cardiac reserve was correlated with events that were emotionally significant to the individual patient. Two classes of interpersonal events were identified: those leading to feelings of frustration and rage and those leading to a feeling of rejection in which the threat of loss of security predominated.

The course of the disease may be modified by the ministrations of a benign and supportive physician combined with the use of drugs (Shapiro and Teng, 1957; Shapiro et al., 1954) or by a thoughtful physician on whom the patient can depend (Moses et al., 1956; Reiser et al., 1951a; Weiss and English, 1957).

Psychological studies of patients after the onset of EH have the implied purpose of uncovering those features of the personality that may play a role in the etiology, pathogenesis, or maintenance of the disease. Since it has not been established that features of the personality studied after disease onset play an etiological or pathogenetic role in EH (Glock and Lennard, 1957), the logic of this implied research goal is open to question. To circumvent this problem, a more careful assertion should be made: Personality factors that characterize hypertensive patients covary with elevated blood pressure levels. Indeed they may; for in the absence of established fact, the hypothesis could be put forward that both the personality features and the elevated blood pressure levels are but the expression of a third variable—for instance, a genetic one or the effect on the brain of some pathophysiological disturbance, such as raised angiotensin levels.

Earlier studies, usually of male hypertensive patients, tended to focus on the patients' psychological conflicts. The researchers concluded that patients with EH had lifelong conflicts about the expression of hostility, aggression, resentment, rage, rebellion, ambition, or dependency (Alexander, 1939, 1950; Alexander et al., 1968; Ayman, 1933; Barach, 1928; Binger et al., 1945; Dunbar, 1943; Hambling, 1951, 1952; Harris et al., 1953; Hill, 1935; Miller, 1939; Moschowitz, 1919; Moses et al., 1956; O'Hare, 1920; Palmer, 1950; Saslow et al., 1950; Saul, 1939; Thomas, 1964; van der Valk, 1957; Weiss, 1942). They defended themselves against the emergence of these impulses by various traits such as compliance and submissiveness, outer friendliness or self-control (Alexander, 1939; Saul, 1939). Other patients were perfectionistic or had difficulties with those in authority, especially if they rebelled against them (Saslow et al., 1950). The conflicts in some of these patients made them anxious; other patients were depressed.

Binger et al. (1945) agreed that male hypertensive patients were angry but stressed that these patients lacked the psychological capacity adequately to integrate, handle, or resolve their conflicts about aggression. Patients were made insecure because they could not be certain that they could handle their anger, external danger, or the fear of separation. Fifty percent of their subjects were sensitized to separation by previous life experiences. In fact, 23 of 24 subjects developed hypertension in a setting of actual or threatened bereavement.

The relationships of some hypertensive women to other people were often hostile, combative, and "abrasive." The hypertensive women were less attractive physically. They could not accept and were resentful of their feminine role. They were careful not to express their angry feelings. They bore secret grudges longer than others. Their marriages were frequently unhappy. Their capacity to be anything but truculent was limited (Harris and Singer, 1968). These women did not adapt well in new social environments. Their truculence only made it more difficult for them to gain the help and support of others in new settings or when social change occurred. When exposed to danger they fought; when divorced they savored their misfortune.

Many studies, including cross-cultural ones, have confirmed the fact that many male hypertensive patients, sometime in the course of the syndrome, are overtly less assertive, or submissive, to other persons while being covertly angry (Esler et al., 1977; Harburg et al., 1964; Julius, 1964; Safar et al., 1978). It may be, however, that this combination of personal characteristics occurs in some but not all hypertensive patients. Nonetheless, it is of some interest that Torgersen and Kringlen (1971) studied the blood pressure levels of 48 adult monozygotic (Mz) twins. They found that the more obedient, quiet, reserved, submissive, insecure, depressed, and withdrawn member of each pair of twins had higher systolic blood pressure levels than the other. The systolic blood pressure levels in some instances ranged from 97 to 227 mm Hg.

The submissiveness of (some) hypertensive patients seems to protect them against their latent hostility, which may, however, have additional and variable personal effects. Wolf and Wolff (1951) and their associates (Wolf et al., 1948, 1955; Wolff, 1953) studied 103 hypertensive patients and concluded that their latent hostility alerted and prepared them to take offensive action against other people. In contrast with members of a hospital staff, normotensive patients, and patients who suffered from bronchial asthma and vasomotor rhinitis, many of the hypertensive patients preferred offensive action to thoughtful reflection. They were tense, suspicious, and wary. Others tried to please and placate those that they feared, rather than take offensive action against them. Hypertensive patients who were prepared to fight were often outwardly calm, easygoing, and restrained.

It is remarkable how consistent the clinical descriptions of hypertensive patients have been. Nonetheless, they should be verified by psychological tests, such as those done by Saslow and his co-workers (1950). They confirmed the fact that hypertensive patients had certain traits: They were less overtly assertive and manifested compulsive character traits more often than normotensive patients who had personality disorders. Wolf and Wolff's studies emphasized that the latent hostility of hypertensive patients was directed at other people, but it was hidden from them by various traits. Thaler and her co-workers (1957) and Weiner and his (1962) attempted to specify the nature of the hypertensive patient's interpersonal relationships by studying how these patients perceive and interact with their physicians. The implicit aim of these studies was to identify how hypertensive patients perceive other people and how that perception affects their relationships to them. These studies made no explicit or implicit assumption that the patient's perception of or relationships with others had etiologic or pathogenetic significance for the disease. They found that hypertensive subjects perceive other people as dangerous, derisive, and untrustworthy. Because of this perception, patients attempt to maintain a distant relationship. Paradoxically, they provoke others and are alert to anger and hostility—the very reactions they most fear. When hypertensive patients successively maintained their distance and avoided relationships, the blood pressure levels remained unchanged, but when this habitual defensive style failed, critical elevations of blood pressure occurred.

This interpersonal style—the manner with which hypertensive subjects defend against personal involvements—was also described by Grace and Graham (1952), who verified their findings in a later study (Graham et al., 1962). The characteristic attitude of hypertensive patients consists of an "awareness of threat of bodily harm, without any possibility of running away or fighting back." Implicit in this description was an inhibited desire to fight danger.

The observations of Thaler and co-workers (1957) were put to the test by Sapira and co-workers (1971) by a different method: 19 hypertensive and 15 normotensive patients were shown two movies; one depicted a rude and disinterested physician, the other a physician who was at ease and related with patients in a warm and kindly manner. The hypertensive patients had significantly greater blood pressure and heart rate responses while viewing the two films and during a later interview, and they denied perceiving any differences between the actions and attitudes of the two physicians. The normotensive group could tell the difference in the behavior of the two physicians. The interviewer evoked greater blood pressure response in hypertensive patients when he played the roles of the physician in the movies than when he did not. The authors postulate that the hypertensive patients "screen out" the perception of the differences between the "good" and "bad" doctor (while still showing exaggerated blood pressure responses) in order to defend against their cardiovascular hyperreactivity. The patients in this study did not recognize the difference between a "good" and "bad" doctor because to admit that they saw one would be tantamount to seeing the other.

These psychological traits and psychological states appear to occur in some, but not in all, hypertensive patients. There is psychological heterogeneity. On the other hand, a relationship exists between emotionality, excessive vascular hyperreactivity, and blood pressure variability in patients with essential and renovascular hypertension.

All these studies are correlative and, therefore, their interpretation is suspect. Yet, Thomas (1957, 1958, 1961, 1964, 1967) and her co-workers (Bruce and Thomas, 1953; Thomas et al., 1964; Thomas and Ross, 1963) have carried out a prospective study. They administered psychological tests to 1,200 medical students and their parents in 1953. By 1967, 400 parents had died. Of these, 100 had died of the complications of hypertensive or coronary artery disease. No striking definitive psychological differences were found between the offspring of parents who died of hypertensive heart diseases and the offspring of parents dead of other diseases or those still alive and well. The children of hypertensive parents, however, tended to be more aggressive and hostile and to feel more inadequate. They had compulsive character traits. Although no great differences were uncovered between the offspring of hypertensive parents and the offspring of those who were not hypertensive, these studies tend to confirm the observations obtained by retrospective studies.

Taken together the studies reviewed above allow one to conclude that many hypertensive patients harbor strong feelings of resentment and anger that are either covered over by submissiveness to others and nonassertiveness, or by a tendency to avoid relationships and confrontations; at other times their feelings are expressed explosively. Also, many hypertensive patients are vigilant and particularly prone to detect disinterest and hostility in others, or to euphemize this very perception. Many hypertensive patients are also physiologically hyperreactive to a large variety of stimuli: They respond by larger and more persistent increases in blood pressure.

These data suggested to Shapiro (1979) that the inhibition of anger and the avoidance of confrontation is the hypertensive patient's attempt to maintain stable blood pressure levels or to lower them. However, caution must be exercised before arriving at any firm conclusions because these personality traits may occur only in some forms of EH, or may be evident only at certain stages of the syndrome. Finally, the correlation between these traits and high blood pressure cannot as yet be regarded as a causal one: These traits may or may not antecede EH. Both might be a product of some other process, such as an altered state of the brain.

Psychophysiological Properties of Hypertensive Persons

In an attempt to verify the hypotheses that patients with hypertension are distinct from normotensive persons, a wide variety of techniques have been employed to correlate their blood pressure levels with their personal characteristics, or to mobilize blood pressure responses under laboratory conditions or in everyday (naturalistic) settings. In general, the results of these studies demonstrate that hypertensive patients have brisker and longer-lasting blood pressure responses to a variety of inciting measures than do their normotensive peers.

The most sophisticated study to date related the psychological features of patients to various measures of their circulation. By the use of the proper controls, hypertensive patients were found to be more emotional, tense, unstable, excitable, guilt-ridden, timid, insecure, and sexually inhibited than normotensive patients. They were deferential to others and abased themselves. The more deferential they were, the greater their peripheral resistance and resting blood pressure levels. The more they abased themselves, the higher the resting blood pressure levels. The more they were emotionally stimulated, the greater were the changes in diastolic and systolic blood pressure levels. Those hypertensive patients who expressed interest in members of the opposite sex had high heart rates and diastolic blood pressure levels. The more anxious and tense they were, the higher the basal peripheral resistance, and the more it increased on stimulation (Pilowsky et al., 1973).

Because of the repeated clinical observation that patients with EH harbor strong feelings of anger, there have been attempts to correlate anger with cardiovascular responses (Moses et al., 1956; Schachter, 1957) and to contrast these responses to those obtained when fear, pain, or anxiety are elicited. Studies have produced pain by immersion of the patient's hand in ice water at 3° C for one minute, anger by insulting and abusing the subject, and fear by a mild electric shock (Ax, 1953). In the hypertensive patients greater increments in blood pressure occurred in these three situations (Schachter, 1957). In both the pain and anger conditions, diastolic blood pressure rose significantly because of an increased peripheral resistance, whereas fear produced increases in systolic blood pressure as the cardiac output increased. In Schachter's experiment, the situation designed to produce pain is also conducive to vasoconstriction; immersion of a limb in ice water has often been used to measure blood pressure reactivity in normal and hypertensive subjects. Therefore, the effects of mild pain and vasoconstriction are confounded in this experiment. Pain and other feelings interact with vasoconstriction; blood pressure reactivity is greater if the cold-immersion test is given to anxious patients (White and Gildea, 1937). The blood pressure reactivity also is greater in neurotic (Malmo and Shagass, 1952) and angry patients than in calm ones (Cranston et al., 1949). Heart rate and blood pressure changes have been used to infer (Schachter, 1957) or measure the associated humoral changes that correlate with specific affects. When aggression and active emotional states are elicited in subjects, norepinephrine secretion occurs, whereas, when anger is handled intrapunitively, urinary epinephrine levels are increased in normal subjects (Cohen et al., 1957; Cohen and Silverman, 1959; Elmadjian et al., 1957).

The relationship between the blood pressure, catecholamine excretion, and mental stress depends in part on the state and stage of hypertension. Borderline cases or young male hypertensive patients have different cardiovascular dynamics with different catecholamine excretion levels than do patients with well-established hypertension or normals. Nestel (1969) reexamined this problem by studying 17 normotensive subjects and 20 hypertensive patients with a mean resting blood pressure of 147/95 mm Hg. Basal urinary excretion levels of norepinephrine and epinephrine were the same in both groups. The subjects were asked to solve visual puzzles—the Raven's matrix test—for 40 minutes. Much greater increments in systolic (Δ = 35 mm Hg) and diastolic (Δ = 25 mm Hg) blood pressure occurred in the labile hypertensive group than in the normotensive group. The urinary output of norepinephrine and epinephrine rose in all subjects, but the increases were significantly greater in the hypertensive patients, rising in 17 of the 20. By comparison, urinary catecholamine output rose in only seven of the 17 normotensive subjects. Mean postexperimental levels of both catecholamines were also higher in the patient group. The changes in urinary catecholamine levels correlated significantly with changes in blood pressure levels, particularly in the labile hypertensive group. Apparently patients with labile hypertension respond to a complex psychological task by increased sympathetic nervous activity and greater blood pressure responses.

Whether discernible differences in physiological responses occur in different affective states continues to be a moot point (Buss, 1961). Harris and his co-workers (1965) do not believe in such differences. They performed cardiac catheterization and serial blood-chemical studies while intense, life-like fear and anger were induced in their subjects under hypnosis. Similar physiological responses accompanied fear and anger. Fear and angry responses were both associated with a 33 percent increase in cardiac index, with a 50 percent rise in the heart rate, a 20 percent fall in stroke volume, a 10 mm Hg increase in blood pressure, and a 13 percent fall in peripheral resistance. The respiratory rate doubled and six subjects developed a respiratory alkalosis. Mean levels of plasma hydrocortisone and plasma nonesterified fatty acids doubled. A β-adrenergic blocking agent reduced the cardioaccelerator response due to fear but not due to anger. The agent failed to block the increases of cardiac output, plasma hydrocortisone, and free fatty acids. The entire experiment was repeated several weeks later and the results were replicated. Therefore, under hypnosis it is impossible to discriminate between the physiological correlates of fear and anger in normal subjects.

In other experiments, anger produces qualitatively similar but quantitatively greater cardiovascular responses. Hokanson (1961a and b) harassed subjects while they were counting. He found that the more hostile subjects had brisker increases in systolic and diastolic blood pressure. Those who expressed their anger and hostility openly had a great fall in systolic blood pressure when the experiment was over, which suggested, Hokanson argued, that the failure to express these feelings, because of guilt or anxiety, delayed the fall in blood pressure to preexperimental levels. Graham et al. (1960, 1962) hypnotized two groups of normal subjects. A psychological attitude correlated with hives was suggested to one group, and an attitude of unexpressible rage to another group. Significant skin temperature changes occurred when hives were suggested, and increases in diastolic blood pressure when rage was suggested.

Gottschalk and Hambidge (1955) evaluated inhibited or partially expressed hostile verbal content in awake subjects while measuring blood pressure. Using their technique, Kaplan et al. (1960) found that, while hypertensive subjects spoke, their blood pressures rose. In contrast, while normotensive subjects spoke, their blood pressures fell. In hypertensive subjects a significant relationship was found between the intensity of the hostile content of speech and the diastolic blood pressure levels. Psychophysiological studies in normal subjects may be relevant to the etiology of high blood pressure, but they do not prove that anger or hostility specifically raise the blood pressure any more than fear does. Responses to feelings in normal subjects are often different in degree, duration, or kind than in hypertensive subjects. Many studies have been designed to show that psychological stimuli of various kinds in the laboratory do elicit changes in blood pressure in hypertensive subjects, and that these changes are greater or longer-lasting than in normal subjects (Jost et al., 1952).

Wolf and Wolff (1951) interviewed 203 normotensive subjects and 103 subjects with blood pressure levels of 160/95 mm Hg or more. Although the hypertensive subjects were usually affable and friendly to the experimenter, their blood pressure rose more during the interview. It did not do so consistently, however, because different changes in cardiovascular dynamics occurred with different feelings. When the predominant feeling in the interview was restrained hostility or anxiety, the cardiac output did not change, but the peripheral resistance rose. With overt anxiety, the cardiac output increased and the peripheral resistance fell. With feelings of despair and of being overwhelmed, both cardiac output and peripheral resistance fell.

An association between specific feelings and specific changes in the circulation has not always been observed. Changes in blood pressure do occur during interviews, but the changes may have more to do with the speed with which the subject talks than with the feelings he or she expresses. Nonetheless, hypertensive patients differ from normotensive ones—even when they talk with the same speed, their blood pressure responses last longer, even after they fall silent (Innes et al., 1959). Innes also found that some neurotic and some hypertensive patients share a common psychological characteristic that he called "emotional lability" (Davies, 1971).

Whether or not specific emotions produce specific alterations of cardiovascular function has not been settled. Individual response specificity to various stimuli has also been observed in hypertensive patients (Engel and Bickford, 1961); they responded to various stimuli (such as lights, sounds, mental arithmetic, exercise, and the cold-pressor test) by increases in systolic blood pressure and not by other cardiovascular reactions. Their systolic blood pressure responses were greater than in normal subjects and did not depend on the stimulus used. The magnitude of these responses was always greater than in normal subjects. Larger responses are elicited by psychological stimuli as well as such physical stimuli as sounds and immersing the hand in cold water (Reiser et al., 1951a). In some patients, the blood pressure responses to cold lasted for several days.

Pfeiffer and Wolff (1950) used the stress interview to study the renal circulation in 23 hypertensive and 13 normotensive subjects. The renal blood flow fell and the filtration fraction increased in both groups. Presumably, these changes were caused by constriction of the renal glomerular arterioles, and they could be conducive to the release of renin. It may well be that such renal changes in association with psychological stimuli are important in hypertensive subjects, but some additional factors must be involved in the pathogenesis of hypertension, because both groups showed the same changes in renal function. Stressful interviews that had personal significance to hypertensive patients reduced renal blood flow (Wolf et al., 1948) and elicited brisk pressor responses—a rise of 14 mm Hg (Wolf et al., 1955)—and even greater mean blood pressure responses—26.5 mm Hg—in another study (Hardyck and Singer, 1962).

But blood pressure changes in normotensive subjects and hypertensive patients are not only produced by feelings; intellectual tasks and pain also elicit brisk responses. Brod (1960, 1970) and Brod et al. (1959, 1962) used mental arithmetic performed under duress to produce increases in arterial blood pressure, muscle blood flow, splanchnic vasoconstriction, and cardiac output in normotensive and hypertensive subjects. More renal vasoconstriction and less vasodilation in muscle was found in hypertensive subjects. The hemodynamic changes and elevations of blood pressure persisted longer in the hypertensive subjects than in the normotensive group. These results must be evaluated bearing in mind that six of the eight normotensive subjects, but only two of the 10 hypertensive subjects, were women. (Sex differences in cardiovascular reactivity are known to occur.)

With simple painful stimuli, hypertensive and normotensive subjects with a family history of hypertension have more rapid and brisker blood pressure responses than normal subjects have. No significant changes in peripheral resistance occur in hypertensive patients with pain. Subjects with a family history of hypertension increase their cardiac output and, therefore, their blood pressure (Shapiro, 1960a and b). The degree and duration of the blood pressure responses to various stimuli and tasks are greater in hypertensive patients than in normal subjects. This increased responsivity occurs both in essential and renovascular hypertension (Ostfeld and Lebovitz, 1959, 1960). In patients with essential hypertension and renovascular hypertension, anxiety produces similar elevations of blood pressure that last equally long. The similar blood pressure responses in different forms of hypertension have been interpreted to mean that psychological factors play no etiological role in essential hypertension. Alternative interpretations are possible: Anxiety may interact with some mechanism common to both forms of hypertension to raise the blood pressure. Although anxiety may not play an etiological role, it may help to sustain both forms of hypertension by repeatedly raising blood pressure further.

Psychophysiological studies have shown that each person responds physiologically to many different stimuli in his or her own manner; hypertensive persons also have larger blood pressure responses. Subjects in the psychophysiological laboratory also respond psychologically in their own particular ways. In most studies, the experimenter has attempted to provoke a particular feeling in the subject. In more recent studies, instead of provoking feelings, the experimenter or an observer of the experimenter and subject's interaction watched the individual psychological style of the subject. Innes and his colleagues (1959) showed that the speed with which a subject talks is individual and is related to his or her blood pressure responses.

Other experimental observations focused on the style in which the subject and experimenter related to each other, while the blood pressure and other hemodynamic changes were measured. Weiner et al. (1962) found that hypertensive subjects were less reactive physiologically than normotensive ones, because they interacted little with the experimenter. One hypertensive subject, who had previously not responded physiologically, was persuaded against his will to undergo the laboratory procedure a second time. He equated the second experiment with a threat to his life, his distant style crumbled, and a very brisk, long-lasting blood pressure response occurred. These experiments demonstrate that the nature of the experimenter-subject relationship and the effectiveness of a habitual style of relating to the experimenter may be the critical determinants in producing cardiovascular changes in the laboratory. As long as a style "works," no changes occur in normotensive or hypertensive subjects. The detailed findings of this study have been verified (McKegney and Williams, 1967; Williams and McKegney, 1965; Williams et al., 1972). The findings shed some light on the complex interactions between the nature of the subject-experimenter relationship, the manner in and success with which subjects cope with a task and an experimenter, and changes in cardiovascular function.

Hypertensive patients have individual styles of relating to physicians and experimenters in the laboratory. They keep their distance from them and avoid close personal involvements. They eschew relationships because they perceive the physician as hostile, dangerous, coercive, or ungiving. If they cannot avoid the relationship, their blood pressure responses are brisker and more prolonged than those of normotensive patients (Shapiro, 1973; Thaler et al., 1957; Weiner et al., 1962).

Human "coping" and "defensive" styles may be the critical intervening variables between the perception of a psychosocial stimulus, the psychological response (including the emotional one) to that perception, and the individual physiological response to the stimulus. If these styles are successful, little physiological change occurs. If not successful, changes do occur. The changes are greater and last longer in hypertensive patients than in normotensive ones. The specific feelings that a stimulus provokes are not associated with specific physiological changes. Anger does not uniquely raise the blood pressure—other feelings such as fear and pain also do. Rather, each person responds physiologically in his or her own manner to a variety of feelings and stimuli. Hypertensive patients respond with brisker blood pressure increases that last longer to a variety of psychological tasks and feelings, as well as to cold and pain. Their cardiovascular responses are predetermined, individual, and hyperreactive for unknown reasons. Their responses may reflect an intrinsic defect in the regulation of blood pressure that may antedate the disease. Hypertensive patients also have individual psychological responses to the experimenter and laboratory and they cope differently with pain, cold, and cognitive tasks.

Psychophysiological Studies of Blood Pressure in a Naturalistic Setting

Much has been learned about the correlations between psychological and physiological variables from laboratory and conditioning studies. Variations in blood pressure could not be studied over the long term and in everyday settings until a method had been developed that would measure the blood pressure continuously. With this nonintrusive method, it becomes possible to relate changes in blood pressure to daily events and the psychological responses that they elicit. Sokolow and his co-workers (1970) studied 124 hypertensive patients in this manner, finding that marked variations in blood pressure occurred depending on the changing events of the day. One middle-aged student, for example, had a blood pressure of 160/95 mm Hg while anticipating a campus interview, and 100/82 mm Hg while at home talking to her son.

An analysis of the changes in 50 hypertensive patients leads to the conclusion that the highest systolic blood pressure levels and pulse rates occur when patients are alert, anxious, or under pressure. The highest diastolic blood pressure levels occur when the patients are anxious or pressured. Contentment lowers levels. Sokolow and his co-workers (1970) also found that the most anxious, hostile, and depressed patients were most likely to develop hypertensive disease and all its complications. This finding should not be surprising, as these patients also had the highest blood pressure levels.

These studies relating high blood pressure levels to the emotional state of patients should be viewed with caution. Blood pressure levels vary with behavioral as well as emotional states. They are low in sleep and increase markedly on awakening. Acute increases occur with pain or during coitus. Blood pressure levels are not a stable function—they are subject to circadian rhythms upon which pain, excitement, mental work, anxiety, and anger are superimposed.

THE HETEROGENEITY OF BORDERLINE ESSENTIAL HYPERTENSION

There are no established ways of identifying persons at risk for the development of EH. Two strategies have, therefore, been devised in the past few years. The first is to classify hypertensive patients according to physiological patterns that consist of deviations of cardiac output, plasma renin activity (PRA), or plasma volume (Julius and Esler, 1975; Laragh et al., 1972; Tarazi et al., 1970). Yet these pathophysiological patterns may not necessarily indicate differences in the etiology or pathogenesis of EH; they might simply reflect a different state of the disease. High PRA may, for example, occur early, or very late at the end stages of the disease. Nevertheless, elevations of PRA at these stages are believed to come about by different mechanisms. The manner of classifying patients does not, however, prove that different forms of EH exist. The second and the best research strategy available is to study patients very early in the disease process, before (mal)adaptive changes to high blood pressure itself occur. Some of these secondary adaptations consist of a diminution in the sensitivity of the arterial baroreceptors (Korner et al., 1974), an increase in peripheral resistance in response to an increase in cardiac output, structurally increased resistance to regional blood flow (Folkow and Hallbäck, 1977), and changes in cardiac performance (Frohlich et al., 1971).

Other changes in many systems are also found in abiding EH. To mention just two, significant increases in the plasma concentration of aldosterone occur with age in essential hypertension, in contrast to a decline with age of plasma aldosterone levels in normotensive subjects (Genest et al., 1978), and (as mentioned) PRA is markedly increased during the development of the malignant phase of hypertensive disease and renal failure. Complex changes also occur in renal dynamics; these are believed to be the consequence of a subform of the borderline hypertensive state, in which an increased activity of the sympathetic nervous system (and probably diminished parasympathetic activity) occurs. Renal blood flow is reduced by reversible intrarenal vasoconstriction, and increases in circulating norepinephrine and in sympathetic drive both reduce the urinary excretion of sodium and water (Brown et al., 1977; Hollenberg and Adams, 1976). But the rise in BP should cause an increased excretion of sodium and water, which at first does and later does not occur. Therefore, a progressive resetting of the relationship of BP to sodium and water excretion—a regulatory disturbance—is produced. Progressive renal changes ensue to account for the change from borderline labile hypertension to essential hypertension. In short, the BP increases that were initiated elsewhere are maintained by the kidney by a fall in renal blood flow and renin and a rise in total and renal vascular resistance (Brown et al., 1977).

Not all patients with borderline essential hypertension go on to essential hypertension. Groups of patients with borderline hypertension tend to have some increase in cardiac output, increased cardiac contractility and heart rate. Their plasma catecholamine levels are likely to be higher and the urinary excretion of catecholamines is excessive on standing. Tilting the patient upright or the stimulus of the cold pressor test produce exaggerated catecholamine and BP responses. Ganglionic blocking agents produce a fall in BP that closely correlates with a fall in plasma norepinephrine levels (DeChamplain et al., 1976; DeQuattro and Miura, 1973; Engelman et al., 1970; Julius and Esler, 1975; Kuchel, 1977; Lorimer et al., 1971; Louis et al., 1973).

Patients with borderline hypertension differ as a group (but not necessarily as individuals) from normotensive subjects. The patients also differ from each other. Not all patients with borderline hypertension have an elevated cardiac output: In 30 percent the cardiac output is two standard deviations beyond the mean for normal age-matched subjects. In this subgroup of patients, the total peripheral resistance is inappropriately normal at rest (it should be decreased when increased tissue perfusion is brought about by the increased cardiac output). In other patients with borderline hypertension who have normal cardiac output and heart rate, the total peripheral resistance is increased at rest, possibly because of increased alpha-adrenergic vasoconstrictor tone. Blood volume is unevenly distributed in the circulation (mainly in the cardiopulmonary bed) in borderline hypertension, but only in those patients with an increased cardiac output. In about 30 percent of all patients with borderline hypertension, PRA and norepinephrine concentration are elevated (DeQuattro et al., 1975, 1977; Esler et al., 1977). Other patients increase their PRA excessively with postural changes. Yet the increased PRA does not seem to maintain the heightened BP levels through its effect on angiotensin II and aldosterone production. The increased heart rate, cardiac output, and PRA may be reduced to normal levels with propranolol, but the plasma norepinephrine concentration and BP continue to remain elevated. Therefore, the enhanced PRA is believed to be a result of increased sympathetic activity and is not the primary pathogenetic factor in raising the BP (Esler et al., 1977; Julius and Esler, 1975). (The reverse causal sequence is, however, believed to account for the malignant phase of hypertension when high PRA is found.)

Nonetheless, many borderline hypertensive patients have normal and some have low PRA (Esler et al., 1975). Patients whose PRA is normal tend to be those with diminished stroke volume and cardiac index, normal pulse rate, but increased total peripheral resistance. Their plasma norepinephrine concentration is higher than normal but lower than in borderline hypertensive patients with high PRA. The increased peripheral resistance and BP in patients with borderline hypertension and low or normal PRA is unaffected by the administration of the drugs which cause a fall in BP and peripheral resistance in patients with high PRA borderline hypertension (Esler et al., 1975, 1977).

These results suggest that borderline hypertension—a harbinger of essential hypertension—is a heterogeneous disturbance with perhaps three different physiological and humoral profiles. These profiles in turn reflect different pathogeneses for borderline hypertension. In fact, the endocrine changes in other groups of borderline hypertensive patients also are not completely uniform. (These patients may not, however, be the same ones as those who have been studied for their cardiovascular dynamics, their responses to sympathetic and parasympathetic blocking agents, and their PRA.) In any case, patients with borderline hypertension may be divided into those whose BP falls below 140/90 mm Hg with reassurance and rest and those in whom no fall occurs (Genest et al., 1978). In both groups a significant mean increase in plasma aldosterone concentration is found; this reverts to normal levels, but only in those who become normotensive. Both groups of patients, when recumbent, show a decreased metabolic clearance rate of aldosterone when compared to normal control subjects. Usually an upright posture considerably decreases the metabolic clearance of aldosterone, but not in patients with mild borderline hypertension. Although other alterations in aldosterone metabolism, binding of the hormone to a specific plasma globulin, and responses to stimulation occur in borderline hypertensive patients, the point of this discussion is that borderline patients with mild hypertension are similar in some ways and different in others.

Substance has also been added to the speculation, which appears in previous sections, that the physiological heterogeneity of patients with EH is also reflected in their psychological heterogeneity. Esler and his co-workers (1977) have reported that 16 men, 18 to 35 years of age, experiencing the subform of borderline hypertension with high PRA and increased plasma norepinephrine levels, differ psychologically from 15 borderline hypertensive men with normal PRA and from 20 men with normal blood pressures. The patients with high-renin EH differ significantly from both the normotensive patients and the hypertensive patients with normal plasma renin activity on a number of psychological measures that signify that they are controlled, guilt-ridden, submissive persons with higher levels of unexpressed or unexpressible anger. But neither hypertensive group scored higher on anxiety ratings than did the control groups. The only tendency that differentiated the control group from the hypertensive patients with normal PRA is that the latter appeared to be more resentful, though as capable of expressing this resentment as were their normotensive peers.

Esler and his colleagues' study documents the psychological heterogeneity of hypertensive patients; it also confirms the psychiatric description of hypertensive patients that we owe to Alexander (1950). Nonetheless, the meaning of this important study is not clear. Julius and Esler (1975) and Esler and colleagues (1977) have argued that the pathogenesis of high-renin borderline hypertension is neurogenic—that the high PRA is secondary to increased sympathetically mediated renin release because the effect of propranolol is to lower PRA but not BP in these patients (Stumpe et al., 1976). The Esler group concluded that, in this subform of EH, either increased sympathetic nervous system activity or both sympathetic nervous system enhancement and diminished parasympathetic inhibition, caused by a disturbance in central autonomic regulation, account for their findings. The increased sympathetic nervous system activity would account for all the findings in this subform of EH.

It would also be enticing to explain the increased sympathetic nervous system activity on the basis of suppressed hostility. However, the findings of Esler and his co-workers are of a correlational nature: The chronically suppressed hostility may not antecede the increased sympathetic drive—it might result from it; perhaps both are expressions of some altered central nervous system state. Psychosomatic investigators in the past were guided largely by the concept that suppressed hostility, such as that found by Esler and his co-workers, initiates all forms of hypertension. Clearly, the Esler study does not support this contention—other patients with borderline essential hypertension do not show this psychological trait. Besides, the hostility itself does not explain the pathogenesis of this one form, let alone all forms, of hypertension. But hostile subjects may also develop diseases other than hypertension.

In addition, patients in whom one or other forms of borderline EH become sustained go through a series of psychological (as well as physiological) changes as this process progresses. Safar et al. (1978) studied patients longitudinally using Rorschach tests. Early in the course, during the borderline phase, patients tended to be emotionally labile, to sweat easily, to show the physiological correlates of anxiety, to evidence covert aggressive tendencies that they imagined were dangerous, and to have an impoverished fantasy life. As their hypertension became sustained, they became more conventional and conforming in their ways, and less sociable. They showed less evidence of anxiety, but the hostile trends were maintained and were expressed somewhat more frankly in fantasy.

It would be tempting to ascribe causality to these associations between the psychology and physiology of hypertensive patients at various stages of their disease, but it would be premature to do so. Work on animal models of high blood pressure tells us that changes in behavior do not invariably antecede the development of high blood pressure; they may be associated with its inception. In still other instances both the behavior and the high blood pressure are the product of an altered central neural state. These assertions are supported by the following data.

The Multiple Relationship Between Behavior and Blood Pressure Levels: Animal Studies

The complex interactions of previous experience (that alters later social behavior), brain mechanisms, and the physiology of mice, which together produce high blood pressure, have been described by Henry et al. (1967) and Henry and Stephens (1977). Their studies are the most persuasive and systematic ones ever published on the role played by social experience in producing sustained systolic high blood pressure in animals. Mixing male mice from different boxes, aggregating them in small boxes, exposing mice to a cat for six to 12 months, and producing territorial conflict in colonies of mixed males and females resulted in sustained elevations of systolic blood pressure, which were higher in male than in female mice. Henry and Stephens (1977) also found that male mice, when first raised apart and then placed back in a colony, became the dominant animals but developed high blood pressure and died of an interstitial nephritis. When young mice were raised together rather than apart, and were later crowded together or made to fight for territory, food, and females, their blood pressure did not show the increases seen in those brought up in isolation from weaning to maturity. Henry and his co-workers (1971a and b) have worked out some of the mechanisms associated with the hypertension. Socially isolated mice first showed a decreased activity of tyrosine hydroxylase (TH) and phenylethanolamine N-methyltransferase (PNMT) activity in the adrenal gland. But the activity of both enzymes and of monoamine oxidase, and the levels of norepinephrine and epinephrine became elevated in animals that were subsequently stimulated by contact with other animals. The mechanism of these increases was worked out by Thoenen and co-workers (1969). A reflex increase of sympathetic nerve activity on transsynaptic stimulation induced enzyme activity in the adrenal gland after one to three days. Adrenal TH activity decreased after the splanchnic (sympathetic) nerve to the adrenal gland was cut. Therefore, the increase in TH activity in the adrenal gland was the result of increased sympathetic activity and not increased pituitary or adrenocortical steroid activity.

Other experiments have shown, however, that social stimulation (such as fighting) may increase the levels of adrenocortical steroids (Bronson, 1967; Christian et al., 1965), constrict renal vessels (Bing and Vinthen-Paulsen, 1952), and raise levels of epinephrine, norepinephrine, and serotonin in the brain (Welch and Welch, 1965, 1971). In mice, daily fighting that is sustained for 14 days induces elevations of brain catecholamine levels and levels of epinephrine (but not norepinephrine) in the adrenal glands, causes the kidneys to be "shrunken and contracted," and the adrenal glands, hearts, and spleens to be enlarged.

A salt-sensitive strain of rats has been bred that regularly develops hypertension after eating small amounts of salt, but it takes time for them to do so (Dahl et al., 1962; Jaffe et al., 1969). Even a diet containing only 0.38 percent of salt causes salt-sensitive rats to have higher blood pressure levels (134 mm Hg, mean) than salt-resistant ones (112 mm Hg, mean). Salt-sensitive rats also differ behaviorally from salt-resistant animals, even before they develop high blood pressure; therefore, a relationship exists between specific behavior patterns and the predisposition to experimental hypertension in this strain. Haber and her colleagues (1979) compared normotensive salt-sensitive and salt-resistant rats on a number of behavioral measures and found that most of the salt-sensitive ones were more active and explored their environments more, especially when they were about nine weeks old. Behavioral differences may, therefore, antecede the development of experimental hypertension in rats, but this does not mean that the relationship is a causal one; both might be functionally related to altered brain function. This alteration is, for example, already manifest in the spontaneously hypertensive strain of rats before high blood pressure develops, and expresses itself as an increased reactivity to environmental stimuli (Okamoto, 1972).

These two examples support the idea that the behaviors of some animals differ before the inception of high blood pressure. Other information suggests, however, that one may not generalize from these examples: In the spontaneously hypertensive strain of rats, other altered behaviors are associated in time with the inception of high blood pressure; that is, spontaneously hypertensive rats, although unusually hyperreactive to environmental stimuli, also showed altered behaviors only during the initial phases of the disease. Rifkin et al. (1974) found that 33-week-old spontaneously hypertensive rats, which already had elevated blood pressure levels, were much more likely to kill mice introduced into their cages than were matched normotensive rats. In the group of hypertensive rats, those who committed muricide had a more labile blood pressure and somewhat lower levels than did hypertensive nonkillers.

Other data suggest, however, that the behavior of other animals changes once high blood pressure is installed. In such cases, both the behavioral changes and the high blood pressure levels are the product of an altered central neural state; they cannot be assumed causally to produce each other. Rather some alteration of state of brain may both raise blood pressure and cause the organism to respond in a new manner to the environment. In support of this hypothesis McCubbin (1967) has found that, after very small doses of angiotensin II, which had no immediate effect on blood pressure levels, had been infused for several days into dogs, the arterial blood pressure became elevated and labile. When the dogs were surrounded by everyday activity in the laboratory, the arterial pressures were labile and high. If the laboratory was quiet, minor distractions caused marked further increases in arterial pressure. After the injection of angiotensin II, the dogs became sensitized to the administration of tyramine which releases endogenous stores of norepinephrine. Tyramine injection produced further elevations of the dogs' arterial pressures. The results of McCubbin's experiments strongly suggest that angiotensin II plays a role in the initiation of high blood pressure levels and alters the reactivity of the animal to environmental stimuli. Once these changes have occurred, the animal overreacts even to trivial stimuli. Environmental stimuli or drugs, such as tyramine, produce excessive responses that did not occur before treatment with angiotensin II. One may conclude, therefore, that psychological stimuli do not necessarily initiate high blood pressure levels. Angiotensin II alters the reactivity of dogs to environmental stimuli by mechanisms that may include the effects of angiotensin II on the brain. It may alter the function of the brain so that it responds in new ways to environmental stimuli by changing levels or turnover rates of brain catecholamines (Chalmers, 1975).

Another example of the association of high blood pressure levels and behavioral change is provided by the effects of bilateral lesions of the nucleus of the tractus solitarius (NTS) in cats (Reis, 1980). After lesions are made in the NTS, elevated levels of blood pressure occur that last for 24 hours, only to subside to mildly elevated basal levels. However, the BP also becomes extremely labile despite the fact that the animal is quietly at rest; the lability is much greater during the day than at night, and can be reduced if the animal is housed in a sound-proof room (Nathan et al., 1977). Therefore, the lability seems to be associated with banal, everyday sounds heard in a laboratory. Furthermore, marked increases in blood pressure occur during grooming, feeding, stimulation such as petting, or the presentation of novel or conditioning stimuli.

Cats with NTS lesions show a persistent, stable tachycardia throughout the day and night, uninfluenced by the behaviors and stimuli that produce such marked blood pressure changes. The lesions also abolish all baroreceptor reflexes (Miura and Reis, 1972). Reis (1980) has suggested that baroreceptor reflexes usually buffer blood pressure responses to emotions, environmental or conditioning stimuli; only if these reflexes are impaired do these contingencies produce elevations of blood pressure in animals.

The baroreceptor mechanism buffers the effect of sensory stimuli or emotion against an increase in sympathetically mediated vasomotor discharge. Further support is given to this statement by the fact that destruction of brain structures (by decerebration) rostral to the NTS and before they are bilaterally lesioned prevents the development of high blood pressure, or lowers the blood pressure levels after these nuclei are destroyed (Doba and Reis, 1973). More localized lesions—i.e., of the anterior basal hypothalamus—also abolish the hypertension that follows NTS lesions (Brody et al., 1980).

One may conclude, therefore, that the relationship of environmental stimuli, behavior, and high blood pressure in animals is complex. Some animals prone to high blood pressure demonstrate different behaviors before its development. In other animals, previous experience alters later social behavior to eventuate in high blood pressure. A third group of animals shows altered behaviors during the inception of high blood pressure. In a fourth group of animals, levels of high blood pressure are determined by sensory stimulation or conditioning techniques.

REFERENCES

ADER, R. 1980. Psychosomatic and psychoimmunologic research. *Psychosom. Med.*, 4:307-321.
ALEXANDER, F. 1939. Psychoanalytic study of a case of essential hypertension. *Psychosom. Med.*, 1:139.

ALEXANDER, F. 1950. *Psychosomatic Medicine.* New York: Norton.
ALEXANDER, F., FRENCH, T. M., and POLLOCK, G. H. 1968. *Psychosomatic Specificity.* Chicago: University of Chicago Press.
AX, A. F. 1953. The physiological differentiation between fear and anger in humans. *Psychosom. Med.*, 15:433.
AYMAN, D. 1933. The personality traits of patients with arteriolar essential hypertension. *Am. J. Med. Sci.*, 186:213.
BARACH, J. H. 1928. The constitutional factors in hypertensive disease. *J.A.M.A.*, 91:1511.
BING, J., and VINTHEN-PAULSEN, N. 1952. Effects of severe anoxia on the kidneys of normal and dehydrated mice. *Acta Physiol. Scand.*, 27:337.
BINGER, C. A., ACKERMAN, A. E., COHEN, A. E., SCHROEDER, H. A., and STEELE, J. M. 1945. Personality in arterial hypertension. *Psychosomatic Monographs.* New York: R. Brunner.
BROD, J. 1960. Essential hypertension—hemodynamic observations with bearing on its pathogenesis. *Lancet*, ii:773.
BROD, J. 1970. Hemodynamics and emotional stress. *Bibl. Psychiatr.*, 144:13.
BROD, J., FENCL, V., HEJL, Z., and JIRKA, J. 1959. Circulatory changes underlying blood pressure elevation during acute emotional stress (mental arithmetic) in normotensive and hypertensive subjects. *Clin. Sci.*, 18:269.
BROD, J., FENCL, V., HEJL, Z., JIRKA, J., and ULRYCH, M. 1962. General and regional hemodynamic pattern underlying essential hypertension. *Clin. Sci.*, 23:339.
BRODY, M. J., HAYWOOD, J. R., and TOUW, K. B. 1980. Neural mechanisms in hypertension. *Ann. Rev. Physiol.*, 42:441-453.
BRONSON, F. H. 1967. Effects of social stimulation on adrenal and reproductive physiology of rodents. In M. L. Conalty (ed.), *Husbandry of Laboratory Animals.* New York: Academic Press.
BROWN, J. J., FRASER, R., LEVER, A. J., MORTON, J. J., ROBERTSON, J. I. S., and SCHALEKAMP, M. A. D. H. 1977. Mechanisms in hypertension: A personal view. In J. Genest, E. Koiw, and O. Kuchel (eds.), *Hypertension*, pp. 529–548. New York: McGraw Hill.
BRUCE, J. M., Jr., and THOMAS, C. B. 1953. A method of rating certain personality factors as determined by the Rorschach test for use in a study of the precursors of hypertension and coronary artery disease. *Psychiatr. Q.* 27(suppl.):207.
BUSS, A. H. 1961. The *Psychology of Aggression.* New York: Wiley.
CHALMERS, J. P. 1975. Brain amines and models of experimental hypertension. *Circ. Res.*, 36:469-480.
CHAMBERS, W. W., and REISER, M. F. 1953. Emotional stress in the precipitation of congestive heart failure. *Psychosom. Med.*, 15:38.
CHRISTENSON, W. N., and HINKLE, L. E. 1961. Differences in illness and prognostic signs in two groups of young men. *J.A.M.A.*, 177:247.
CHRISTIAN, J. J., LLOYD, J. A., and DAVIS, D. 1965. The role of endocrines in the self-regulation of mammalian populations. *Recent Prog. Horm. Res.*, 22:501-578.
COBB, S., and ROSE, R. M. 1973. Hypertension, peptic ulcer, and diabetes in air traffic controllers. *J.A.M.A.*, 224:489-492.
COHEN, S. I., and SILVERMAN, A. J. 1959. Psychophysiological investigations of vascular response variability. *J. Psychosom. Res.*, 3:185.
COHEN, S. I., SILVERMAN, A. J., ZUIDEMA, G., and LAZAR, C. 1957. Psychotherapeutic alteration of a physiologic stress response. *J. Nerv. Ment. Dis.*, 125:112.
CRANSTON, R. W., CHALMERS, J. H., TAYLOR, H. L., HENSCHEL, A., and KEYS, A. 1949. Effects of a psychiatric interview on the blood pressure response to cold stimuli. *Fed. Proc.*, 8:30.
CRUZ-COKE, R. 1960. Environmental influences and arterial blood pressure. *Lancet*, 2:885.
DAHL, L. K., HEINE, M., and TASSINARI, L. 1962. Role of genetic factors in susceptibility to experimental hypertension due to chronic excess salt ingestion. *Nature*, 194:480-482.
D'ATRI, D. A., and OSTFELD, A. M. 1975. Crowding: Its effects on the elevation of blood pressure in a prison setting. *Prev. Med.*, 4:550-556.

DAVIES, M. 1971. Is high blood pressure a psychosomatic disorder? *J. Chron. Dis.*, 24:239.

DECHAMPLAIN, J., FARLEY, L., COSINEUA, D., and AMERINGEN, M. 1976. Circulating catecholamine levels in human and experimental hypertension. *Circ. Res.*, 38:109-114.

DEQUATTRO, V., BARBOUR, B. H., and CAMPESE, V. 1977. Sympathetic nerve activity in high-renin hypertension: Effects of saralasin infusion. *Mayo Clin. Proc.*, 52:369-373.

DEQUATTRO, V., and MIURA, Y. 1973. Neurogenic factors in human hypertension: Mechanism or myth? *Am. J. Med.*, 55:362.

DEQUATTRO, V., MIURA, Y., and LURVEY, A. 1975. Increased plasma catecholamine concentrations and vas deferens norepinephrine biosynthesis in men with elevated blood pressure. *Circ. Res.*, 36:118-126.

DOBA, N., and REIS, D. J. 1973. Acute fulminating neurogenic hypertension produced by brainstem lesions in rat. *Circ. Res.*, 32:584-593.

DOYLE, A. E., and FRASER, J. R. E. 1961. Essential hypertension and inheritance of vascular reactivity. *Lancet*, ii:509.

DUNBAR, H. F. 1943. *Psychosomatic Diagnosis*. New York: Hoeber.

ELMADJIAN, F., HOPE, J. M., and LAMSON, E. T. 1957. Excretion of epinephrine and norepinephrine in various emotional states. *J. Clin. Endocrinol. Metab.*, 17:608.

ENGEL, B. T., and BICKFORD, A. F. 1961. Response specificity. *Arch. Gen. Psychiatry*, 5:82.

ENGELMAN, K., PORTNOY, B., and SJOERDSMA, A. 1970. Plasma catecholamine concentrations in patients with hypertension. *Circ. Res.* (suppl. 1), 27:141-146.

ESLER, M. D., JULIUS, S., RANDALL, O. S., ELLIS, C. N., and KASHIMA, T. 1975. Relation of renin status to neurogenic vascular resistance in borderline hypertension. *Am. J. Cardiol.*, 36:708.

ESLER, M. D., JULIUS, S., ZWEIFLER, A., RANDALL, O., HARBURG, E., GARDINER, H., and DEQUATTRO, V. 1977. Mild high-renin essential hypertension. *N. Engl. J. Med.*, 296:405.

FISCHER, H. K. 1961. Hypertension and the psyche. In A. N. Brest and J. H. Moyer (eds.), *Hypertension—Recent Advances: The Second Hahnemann Symposium on Hypertensive Disease*. Philadelphia: Lea & Febiger.

FOLKOW, B. U. G., and HALLBÄCK, M. I. L. 1977. Physiopathology of spontaneous hypertension in rats. In J. Genest, E. Koiw, and O. Kuchel (eds.), *Hypertension*, pp. 507-529. New York: McGraw-Hill.

FROHLICH, E. D., TARAZI, R. C., and DUSTAN, H. P. 1971. Clinical-physiological correlation in the development of hypertensive heart disease. *Circulation*, 44:446-455.

GENEST, J., NOWACZYNSKI, W., BOUCHER, R., and KUCHEL, O. 1978. Role of the adrenal cortex and sodium in the pathogenesis of human hypertension. *Can. Med. Assoc. J.*, 118:538-549.

GLOCK, C. Y., and LENNARD, H. L. 1957. Studies in hypertension. 5. Psychologic factors in hypertension: An interpretative review. *J. Chronic Dis.*, 5:174.

GORLIN, R. 1962. The hyperkinetic heart syndrome. *J.A.M.A.*, 182:823.

GOTTSCHALK, L., and HAMBIDGE, G. 1955. Verbal behavior anlysis: A systematic approach to the problem of quantifying psychologic processes. *J. Project. Psychol.*, 19:387.

GRACE, W. J., and GRAHAM, D. T. 1952. Relationship of specific attitudes and emotions to certain bodily diseases. *Psychosom. Med.*, 14:253.

GRAHAM, D. T., KABLER, J. D., and GRAHAM, F. K. 1960. Experimental production of predicted physiological differences by suggestion of attitude. *Psychosom. Med.*, 22:321.

GRAHAM, D. T., KABLER, J. D., and GRAHAM, F. K. 1962. Physiological response to the suggestion of attitudes specific for hives and hypertension. *Psychosom. Med.*, 24:159.

GRAHAM, J. D. P. 1945. High blood pressure after battle. *Lancet*, 1:239-240.

HABER, S. B., FRIEDMAN, R., and IWAI, J. 1979. The relationship between genotype and behavior in experimental hypertension. Submitted for publication.

HAMBLING, J. 1951. Emotions and symptoms of essential hypertension. *Br. J. Med. Psychol.*, 24:242.

HAMBLING, J. 1952. Psychosomatic aspects of essential hypertension. *Br. J. Med. Psychol.*, 25:39.

HARBURG, E., ERFURT, J. C., HAUENSTEIN, L. S., CHAPE, C., SCHULL, W. J., and SCHORK, M. A. 1973. Socio-ecological stress, suppressed hostility, skin color, and black-white male blood pressure: Detroit. *Psychosom. Med.*, 35:276.

HARBURG, E., JULIUS, S., MCGINN, N. F., MCLEOD, J., and HOOBLER, S. W. 1964. Personality traits and behavior patterns associated with systolic blood pressure levels in college males. *J. Chronic Dis.*, 17:405-414.

HARDYCK, C., and SINGER, M. T. 1962. Transient changes in affect and blood pressure. *Arch. Gen. Psychiatry*, 7:15.

HARRIS, R. E., and SINGER, M. T. 1968. Interaction of personality and stress in the pathogenesis of essential hypertension. In *Hypertension. Neural Control of Arterial Pressure*, vol. 16, *Proceedings of the Council for High Blood Pressure Research.* New York: American Heart Association.

HARRIS, R. E., SOKOLOW, M., CARPENTER, L. G., FREEDMAN, M., and HUNT, S. P. 1953. Response to psychologic stress in persons who are potentially hypertensive. *Circulation*, 7:874.

HARRIS, W. S., SCHOENFELD, C. D., GWYNNE, P. H., WEISSLER, A. M., and WARREN, J. V. 1965. Circulatory and humoral responses to fear and anger. *J. Lab. Clin. Med.*, 64:867.

HENRY, J. P., and CASSEL, J. C. 1969. Psychosocial factors in essential hypertension. Recent epidemiologic and animal experimental evidence. *Am. J. Epidemiol.*, 90:171.

HENRY, J. P., ELY, D. L., and STEPHENS, P. M. 1971a. Role of the autonomic system in social adaptation and stress. *Proceedings of International Union of Physiological Scientists*, 8:50.

HENRY, J. P., MEEHAN, J., and STEPHENS, P. M. 1967. The use of psychosocial stimuli to induce prolonged systolic hypertension in mice. *Psychosom. Med.*, 29:408-432.

HENRY, J. P., and STEPHENS, P. M. 1977. *Stress, Health, and the Social Environment.* New York: Springer-Verlag.

HENRY, J. P., STEPHENS, P. M., AXELROD, J., and MUELLER, R. A. 1971b. Effect of psychosocial stimulation on the enzymes involved in the biosynthesis and metabolism of noradrenaline and adrenaline. *Psychosom. Med.*, 33:227-237.

HILL, L. B. 1935. A psychoanalytic observation on essential hypertension. *Psychoanal. Rev.*, 22:60.

HOKANSON, J. E. 1961a. The effects of frustration and anxiety on overt aggression. *J. Abnorm. Psychol.*, 62:346.

HOKANSON, J. E. 1961b. Vascular and psychogalvanic effects of experimentally aroused anger. *J. Pers.*, 29:30.

HOLLENBERG, N. K., and ADAMS, D. F. 1976. The renal circulation in hypertensive disease. *Am. J. Med.*, 60:773-784.

INNES, G., MILLER, W. M., and VALENTINE, M. 1959. Emotion and blood pressure. *J. Ment. Sci.*, 105:840.

JAFFE, D., DAHL, L. K., SUTHERLAND, L., and BARKER, D. 1969. Effects of chronic excess salt ingestion: Morphological findings in kidneys of rats with differing genetic susceptibility to hypertension. *Fed. Proc.*, 28:422.

JOST, H., RUILMANN, C. J., HILL, T. S., and GULO, M. J. 1952. Studies in hypertension 2: Central and autonomic nervous system reactions of hypertensive individuals to simple physical and psychologic stress situations. *J. Nerv. Ment. Dis.*, 115:152.

JULIUS, S. 1964. Psihosomatske Znacajke Studenata s Provisenim Sistollicken Tlakom. (Psychosomatic studies of students with systolic blood pressure increases.) Thesis for Sc.D. Degree, Zagreb, Yugoslavia.

JULIUS, S., and ESLER, M. 1975. Autonomic nervous cardiovascular regulation in borderline hypertension. *Am. J. Cardiol.*, 36:685-696.

KAPLAN, S. M., GOTTSCHALK, L. A., MAGLIOCCO, B., ROHOVIT, D., and ROSS, W. D. 1960. Hostility in verbal productions and hypnotic "dreams" of hypertensive patients (comparisons between hypertensive and normotensive groups and within hypertensive individuals). *Psychosom. Med.*, 22:320.

KASL, S. V., and COBB, S. 1970. Blood pressure changes in men undergoing job loss: A preliminary report. *Psychosom. Med.*, 32:19-38.

KORNER, P. I., WEST, M. J., SHAW, J., and UTHER, J. B. 1974. "Steady state" properties of the baroreceptor-heart rate reflex in essential hypertension in man. *Clin. Exp. Pharmacol. Physiol.*, 1:65.

KUCHEL, O. 1977. Autonomic nervous system in hypertension: Clinical aspects. In J. Genest, E. Koiw, and O. Kuchel (eds.), *Hypertension.* New York: McGraw-Hill.

LARAGH, J. H., BAER, L. H., BRUNNER, H. R., BÜHLER, R. F., SEALEY, J. E., and VAUGHAN, JR., E. D. 1972. Renin, angiotensin and aldosterone in pathogenesis and management of hypertensive vascular disease. *Am. J. Med.*, 52:633.

LORIMER, A. R., MCFARLANE, P. W., PROVAN, G., DUFFY, T., and LAWRIE, T. D. V. 1971. Blood pressure and catecholamine responses to stress in normotensive and hypertensive subjects. *Cardiovasc. Res.*, 5:169.

LOUIS, W. J., DOYLE, A. E., ANAVEKAR, S. N., and CHUA, K. G. 1973. Sympathetic activity and essential hypertension. *Clin. Sci. Mol. Med.*, 45:1195.

MALMO, R. B., and SHAGASS, C. 1952. Studies of blood pressure in psychiatric patients under stress. *Psychosom. Med.*, 14:82.

MCCUBBIN, J. W. 1967. Interrelationships between the sympathetic nervous system and the renin-angiotensin system. In P. Kezdi (ed.), *Baroreceptors and Hypertension.* New York: Pergamon.

MCKEGNEY, F. P., and WILLIAMS, R. B., JR. 1967. Psychological aspects of hypertension: II. The differential influence of interview variables on blood pressure. *Am. J. Psychiatry,* 123:1539.

MIASNIKOV, A. L. 1961. The significance of higher nervous activity in the pathogenesis of essential hypertension. In J. H. Cort, V. Fencl, Z. Hejl, and J. Jirka (eds.), *The Pathogenesis of Essential Hypertension,* pp. 152-162. Prague: State Medical Publishing House.

MILLER, M. L. 1939. Blood pressure and inhibited aggression in psychotics. *Psychosom. Med.*, 1:162.

MIURA, M., and REIS, D. J. 1972. The role of the solitary and paramedian reticular nuclei in mediating cardiovascular reflex responses from carotid baro- and chemoreceptors. *J. Physiol.* (London), 223:525-548.

MOSCHOWITZ, E. 1919. Hypertension: Its significance, relation to arteriosclerosis and nephritis, and etiology. *Am. J. Med. Sci.*, 158:668.

MOSES, L., DANIELS, G. E., and NICKERSON, J. L. 1956. Psychogenic factors in essential hypertension: Methodology and preliminary report. *Psychosom. Med.*, 18:471.

NATHAN, M. A., SEVERINI, W. A., TUCKER, L. W., and REIS, D. J. 1977. Effect of environment on labile arterial hypertension. *Circulation* (suppl.) 3:242.

NESTEL, P. J. 1969. Blood pressure and catecholamine excretion after mental stress in labile hypertension. *Lancet*, i:692.

O'HARE, J. P. 1920. Vascular reactions in vascular hypertension. *Am. J. Med. Sci.*, 159:371.

OKAMOTO, K. 1972. *Spontaneous Hypertension.* Tokyo: Igaku Shoin.

OSTFELD, A. M., and LEBOVITZ, B. Z. 1959. Personality factors and pressor mechanisms in renal and essential hypertension. *Arch. Intern. Med.*, 104:497.

OSTFELD, A. M., and LEBOVITZ, B. Z. 1960. Blood pressure lability: A correlative study. *J. Chronic Dis.*, 12 (4):428-439.

PALMER, R. S. 1950. Psyche and blood pressure. *J.A.M.A.*, 144:295.

PFEIFFER, J. B., JR., and WOLFF, H. G. 1950. Studies in renal circulation during periods of life stress and accompanying emotional reactions in subjects with and without essential hypertension: Observations on the role of neural activity in the regulation of renal blood flow. *Res. Publ. Assoc. Res. Nerv. Ment. Dis.*, 29:929.

PILOWSKY, I., SPALDING, D., SHAW, J., and KORNER, P. I. 1973. Hypertension and personality. *Psychosom. Med.*, 35:50.

REIS, D. J. 1980. Brain stem mechanisms in experimental hypertension. In H. Weiner, M. A.

Hofer, and A. J. Stunkard (eds.), *Brain, Behavior and Bodily Disease, Proceedings of the Association for Research in Nervous and Mental Disease*, vol. 59. New York: Raven Press.

REISER, M. F., BRUST, A. A., FERRIS, E. B., SHAPIRO, A. P., BAKER, H. M., and RANSOHOFF, W. R. 1951a. Life situations, emotions and the course of patients with arterial hypertension. *Psychosom. Med.*, 13:133-139.

REISER, M. F., BRUST, A. A., SHAPIRO, A. P., BAKER, H. M., RANSCHOFF, W., and FERRIS, E. B. 1950. Life situations, emotions and the course of patients with arterial hypertension. *Res. Publ. Assoc. Res. Nerv. Ment. Dis.*, 29:870.

REISER, M. F., ROSENBAUM, M., and FERRIS, E. B. 1951b. Psychologic mechanisms in malignant hypertension. *Psychosom. Med.*, 13:147-159.

RIFKIN, R. J., SILVERMAN, J. M., CHAVEZ, F. T., and FRANKL, G. 1974. Intensified mouse killing in the spontaneously hypertensive rat. *Life. Sci.*, 14:985-992.

ROSE, R. M., and LEVIN, M. A. 1979. The role of stress in human hypertension. *J. Human Stress*, 5:7-26.

RUSKIN, A., BEARD, O. W., and SCHAFFER, R. L. 1948. "Blast hypertension": Elevated arterial pressure in victims of the Texas City disaster. *Am. J. Med.*, 4:228.

SAFAR, M. E., KANIENIECKA, H. A., LEVENSON, J. A., DIMITRIU, V. M., and PAULEAU, N. F. 1978. Hemodynamic factors and Rorschach testing in borderline and sustained hypertension. *Psychosom. Med.*, 40:620-630.

SAPIRA, J. D., SCHEIB, E. T., MORIARTY, R., and SHAPIRO, A. P. 1971. Differences in perception between hypertensive and normotensive populations. *Psychosom. Med.*, 33:239-250.

SASLOW, G., GRESSEL, G. C., SHOBE, F. O., DUBOIS, P. H., and SCHROEDER, H. A. 1950. Possible etiological relevance of personality factors in hypertension. *Psychosom. Med.*, 12:292.

SAUL, L. J. 1939. Hostility in cases of essential hypertension. *Psychosom. Med.*, 1:153.

SCHACHTER, J. 1957. Pain, fear and anger in hypertensives and normotensives: A psychophysiologic study. *Psychosom. Med.*, 19:17.

SCOTCH, N. A. 1961. Blood pressure measurements of urban Zulu adults. *Am. Heart J.*, 61:173.

SHAPIRO, A. P. 1960a. Comparative studies of the blood pressure response to different noxious stimuli. *Psychosom. Med.*, 22:320.

SHAPIRO, A. P. 1960b. Psychophysiologic mechanisms in hypertensive vascular disease. *Ann. Intern. Med.*, 53:64.

SHAPIRO, A. P. 1973. Essential hypertension—Why idiopathic? *Am. J. Med.*, 54:1.

SHAPIRO, A. P. 1979. The role of stress in hypertension. *J. Human Stress*, 5:18-19.

SHAPIRO, A. P., ROSENBAUM, M., and FERRIS, E. B. 1954. Comparison of blood pressure response to veriloid and to the doctor. *Psychosom. Med.*, 16:478.

SHAPIRO, A. P., and TENG, H. C. 1957. Technic of controlled drug assay illustrated by a comparative study of rauwolfia serpentina, phenobarbital and placebo in the hypertensive patient. *N. Engl. J. Med.*, 256:970.

SIMONSON, E., and BROZEK, J. 1959. Russian research on arterial hypertension. *Ann. Intern. Med.*, 50:129.

SOKOLOW, M., and HARRIS, R. E. 1961. The natural history of hypertensive disease. In A. N. Brest and J. H. Moyer (eds.), *Hypertension—Recent Advances. The Second Hahnemann Symposium on Hypertensive Disease*. Philadelphia: Lea & Febiger.

SOKOLOW, M., WERDEGAR, D., PERLOFF, D. B., COWAN, R. M., and BRENENSTUHL, H. 1970. Preliminary studies relating portably recorded blood pressures to daily life events in patients with essential hypertension. *Bibl. Psychiatr.*, 144:164.

STAMLER, J., STAMLER, R., and PULLMAN, T. 1967. *The Epidemiology of Essential Hypertension.* New York: Grune & Stratton.

STUMPE, K. O., KOLLOCH, R., VETTER, H., GRAMMAN, W., KRUCK, F., RESSEL, C., and HIGUCHI, M. 1976. Acute and long-term studies of the mechanisms of action of beta-blocking drugs in lowering blood pressure. *Am. J. Med.*, 60:853-865.

SYME, S. L., HYMAN, M. D., and ENTERLINE, P. E. 1964. Some social and cultural factors associated with the occurrence of coronary heart disease. *J. Chronic Dis.*, 17:277.

TARAZI, R. C., DUSTAN, H. P., FROHLICH, E. D., GIFFORD, JR., R. W., and HOFFMAN, G. C. 1970. Plasma volume and chronic hypertension. Relationship to arterial pressure levels in different hypertensive diseases. *Arch. Intern. Med.*, 125:835.

THALER, M., WEINER, H., and REISER, M. F. 1957. Exploration of the doctor-patient relationship through projective techniques. *Psychosom. Med.*, 19:228.

THOENEN, H., MUELLER, R. A., and AXELROD, J. 1969. Trans-synaptic induction of adrenal tyrosine hydroxylase. *J. Pharmacol. Exp. Ther.*, 169:249.

THOMAS, C. B. 1957. Characteristics of the individual as guideposts to the prevention of heart disease. *Ann. Intern. Med.*, 47:389.

THOMAS, C. B. 1958. Familial and epidemiologic aspects of coronary disease and hypertension. *J. Chronic Dis.*, 7:198.

THOMAS, C. B. 1961. Pathogenetic interrelations in hypertension and coronary artery disease. *Dis. Nerv. Syst.*, 22 (suppl.):39.

THOMAS, C. B. 1964. Psychophysiologic aspects of blood pressure regulation: A clinician's view. *J. Chronic Dis.*, 17:599.

THOMAS, C. B. 1967. The psychological dimensions of hypertension. In J. Stamler, R. Stamler, and T. N. Pullman (eds.), *The Epidemiology of Essential Hypertension*. New York: Grune & Stratton.

THOMAS, C. B., and ROSS, D. C. 1963. A new approach to the Rorschach test as a research tool. *Bull. Johns Hopkins Hosp.*, 112:312.

THOMAS, C. B., ROSS, D. C., and FREED, E. S. 1964. *An Index of Rorschach Responses: Studies on the Psychological Characteristics of Medical Students*. Baltimore: Johns Hopkins University Press.

TORGERSEN, S., and KRINGLEN, E. 1971. Blood pressure and personality. A study of the relationship between intrapair differences in systolic blood pressure and personality in monozygotic twins. *J. Psychosom. Res.*, 15:183.

VAN DER VALK, J. M. 1957. Blood pressure changes under emotional influences in patients with essential hypertension and control subjects. *J. Psychosom. Res.*, 2:134.

WEINER, H. 1977. *Psychobiology and Human Disease*. New York: Elsevier North-Holland.

WEINER, H. 1979. *Psychobiology of Essential Hypertension*. New York: Elsevier North-Holland.

WEINER, H., SINGER, M. T., and REISER, M. F. 1962. Cardiovascular responses and their psychophysiologic correlates. A study in healthy young adults and patients with peptic ulcer and hypertension. *Psychosom. Med.*, 24:477-498.

WEISS, E. 1942. Psychosomatic aspects of hypertension. *J.A.M.A.*, 120:1081.

WEISS, E., and ENGLISH, O. S. (eds.) 1957. *Psychosomatic Medicine*, 3rd edition. Philadelphia: Saunders.

WELCH, B. L., and WELCH, A. S. 1965. Effect of grouping on the level of brain norepinephrine in white Swiss mice. *Life. Sci.*, 4:1011.

WELCH, B. L., and WELCH, A. S. 1971. Isolation, reactivity and aggression: Evidence for an involvement of brain catecholamines and serotonin. In B. E. Eleftherious and J. P. Scott (eds.), *The Physiology of Aggression and Defeat*. New York: Plenum.

WHITE, B. V., JR., and GILDEA, E. F. 1937. "Cold pressor test" in tension and anxiety: A cardiochronographic study. *Arch. Neurol. Psychiatry*, 38:914.

WILLIAMS, R. B., JR., KIMBALL, C. P., and WILLIARD, H. N. 1972. The influence of interpersonal interaction on diastolic blood pressure. *Psychosom. Med.*, 34:194.

WILLIAMS, R. B., JR., and MCKEGNEY, F. P. 1965. Psychological aspects of hypertension: I. The influence of experimental variables on blood pressure. *Yale J. Biol. Med.*, 38:265.

WOLF, S., CARDON, P. V., JR., SHEPHARD, E. M., and WOLFF, H. G. 1955. *Life Stress and Essential Hypertension*. Baltimore: Williams & Wilkins.

WOLF, S., PFEIFFER, J. B., RIPLET, H. S., WINTER, O. S., and WOLFF, H. G. 1948. Hypertension as a reaction pattern to stress: Summary of experimental data on variations in blood pressure and renal blood flow. *Ann. Intern. Med.*, 29:1056-1076.

WOLF, S., and WOLFF, H. G. 1951. A summary of experimental evidence relating life stress to the pathogenesis of essential hypertension in man. In E. T. Bell (ed.), *Essential Hypertension.* Minneapolis: University of Minnesota Press.

WOLFF, H. G. 1953. *Stress and Disease.* Springfield, IL: Charles C Thomas.

V.
SLEEP

13

ANXIETY AND SLEEP

ROBERT L. WILLIAMS, M.D.

Few physicians are surprised when an anxious patient also complains of disturbed sleep. This clinical experience, supplemented by medical studies often cited in the literature, has led them to assume that anxiety invariably keeps its unwilling victims tossing and turning well past midnight. When the anxious patient finally does sleep, he falls in and out of sleep throughout the night. The assumption that anxiety increases sleep latency and the number of awakenings during the night has been supported by both subjective and objective evidence—some rooted in common sense, some well documented in the psychiatric literature, but most not so well supported by sleep laboratory studies. Furthermore, both somatic and cognitive theories of insomnia implicate anxiety as a contributing factor; autonomic arousal and intrusive cognition, respectively, are among the clinically established symptoms of anxiety.

COMMON SENSE ASSUMPTIONS

Perhaps the most convincing justification—to patient and doctor alike—for assuming an unhappy union between anxiety and sleep is common sense: Tense, worried, apprehensive patients do not need the well-replicated results of a controlled experiment to convince themselves or their doctor that this uncomfortable state is keeping them awake. Certainly, the reasons patients consistently give their doctors for their sleeplessness—restlessness, worrying about their family finances, ruminations about past mistakes, generalized nervousness—imply the presence of some anxiety. Such reports are supported by the clinically accepted definitions of anxiety, all of which include components of both physiologic and cognitive arousal.

INFERENCES FROM DRUG EFFICACY STUDIES

An association between anxiety and sleep can also be inferred from drug efficacy studies. It is well known that benzodiazepines, often prescribed to relieve insomnia, have both hypnotic and anxiolytic properties. Further studies to better characterize their precise mechanism of action might help reveal the nature of that relationship. In a study designed to test clinical effects and psychological performance the week following diazepam treatment, Zimmerman Tansella et al. (1979) found that diazepam significantly improved subjective anxiety and insomnia in inpatients with anxiety neurosis. Interestingly, however, amylobarbitone improved only the self-rated quality of sleep in this study. Hindmarch and Parrott (1979) found that the anxiolytics, dipotassium chlorazepate (a precursor of diazepam) and clobazam, when administered at bedtime improved the self-rated quality of sleep and reduced anxiety scores the next afternoon. Other European tests of the efficacy of Trancopal (chlormezanone), a new anxiolytic, revealed that nighttime administration of the drug relieves mild neurotic anxiety and improves self-rated sleep (Ali-Khan, 1979; Warnock, 1978).

CLINICAL EVIDENCE

As convincing as the inferences from such studies may seem, the results of objective studies which directly measure insomnia in anxious patients and, conversely, anxiety in insomnia patients would extend the credibility of a close relationship between anxiety and poor sleep. On personality inventories, insomnia patients typically show elevated anxiety and depression (Coursey et al., 1975; Kales et al., 1976), with worry about falling asleep exacerbating the sleep disturbance (Ascher and Efran, 1978; Kales et al., 1976; Storms and Nisbett, 1970). Lichstein and Rosenthal (1980) confirmed that insomnia patients attribute their sleep problems to intrusive cognitions and other indications of cognitive arousal, established components of anxiety.

Clinical assessments support the high evidence of insomnia in anxiety neurotics. Cohen and White (1950) reported insomnia in 54 percent of anxious patients but only 4 percent of normal controls. In another clinical study (Stonehill et al., 1976), 376 psychiatric patients admitted for mood disorders were assigned to standard diagnostic categories and rated on four scales—anger, anxiety, sadness, and tension. According to observers, sleep latency was longest in the anxious patients. Those patients diagnosed as having primary anxiety states both fell asleep and awakened later than the other patients.

Sleep Laboratory Studies

Electroencephalographic (EEG) recordings of sleep would complement the findings of psychological tests and psychiatric interviews in clarifying the relationship between anxiety and sleep. Despite physicians' expectations and clinical evidence of the adverse effects of anxiety on sleep, sleep laboratory studies draw only tentative associations, if any. Two kinds of sleep laboratory studies have been done—one inducing anxiety in normal subjects and the other statistically examining the anxiety scales of EEG-evaluated insomnia patients. Both of these research designs have flaws which preclude making definite statements about the role of anxiety in disturbing sleep. Some researchers doubt that the former can be considered a true paradigm of anxiety. Patients in the latter are often suffering from several levels of psychiatric disturbance which may or may not be discussed in the results. The anxiety observed in these patients may actually be secondary to depression which could be primarily responsible for the sleep disturbance recorded.

Data from studies of anxiety induced in normal subjects tend to show that anxiety increases sleep latency, probably decreases the amount of slow-wave sleep, increases the frequency of arousals, and probably has little effect on rapid eye-movement (REM) sleep. The well-documented "first-night effect," attributed to anxiety resulting from situational unfamiliarity, is often used as a model of insomnia. Goodenough et al. (1975) induced psychometrically documented anxiety in normal subjects by showing them at bedtime a documentary of an Australian circumcision ceremony. Sleep-onset insomnia resulted, but this effect on sleep may have been produced by hostility or depression—also indicated by the test scales—rather than anxiety. Two studies suggest that anxiety-associated arousal disturbs sleep. A study of medical students' reactions to pending exams (Lester et al., 1967) and a Minnesota Multiphasic Personality Inventory (MMPI) evaluation of undergraduate student volunteers (McDonald et al., 1976) disclosed positive correlations between anxiety, increased galvanic skin response, and reduced slow-wave sleep.

Unfortunately, studies of insomnia patients do not consistently find a strong relationship between anxiety and sleep. The variations found in the effects of anxiety on sleep probably reflect the assortment of methods used and patient populations observed. However, such studies do tentatively support the above-described arousal model of anxiety often used when anxiety is artificially induced in normal subjects. When Monroe's (1967) polysomnographic evaluations revealed increased levels of autonomic arousal in

insomnia patients, he proposed that they might reflect the physiologic outcome of anxiety. At that time, there was little evidence for the validity of
a physiologic model of anxiety. In fact, Freedman and Papsdorf's (1976)
failure to find a significant relationship between levels of presleep autonomic
activity and initial sleep-onset duration in a group of sleep-onset insomnia
patients seemed to refute this model. The more recent findings of Kazarian
et al. (1978) support both the physiologic arousal model and the stimulus
control model of insomnia, the former for overall insomnia and the latter for
sleep-onset insomnia only. In patients admitted to the London Psychiatric
Hospital, the Manifest Anxiety Scale significantly discriminated between
those who reported sleep difficulties and those who did not (Kazarian et al.,
1978).

In a limited study of 10 anxious patients, Foster et al. (1977) recorded
significantly increased sleep latencies, decreased total sleep time, decreased
sleep efficiency, and reduced delta sleep. These findings did not differ significantly, however, from those of depressed patients in the same study.
According to Ware (1979), patients presenting at the Baylor Sleep Disorders
Center with complaints of disturbed sleep typically show elevated anxiety
scores on scales designed to measure this parameter. This association is not
substantiated by the Peter Bent Brigham Sleep Clinic, where no causal
relationship between anxiety and insomnia has been found (Regestein, 1979).

At the Baylor College of Medicine Sleep Disorders Center a controlled
study was designed to clarify such inconsistencies (Williams et al., 1979).
Twenty-five insomnia patients were assigned to either a drug (mood or sleep-
altering) or nondrug group and matched to a control group. The subjects
were assessed for anxiety on the t-scale of the Profile of Mood States (POMS-
T), the State-Trait Anxiety Index, and several MMPI-derived indices and
standard EEG measures were done. The insomnia, nondrug group proved
to be significantly more anxious and depressed than the controls. This group
also exhibited decreased sleep efficiency and increased sleep latency. However, analyses of covariance determined that depression and age differences
between the subject groups, rather than anxiety, accounted for the altered
sleep parameters. Only when anxiety was covaried with depression was
elevated anxiety related to increased sleep latency. The insomnia, drug
group not only was more extreme on all psychometric measures but also
showed a positive correlation between sleep latency and anxiety. With the
exception of this finding, the results of this study seemed to indicate that
the disordered sleep of insomnia patients is not caused by anxiety. However,
these results may be a function of the selection of patients for sleep complaints rather than for a full range of anxiety symptoms.

CONCLUSION

When subjective and objective indications of an association between anxiety and disturbed sleep are compiled, the symptoms of anxiety seem to potentiate insomnia. However, the variable effect of anxiety on sleep parameters, observed in polysomnographic evaluations of both insomnia patients and anxiety-induced normal subjects, may indicate that anxiety sometimes plays a secondary rather than a primary role in the etiology of disorders of initiating and maintaining sleep. Anxiety may occur in isolation from other psychopathology, but it more often accompanies other psychiatric disturbances ranging from depression to schizophrenia. In particular, the effects of anxiety need to be separated from the effects of depression since they tend to occur together in insomnia patients. To permit the study of more uniform patient populations, more objective markers of mood disorders than those presently available must be developed.

Perhaps the present array of EEG parameters measured in the sleep laboratory are not sufficiently sensitive to detect subtle differences between anxious patients and normal subjects. A better understanding of the relationship between psychological states and sleep may depend on our ability to apply computer technology to the development of more refined EEG sleep measures.

Further research on the mechanism of the sedative, hypnotic action of benzodiazepines could more thoroughly explicate the nature of the relationship between anxiety and sleeplessness. An unequivocal determination of how anxiety affects sleep awaits such advances.

REFERENCES

ALI-KHAN, G. 1979. Treatment of anxiety-related insomnia with chlormezanone. *Curr. Med. Res. Opin.*, 6:259-262.
ASCHER, L. M., and EFRAN, J. S. 1978. Use of paradoxical intention in a behavioral program for sleep onset insomnia. *J. Consult. Clin. Psychol.* 46:547-550.
COHEN, M., and WHITE, P. 1950. Life situations, emotions, and neurocirculatory asthenia (anxiety neurosis, neurasthenia effort syndrome). *Res. Publ. Assoc. Res. Nerv. Ment. Dis.*, 29:832-869.
COURSEY, R. D., BUCHSBAUM, M., and FRANKEL, B. L. 1975. Personality measures and evoked responses in chronic insomniacs. *J. Abnorm. Psychol.*, 84:239-249.
FOSTER, G., GRAU, T., SPIKER, D. G., et al. 1977. EEG sleep in generalized anxiety disorder (abstract). *Sleep Research*, 6:145.
FREEDMAN, R., and PAPSDORF, J. D. 1976. Biofeedback and progressive relaxation treatment of sleep-onset insomnia. *Biofeedback Self. Regul.*, 1:253.
GOODENOUGH, D. R., WITKIN, H. A., KOULACK, O., and COHEN, H. 1975. The effects of stress films on dream affect and on respiration and eye-movement activity during rapid-eye-movement sleep. *Psychophysiology*, 12:313-320.

HINDMARCH, I., and PARROTT, A. C. 1979. The effects of repeated nocturnal doses of clobazam, dipotassium chlorazepate and placebo on subjective ratings of sleep and early morning behaiour and objective measures of arousal, psychomotor performance and anxiety. *J. Clin. Pharmacol.*, 8:325-329.
KALES, A., CALDWELL, A. B., PRESTON, T. A., HEALEY, S., and KALES, J. D. 1976. Personality patterns in insomnia. *Arch. Gen. Psychiatry*, 33:1128-1134.
KAZARIAN, S. S., HOWE, M. G., MERSKEY, H., and DEINUM, E. J. L. 1978. Insomnia: Anxiety, sleep-incompatible behaviors and depression. *J. Clin. Psychol.*, 34:865-869.
LESTER, B. K., BURCH, N. R., and DOSSETT, R. C. 1967. Nocturnal EEG-GSR profiles: The influence on presleep states. *Psychophysiology*, 3:238-248.
LICHSTEIN, K. L., and ROSENTHAL, T. L. 1980. Insomniacs' perceptions of cognitive versus somatic determinants of sleep disturbance. *J. Abnorm. Psychol.*, 89:105-107.
MCDONALD, D. G., SHALLENBERGER, H. D., KORESKO, R. L., and KINZY, B. G. 1976. Studies of spontaneous electrodermal responses in sleep. *Psychophysiology*, 13:128-134.
MONROE, L. J. 1967. Psychological and physiological differences between good and poor sleepers. *J. Abnorm. Psychol.*, 72:255.
REGESTEIN, O. R. 1979. Practical ways to manage chronic insomnia. *Med. Times*, 107:19-23.
STONEHILL, E., CRISP, A. H., and KOVAL, J. 1976. The relationship of reported sleep characteristics to psychiatric diagnosis and mood. *Br. J. Med. Psychol.*, 49:381.
STORMS, M. D., and NISBETT, R. E. 1970. Insomnia and the attribution process. *J. Pers. Soc. Psychol.*, 16:319-328.
WARE, J. C. 1979. The symptom of insomnia: Causes and cures. *Psychiatric Annals*, 9:27-49.
WARNOCK, J. M. T. 1978. A controlled study of trancopal in the treatment of sleep disturbances due to anxiety. *J. Int. Med. Res.*, 6:115-120.
WILLIAMS, R. L., WARE, J. C., ILARIA, R. L., and KARACAN, I. 1979. Disturbed sleep and anxiety. In W. E. Fann, I. Karacan, A. D. Pokorny, and R. L. Williams (eds.), *Phenomenology and Treatment of Anxiety*, pp. 211-223. New York: Spectrum.
ZIMMERMAN TANSELLA, C., TANSELLA, M., and LADER, M. 1979. A comparison of the clinical and psychological effects of diazepam and amylobarbitone in anxious patients. *J. Clin. Pharmacol.*, 7:605-611.

14

SLEEP AND PSYCHOSOMATIC ILLNESS

HARVEY MOLDOFSKY, M.D.

Psychosomatic disorders involve the study of psychologic, social, and biologic factors that relate to health and disease. The theories and studies of the psychobiology of disease involve the association of a type of psychologic experience with brain function and how this association is translated into disease activity. Such psychologic concepts as emotional conflict, stress, and bereavement (Weiner, 1977) involve the individual's waking experience. Somehow this waking experience is transduced into specific biologic changes that influence the emergence and evolution of disease. There are, however, certain psychosomatic disorders that may also appear outside daytime wakefulness or relate to the circadian sleep-wake cycle.

Until recently no specific feature of sleep physiology was believed to influence the clinical features or course of medical disorders. But the discovery by Aserinsky and Kleitman (1953) (subsequently verified by numerous investigators) of two states of sleep with distinct physiologic and psychologic features heralded a new era of psychobiologic investigation. These distinct states are now known as rapid eye-movement sleep (REM, dreaming, D, paradoxical or active sleep) and nonrapid eye-movement sleep (NREM, slow-wave, S-sleep, quiet or orthodox sleep). The physiologic and psychologic features of these two sleep states, which alternate at about 90-minute intervals in the normal adult, are summarized in Table 1. The application of sleep physiologic technology to the study of disease has produced important advances in the understanding of pathology. Specific physiologic features that are unique to sleep provoke or complicate certain medical and behavioral disorders. Sleep apnea, for example, has been associated with right heart failure, secondary polycythemia, hypertension, sexual impotence, excessive daytime sleepiness, and impairment of intellectual functioning (Guillemi-

The assistance of Ontario Mental Health Foundation Grant No. 793-80/82 is acknowledged.

241

Table 1

Characteristics of Sleep
(Normal Young Adult)

Sleep States	Physiologic Features		Psychological Features	Proportion of Total Sleep Time
Rapid Eye-Movement (REM) Sleep	EEG: low-voltage, mixed-frequency "saw tooth" waves Phasic bursts of extraocular and middle-ear muscle activity Motor inhibition of major antigravity and locomotor muscles Penile tumescence, increased vaginal blood flow Autonomic variability (irregular heart and respiratory rates) Increased cerebral neuronal activity Increased cerebral blood flow Increased brain temperature Poikilothermia Diminished or absent CO_2 chemoreceptor sensitivity, and pulmonary stretch reflexes		Vivid dreaming	20-25%
Nonrapid Eye-Movement (NREM) Sleep	EEG sleep stages:	I Low-voltage, mixed-frequency, slow eye movements	Fantasy	1-5%
		II Sleep spindles, K complexes	Occasional, vague, or fragmented ideas or thoughts	40-60% 10-20%
		III High-voltage,		
		IV slow (delta) waves		
	Growth hormone secretion in stages 3 and 4 sleep Decrease in heart rate and blood pressure Slow and regular respiration Decreased body temperature			

nault et al., 1978). Similarly, the physiology of sleep and wakefulness is important in medical disorders in which psychologic influences have been implicated.

Three categories of sleep-wake physiologic conditions are associated with psychosomatic disorders. First, there are psychosomatic disorders that appear in the context of sleep. For example, attacks of angina, peptic ulcer pain, asthma, or migraine may suddenly erupt out of sleep. Second, the clinical course of psychosomatic illness may be affected by disruptions in the sleep-wake schedule. For example, disruption of the circadian rhythm of sleep-wakefulness in hospital intensive care units contributes to clinical and behavioral problems of cardiac patients. Last are the psychosomatic disorders that are especially disabling after awakening from sleep. For example, upon awakening in the morning, people with fibrositis syndrome or rheumatoid arthritis usually experience much pain, stiffness, and emotional distress. Recent observations on the role of sleep physiology in these three categories of sleep-related psychosomatic disorders will be reviewed.

Psychosomatic Disorders that Interrupt Sleep

For psychosomatic disorders that may interrupt the continuity of sleep, attempts have been made to relate the sudden attack to a specific physiologic state of sleep, that is, REM vs. NREM sleep. Nocturnal attacks of angina, peptic ulcer, asthma, or migraine might be expected to occur during REM sleep when there is a considerable increase in autonomic nervous system activity. However, the studies have not shown a consistent relationship of the REM state to nocturnal attacks of angina, duodenal ulcer pain, or asthma.

Nocturnal Angina Pectoris

Early reports on angina patients suggested a relationship of recurrent nocturnal angina symptoms and REM-associated electrocardiographic (EKG) changes (King et al., 1973; Knowlin et al., 1965; Murao et al., 1972). Patients would awaken from REM sleep with chest pain and/or show depressed EKG S-T segments. Later studies (Broughton and Baron, 1978; Karacan et al., 1973; Stern and Tzivoni, 1973) failed to show this relationship. Broughton and Baron found that only two of 12 documented nocturnal attacks occurred during REM. They found a tendency for the anginal episodes to occur in the deepest electroencephalographic (EEG) stages of NREM sleep in patients who had suffered acute myocardial infarction. Typically, tachycardia and EKG ST deviation began in sleep with the patient awakening; then there was decrease in EKG amplitude and complaints of anginal pain. The researchers suggested the possibility of sustained hypotension during this sleep period as a predisposing factor to their findings. But no definitive conclusions can be drawn from these studies, given the unavoidable confounding influences of varying medications and dosages, and the heterogeneity of disease and disease severity.

Nocturnal Duodenal Ulcer Pain

Armstrong et al. (1965) monitored sleep physiology and continuously aspirated gastric contents overnight in five patients acutely ill with duodenal ulcer. They suggested that duodenal ulcer patients had bursts of gastric acid secretion during REM. No specific pattern of acid secretion was found in normal persons. A later report by Orr et al. (1974) casts doubt on the specificity of sleep state and acid secretion even though their study was of two patients with duodenal ulcer disease. Orr et al. showed no significant relationship between acid secretion or concentration, or serum gastrin levels, and specific stages of sleep. They found that acid secretion was sustained throughout the night, but not in the normal subjects in whom acid secretion diminished within the hour of falling asleep.

Nocturnal Bronchial Asthma

Nocturnal asthma attacks, although a common feature of asthma, have not yet been studied adequately. Studies are few and involve a small number of subjects, so that the mechanisms involved are not well understood. Furthermore, the studies do not demonstrate conclusively that sleep state is a specific triggering factor in the nocturnal attacks. Kales and Kales's (1973) study of 12 adult asthmatic patients showed no clear relationship of asthma attacks to sleep stages or time, but there was a reduction in stage 4 sleep. In a study of children, they noted a diminished tendency for asthmatic episodes to occur during the first third of the night in conjunction with slow-wave sleep. Kales and Kales suggest that exercise with its concomitant increase in slow-wave sleep may be associated with a reduction in nocturnal asthma attacks, but as yet no studies have been done to test this hypothesis. On the other hand, Ravenscroft and Hartmann (1968) found that the three patients they studied experienced frequent nocturnal asthma attacks during REM sleep and that attacks during NREM sleep were often related to the patients' reports of dreaming. Tabachnick et al. (in press) found a marked increase in the work of breathing in asthmatic children during REM sleep; this increased mechanical activity might impair the continuity of sleep. The increased autonomic reactivity that influences marked fluctuations in tracheobronchial smooth-muscle tone during REM in Sullivan et al.'s (1979) study of sleeping dogs suggests a possible triggering mechanism of an acute attack in patients with increased airway reactivity. Circadian biochemical rhythms may be important in changes in this airway reactivity. Barnes et al. (1980) found that the greatest reduction of peak expiratory flow rate in extrinsic asthma occurred about 4 a.m. The narrowing of airways coincided with a peak in plasma histamine not found in normal persons, and a nadir in plasma epinephrine. The stimulating effect of histamine on bronchoconstriction in a situation of inadequate adrenergic bronchodilatory activity may influence early-morning wheezing. But the trigger of bronchoconstriction and the nocturnal asthmatic attack is unknown. The special roles of sleep-related tracheobronchial reactivity, mucociliary clearance, respiratory mechanics, biochemical rhythms, action of asthma drugs during sleep, and the significance of mentation or dreaming need investigation in asthmatic children and adults who have nocturnal respiratory symptoms.

Nocturnal Migraine

Studies in persons who are predisposed to nocturnal headaches have shown that REM sleep is temporally related to attacks of migraine, cluster headaches, and chronic paroxysmal hemicrania (Dexter and Weitzman, 1970; Hsu et al., 1977; Kayed et al., 1978). Subjects awaken with headache attacks out of REM sleep, or within 10 minutes of the end of a REM episode. Hsu et al. (1977) showed that nocturnal biochemical changes may contribute to the attack. Plasma catecholamine levels were found to be elevated in the three-hour period before the subjects awakened with a migraine headache.

But these studies leave unanswered why nocturnal symptoms—for example, peptic ulcer pain and headache attacks—do not occur during every REM episode. If emotional factors are significant to headache and, possibly, to the other sleep-related disorders, could sleep mentation or dream content and the emotions experienced contribute to the evolution of the attack? To date, no one has examined this psychosomatic hypothesis of the relative contributions of physiologic and metabolic changes and psychologic state to these nocturnal symptoms.

SLEEP-WAKE DISORDERS AND COURSE OF PSYCHOSOMATIC ILLNESS

Disorders of Initiating and Maintaining Sleep Associated with Illness Behavior

Naturally, illness, whether physical or psychiatric, may result in sleep difficulty. Patients may have problems falling asleep or staying asleep because of their somatic or emotional distress. Often patients complain bitterly about their sleep problems. They claim that if they could sleep better, they would feel better. The chronic use of sleeping pills may then become a way of life. In turn, the drug dependence may adversely affect the course of illness. The patients may be afraid to stop taking the pills lest their physical and emotional symptoms reappear. Such hypnotics as barbiturates lose their efficacy within a few weeks and patients experience unpleasant withdrawal symptoms when they attempt to stop taking these sleeping pills (Kales et al., 1974). All these factors contribute to hypnotic drug dependence and difficulties in managing illness.

Disorders of Sleep-Wake Schedule and Course of Disease

Acute irregular sleep-wake pattern and cardiac intensive care units. Hospitalization for medical illness may trigger alterations in sleep-wake schedule that may subsequently complicate the course of illness. For example, patients admitted to intensive care units or acute coronary care units often experience fragmentation of their sleep-wake rhythm by the environmental intrusions—noise from medical personnel, intrusion of monitoring equipment, lighting—and by the anxiety and physical discomfort that often accompany such stressful situations. The sleep disturbance is difficult to disentangle from a variety of drug, metabolic, and psychologic factors (hypnotic sedatives, analgesics, drug withdrawal states, steroids, metabolic and physiologic factors relating to the illness, the environment, communication difficulties from, for example, tracheostomies, and disrupted human relationships) that have been suggested as provoking delirium (Kimball, 1979). Two studies reported major disruptions in sleep in patients who had undergone open-heart surgery: initial absence of sleep on the first postoperative day, then prolonged suppression of REM and slow-wave sleep (Elwell et al., 1974; Orr and Stahl, 1977). While Elwell et al. reported postoperative delirium, no postoperative neurologic or psychiatric disorders were found in Orr and Stahl's study. Therefore, disturbance in sleep physiology may not be the critical factor in inducing major psychiatric disorder in patients managed on intensive care units for myocardial infarction or postoperative cardiac surgery (Broughton and Baron, 1978; Karacan et al., 1973). Moreover, there is no information on whether specific disturbances in sleep-wakefulness have any significant effect on the rate of convalescence from myocardial infarction, cardiotomy procedures, or aortocoronary bypass surgery. Studies of this matter may be important, given the observation that myocardial proteins of rodents are more rapidly synthesized during rest and sleep (Rau and Meyer, 1975) and the general viewpoint of Adam and Oswald (1977) that synthetic, restorative processes are favored during inactivity and sleep.

Chronic irregular sleep-wake pattern and illness behavior. Hospitalization may also change an individual's usual day-night behavior, triggering long-lasting alterations in sleep-wake patterning that may eventually impair psychologic and social functioning. For example, one patient who required a long hospital stay for treatment of his peripheral vascular disease completely reversed his sleep-wake behavior so that he napped episodically during the day and remained awake during the night. He found that he enjoyed staying awake all night to talk with the nurses whose ward duties were less demanding at night. Thus, the patient received the attention and sympathy he craved but did not receive from his family and from the busy day nurses. After leaving the hospital he was unable to revert to his previous day-wake/night-sleep schedule because he continued his self-induced circadian rhythm disorder by heavy use of coffee, cigarettes, and alcohol at the local pub until the early hours of the morning and by taking diazepam and narcotic analgesics during the day. He was forced to leave his daytime job, his marriage failed, and his psychologic and social functioning became severely impaired.

PSYCHOSOMATIC DISORDERS WITH NONRESTORATIVE SLEEP SYMPTOMS

In the third group of psychosomatic disorders in which disabling symptoms occur upon morning awakening, the quality of sleep influences the severity of morning symptoms. That is, patients with either "fibrositis syndrome" or rheumatoid arthritis often have more nonarticular aching and stiffness upon awakening in the morning than at bedtime. They experience sleep to be light and restless, with frequent arousals. They fail to be restored by their sleep. Although we have assumed that the sleep disturbance is secondary to the pain, recent research (Moldofsky et al., 1975, 1979) suggests that a specific disturbance in sleep physiology has an important relationship to the morning symptoms and, possibly, the evolution of these rheumatic disorders.

"Fibrositis Syndrome"

"Fibrositis syndrome" is a common chronic, nonarticular rheumatic disorder which has no known organic pathology (Smythe, 1979). Physical and emotional stress or adverse weather change aggravates the disorder. The key features of this syndrome include chronic, widespread and variable musculoskeletal aching and stiffness, localized areas of tenderness in specific anatomic regions (Smythe and Moldofsky, 1977), nonrestorative sleep, easy fatigability, emotional distress (anxiety, irritability, depression), and no biochemical, serologic, inflammatory, or structural pathology that can be demonstrated or attributed to the symptoms. In our initial study, most patients reported major stressful life situations had happened to them at the time their symptoms began to appear. Typically, they had experienced a frightening, but minor, automobile or industrial accident, or they had become helplessly involved in insoluble domestic difficulties. They showed an overnight increase in muscle tenderness and pain and coincident physiologic sleep disturbance, that is, alpha-delta or alpha EEG frequency in NREM sleep. This sleep anomaly had been reported previously in patients with chronic somatic malaise and fatigue (Hauri and Hawkins, 1973).

A similar alpha NREM sleep anomaly and coincident musculoskeletal and mood symptoms were artificially induced in healthy sedentary subjects in the context of noise-induced stage 4 (delta) NREM sleep disruption (Moldofsky and Scarisbrick, 1976). The symptoms in both the "fibrositis" patients and healthy subjects may reflect the reduction of the efficacy of the restorative functions of sleep and the resultant morning symptoms. The nonrestorative sleep is caused by an arousal mechanism competitive with sleep, evident in the "light" sleep experienced by these affected people and the prominent alpha EEG sleep anomaly. The nonrestorative sleep syndrome may have been triggered by a significant frightening event or ongoing emotional distress. A vicious cycle ensues with the nonrestorative sleep together with the pain and mood symptoms having a mutual influence on one another. Furthermore, consistent with this theory, the quantity of EEG alpha and delta frequencies during sleep is related to overnight change in pain and mood symptoms. The alpha frequency is directly related to overnight change in these symptoms. Conversely, the sleep EEG delta frequency, which has been thought to be associated with the restorative function of sleep (Hartmann, 1974), is inversely related to these overnight changes in pain and mood symptoms (Moldofsky and Lue, 1980). This theory would account for the observation of an alpha NREM sleep disturbance, chronic musculoskeletal pain, and emotional distress in Israeli war veterans who had survived the highly stressful Yom Kippur War (Lavie et al., 1979) and for similar features found in workmen who become chronically disabled with widespread musculoskeletal pain and fatigue after minor, yet frightening, industrial accidents. Likely there are other specific situations that evolve into this final common symptom pathway. Alcohol or opiate dependence withdrawal states and nocturnal myoclonus have been reported to be associated with the alpha NREM sleep anomaly.

There is no definite explanation of how the sleep-physiologic disturbance causes the morning symptoms in these patients. Perhaps disturbances of central nervous system serotonin and endorphin metabolism may be among the links connecting the sleep disorder to the pain and mood symptoms (Moldofsky and Warsh, 1978).

Rheumatoid Arthritis

Morning pain, stiffness, and fatigue are the most common and some of the most disabling symptoms of acute rheumatoid arthritis. Motor immobility during sleep has been suggested to produce "jelling." But there has been no satisfactory biochemical or physiologic evidence to account for these morning symptoms. Moldofsky et al. (1979) found the alpha NREM sleep anomaly and overnight increase in articular and muscle pain and tenderness in patients who were experiencing a flare in their rheumatoid arthritis. Considerable time, as well, was spent in wakefulness or light (stage 1) sleep. One patient, whose articular inflammatory symptoms and muscle aching and tenderness remitted, showed a coincidental reduction in the amount of alpha frequency during NREM sleep. His mean percentage of time in the alpha frequency band width fell from 20 percent during the initial acute stage of illness to 7-9 percent during the period of remission two weeks later. At the same time, the mean percentage of time in NREM delta frequency band went from 30 percent to 41 percent. The study suggests that the pain from inflammatory joint disease produces an arousal state in sleep as shown by the alpha frequency during sleep. This arousal state or alpha NREM sleep is followed by the nonrestorative sleep symptoms: morning muscle aching, stiffness, and fatigue. Although the sleep physiology and morning symptoms are similar in fibrositis syndrome and rheumatoid arthritis, there are differences in the genesis of the arousal state manifested by the alpha NREM sleep. In fibrositis syndrome, the alpha NREM may be precipitated by exogenous factors or psychologic distress, whereas in rheumatoid arthritis, this sleep disturbance may be triggered by endogenous factors or painful inflammatory articular stimuli that intrude into sleep. These observations on alpha NREM sleep do not necessarily imply a causal relationship to pain, mood, and fatigue symptoms. The sleep anomaly may be an important biologic index of the neurophysiologic arousal response mediating intervening psychobiologic (psychologic and metabolic) factors that transduce pain stimuli.

Since a variety of exogenous (psychologic, environmental) and endogenous (inflammatory, metabolic) conditions may influence the sleep and pain symptoms, a new diagnostic label of "rheumatic pain modulation syndrome" is suggested (Moldofsky, in press). The rheumatic pain modulation syndrome describes the final common pathway of alpha NREM sleep and nonarticular pain and fatigue that characterize differing rheumatic disorders. This new concept is useful clinically. Symptoms of this syndrome that are associated with articular inflammatory disease must be discriminated from similar symptoms provoked by emotional distress. Unwarranted or potentially harmful drugs (steroids, immunosuppressant drugs) or surgical procedures can then be avoided in rheumatoid patients who bitterly complain of widespread muscle pain but show no objective evidence of active joint disease. Similarly, inappropriate medications used for joint inflammatory disease should be avoided in those with fibrositis syndrome.

SUMMARY

Three categories of sleep-related symptoms are found in psychosomatic disorders. First, there are those nocturnal disorders—angina, duodenal ulcer pain, bronchial asthma, migraine—which interrupt the course of sleep. Although a sleep physiologic state, that is, REM vs. NREM sleep, has been inconsistently implicated in these nocturnal attacks, REM-associated symptoms have been clearly demonstrated only in nocturnal migraine. Second, sleep-wake disorders influence the course of illness. Disorders of initiating or maintaining sleep that accompany illness are commonly perpetuated by hypnotic drug dependence. Hospitalization for major illness—myocardial infarction, heart surgery—may precipitate acute sleep-wake schedule disturbances that contribute to neuropsychiatric disorder (delirium). Furthermore, the hospital environment may initiate chronic irregular sleep-wake patterns and provoke drug dependence, social and behavioral difficulties. Third, there are psychosomatic disorders—fibrositis syndrome and rheumatoid arthritis—in which morning symptoms are associated with a nonrestorative sleep physiologic disturbance, alpha NREM sleep. The constellation of alpha NREM sleep and musculoskeletal pain and fatigue comprises a syndrome termed rheumatic pain modulation disorder.

REFERENCES

ADAM, K., and OSWALD, I. 1977. Sleep is for tissue restoration. *J. R. Coll. Physicians, Lond.*, 11:376-388.

ARMSTRONG, R. H., BURNAP, D., JACOBSON, A., KALES, A., WARD, S., and GOLDEN, J. 1965. Dreams and gastric secretions in duodenal ulcer patients. *New Physician*, 14:241-243.

ASERINSKY, E., and KLEITMAN, N. 1953. Regularly occurring periods of eye motility, and concomitant phenomena, during sleep. *Science*, 118:273-274.

BARNES, P., FITZGERALD, G., BROWN, M., and DOLLERY, C. 1980. Nocturnal asthma and changes in circulating epinephrine, histamine and cortisol. *N. Engl. J. Med.*, 303(5):263-267.

BROUGHTON, R. J., and BARON, R. 1978. Sleep patterns in the intensive care unit and on the ward after acute myocardial infarction. *Electroencephalogr. Clin. Neurophysiol.*, 45:348-360.

DEXTER, J. D., and WEITZMAN, E. D. 1970. The relationship of nocturnal headaches to sleep stage patterns. *Neurology*, 20:513-518.

ELWELL, E. L., FRANKEL, B. L., and SNYDER, F. 1974. A polygraphic sleep study of five cardiotomy patients. *Sleep Research*, 3:133.

GUILLEMINAULT, C., VAN DEN HOED, J., and MITLER, M. 1978. Clinical overview of the sleep apnea syndromes. In C. Guilleminault and W. C. Dement (eds.), *Sleep Apnea Syndromes*, pp. 1-12. New York: Liss.

HARTMANN, E. 1974. *The Functions of Sleep.* New Haven: Yale University Press.

HAURI, P., and HAWKINS, D. R. 1973. Alpha-delta sleep. *Electroencephalogr. Clin. Neurophysiol.*, 34:233-237.

HSU, L. K. G., CRISP, A. H., KALUCY, R. S., KOVAL, J., CHEN, C. N., CARUTHERS, M., and ZILKHA, K. J. 1977. Early morning migraine nocturnal plasma levels of catecholamines tryptophan, glucose and free fatty acids, and sleep encephalogram. *Lancet*, 1:447-450.

KALES, A., BIXLER, E. O., TAN, T. L., SCHARF, M. B., and KALES, J. D. 1974. Chronic hypnotic drug use: Ineffectiveness, drug withdrawal, insomnia and hypnotic drug dependence. *J.A.M.A.*, 277:513-517.

KALES, A., and KALES, J. 1973. Recent advances in the diagnosis and treatment of sleep disorders. In G. Usdin (ed.), *Sleep Research and Clinical Practice*, pp. 61-94. New York: Brunner-Mazel.

KARACAN, I., GREEN, J. R., TAYLOR, W. J., WILLIAMS, J. C., ELIOT, R. S., THORNBY, J. I., SALIS, P. J., and WILLIAMS, R. L. 1973. Sleep characteristics of acute myocardial infarct patients in an ICU. *Sleep Research*, 2:159.

KAYED, K., GODTLIBSEN, O. B., and SJAASTAD, O. 1978. Chronic paroxysmal hemicrania IV: "REM sleep locked" nocturnal headache attacks. *Sleep*, 1:91-95.

KIMBALL, C. P. 1979. Reactions to illness: The acute phase. The interplay of environmental factors in intensive care units. In C. P. Kimball (ed.), *Symposium on Liaison Psychiatry, The Psychiatric Clinics of North America*, 2(2):307-319. Toronto: Saunders.

KING, M. J., ZIR, L. M., KALTMAN, A. J., and FOX, A. D. 1973. Variant angina associated with angiographically demonstrated coronary artery spasm and REM sleep. *Am. J. Med. Sci.*, 265:419-422.

KNOWLIN, B. J., TROYER, W. G., COLLINS, W. S., SILVERMAN, G., NICHOLAS, C. R., McINTOSH, H. D., ESTES, E. H., and BOGDONOFF, M. D. 1965. The association of nocturnal angina with dreaming. *Ann. Intern. Med.*, 63:1040-1046.

LAVIE, P., HEFEZ, A., HALPERIN, G., and ENOCH, D. 1979. Long term effects of traumatic war-related events on sleep. *Am. J. Psychiatry*, 130(2):175-178.

MOLDOFSKY, H. Rheumatic pain modulation syndrome: Interrelationships between sleep, central nervous system serotonin and pain. In M. Critchley, A. Friedman, S. Sicuteri, S. Gorini (eds.), *International Headache Congress 1980*. New York: Raven Press, in press.

MOLDOFSKY, H., and LUE, F. 1980. The relationships of alpha and delta EEG sleep to pain and mood in "fibrositis" patients treated with chlorpromazine and L-tryptophan. *Electroencephalogr. Clin. Neurophysiol.*, 50:71-80.

MOLDOFSKY, H., LUE, F., and SMYTHE, H. 1979. Alpha EEG sleep and pain in rheumatoid arthritis. *Sleep Research*, 8:236.

MOLDOFSKY, H., and SCARISBRICK, P. 1976. Induction of neurasthenic musculoskeletal pain syndrome by selective sleep stage deprivation. *Psychosom. Med.*, 38:35-44.

MOLDOFSKY, H., SCARISBRICK, P., ENGLAND, R., and SMYTHE, H. 1975. Musculoskeletal symptoms and Non-REM sleep disturbance in patients with "fibrositis syndrome" and healthy subjects. *Psychosom. Med.*, 37:341-351.

MOLDOFSKY, H., and WARSH, J. J. 1978. Plasma tryptophan and musculoskeletal pain in nonarticular rheumatism (fibrositis syndrome). *Pain*, 5:65-71.

MURAO, S., HARUMI, K., KATAYAMA, S., MASHIMA, S., SHIMOMURA, K., MURAYAMA, M., MATSUO, H., YAMAMOTO, H., KATO, R., and CHEN, C. 1972. All night polygraphic studies of nocturnal angina pectoris. *Jpn. Heart J.*, 13:295-306.

ORR, W. C., HALL, W. H., STAHL, M., DURKIN, M. G., GRIFFITHS, W., and WHITSETT, T. L. 1974. Gastric secretions and sleep patterns in ulcer patients and normals. *Sleep Research*, 3:34.

ORR, W. C., and STAHL, M. L. 1977. Sleep disturbances after open heart surgery. *Am. J. Cardiol.*, 39:196-201.

RAU, E., and MEYER, D. K. 1975. A diurnal rhythm of incorporation of L-(3H) leucine in myocardium of the rat. *Recent Adv. Stud. Cardiac Struct. Metab.*, 7:105-110.

RAVENSCROFT, D., and HARTMANN, E. 1968. The temporal correlation of nocturnal asthmatic attacks and the D-state. *Psychophysiology*, 4:396-397.

SMYTHE, H. A. 1979. "Fibrositis" as a disorder of pain modulation. *Clinics in Rheumatic Disease*, 5(3):823-832.

SMYTHE, H., and MOLDOFSKY, H. 1977. Two contributions to understanding of the "fibrositis" syndrome. *Bull. Rheum. Dis.*, 28:928-931.

STERN, S., and TZIVONI, D. 1973. Dynamic changes in the ST-T segment during sleep in ischemic heart disease. *Am. J. Cardiol.*, 32:17-20.

SULLIVAN, C. E., ZAMEL, N., KOZAR, L. F., MURPHY, E., and PHILLIPSON, E. A. 1979. Regulation of airway smooth muscle tone in sleeping dogs. *Am. Rev. Respir. Dis.*, 119(1):87-99.

TABACHNICK, E., MULLER, N., LEVISON, H., and BRYAN, A. C. Mechanics of breathing in adolescent asthmatics during sleep. *Am. Rev. Respir. Dis.*, in press.

WEINER, H. 1977. *Psychobiology and Human Disease.* New York: Elsevier.

15

EVALUATION AND TREATMENT OF INSOMNIA

ISMET KARACAN, M.D., D.Sc. (Med.),
and CONSTANCE A. MOORE, M.D.

The evaluation and treatment of insomnia—difficulty falling asleep and/or staying asleep—have become more and more critical over the past decade as epidemiological studies have revealed the prevalence of sleep complaints and hypnotic-drug use and abuse in the United States. In a number of surveys (Balter and Bauer, 1975; Kales et al., 1974; Karacan et al., 1976b), about one-third of adult respondents reported a sleep disturbance. Socio-demographic factors that have been significantly associated with insomnia include sex, age, education, income level, occupation, and marital status. According to most (Balter and Bauer, 1975; Dupuy et al., 1970; Hammond, 1964; Karacan et al., 1976b; McGhie and Russell, 1962; Raybin and Detre, 1969; Thornby et al., 1977) but not all (Kales et al., 1974; Thomas and Pederson, 1963; Tune, 1969) authors, more women than men across all age ranges complain of insomnia. Normative polysomnographic evaluations indicate, however, that normal women have more restful sleep, with fewer awakenings and more stages 3 and 4 than normal men (Williams et al., 1974). That sleep disturbance increases with age has yet to be disputed by any study of insomnia. A survey in the Houston metropolitan area (Thornby et al., 1977) found that sleeping difficulty was inversely related to education and income level. Housewives consistently reported greater problems with sleep than did people in most other occupations. Being divorced, widowed, or separated (Clift, 1975; Thornby et al., 1977), sleeping alone (Clift, 1975; Weiss et al., 1962), being pregnant (Karacan et al., 1968; Schweiger, 1972), or being a perimenopausal woman (Ballinger, 1976) have also been associated

The authors wish to thank Ms. Carol Howland for her editorial assistance in preparing this article.

with difficulty in sleeping. In addition, sleep disturbance has been found to accompany medical, surgical, and psychiatric illnesses (Detre, 1966; Johns et al., 1970; Ward, 1968; Weiss et al., 1962), particularly schizophrenia, depression, anxiety, and alcoholism.

An estimated 10 to 11 percent of the United States population takes prescription hypnotic drugs (Abelson et al., 1973; Karacan et al., 1976b). Pill-taking is higher in women than in men, in divorced, widowed, or separated persons, and especially in physically or psychiatrically ill patients. Sleeping pill use also increases with age. In three studies, 26 percent (Marttila et al., 1977), over 50 percent (Mulligan and O'Grady, 1971), and 100 percent (Derbez and Grauer, 1967) of elderly institutionalized patients were receiving or had received hypnotic drugs routinely or nightly. Use is even greater when over-the-counter sleeping pills and alcohol are considered.

With the exception of flurazepam, the number of prescriptions for hypnotic drugs has been declining steadily since 1971. Most hypnotics are dispensed on an outpatient basis and by three medical specialties—family/general practice, internal medicine, and psychiatry/neurology. The average hypnotic prescription to relieve insomnia is written for a duration inconsistent with well-substantiated findings on tolerance.

Despite some consensus among researchers, the most consistent finding about patients who complain of insomnia is that the findings are inconsistent. This is not surprising considering the differences in research methods, patient selection, and other parameters among the available studies. Perhaps the most important confounding variable is the heterogeneity of the population complaining of insomnia. Therefore, before embarking on treatment programs for the patient with insomnia, the physician should diligently search for etiologic factors. Treatment for insomnia should not only be directed toward the underlying cause, but also vary with the symptom complex, severity, and duration.

The new Diagnostic Classification of Sleep and Arousal Disorders (1979), prepared jointly by the Association of Sleep Disorders Centers (ASDC) and the Association for the Psychophysiological Study of Sleep (APSS), identifies four clusters of sleep and arousal disorders: disorders of initiating and maintaining sleep (DIMS), disorders of excessive somnolence (DOES), disorders of the sleep-wake schedule, and dysfunctions associated with sleep, sleep stages, or partial arousals. Insomnia generally refers to DIMS. This cluster of disorders includes:

1. Psychophysiological
   a. Transient and situational
   b. Persistent

2. Associated with psychiatric disorders
   a. Symptom and personality disorders
   b. Affective disorders
   c. Other functional psychoses
3. Associated with use of drugs and alcohol
   a. Tolerance to or withdrawal from central nervous system (CNS) depressants
   b. Sustained use of CNS stimulants
   c. Sustained use of or withdrawal from other drugs
   d. Chronic alcoholism
4. Associated with sleep-induced respiratory impairment
   a. Sleep apnea DIMS syndrome
   b. Alveolar hypoventilation DIMS syndrome
5. Associated with sleep-related (nocturnal) myoclonus and "restless legs"
   a. Sleep-related (nocturnal) myoclonus DIMS syndrome
   b. "Restless legs" DIMS syndrome
6. Associated with other medical, toxic, and environmental conditions
7. Childhood-onset DIMS
8. Associated with other DIMS conditions
   a. Repeated rapid eye-movement (REM) sleep interruptions
   b. Atypical polysomnographic features
   c. Not otherwise specified
9. No DIMS abnormality
   a. Short sleeper
   b. Subjective DIMS complaint without objective findings
   c. Not otherwise specified

Evaluation of Insomnia

Whenever patients complain of insomnia or disturbed sleep, physicians should question them to estimate if they suffer from a disorder of initiating and maintaining sleep, a disorder of excessive somnolence, a sleep-wake schedule disorder, or one of the parasomnias. If insomnia is suspected, the duration of the symptoms should be noted. If the sleep problem has a recent onset (less than a month) and is a short-term or transient disorder, the physician should—through a careful history, physical examination, and routine laboratory tests—make a presumptive diagnosis and, on that basis, prescribe an appropriate treatment. If the sleep disturbance has persisted more than a month and appears to be of a chronic nature, referral for sleep laboratory evaluation is often indicated. Sleep laboratory evaluation is important because a sleep disorder may be not only impossible to diagnose accurately through the patient history and routine examination, but life-threatening as well. Prescribing a hypnotic for a patient with sleep apnea, for example, could easily become a death sentence.

Figure 1 is a flow chart of the steps followed and parameters measured in our sleep laboratory. The routine sleep laboratory evaluation of a patient who complains of insomnia begins with the sleep complaint, drug usage, family, and medical history followed by physical and neurologic examinations—all performed by sleep disorders experts. The patient's bed partner is also interviewed at this time to identify symptoms such as snoring, cessation of breathing, restlessness, or myoclonus. A psychiatric interview is then conducted and the patient receives a standard packet of psychological tests: Minnesota Multiphasic Personality Inventory (MMPI), State-Trait Anxiety Index, Profile of Mood States, Self-Evaluation Questionnaire, Shipley Institute of Living Scale, Sentence Completion for Men or Women, Internal-External Locus of Control. After the interviews, the patient is typically scheduled for up to three consecutive nights of sleep at the sleep disorders center. The patient reports to the laboratory an hour before normal bedtime in order to complete a Sleep Index, which assesses recent sleeping habits and helps identify problems with sleep hygiene. The patient then retires at his or her customary bedtime and spends his or her normal number of sleep hours in a temperature- and sound-controlled bedroom.

Polysomnographic measurements that are routinely recorded while the patient sleeps are the electroencephalogram/electro-oculogram (EEG/EOG), electrocardiogram (EKG), electromyogram (EMG; chin, tibial), and respiration (nasal). The objective polysomnographic variables routinely evaluated include sleep latency, total sleep time, frequency and duration of spontaneous arousals, duration and sequence of sleep stages, and body movement analysis, while the sleep parameters subjectively evaluated are sleep latency, total sleep time, number of awakenings, and morning restoration. For a comprehensive explanation of sleep polysomnographic evaluation, see Williams et al. (1974).

At the physician's discretion, additional, nonroutine polysomnographic measures may be ordered. These include continuous blood sampling, cerebrospinal fluid (CSF) metabolites, systemic and pulmonary hemodynamic variables, clinical EEG, pharyngeal EMG, blood gases, and intrathoracic respiration. Many of these nonroutine variables are necessary to determine the severity of sleep apnea.

If the sleep laboratory evaluation discloses no objective abnormalities, the patient is diagnosed as having no DIMS abnormality or, possibly, an environmental, situational, transient or intermittent disorder that is not experienced in the sleep laboratory.

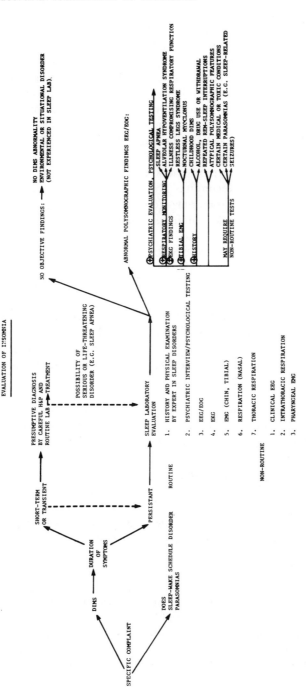

Figure 1

Sleep laboratory evaluation may reveal, on the other hand, abnormalities in one or more of the polysomnographic measurements that are useful in diagnosing the type of DIMS. The psychiatric evaluation and psychological testing may designate emotional factors as the primary cause of insomnia. Irregularities in respiratory monitoring may disclose sleep apnea, alveolar hypoventilation syndrome, or another illness which compromises the respiratory function. The restless legs syndrome and nocturnal myoclonus produce typical bursts of tibial EMG tracings. Recent alcohol and drug use or withdrawal can be identified by sleep EEG. The presence of repeated REM-sleep interruptions and atypical polysomnographic features will also be evident in the EEG/EOG recordings. Symptoms and signs of certain medical or toxic conditions and parasomnias (e.g., sleep-related seizures) may call for nonroutine tests to make a definitive diagnosis.

TREATMENT OF INSOMNIA

Hypnotic Drugs

Treatment of insomnia is most commonly pharmacologic. Hypnotic drugs taken to relieve sleep disturbance include alcohol, barbiturates, benzodiazepines, nonbarbiturate, nonbenzodiazepine drugs, and nonprescription drugs. Table 1 shows the oral dose range for commonly used hypnotic preparations.

Alcohol. Alcohol is one of the oldest and most widely "self-prescribed" hypnotics. Unfortunately, few of those who have a nightcap (or several) before bedtime to help them relax realize that alcohol actually disturbs sleep with both acute and chronic intake. Ethanol ingestion before bedtime disturbs the normal sleep architecture, decreasing sleep latency and REMS (Rundell et al., 1972; Yules et al., 1966, 1967) while increasing slow-wave sleep (MacLean and Cairns, 1974; Williams and Salamy, 1972; Yules et al., 1966, 1967) in the first half of the night and sometimes leading to restless sleep with frequent awakenings in the second half of the sleep period. These effects are more severe in alcoholics following heavy alcohol intake (Gross et al., 1972; Lester et al., 1973). In chronic alcoholism, slow-wave sleep, but not REMS, is decreased. Besides causing abnormal sleep architecture, alcohol can lead to respiratory depression followed by death if ingested with CNS depressants such as sleeping pills.

Barbiturates. Barbiturates are well-known hypnotic drugs with a long history of use in medical practice. They have certain advantages over other hypnotics; full efficacy is achieved on the first night of use and long-acting

Table 1

Commonly Used Hypnotic Preparations

Generic Name	Trade Name	Oral Hypnotic Dose Range (Adults)
Barbiturates		
Amobarbital	Amytal	100-200 mg
Pentobarbital	Nembutal	100 mg
Phenobarbital	Luminal	100 mg
Secobarbital	Seconal	100 mg
Benzodiazepines		
Flurazepam	Dalmane	15-30 mg
Chloral derivatives		
Chloral hydrate	Notic, Somnos	500-1000 mg
Chloral betaine	Beta-chlor	870-1740 mg
Trichloroethyl phosphate	Triclos	1500 mg
Paraldehyde	Paral	5-10 ml
Piperadinediones		
Glutethimide	Doriden	500 mg
Methyprylon	Noludar	200-400 mg
Quinazolines		
Methaqualone	Quaalude, Sopor	150-300 mg
Aliphatic alcohols		
Ethchlorvynol	Placidyl	500 mg
Antihistamines		
Diphenhydramine	Benadryl	50 mg

metabolites do not accumulate when the drug is used over several nights. Their primary action is depression of the CNS, resulting in effects ranging from mild sedation in therapeutic dosages to coma and death when taken in overdose. They seem to exert depressing effects on repetitive activity in multineuronal networks that may be important in the maintenance of wakefulness (Harvey, 1975). The most commonly prescribed barbiturates are phenobarbital, pentobarbital, amobarbital, and secobarbital. Physicians often prefer the latter two because of their relatively short plasma half-lives (14 to 42 hours). However, the long-acting phenobarbital gives no more subjective sense of hangover than the short-acting drugs (Mark, 1963).

Most barbiturates alter a number of sleep parameters, although there is some variation in these effects. All of them have been observed to decrease REMS (Baekeland, 1967; Borenstein and Cujo, 1974; Fujii, 1973; Haider and Oswald, 1971; Hartmann, 1968a; Karacan, in press; Williams and Agnew, 1969) and body movements (Brazier, 1966; Feinberg et al., 1969b; Haider, 1969; Haider and Oswald, 1971; Karacan, in press). In addition, pentobarbital and phenobarbital decrease the number of awakenings (Baekeland,

1967; Feinberg et al., 1969b; Kales et al., 1975) and increase REM latency, while amobarbital decreases REM latency (Haider, 1969; Haider and Oswald, 1971). Amobarbital and pentobarbital increase spindle sleep (Perkins and Hinton, 1974; Williams and Agnew, 1969), while phenobarbital has little effect on spindle activity (Karacan, in press). The effects, if any, of barbiturates on slow-wave sleep have varied in different studies (Brazier, 1966; Feinberg et al., 1969b; Kales et al., 1970b; Karacan, in press; Lester and Guerrero-Figueroa, 1966).

Benzodiazepines. The most frequently prescribed drugs in the United States, benzodiazepines were dispensed under 68 million prescriptions in 1978, according to the Food and Drug Administration (Greiner, 1980). All benzodiazepines have some hypnotic effects although some, such as diazepam, are primarily prescribed to relieve anxiety. Flurazepam is the most widely used hypnotic in America, while nitrazepam, triazolam, and lorazepam are preferred in Europe. Despite their extensive use, their mechanism of hypnotic action remains uncertain, although it has been proposed to be related to gamma-aminobutyric acid (GABA)-mediated transmission (Guidotti, 1978).

There is some controversy concerning the long-range effects of benzodiazepines, especially following withdrawal. Unlike barbiturates, benzodiazepines produce psychoactive metabolites with long half-lives. Consequently, first-night efficacy is limited, side effects become more frequent and severe with nightly use, and clinical benefits or side effects may persist for several days after discontinuance of the drug. Hindmarch (1981) suggests that, since short-acting benzodiazepines such as triazolam (half-life—four to six hours) show a relative lack of morning-after effects yet possess equipotent hypnotic activity, they should be prescribed instead of the longer-acting drugs. However, the studies of Kales et al. (1979) indicate that, unlike long-acting drugs, short and intermediate half-life drugs consistently cause rebound insomnia—severe worsening of sleep upon withdrawal. They conclude that the shorter-acting benzodiazepines are more likely to lead to hypnotic drug dependence because the patient will take more of the drug to treat the rebound insomnia. Kales et al. (1979) also caution against the tendency to consider benzodiazepines to be alike in their actions.

Like the barbiturates, benzodiazepines disrupt normal sleep architecture. Studies indicate that flurazepam, for example, decreases sleep latency (Dement et al., 1973; Fujii, 1973; Johns and Masterton, 1974; Kales et al., 1970a, 1971a; Vogel et al., 1972), number of awakenings (Johns and Masterton, 1974; Kales et al., 1970a, 1971a), slow-wave sleep (Fujii, 1973; Kales et al., 1970a, 1975), REMS (Fujii, 1973; Kales et al., 1970a), and alpha activity (Karacan, in press), and increases total sleep time, EEG beta activity during REMS (Itil et al., 1974), REM latency (Kales et al., 1975), spindling (Karacan, in press), and stage 2 sleep (Karacan, in press). The significance in changes in architecture is unknown, but decreases in certain stages, for example, REMS and slow-wave sleep, may have serious consequences in the long run. REM deprivation results in a rebound effect often accompanied by disturbing nightmares. Slow-wave sleep is believed to have a physically restorative role.

Nonbarbiturate, nonbenzodiazepine drugs. Nonbarbiturate, nonbenzodiazepine prescription hypnotics include chloral hydrate, paraldehyde, glutethimide, methaqualone, ethchlorvynol, methyprylon, as well as antihistamines (e.g., diphenhydramine), neuroleptics (e.g., chlorpromazine), antidepressants (e.g., doxepin), and L-tryptophan.

Chloral hydrate, the oldest hypnotic in current use, is often chosen for its paucity of undesirable effects in therapeutic doses. It does not lower blood pressure, affect respiration, or depress the reflex system as do some of the other hypnotics. Disruption of sleep architecture is minimal. However, like barbiturates, it is toxic or lethal in relatively low overdoses and may displace or potentiate concurrent medications which are also albumin-bound.

L-tryptophan's efficacy has not yet been well-established and its hypnotic effects appear to be relatively weak. However, it is considered a particularly promising hypnotic agent due to its theoretical appeal. According to Hartmann (1978), it is potentially the first safe and rational sleeping medication for which the mechanism of action is based on the biochemical basis of sleep. Limited studies have shown that L-tryptophan increases total sleep time and/or slow-wave sleep (Cazullo et al., 1969; Williams et al., 1969; Wyatt et al., 1970) and shortens sleep latency and wakefulness without altering other sleep parameters (Hartmann et al., 1973).

Although a relatively weak hypnotic, diphenhydramine is the most effective antihistamine for inducing sleep (Sunshine et al., 1978; Teutsch et al., 1975). It has few toxic side effects in therapeutic doses and a low potential for abuse, but does decrease REMS (Kales et al., 1969b) in healthy subjects.

Most of the other hypnotics in this group are not sufficiently more effective to warrant their disadvantages, which may include extreme toxicity, high abuse potential, confusion and emotional distress, tardive dyskinesia, or excessive disturbance of normal sleep architecture.

Nonprescription sedative hypnotics. Most over-the-counter (OTC) hypnotics contain an antihistamine or a combination of an antihistamine and scopolamine. Many of them contained methapyriline until late 1978, when it was implicated as a carcinogen in laboratory rats (Food and Drug Administration, 1978). Since then, pyrilamine maleate has replaced methapyrilene in such compounds as Nytol, Sleep-eze, and Compoz. Little is known about the efficacy of OTC hypnotics despite their popularity. The few studies done reveal little effect on sleep parameters (Kales et al., 1971b), although scopolamine alone has been reported to increase spindle sleep and REM latency and decrease REMS (Sagales et al., 1969).

Potentially Hazardous Characteristics

When deciding which hypnotic to prescribe, or whether to prescribe one at all, the physician should consider their potential hazards. These include overdose toxicity; additive toxicity with alcohol and other CNS depressants; adverse interactions with other prescribed drugs; hangover effects on daytime coordination, cognition, mood, and driving; difficulty awakening from sleep to respond to emergencies; development of nightly reliance on drugs for sleep; possible exacerbation of insomnia; rapid development of tolerance; disruption of normal sleep stages; and susceptibility to drug abuse (Institute of Medicine, 1979, p. 104).

The risk of each of these hazards varies with the type of drug used. Relatively low doses of barbiturates can result in death; the number of prescriptions written for them has therefore declined. Both short-acting and long-acting barbiturates cause a morning-after sense of hangover (Mark, 1963). Psychomotor impairment can last from 10 to 22 hours after a bedtime oral dose (McKenzie and Elliott, 1965). Tolerance to the sedative-hypnotic effects of barbiturates is easily reached due to their ability to increase the rate of their own metabolism as well as that of other drugs. Physical dependence is common and sudden withdrawal after chronic use can result in serious withdrawal symptoms. Upon withdrawal of barbiturates, insomnia or REM rebound resulting in nightmares and restlessness may occur (Oswald and Priest, 1965). Even at therapeutic doses, possible side effects include respiratory depression, allergic reactions, gastrointestinal disturbances, paradoxical excitement, and neuralgic or arthritic pain.

Although fatal overdoses following benzodiazepine ingestion are rare, habituation to these drugs is common and, similar to barbiturates, tolerance and physical dependence with marked withdrawal syndrome can accompany chronic administration of high doses (Goth, 1976). Benzodiazepines also have many side effects, which increase with nightly use and sometimes persist for several days after withdrawal. Common side effects include drowsiness, incoordination, ataxia, syncope, paradoxical excitement, nausea and vomiting, rash, blurred vision, dry mouth, and mental sluggishness.

The wide availability of hypnotics leads to public health problems. Suicide or accidental overdose results in mortality or high treatment costs for nonfatal emergencies; addiction repercussions range from increased crime and lost production to needless deaths; driving or operating motor vehicles while "hung-over" threatens public and personal safety on the highway and on the job (Institute of Medicine, 1979, p. 7).

Other potential hazards are the unknown, long-term consequences (possibly neuroendocrine and neurotransmitter imbalance) and repercussions from interference with normal sleep. Hazards are minimized when hypnotics are prescribed a few pills at a time in low dosages and patients are closely monitored for untoward effects and potential dependence. When the use of hypnotic drugs for more than two weeks is unavoidable, the patient should be advised to reserve a couple of drug-free nights each week.

Choice of Drug

In choosing a drug to alleviate insomnia, there is no "ideal hypnotic." Since no drug is totally without hazards and the available hypnotics are similar in clinical efficacy, the physician's goal should be to choose the most appropriate, least hazardous approach to providing relief for each insomnia patient. Therefore, selection should include consideration of disruption of normal sleep architecture, intensity and duration of hangover after-effects, cost, therapeutic index, drug interactions, toxicities, potential for abuse, addiction, and withdrawal syndromes. The drug should also be matched to each patient's particular medical and psychosocial characteristics. This requires diagnosis of any underlying disorders as well as of the specific sleep disorder leading to the insomnia complaint. Flurazepam or a barbiturate, for example, would be a poor choice for a patient with liver disease, while a depressed patient with suicidal ideation would be a poor candidate for a barbiturate. For some patients, any hypnotic is a poor or dangerous choice, especially if alcoholism or sleep apnea is suspected.

In general, the older hypnotics such as ethchlorvynol are poor prescription choices due to their toxicity and abuse potential. There is a growing preference for prescribing the newer benzodiazepines rather than barbiturates and the older compounds. It has been suggested that the benzodiazepines gradually replace barbiturates as the primary hypnotic choice. However, removing barbiturates from the market is not advised because they may prove less toxic on chronic administration, because certain patients have proven capable of safely regulating their own barbiturate use while sustaining hypnotic benefits, and because barbiturates are much less expensive than benzodiazepines.

Another important factor in hypnotic choice is dosage selection. To minimize toxic side effects, any drug selected, especially for the geriatric patient, should be prescribed in the lowest possible dose to obtain the desired effect on sleep. For example, although the drug manufacturer continues to recommend a 30 mg dose of flurazepam, clinical investigators (Dement et al., 1978; Kales et al., 1976; Salkind and Silverstone, 1975) would reduce this usual dose to 15 mg because there is little difference in symptomatic relief between the two dose levels.

Risks and Benefits of Hypnotic Drugs

Medical professionals sometimes question whether the potential benefits of hypnotic use are worth their risks. This is not surprising, considering that:

1. Hypnotics are involved in nearly 20 percent of all drug-related deaths (Cooper, 1977, p. vii).
2. Seventy-five percent of all hospital admissions for barbiturates are patients under 25 years of age (Cooper, 1977, p. 70).
3. Forty to sixty percent of those admitted to emergency rooms for hypnotic abuse obtain their medication by prescription (Cooper, 1977, p. xii).
4. Chronic use of all hypnotics eventually generates a cycle of tolerance and dependence which actually worsens sleep in the long run (see Figure 2), yet physicians' prescription patterns demonstrate that these drugs are distributed for periods beyond their proven effectiveness (Belleville and Fraser, 1957; Dement et al., 1975; Kales et al., 1974).
5. Insufficient attention is paid to hypnotic hangover effects, even though the greatest volume of hypnotics are dispensed on an outpatient basis (Cooper, 1977, p. 65)

Of course, a certain degree of risk can be tolerated if hypnotics do, indeed, effectively treat insomnia, but clinicians are having difficulty agreeing on what should constitute adequate criteria for hypnotic efficacy. A drug effectively treats insomnia, by definition, if it significantly reduces sleep latency, reduces the number of awakenings, or maintains an adequate sleep duration. Yet EEG studies indicate that, typically, hypnotics shorten sleep latency by a maximum of 10 to 20 minutes and lengthen total sleep time by only 30 to 40 minutes (Institute of Medicine, 1979, p. 155). Furthermore, clinicians question whether hypnotics can be considered of much benefit to patients when sleep deprivation studies demonstrate that sleeplessness does not significantly impair daytime cognitive and motor functions unless it continues over at least two consecutive nights (Naitoh and Townsend, 1979; Pasnau

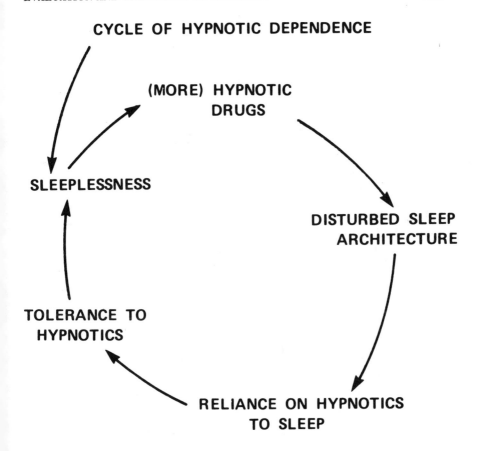

Figure 2

et al., 1978; Wilkinson et al., 1966). On the other hand, a lack of objective documentation of efficacy may be irrelevant if patients and physicians perceive that hypnotics improve sleep and alleviate a subjective sense of distress. This subjective satisfaction is confirmed by surveys (Boston Collaborative Drug Surveillance Program, 1972; Jick, 1967; Shapiro et al., 1969).

Nonpharmacologic Therapy

Accompanying the growing medical knowledge which challenges the long-term use of hypnotic drugs is progress in the development of nonpharmacologic means of relieving insomnia. Behavioral therapy includes educating the patient about good sleep hygiene, relaxation training, practicing positive thinking about oneself and one's environment (Coates and Thoresen, 1977), and psychotherapy to ameliorate underlying anxiety. Behavioral therapy is the best therapeutic choice when insomnia is long-standing and chronic, especially in elderly patients who may not tolerate drugs well. It is indicated particularly when patients report inability to sleep whenever they *try* to sleep, ability to sleep better in a setting other than their bedrooms, frequent daytime napping with little nighttime sleep, or excessive concern about occasional sleepless nights (Hauri, 1979). Patients with medical or psychiatric problems may have acquired sleep-habit problems over the years that would benefit from behavioral therapy.

Behavioral changes that enhance restful sleep include: limiting the amount of time spent in bed each night; retiring and arising at about the same time daily; avoiding heavy meals, heavy exercise, alcohol, coffee, cola, and cigarettes the few hours before bedtime; getting some exercise earlier in the day; winding down from the day's pressures by enjoying quiet activities before bedtime; avoiding napping; and using the bedroom only for sleeping and sex, and not for stressful activities such as financial discussions and homework (Ware, 1979). To reestablish good sleep hygiene, the elderly may need help in establishing a new routine for rising, meals, exercise, and so forth (Institute of Medicine, 1979, p. 127). Informal community social support systems can supplement professional care by nurses and social workers (President's Commission on Mental Health, 1978).

Several studies have demonstrated the efficacy of relaxation training in the treatment of sleep-onset insomnia (Borkovec and Fowles, 1973; Borkovec and Weerts, 1976; Lick and Heffler, 1977; Nicassio and Bootzin, 1974; Steinmark and Borkovec, 1974; Woolfolk et al., 1976). Some researchers have attributed this success to a placebo effect, but Carr-Kaffashan and Woolfolk (1979) found in their study that only subjects trained in relaxation techniques improved significantly; active treatment was much more effective than the placebo in reducing sleep onset latency.

Appropriate Therapy for Each Class of Insomnia

DIMS with psychophysiological causes. DIMS with psychophysiological causes can be either transient and situational or persistent.

Transient and situational DIMS, usually initiated by acute emotional reaction to a disturbing event or a significant life change, usually lasts less than three weeks from the onset of the precipitating event. Its main symptoms—difficulty falling asleep, intermittent awakenings, and early morning arousal—are readily ameliorated by short-term, low-dose hypnotic therapy (benzodiazepine or barbiturate). In less severe cases, no treatment may be necessary since the emotional cause of the disorder is typically resolved in a short time. Sleep laboratory evaluation is rarely necessary; most transient DIMS are managed successfully by the family physician.

Persistent psychophysiological DIMS are caused by long-standing tension or anxiety, internal arousal, or negative conditioning to sleep. Patients with this type of DIMS tend to somatize and to sleep better on weekends, holidays, or vacations. They typically complain of difficulty falling asleep or inability to return to sleep after awakening at night. Differential diagnosis is difficult to make from a history and physical exam alone; therefore sleep laboratory evaluation is usually indicated. Since the possible adverse effects of long-term hypnotic drug use are unknown, and hypnotics lose efficacy with chronic use, nonpharmacologic therapy is the preferred treatment.

DIMS associated with psychiatric disorders. DIMS are found in symptom and personality disorders, affective psychoses, and other functional psychoses. DIMS may result from the symptoms of personality disorders, anxiety disorders, somatoform disorders, and any other nonaffective and nonpsychotic psychiatric disorder. Nonpharmacologic treatment of the patient's symptoms is recommended, supplemented by short-term hypnotic treatment when the sleep disturbances are exacerbated.

Sleeplessness has long been observed as one of the major symptoms of affective disorders. Insomnia is often associated with both manic and depressive episodes; the severity of the DIMS tends to parallel the severity of the affective disorder. Often preceding the clinical signs of depression, sleep disturbance may be a clue to impending depression. Most typically reported are frequent nocturnal awakenings and early morning awakenings, although in comparison to normal subjects, the sleep of depressed patients varies greatly from night to night.

Depression which accompanies other psychiatric or medical syndromes often mimics the transient DIMS and therefore responds well to short-term hypnotic treatment combined with depression-oriented therapy.

Normal sleep parameters are altered in 96 percent of patients with a major depression (Jovanovic, 1973). The most common alterations are increased stage 1 sleep, reduced slow-wave sleep, and shortened REM latency, and, sometimes, rapid sleep-stage shifts (Gillin et al., 1975; Kupfer and Foster, 1975, 1978). These sleep parameters usually return to normal following clinical recovery from depression.

The most rational treatment for this type of DIMS is directed to the underlying depressive disorder. Tricyclic antidepressants are the best choice for moderate to severe depression, especially if the "endogenous cluster of symptoms"—diurnal mood variation with the saddest mood in the morning,

psychomotor retardation or agitation, loss of libido and interest in life, suicidal ideation, anorexia and weight loss, constipation, and inappropriate
guilt feelings—are prominent (Goodwin, 1977). The sedative-hypnotic effects of the six types of tricyclic antidepressants available in the United States
vary. Depressed patients experiencing agitation, anxiety, and insomnia are
reported to be most responsive to amitriptyline and doxepin, while patients
with psychomotor retardation and apathy are frequently believed to be more
effectively treated by protriptyline—a relatively stimulating drug. The tricyclic antidepressants markedly suppress REMS (Dunleavy et al., 1972;
Fujii, 1973; Hartmann, 1968a; Hartmann and Cravens, 1973; Okuma et al.,
1975; Passouant et al., 1975; Saletu et al., 1974; Takahashi, 1976; Toyoda,
1964; Zung, 1969), an effect suggested to be instrumental in the reversal of
depression because behavioral suppression of REMS similarly improves
depression (Kay et al., 1976). Consequently, tricyclic withdrawal has produced REMS rebound. These agents have also been shown to increase
spindle sleep (Hartmann and Cravens, 1973; Nakazawa et al., 1975; Takahashi, 1976; Toyoda, 1964), slow-wave sleep (Hartmann and Cravens, 1973;
Karacan et al., 1975; Saletu et al., 1974), and total sleep time (Karacan et
al., 1975), while decreasing nighttime wakefulness (Karacan et al., 1975) and
the number of awakenings per night (Karacan et al., 1975). Tricyclic antidepressants have abundant possible untoward effects—mainly anticholin-
ergic but also cardiovascular and CNS—requiring close monitoring of their
use. Treatment with monoamine oxidase inhibitors, due to their higher
toxicity potential, is limited to patients whose symptoms are not relieved by
the tricyclics.

In the bipolar type of affective disorder, the nature of the sleep disturbance
depends on whether the manic or depressed phase is ascendant. Mania-as-
sociated sleep has been described as short, restful, and deep with few interruptions (Jovanovic et al., 1973; Platman and Fieve, 1970) and depression-
associated sleep as either longer than normal or low to normal in total sleep
time (TST) (Hartmann, 1968b), with increased awakenings (Platman and
Fieve, 1970) and REMS (Hartmann, 1968b), decreased REM latency (Hartmann, 1968b), followed by daytime fatigue. Although sleep-onset insomnia
and a TST of only two to four hours is common in patients in the manic
phase, they seldom complain of disturbed sleep. As in unipolar depression,
sleep disturbance in the bipolar disorder is ameliorated by treating the
psychiatric disturbance. Lithium carbonate, the established treatment, has
been found to decrease REMS and increase REMS latency in both manic
and depressed patients (Chernik and Mendels, 1974; Kupfer et al., 1970a,
1974; Mendels and Chernik, 1973) as well as increasing TST and slow-wave
sleep.

The functional psychosis most clearly associated with insomnia is schizophrenia. Symptoms associated with psychosis such as anxiety, increased motor activity, delusions, and hallucinations lead to severe sleep-onset insomnia and, in the acute stages, to partial or total sleep loss. Typically, the schizophrenic patient's arising time gradually shifts into the afternoon, leading to a partial or complete inversion of day-night sleep cycles (Kupfer et al., 1970b). Although it is generally understood that schizophrenia alters some sleep parameters, sleep evaluation has yielded inconsistent results (Zarcone, 1979). Slow-wave sleep is reduced (Caldwell and Domino, 1967; Feinberg et al., 1969a; Kupfer et al., 1970b; Lairy et al., 1965; Stern et al., 1969; Traub, 1972; Wilczak et al., 1968), REM latency is shorter, and some (Azumi, 1966; Azumi et al., 1967; Gillin et al., 1974; Zarcone et al., 1968, 1975) but not all (de Barros-Ferreira et al., 1973; Vogel and Traub, 1968) researchers have noted that, unlike normal controls, actively psychotic schizophrenic patients lack REM rebound after REM deprivation nights. Regarding the role of sleep in schizophrenia, an interesting hypothesis attributes nonparanoid schizophrenic symptoms to the intrusion of REM-phasic events, triggered by serotonin synthesis malfunction, into wakefulness (Dement et al., 1969; Wyatt, 1972; Zarcone, 1979). Treatment with neuroleptic drugs relieves psychosis-related insomnia. Chlorpromazine has been found to increase stage 4 sleep (Feinberg et al., 1969b; Kaplan et al., 1974; Lester and Guerrero-Figueroa, 1966; Sagales et al., 1969); a deficit in this stage is the most consistent sleep abnormality found in schizophrenia (Feinberg and Hiatt, 1978).

DIMS associated with drugs and alcohol. Insomnia may accompany tolerance to or withdrawal from CNS depressants used as hypnotics which have been taken nightly for at least 30 days. The most prominent sleep disturbance associated with chronic use of hypnotic drugs is sleep interruption during the second half of the night as the drug's effects decline. Chronic users of sleeping pills have disturbed sleep architecture with decreased slow-wave sleep and REMS, increased stages 1 and 2 sleep, frequent stage shifts, as well as reduced spindles, K-complexes, delta activity, and rapid eye movements (Kales et al., 1969a).

The sustained use of CNS stimulants—analeptic agents, amphetamines, diet pills, and caffeine—also causes insomnia (Karacan et al., 1976a), especially if they are consumed later in the day or in excessive amounts (Derman et al., 1981). These drugs reduce both SWS and REMS (Oswald, 1969).

Other drugs for which chronic use and withdrawal lead to DIMS include antimetabolites, cancer chemotherapeutic agents, ACTH, oral contraceptives and propranolol, as well as illicit drugs such as marijuana and cocaine

(Kay et al., 1976). These drugs usually interfere with sleep onset. The successful treatment of drug- or alcohol-associated insomnia requires gradual withdrawal of the agent as recommended for the particular drug addiction. Hypnotics should not be prescribed unless a patient is already taking them, and then only in gradually decreasing amounts under medical supervision.

DIMS associated with sleep-induced respiratory impairment. Sleep-induced respiratory disorders which may cause insomnia are the sleep apnea syndrome (Guilleminault et al., 1976) and alveolar hypoventilation. The many episodes of respiration cessation in the sleep apnea syndrome are terminated by lightening of sleep or awakening. Although apnea patients may experience over 500 nighttime arousals, they are rarely aware of them. However, a bed partner may report important clinical signs of the disorder such as fitful snoring and restless movement.

Based on the respiratory motor output of the CNS, there are three types of sleep apnea syndromes: obstructive or upper airway, central, and mixed. Blockage of the upper airways characterizes the obstructive type; the central type results from cessation of diaphragmatic and intercostal muscle efforts; mixed is a combination of the other two.

Each of these types calls for different treatment. Hypnotics should never be prescribed when sleep apnea is suspected because they exacerbate the already inadequate airflow, causing severe respiratory depression which can lead to death. Instead, treatment of the respiratory impairment is indicated. Possible treatments for obstructive or mixed sleep apnea syndrome include weight reduction for the obese patient, surgical removal of obstructive tissues, and tracheostomy with positioning of a permanent tracheal valve capable of daytime closure (Glenn et al., 1976; Guilleminault and Dement, 1978; Guilleminault et al., 1975; Hishikawa et al., 1972; Imes et al., 1977; Lugaresi et al., 1973). A newly developed procedure, nocturnal diaphragm pacing, ameliorates some central sleep apnea syndromes (Glenn et al., 1976, 1978). Experimentation with drug treatment for the central type of disturbance has yielded little success; there is no well-established recommended treatment for this type.

Alveolar hypoventilation syndrome results from ventilatory impairment which is increased by sleep. It is distinguished from sleep apnea by the lack or infrequency of apnea episodes and by the existence of some respiratory impairment while awake. Insomnia results from this exacerbation of symptoms during sleep. Although associated with gross overweight (Rochester and Enson, 1974), myotonic dystrophy, narcolepsy, poliomyelitis, and other CNS pathology, its specific cause is uncertain. As with sleep apnea, treating this disorder with hypnotics is definitely contraindicated; it poses a serious threat to the patient's survival. Again, the underlying respiratory disorder should be treated whenever possible.

DIMS associated with sleep-related nocturnal myoclonus and restless legs. In nocturnal myoclonus, the patient is partially aroused or awakened after numerous episodes of repetitive, abrupt leg muscle contractions. The myoclonus does not occur when the patient is awake. Sleep laboratory evaluation is usually required when this disorder is suspected; an EMG recording can differentiate it from generalized body movements during sleep. Myoclonus should be treated only if the patient complains of nocturnal awakenings. We have had some success in our sleep laboratory with using clonopin to treat myoclonus. Determining the optimal therapeutic dose, however, is difficult. It usually ranges from 1 to 2 mg.

The restless legs DIMS syndrome (RLS), deep creeping sensations in the resting calves which lead to an urge to move the legs, is almost always accompanied by nocturnal myoclonus. The cause of this syndrome is unknown, but a genetic basis is suspected. In one EEG study, 85 percent of muscle twitches occurred during stages 1 and 2 sleep, 15 percent during REMS, and none during slow-wave sleep (Frankel et al., 1974). RLS, like nocturnal myoclonus, has no recognized treatment. However, 1 to 2 mg of clonopin at bedtime alleviated nighttime dysesthesia and insomnia in one patient with a 50-year history of RLS who was treated at our sleep disorders center. In our experience, many RLS patients have been given percodan for symptomatic relief. Although this treatment does decrease RLS, we do not recommend it because it has a high addiction potential.

DIMS associated with medical, toxic, and environmental conditions. DIMS may be instigated or aggravated by an assortment of central nervous system conditions (Freemon, 1978), endocrine and metabolic diseases, renal failure, bacterial, viral, and parasitic infections, arthritic and rheumatoid disease, gastrointestinal disease (Kales and Tan, 1969; Williams, 1978), alcohol-associated pathologies, allergies, symptoms of diseases such as pain, paresthesia, pruritus, and persistent cough, parasomnias, noxious environmental stimuli, and toxic effects of arsenic, mercury, alcohol, and tobacco. Pain is probably the most prevalent cause of this type of DIMS.

Treatment of insomnia associated with medical, toxic, and environmental conditions should emphasize modifying the offending environment or treating the underlying disorder whenever possible. Regardless of the type or cause of DIMS, chronic use of hypnotics should be avoided.

Childhood-onset DIMS. Childhood-onset DIMS is a sleep-onset and sleep-maintenance insomnia which begins before puberty and continues into adult-hood. The patient's history indicates that the poor sleep patterns are rela-tively independent of variations in emotional adaptation. That early-onset DIMS is particularly resistant to treatment compared to other types of DIMS implicates a possible CNS imbalance of sleep-wake mechanisms (Anders and Guilleminault, 1976). Patients' reports of daytime symptoms (fatigue, etc.) indicate that this group requires more sleep than they typically get, which differentiates them from short sleepers.

Children who have insomnia do not respond to drugs as well as adults. Therefore, drug treatment of childhood DIMS should be avoided or given with extreme caution. Nonpharmacologic and supportive types of treatment are recommended for children as well as for adults whose insomnia has persisted since childhood.

DIMS associated with other DIMS conditions. Other DIMS conditions can be detected only through sleep laboratory polysomnographic evaluation. Sleep-maintenance insomnia may result from repeated awakenings during every REM sleep period. Differential diagnosis is important because many conditions—hyperthyroid problems, paroxysmal nocturnal dyspnea, epi-lepsy, and apnea—may clinically simulate REMS interruptions. Typical con-tributing factors involve depression or other psychopathology, or avoidance of dysphoric dreams. Because of its rare occurrence, the best treatment for this condition is unknown. If the interruptions are associated with depres-sion, therapy with antidepressant drugs is indicated.

Persons with insomnia caused by atypical polysomnographic features com-plain of poor sleep quality, frequent awakenings, and feeling unrefreshed in the morning. EEG tracings are abnormal, with high-voltage alpha waves often superimposed on slow waves. There is no established treatment for this disorder.

No DIMS abnormality. A complaint of insomnia does not necessarily in-dicate the presence of a sleep disturbance. Some people consistently require fewer than six hours of sleep nightly to feel rested the next day. However, the short sleeper may try to sleep longer to conform to social expectations and eventually seek medical evaluation for the "abnormality." The patient should be reassured that his or her sleep length is normal and that phar-macologic or other treatment is unnecessary. Unfortunately, physicians sometimes mistake normal sleep for insomnia in such cases, or recommend longer sleep to compensate for a health problem, and prescribe a hypnotic. The patient may then become dependent on the medication to sleep at all and end up with a true sleep disorder.

No psychopathology or objective laboratory evidence of abnormal sleep can be detected in nearly 25 percent of patients who complain of persistent insomnia (Carskadon et al., 1976). This discrepancy between the subjective complaint and objective measures may reflect excessive mentation during sleep, physiologic abnormalities in the sleep tracing that cannot be detected by current recording methods, or inaccurate self-estimates of time spent asleep. Unaware that sleeping less is normal as they age, elderly patients often complain of insomnia even when their daytime functioning is not compromised. Often, the only treatment necessary for unsubstantiated complaints of insomnia is educating patients about what constitutes normal sleep or reassuring them that their sleep is normal. If hypochondriasis is involved, the patient should be referred for psychotherapy. Unfortunately, the potential for drug abuse is great for subjective complainers because physicians too often accept their patients' complaints without sufficient evaluation and prescribe unnecessary medication.

Summary

A physician should never assume that a patient's insomnia is idiopathic and proceed with trial-and-error therapy. Insomnia is not a single disorder but describes a heterogeneous group of conditions involving difficulty in initiating and maintaining sleep. Since there are usually multiple causes, a thorough evaluation of a patient's symptoms should always precede the selection of a suitable treatment for the insomnia complaint. The most current classification system should be consulted to make a differential diagnosis of the sleep disorder which distinguishes among physiologic, psychological, and environmental causes. This detailed diagnostic work-up should include a search for any underlying pathology which could contribute to the sleep disturbance or exclude drugs that are potentially health-endangering. If the patient has a history of insomnia of long duration, referring him or her for sleep laboratory evaluation is usually necessary.

Specific treatment of the underlying pathology and/or alteration of the patient's environment to eliminate sleep-antagonistic stimuli should be considered before deciding to prescribe a hypnotic drug. Generally, hypnotic treatment should be considered a last resort, a temporary measure to relieve transient and situational sleep disturbances, because proof of the drugs' efficacy during nightly use is lacking and tolerance and addiction can lead to refractory disruption of a patient's normal sleep architecture. Behavioral therapy is an effective alternative to pharmacologic therapy in the treatment of chronic insomnia, especially in geriatric patients. Patients whose insomnia is linked to long-term hypnotic, alcohol, or other drug use should have these substances gradually withdrawn, under medical supervision, on a schedule appropriate for the particular drug addiction. When selecting a hypnotic, the differences in the drug's potential side effects, half-life, hangover effects, toxicity, tolerance and dependence potentials, along with the patient's unique psychological and medical characteristics, should be kept in mind.

Future Research Needs

Hypnotic drugs could be more selectively prescribed and effectively used if their relative efficacies were better understood, especially with chronic administration. Possible medical models of insomnia need to be explored and applied to the testing of hypnotic drugs. Due to the potential dangers associated with testing new drugs on insomnia patients and the inconvenience of performing polysomnographic recordings on patients for a length of time sufficient to evaluate the long-term effects, an equivalent means of artificially inducing insomnia in normal subjects would increase opportunities to test drugs. Okuma (1981) constructed a model of insomnia using noise and methylphenidate, a CNS stimulant, and successfully applied it to the investigation of the tolerance-forming tendency of benzodiazepines. Our study (Karacan et al., 1976a) of the insomnia-mimicking effects of coffee and caffeine on sleep suggests that these agents are also potential tools for creating an experimental model of insomnia. This model could be applied to the exploration of the etiology of insomnia as well as of hypnotic drug effects.

Other studies should be directed toward investigating drugs in which the mechanism of action is more directly related to the physiologic inducement or enhancement of sleep. (Most hypnotics are nonspecific CNS depressants). One such drug is L-tryptophan, an essential amino acid which acts as a precursor of serotonin, a neurotransmitter active in the control mechanisms of sleep.

Current and anticipated advances in the computer scoring of sleep stages and data analysis are expected to improve the standardization of EEG recordings in sleep disorder and hypnotic therapy evaluations. Other research areas needing more intensive study are drug-seeking behavior and education programs for both physicians and the general public.

REFERENCES

ABELSON, J., COHEN, R., SCHRAYER, D., and RAPPEPORT, M. 1973. Drug experience, attitudes, and related behavior among adolescents and adults. In *Drug Use in America, Appendix I: Patterns and Consequences of Drug Use*, pp. 488-867. Washington, DC: U.S. Government Printing Office.

ANDERS, T. F., and GUILLEMINAULT, C. 1976. The pathophysiology of sleep disorders in pediatrics. In I. Schulman (ed.), *Advances in Pediatrics*, Vol. 22, pp. 137-174. Chicago: Year Book Medical Publishers.

ASSOCIATION OF SLEEP DISORDERS CENTERS. 1979. *Diagnostic Classification of Sleep and Arousal Disorders*, Ed. 1, prepared by the Sleep Disorders Classification Committee, H. P. Roffwarg, chairman. *Sleep*, 2:17-57.

AZUMI, K., 1966. A polygraphic study of sleep in schizophrenia. *Seishin Shinkeigaku Zasshi*, 68:1222-1241.

AZUMI, K., TAKAHASHI, S., TAKAHASHI, K., MARUYAMI, N., and KIKUTI, S., 1967. The effects of dream deprivation on chronic schizophrenics and normal adults: A comparative study. *Folia Psychiatr. Neurol. Jpn.*, 21:205-225.

BAEKELAND, F., 1967. Pentobarbital and dextroamphetamine sulfate: Effects on the sleep cycle in man. *Psychopharmacologia*, 11:388-396.

BALLINGER, C. B. 1976. Subjective sleep disturbance at the menopause. *J. Psychosom. Res.*, 20:509-513.

BALTER, M. B., and BAUER, M. L. 1975. Patterns of prescribing and use of hypnotic drugs in the United States. In A. D. Clift (ed.), *Sleep Disturbance and Hypnotic Drug Dependence*, pp. 261-293. Amsterdam: Excerpta Medica.

BELLEVILLE, R., and FRASER, J. 1957. Tolerance to some effects of barbiturates. *J. Pharmacol. Exp. Ther.*, 120:469-474.

BORENSTEIN, P., and CUJO, P. 1974. Influence of barbiturates and benzodiazepines on the sleep EEG. In T. M. Itil (ed.), *Psychotropic Drugs and the Human EEG: Modern Problems of Pharmacopsychiatry*, pp. 182-192. Basel: Karger.

BORKOVEC, T. D., and FOWLES, D. C. 1973. Controlled investigation of the effects of progressive and hypnotic relaxation on insomnia. *J. Abnorm. Psychol.*, 82:153-158.

BORKOVEC, T. D., and WEERTS, T. C. 1976. Effects of progressive relaxation on sleep disturbance: An electroencephalographic evaluation. *Psychosom. Med.*, 38:173-180.

Boston Collaborative Drug Surveillance Program. 1972. A clinical evaluation of flurazepam. *J. Clin. Pharmacol.*, 12:217-220.

BRAZIER, M. A. B. 1966. Electroencephalographic studies of sleep in man. In J. B. Dillon and C. M. Ballinger (eds.), *Anesthesiology and the Nervous System. Proceedings of the 1975 Western Biennial Conference on Anesthesiology*, pp. 106-128. Salt Lake City: University of Utah Press.

CALDWELL, D. F., and DOMINO, E. F. 1967. Electroencephalographic and eye-movement patterns during sleep in chronic schizophrenic patients. *Electroencephalogr. Clin. Neurophysiol.*, 22:414-420.

CARR-KAFFASHAN, L., and WOOLFOLK, R. L. 1979. Active and placebo effects in treatment of moderate and severe insomnia. *J. Consult. Clin. Psychol.*, 47:1072-1080.

CARSKADON, M., DEMENT, W., MITLER, M., GUILLEMINAULT, C., ZARCONE, V., and SPIEGEL, R. 1976. Self report versus sleep laboratory findings in 122 drug-free subjects with the complaint of chronic insomnia. *Am. J. Psychiatry*, 133:1382-1388.

CAZZULLO, C. L., PENATI, G., BOZZI, A., and MANGONI, A. 1969. Sleep patterns in depressed patients treated with a MAO inhibitor: Correlation between EEG and metabolites of tryptophan. In A. Cerletti and F. J. Bove (eds.), *The Present Status of Psychotropic Drugs*, vol. 180, pp. 199-203. Amsterdam: Excerpta Medica International Congress Series.

CHERNIK, D. A., and MENDELS, J. 1974. Longitudinal study of the effects of lithium carbonate on the sleep of hospitalized depressed patients. *Biol. Psychiatry*, 9:117-123.

CLIFT, A. D. 1975. Sleep disturbance in general practice. In A. D. Clift, (ed.), *Sleep Disturbance and Hypnotic Drug Dependence*, pp. 155-177. Amsterdam: Excerpta Medica.

COATES, T. J., and THORESEN, C. E. 1977. *How to Sleep Better: A Drug-Free Program for Overcoming Insomnia*. Englewood Cliffs, NJ: Prentice-Hall.

COOPER, J. R. (ed.) 1977. *Sedative-Hypnotic Drugs: Risks and Benefits*, pp. 1-112. Rockville, MD: National Institute on Drug Abuse, U.S. Department of Health, Education and Welfare Publication No. 78-592.

DE BARROS-FERREIRA, M., GOLDSTEINAS, L., and LAIRY, G. 1973. REM sleep deprivation in chronic schizophrenics: Effects on dynamics of fast sleep. *Electroencephalogr. Clin. Neurophysiol.*, 34:561-569.

DEMENT, W. C., CARSKADON, M. A., MITLER, M. M., PHILLIPS, R. L., and ZARCONE, V. P. 1978. Prolonged use of flurazepam: A sleep laboratory study. *Behav. Med.*, 5:25-31.

DEMENT, W. C., PHILLIPS, R. L., MITLER, M., BILLIARD, M., and ZARCONE, V. 1975. Long-term effectiveness of flurazepam 30 mg. H.S. on chronic insomniacs. *Sleep Res.*, 4:94.

DEMENT, W., ZARCONE, V., FERGUSON, J., COHEN, H., PIVIK, T., and BARCHAS, J. 1969. Some parallel findings in schizophrenic patients and serotonin-depleted cats. In D. V. Siva Sankar (ed.), *Schizophrenia: Current Concepts and Research*, pp. 775-811. Hicksville, NY: PJD Publications.

DEMENT, W. C., ZARCONE, V. P., HODDES, E., SMYTHE, H., and CARSKADON, M. 1973. Sleep laboratory and clinical studies with flurazepam. In S. Garattini, E. Mussini, and L. O. Randall (eds.), *The Benzodiazepines*, pp. 599-611. New York: Raven Press.

DERBEZ, R., and GRAUER, H. 1967. A sleep study with investigation of a new hypnotic compound in a geriatric population. *Can. Med. Assoc. J.*, 97:1389-1393.

DERMAN, S., WILLIAMS, R. L., and KARACAN, I. 1981. Sleep disorders and their psychiatric significance. In W. E. Fann, I. Karacan, A. D. Pokorny, and R. L. Williams (eds.), *Phenomenology and Treatment of Psychophysiological Disorders*. New York: Spectrum.

DETRE, T. 1966. Sleep disorder and psychosis. *Can. Psychiatr. Assoc. J.*, 11:S169-S177.

DUNLEAVY, D. L., BREZINOVA, V., OSWALD, I., MACLEAN, A. W., and TINKER, M. 1972. Changes during weeks in effects of tricyclic drugs on the human sleeping brain. *Br. J. Psychiatry*, 120:663-672.

DUPUY, H. J., ENGEL, A., DEVINE, B. K., SCANLON, J., and QUEREC, L. 1970. *Selected Symptoms of Psychological Distress*. Public Health Service Publication No. 1000, Series 11, No. 37. Washington, D.C.: U.S. Government Printing Office.

FEINBERG, I., BRAUN, M., KORESKO, R. L., and GOTTLIEB, F. 1969a. Stage 4 sleep in schizophrenia. *Arch. Gen. Psychiatry*, 21:262-266.

FEINBERG, I., and HIATT, J. F. 1978. Sleep patterns in schizophrenia: A selective review. In R. L. Williams and I. Karacan (eds.), *Sleep Disorders: Diagnosis and Treatment*, pp. 205-231. New York: John Wiley & Sons.

FEINBERG, I., WENDER, P. H., KORESKO, R. L., GOTTLIEB, F., and PIEHUTA, J. A. 1969b. Differential effects of chlorpromazine and phenobarbital on EEG sleep patterns. *J. Psychiatr. Res.*, 7:101-109.

Food and Drug Administration. 1978. Tentative final orders regarding over-the-counter sedatives and sleeping aids.

FRANKEL, B. L., PATTEN, B. M., and GILLIN, J. C. 1974. Restless legs syndrome. Sleep electroencephalographic and neurologic findings. *J.A.M.A.*, 230:1302-1303.

FREEMON, F. R. 1978. Sleep in patients with organic diseases of the nervous system. In R. L. Williams and I. Karacan (eds.), *Sleep Disorders: Diagnosis and Treatment*, pp. 261-283. New York: John Wiley & Sons.

FUJII, S. 1973. Effects of some psychotropic and hypnotic drugs on the human nocturnal sleep. *Psychiatr. Neurol. Jap.*, 75:545-573.

GILLIN, J. C., BUCHSBAUM, M. C., JACOBS, L. S., FRAM, D. H., WILLIAMS, R. L., VAUGHN, T. B., MELLON, E., SNYDER, F., and WYATT, R. J. 1974. Partial REM sleep deprivation, schizophrenia and field articulation. *Arch. Gen. Psychiatry*, 30:653-662.

GILLIN, J. C., BUNNEY, W. E., and BUCHBINDER, R. 1975. Sleep changes in unipolar and bipolar depressed patients as compared with normals. Second International Sleep Research Congress, and 15th Annual Meeting of the Association for Psychophysiological Study of Sleep, Edinburgh, Scotland.

GLENN, W. W., PHELPS, M., and GERSTEN, L. M. 1978. Diaphragm pacing in the management of central alveolar hypoventilation. In C. Guilleminault and W. C. Dement (eds.), *Sleep Apnea Syndromes*, pp. 333-345. New York: Liss.

GLENN, W. W., SHAW, R. K., COLE, D. R., FARMER, W. C., GEE, J. B. L., and BECKMAN, C. B. 1976. Upper airway obstruction complicating central alveolar hypoventilation (Ondine's curse) treated by tracheostomy and diaphragm pacing (abstract). *Am. Rev. Respir. Dis.*, 11 (April suppl.): 262.

GOODWIN, F. K. 1977. Drug treatment of affective disorders: General principles. In M. E. Jarvik (ed.), *Psychopharmacology in the Practice of Medicine*, pp. 241-253. New York: Appleton-Century-Crofts.

GOTH, A. 1976. *Medical Pharmacology Principles and Concepts*. St. Louis: C. V. Mosby.

GREINER, G. E. 1980. Benzodiazepines 1980: Current update: Introduction. *Psychosomatics*, 21 (Supplement):3.

GROSS, M. M., HASTEY, J. M., and LEWIS, E. 1972. Effect of 6 days of heavy drinking on the sleep of alcoholics. In M. H. Chase, W. C. Stern, P. L. Walter (eds.), *Sleep Research*, vol. 1. Los Angeles: Brain Information Service/Brain Research Institute, University of California.

GUIDOTTI, A. 1978. Synaptic mechanisms in the action of benzodiazepines. In M. A. Lipton, A. DiMascio, and K. F. Killam (eds.), *Psychopharmacology: A Generation of Progress*, pp. 1349-1357. New York: Raven Press.

GUILLEMINAULT, C., and DEMENT, W. C. 1978. Sleep apnea syndromes and related sleep disorders. In R. L. Williams and I. Karacan (eds.), *Sleep Disorders: Diagnosis and Treatment*, pp. 9-28. New York: John Wiley & Sons.

GUILLEMINAULT, C., ELDRIDGE, F. L., SIMMON, F. B., and DEMENT, W. C. 1975. Sleep apnea syndrome—Can it induce hemodynamic changes? *West. J. Med.*, 123:7-16.

GUILLEMINAULT, C., TILKIEN, A., and DEMENT, W. C. 1976. The sleep apnea syndromes. *Annu. Rev. Med.*, 27:465-484.

HAIDER, I. 1969. Effects of a hypnotic (sodium amylobarbitone 200 mg.) on human sleep—An electroencephalographic study. *Pakistan Medical Forum*, 4:21-30.

HAIDER, I., and OSWALD, I. 1971. Effects of amylobarbitone and nitrazepam on the electrodermogram and other features of sleep. *Br. J. Psychiatry*, 118:519-522.

HAMMOND, F. C. 1964. Some preliminary findings on physical complaints from a perspective study of 1,064,004 men and women. *Am. J. Public Health*, 54:11-23.

HARTMANN, E. 1968a. The effect of four drugs on sleep patterns in man. *Psychopharmacologia*, 12:346-353.

HARTMANN, E. 1968b. Longitudinal studies of sleep and dream patterns in manic-depressive patients. *Arch. Gen. Psychiatry*, 19:312-329.

HARTMANN, E. 1978. *The Sleeping Pill*. New Haven: Yale University Press.

HARTMANN, E., and CRAVENS, J. 1973. The effects of long term administration of psychotropic drugs on human sleep. III. The effects of amitriptyline. *Psychopharmacologia*, 33:185-202.

HARTMANN, E., CRAVENS, J., and LIST, S. 1973. L-tryptophan as a natural hypnotic: A dose response study in man. Presentation, Association for the Psychophysiological Study of Sleep, San Diego, California.

HARVEY, S. C. 1975. Hypnotics and sedatives. The barbiturates. In L. Goodman and A. Gilman (eds.), *The Pharmacological Basis of Therapeutics*, 5th Ed., pp. 102-123. New York: Macmillan.

HAURI, P. 1979. Behavioral treatment of insomnia. *Med. Times*, 107:36-47.

HINDMARCH, I. 1981. The effect of benzodiazepine hypnotics on aspects of sleep and early morning performance. In I. Karacan (ed.), *Psychophysiological Aspects of Sleep: Proceedings of the Third International Congress on Sleep Research*, pp. 124-132. Park Ridge, NJ: Noyes Medical Publications.

HISHIKAWA, Y., FURUYA, E., WAKAMATSU, H., and YAMAMOTO, J. 1972. A polygraphic study of hypersomnia with periodic breathing and primary alveolar hypoventilation. *Bull. Physiopathol. Resp.*, 8:1139-1151.

IMES, N. K., ORR, W. C., and SMITH, R. O. 1977. Retrognathia and sleep apnea. A life-threatening condition masquerading as narcolepsy. *J.A.M.A.*, 237:1596-1597.

Institute of Medicine, Division of Mental Health and Behavioral Medicine. 1979. *Sleeping Pills, Insomnia, and Medical Practice*. Washington, D.C.: National Academy of Sciences.

ITIL, T. M., SALETU, B., and MARASA, J. 1974. Determination of drug-induced changes in sleep quality based on digital computer "sleep prints." *Pharmakopsychiatr. Neuropsychopharmakol.*, 7:265-280.

JICK, H. 1967. Comparative studies with a hypnotic (R05-6901) under current investigation.

Curr. Ther. Res., 9:355-357.

JOHNS, M. W., EGAN, P., GAY, T. J. A., and MASTERTON, J. P. 1970. Sleep habits and symptoms in male medical and surgical patients. *Br. Med. J.*, 2:509-512.

JOHNS, M. W., and MASTERTON, J. P. 1974. Effect of flurazepam on sleep in the laboratory. *Pharmacology*, 11:358-364.

JOVANOVIC, U. J., DOGAN, S., DURRIGL, V., GUVAREV, N., HAJNSEK, F., ROGINA, V., and STOJANOVIC, V. 1973. Changes in sleep in manic-depressive patients dependent on the clinical state. In U. J. Jovanovic (ed.), *The Nature of Sleep*, pp. 208-211. Stuttgart: Gustar Fischar Verlag.

KALES, A., BIXLER, E. O., LEO, L. A., HEALY, S., and SLYE, E. 1974. Incidence of insomnia in the Los Angeles metropolitan area. In M. H. Chase, W. C. Stern, and P. L. Walter (eds.), *Sleep Research*, vol. 3, p. 139. Los Angeles: Brain Information Service/Brain Research Institute, University of California.

KALES, A., BIXLER, E. O., SCHARF, M., and KALES, J. D. 1976. Sleep laboratory studies of flurazepam: A model for evaluating hypnotic drugs. *Clin. Pharmacol. Ther.*, 19:576-583.

KALES, A., BIXLER, E. O., TAN, T. L., SCHARF, M. B., and KALES, J. D. 1974. Chronic hypnotic drug use: Ineffectiveness, drug withdrawal, insomnia, and dependence. *J.A.M.A.*, 227:513-517.

KALES, A., KALES, J. D., BIXLER, E. O., and SCHARF, M. B. 1975. Effectiveness of hypnotic drugs with prolonged use. Flurazepam and pentobarbital. *Clin. Pharmacol. Ther.*, 18:356-363.

KALES, J., KALES, A., BIXLER, E. O., and SLYE, E. S. 1971a. Effects of placebo and flurazepam on sleep patterns in insomniac subjects. *Clin. Pharmacol. Ther.*, 12:691-697.

KALES, A., KALES, J. D., SCHARF, M. B., and TAN, T. L. 1970a. Hypnotics and altered sleep-dream patterns. II. All-night EEG studies of chloral hydrate, flurazepam, and methaqualone. *Arch. Gen. Psychiatry*, 23:219-225.

KALES, A., MALMSTROM, E. J., SCHARF, M. B., and RUBIN, R. T. 1969a. Psychophysiological and biochemical changes following use and withdrawal of hypnotics. In A. Kales (ed.), *Sleep: Physiology and Pathology*, pp. 331-343. Philadelphia: Lippincott.

KALES, A., MALMSTROM, E. J., and TAN, T. L. 1969b. Drugs and dreaming. In E. Abt and B. F. Riess (eds.), *Progress in Clinical Psychology*, pp. 154-167. New York: Grune & Stratton.

KALES, A., PRESTON, T. A., TAN, T. L., and ALLEN, C. 1970b. Hypnotics and altered sleep-dream patterns. I. All-night studies of glutethimide, methyprylon, and pentobarbital. *Arch. Gen. Psychiatry*, 23:211-218.

KALES, A., SCHARF, M. B., KALES, J. D., and SOLDATOS, C. R. 1979. A potential hazard following withdrawal of certain benzodiazepines. *J.A.M.A.*, 241:1692-1695.

KALES, A. and TAN, T. L. 1969. Sleep alterations associated with medical illness. In A. Kales (ed.), *Sleep: Physiology and Pathology*, pp. 148-157. Philadelphia: Lippincott.

KALES, J., TAN, T. L., SWEARINGEN, C., and KALES, A. 1971b. Are over-the-counter sleep medications effective? All-night EEG studies. *Curr. Ther. Res.*, 13:143-150.

KAPLAN, J., DAWSON, S., VAUGHN, T., GREEN, R., and WYATT, R. J. 1974. Effect of prolonged chlorpromazine administration on the sleep of chronic schizophrenics. *Arch. Gen. Psychiatry*, 31:62-66.

KARACAN, I., BLACKBURN, A. B., THORNBY, J. I., OKAWA, M., SALIS, P. J., and WILLIAMS, R. L. 1975. The effect of doxepin HCL (Sinequan) on sleep patterns and clinical symptomatology of neurotic depressed patients with sleep disturbance. In J. Mendels (ed.), *Sinequan (Doxepin HCL): A Monograph of Recent Clinical Studies*, pp. 4-22. Princeton: Excerpta Medica.

KARACAN, I., HEINE, W., AGNEW, H. W., WILLIAMS, R. L., WEBB, W. B., and ROSS, J. J. 1968. Characteristics of sleep patterns during late pregnancy and the postpartum periods. *Am. J. Obstet. Gynecol.*, 101:579-586.

KARACAN, I., and MOORE, C. A. Psychopharmacological agents in the treatment of sleep disorders. In L. R. Derogatis (ed.), *Pharmacology in Clinical Practice*. New York: Addison Wesley, in press.

KARACAN, I., THORNBY, J. I., ANCH, A. M., BOOTH, G. H., WILLIAMS, R. L., and SALIS, P. J. 1976a. Dose-related sleep disturbances induced by coffee and caffeine. *Clin. Pharmacol. Ther.*, 20:682-689.

KARACAN, I., THORNBY, J. I., ANCH, M., HOLZER, C. E., WARHEIT, G. J., SCHWABB, J. H., and WILLIAMS, R. L. 1976b. Prevalence of sleep disturbance in a primarily urban Florida county. *Soc. Sci. Med.*, 10:239-244.

KAY, D. C., BLACKBURN, A. B., BUCKINGHAM, J. A., and KARACAN, I. 1976. Human pharmacology of sleep. In R. L. Williams and I. Karacan (eds.), *Pharmacology of Sleep*. New York: John Wiley & Sons.

KUPFER, D. J., and FOSTER, F. G., 1975. The sleep of psychotic patients: Does it all look alike?. In D. X. Freedman (ed.), *Biology of the Major Psychoses*, p. 143. New York: Raven Press.

KUPFER, D. J., and FOSTER, F. G., 1978. EEG sleep and depression. In *Sleep Disorders: Diagnosis and Treatment*, pp. 163-204. New York: John Wiley & Sons.

KUPFER, D. J., REYNOLDS, C., WEISS, B. L., and FOSTER, F. G. 1974. Lithium carbonate and sleep in affective disorders: Further considerations. *Arch. Gen. Psychiatry*, 30:79-88.

KUPFER, D. J., WYATT, R. J., GREENSPAN, K., SCOTT, J., and SNYDER, F. 1970a. Lithium carbonate and sleep in affective illness. *Arch. Gen. Psychiatry*, 23:35-40.

KUPFER, D. J., WYATT, R. J., SCOTT, J., and SNYDER, F. 1970b. Sleep disturbance in acute schizophrenic patients. *Am. J. Psychiatry*, 126:1213-1223.

LAIRY, G. C., BARTE, H., GOLDSTEINAS, L., and RIDJANOVIC, S. 1965. Sommeil de nuit de malades mentaux: Etude des bouffées délirantes. In *Le Sommeil de Nuit Normal et Pathologique, Etudes Electroencephalographiques*, p. 353. Paris: Masson.

LESTER, B. K., and GUERRERO-FIGUEROA, R. 1966. Effects of some drugs on electroencephalographic fast activity and dream time. *Psychophysiology*, 2:224-236.

LESTER, B. K., RUNDELL, O. H., COWDEN, L. C., and WILLIAMS, H. L. 1973. Chronic alcoholism, alcohol, and sleep. In M. M. Gross (ed.), Alcohol Intoxication and Withdrawal. Experimental Studies. *Adv. Exp. Med. Biol.*, 35:261-279.

LICK, J., and HEFFLER, D. 1977. Relaxation training and attention placebo in the treatment of severe insomnia. *J. Consult. Clin. Psychol.*, 45:153-161.

LUGARESI, E., COCCAGNA, G., MANTOVANI, M., and BRIGNANI, F. 1973. Effects of tracheostomy in two cases of hypersomnia with periodic breathing. *J. Neurol. Neurosurg. Psychiatry*, 36:15-26.

MACLEAN, A. W., and CAIRNS, J. 1974. Dose-response relationships between ethanol and human sleep. In M. H. Chase, W. C. Stern, and P. L. Walter. (eds.), *Sleep Research*, vol. 4. Los Angeles: Brain Information Service/Brain Research Institute, University of California.

MARK, L. C. 1963. Metabolism of barbiturates in man. *Clin. Pharmacol. Ther.*, 4:504-530.

MARTTILA, J. K., HAMMEL, R. J., ALEXANDER, B., and ZUSTIAK, R. 1977. Potential untoward effects of long-term use of flurazepam in geriatric patients. *J. Am. Pharm. Assoc.*, 17:692-695.

McGHIE, A., and RUSSELL, S. M. 1962. The subjective assessment of normal sleep patterns. *J. Ment. Sci.*, 108:642-654.

McKENZIE, R. E., and ELLIOT, L. L. 1965. Effects of secobarbital and d-amphetamine on performance during a simulated air mission. *Aerospace Med.*, 36:774-779.

MENDELS, J., and CHERNIK, D. A. 1973. The effect of lithium carbonate on the sleep of depressed patients. *Int. Pharmacopsychiatry.*, 8:184-192.

MULLIGAN, A. F., and O'GRADY, C. P. 1971. Reducing night sedation in psychogeriatric wards. *Nurs. Times*, 67:1089-1091.

NAITOH, P., and TOWNSEND, R. E. 1979. The role of sleep deprivation research in human factors. *Human Factors*, 12:575-585.

NAKAZAWA, Y., KOTORII, T., KOTORII, M., HORIKAWA, S., and OSHIMA, M. 1975. Effects of amitriptyline on human REM sleep as evaluated by using partial differential REM sleep deprivation (PDRD). *Electroencephalogr. Clin. Neurophysiol.*, 38:513-520.

NICASSIO, P., and BOOTZIN, R. 1974. A comparison of progressive relaxation and autogenic training as treatments for insomnia. *J. Abnorm. Psychol.*, 83:253-260.

OKUMA, T. 1981. Model insomnia for testing hypnotic medication. In I. Karacan (ed.), *Psychophysiological Aspects of Sleep: Proceedings of the Third International Congress of Sleep Research*, pp. 133-138. Park Ridge, NJ: Noyes Medical Publications.

OKUMA, T., HATA, N., and FUJII, S. 1975. Differential effects of chlorpromazine, imipramine, nitrazepam and amobarbital on REM sleep and REM density in man. *Folia Psychiatr. Neurol. Jpn.*, 29:25-37.

OSWALD, I. 1969. Sleep and dependence on amphetamine and other drugs. In A. Kales (ed.), *Sleep: Physiology and Pathology*, pp. 317-330. Philadelphia: Lippincott.

OSWALD, I., and PRIEST, R. G. 1965. Five weeks to escape the sleeping-pill habit. *Br. Med. J.*, 2:1093-1099.

PASNAU, R. O., NAITOH, P., STIER, S., and KOLLAR, E. J. 1978. The psychological effects of 205 hours of sleep deprivation. *Arch. Gen. Psychiatry*, 18:596-605.

PASSOUANT, P., CADHILAC, J., and BILLIARD, M. 1975. Withdrawal of the paradoxical sleep by the clomipramine: Electrophysiological, histochemical, and biochemical study. *Int. J. Neurol.*, 10:186-197.

PERKINS, R., and HINTON, J. 1974. Sedative or tranquilizer? A comparison of the hypnotic effects of chlordiazepoxide and amylobarbitone sodium. *Br. J. Psychiatry*, 124:435-439.

PLATMAN, S. R., and FIEVE, R. R. 1970. Sleep in depression and mania. *Br. J. Psychiatry*, 116:219-220.

President's Commission on Mental Health. 1978. *Report of the Task Panel on Community Support Systems*, Appendix vol. 2. Washington, DC: U.S. Government Printing Office.

RAYBIN, J. B., and DETRE, T. P. 1969. Sleep disorder and symptomatology among medical and nursing students. *Compr. Psychiatry*, 10:452-462.

RECHTSCHAFFEN, A., and MARON, L. 1964. The effect of amphetamine on the sleep cycle. *Electroencephalogr. Clin. Neurophysiol.*, 16:438-445.

ROCHESTER, D. F., and ENSON, Y. 1974. Current concepts in the pathogenesis of the obesity-hypoventilation syndrome. *Am. J. Med.*, 57:402-420.

RUNDELL, O. H., LESTER, B. K., GRIFFITHS, W. J., and WILLIAMS, H. L. 1972. Alcohol and sleep in young adults. *Psychopharmacologia*, 26:201-218.

SAGALES, T., ERILL, S., and DOMINO, E. F. 1969. Differential effects of scopolamine and chlorpromazine on REM and NREM sleep in normal male subjects. *Clin. Pharmacol. Ther.*, 10:522-529.

SALETU, B., ALLEN, M., and ITIL, T. M. 1974. The effect of Coca-Cola, caffeine, antidepressants, and chlorpromazine on objective and subjective sleep parameters. *Pharmakopsychiatr. Neuropsychopharmakol.*, 254:307-321.

SALKIND, M. R., and SILVERSTONE, T. 1975. A clinical and psychometric evaluation of flurazepam. *Br. J. Clin. Pharmacol.*, 2:223-226.

SCHWEIGER, M. S. 1972. Sleep disturbance in pregnancy: A subjective survey. *Am. J. Obstet. Gynecol.*, 114:879-882.

SHAPIRO, S., SLONE, D., LEWIS, G. P., and JICK, H. 1969. Clinical effects of hypnotics. II. An epidemiologic study. *J.A.M.A.*, 209:2016-2020.

STEINMARK, S. W., and BORKOVEC, T. D. 1974. Active and placebo treatment effects on moderate insomnia under counterdemand and positive demand instructions. *J. Abnorm. Psychol.*, 83:157-163.

STERN, M., FRAM, D. H., WYATT, R., GRINSPOON, L., and TURSKY, B. 1969. All-night sleep studies of acute schizophrenics. *Arch. Gen. Psychiatry*, 20:470-477.

SUNSHINE, A., ZIGHELBOIM, R., and LASKA, E. 1978. Hypnotic activity of diphenhydramine, methapyrilene, and placebo. *J. Clin. Pharmacol.*, 18:425-431.

TAKAHASHI, K. 1976. The action of tricyclics (alone or in combination with methylphenidate) upon several symptoms of narcolepsy. In C. Guilleminault, W. C. Dement, P. Passouant, and E. D. Weitzman (eds.), *Narcolepsy, Advances in Sleep Research*, vol. 3. New York: Spectrum.

TEUTSCH, G., MAHLER, D. L., BROWN, C. R., FORREST, W. H., JR., JAMES, K. E., and BROWN, B. W. 1975. Hypnotic efficacy of diphenhydramine, methapyrilene, and pentobarbital. *Clin. Pharmacol. Ther.*, 17:195-201.

THOMAS, C. D., and PEDERSON, L. A. 1963. Sleep habits of healthy young adults with observations of levels of cholesterol and circulating eosinophils. *J. Chronic Dis.*, 16:1099-1114.

THORNBY, J., KARACAN, I., SEARLE, R., SALIS, P., WARE, C., and WILLIAMS, R. 1977. Subjective reports of sleep disturbance in a Houston metropolitan health survey. Presented at the Seventeenth Annual Meeting of the Association for the Psychophysiological Study of Sleep, Houston.

TOYODA, J. 1964. The effects of chlorpromazine and imipramine on the human nocturnal sleep encephalogram. *Folia Psychiatr. Neurol. Jpn.*, 18:198-221.

TRAUB, A. C. 1972. Sleep stage deficits in chronic schizophrenia. *Psychol. Rep.*, 31:815-820.

TUNE, G. S. 1969. The influence of age and temperament on the adult human sleep-wakefulness pattern. *Br. J. Psychol.*, 60:431-441, 1969.

VOGEL, G. W., HICKMAN, J., THURMOND, A., BARROWCLOUGH, B., and GIESLER, D. 1972. The effect of dalmane (flurazepam) on the sleep cycle of good and poor sleepers (abstract). *Psychophysiology*, 9:96.

VOGEL, G., and TRAUB, A. 1968. REM deprivation. I. The effect on schizophrenic patients. *Arch. Gen. Psychiatry*, 18:287-329.

WARD, J. A. 1968. Alterations of sleep pattern in psychiatric disorder. *Can. Psychiatr. Assoc. J.*, 13:249-257.

WARE, J. C. 1979. The symptom of insomnia: Causes and cures. *Psych. Ann.*, 9:27-49.

WEISS, H. R., KASINOFF, B. H., and BAILEY, M. A. 1962. An explanation of reported sleep disturbance. *J. Nerv. Ment. Dis.*, 134:528-534.

WILCZAK, H., KUBACKI, A., RZEPECKI, J., KILJAN, A., JUS, A., and JUS, K. 1968. Polygraphic studies on night sleep in untreated schizophrenic patients (electroclinical correlations). *Psychiatr. Pol.*, 2:175-181.

WILKINSON, R. T., EDWARDS, R. S., and HAINES, E. 1966. Performance following a night of reduced sleep. *Psychonom. Sci.*, 5:471-472.

WILLIAMS, H. L., LESTER, B. K., and COULTER, J. D. 1969. Monoamines and the EEG stages of sleep. *Acta. Nerv. Super.*, 11:188-192.

WILLIAMS, H. L., and SALAMY, A. 1972. Alcohol and sleep. In B. Kissin and H. Begleiter (eds.), *The Biology of Alcoholism, vol. 2: Physiology and Behavior*, pp. 435-483. New York: Plenum.

WILLIAMS, R. L. 1978. Sleep disturbances in various medical and surgical conditions. In R. L. Williams and I. Karacan (eds.), *Sleep Disorders. Diagnosis and Treatment*, pp. 285-301. New York: John Wiley & Sons.

WILLIAMS, R. L., and AGNEW, H. W., JR. 1969. The effects of drugs on the EEG sleep patterns of normal humans. *Exp. Med. Surg.*, 27:53-64.

WILLIAMS, R. L., KARACAN, I., and HURSCH, C. J. 1974. *Electroencephalography (EEG) of Human Sleep: Clinical Applications*. New York: John Wiley & Sons.

WOOLFOLK, R. L., CARR-KAFFASHAN, L., MCNULTY, T. F., and LEHRER, P. M. 1976. Meditation training as a treatment for insomnia. *Behavior Therapy*, 7:359-365.

WYATT, R. 1972. Behavioral changes of chronic schizophrenic patients given L-5 hydroxytryptophan. *Science*, 177:1124-1126.

WYATT, R. J., FRAM, D., KUPFER, D. J., and SNYDER, F. 1970. Effects of L-tryptophan (a natural sedative drug) on human sleep. *Lancet*, 2:842-846.

YULES, R. B., FREEDMAN, D. X., and CHANDLER, D. A. 1966. The effect of ethyl alcohol on man's electroencephalographic sleep cycle. *Electroencephalogr. Clin. Neurophysiol.*, 20:109-111.

YULES, R. B., LIPPMAN, M. E., and FREEDMAN, D. X. 1967. Alcohol administration prior to sleep. *Arch. Gen. Psychiatry*, 16:94-97.

ZARCONE, V. P., JR. 1979. Sleep and schizophrenia. *Psychiatr. Ann.*, 9:29-40.
ZARCONE, V., AZUMI, K., DEMENT, W., GULEVICH, G., KRAEMER, H., and PIVIK, T. 1975. REM phase deprivation and schizophrenia. II. *Arch. Gen. Psychiatry*, 32:1431-1436.
ZARCONE, V., GULEVICH, G., and PIVIK, T. 1968. Partial REM phase deprivation and schizophrenia. *Arch. Gen. Psychiatry*, 18:194-202.
ZUNG, W. W. K. 1969. Effect of antidepressant drugs on sleeping and dreaming. III. On the depressed patient. *Biol. Psychiatry*, 1:283-287.

AUTHOR INDEX

SUBJECT INDEX